ATLANTIC STUDIES ON SOCIETY IN CHANGE

NO. 104

EVOLUTION OF THE HUNGARIAN ECONOMY 1848–2000

Volume III

Hungary: from Transition to Integration

Edited by
György Csáki
and
Gábor Karsai

Translated and copyedited by
János and Rachel Hideg

Social Science Monographs, Boulder, Colorado
Atlantic Research and Publications, Inc.
Highland Lakes, New Jersey

Distributed by Columbia University Press, New York
2001

EAST EUROPEAN MONOGRAPHS, NO. DXCIV

The publication of this volume was made possible by grants from
the Soros Alapítvány [Soros Foundation], Budapest

ISBN 0-88033-492-4
Library of Congress Catalog Card Number 2001135943

Printed in the United States of America

Table of Contents

Chapter II
Some Critical Issues of Economic Transition

Chapter III
Short-term Macroeconomic Forecast (2001-2002)

Preface to the Series and Acknowledgments

The present volume is a component of a series that is intended to present a comprehensive survey of the many aspects of East Central European society.

The books in this series deal with peoples whose homelands lie between the Germans to the west, the Russians, Ukrainians and Belorussians to the east and north, and the Mediterranean and Adriatic seas to the south. They constitute a particular civilization, one that is at once an integral part of Europe, yet substantially different from the West. The area is characterized by a rich diversity of languages, religions and governments. The study of this complex area demands a multidisciplinary approach, and, accordingly, our contributors to the series represent several academic disciplines. They have been drawn from universities and other scholarly institutions in the United States and Western Europe, as well as East and Central Europe.

The editor-in-chief is responsible for ensuring the comprehensiveness, cohesion, internal balance, and scholarly quality of the series he has launched. He cheerfully accept this responsibility and intend this work to be neither justification nor condemnation of the policies, attitudes, and activities of any person involved. At the same time, because the contributors represent so many different disciplines, interpretations, and schools of thought, our policy in this, as in the past and future volumes, is to present their contributions without major modifications.

The two editors and the contributors of this volume are distinguished scholars of the field the theme of this book belongs to.

Ms. Andrea T. Kulcsár gave extensive help in arranging, and type-setting of the text. I wish to express our gratitude to her.

Budapest, October 23, 2001

Béla K. Király
Editor in Chief

Preface

GKI Economic Research Co. (*GKI Gazdaságkutató Rt.*) is Hungary's leading economic think tank and macroeconomic forecaster: 18 highly qualified and skillful economists are working on macroeconomic analysis as well as on short and medium term forecasts.

Nowadays, Hungary seems to be the most successful transition economy in the central European region: since 1997 Hungary performs year by year 4,6–5,0 percent high growth of GDP, the country has continuously been a favorite target for foreign direct and portfolio investment since as early as 1988, a candidate for EU-accession in the first wave of its eastern enlargement—although five years ago Hungary had the poorest macroeconomic performance in the region. How the country has overcome its critical macroeconomic situation? How has it stabilized its national economy? How the country could find the way out from its severe foreign indebtedness? How Hungary has just become first from one of the worst—in no more than four-five years time?

In their volume, *Hungary: From Transition to Integration*, GKI's 18 analysts provide a large and at the same time comprehensive description and analysis of the Hungarian macroeconomic situation—through the decade of the transition, that is the development from planned to market economy as well as the (re-)integration into the world economy.

In the first part, the volume describes the overall macroeconomic development and the changes of macroeconomic performance of the Hungarian national economy: while following the development of every major industries it does focus on micro- and macroeconomic stabilization, provides a comprehensive description of the macroeconomic stabilization of 1995–96 itself and give an explanation of its extraordinary (and surprisingly fast) success. A special attention is made to the development of the financial situation, the state of the budget and inflation. The volume argues that—based upon the successful stabilization—since 1997, the Hungarian national economy is well on a sustainable development path, therefore, the current dynamism of growth can be maintained on the long term too—hampering either domestic or international equilibrium.

The second part does focus on five topical issues of the transition process, that is: privatization, foreign direct investment inflows, the development of the financial intermediation (banking sector, insurance industry and the capital markets), the development of the corporate sector and last but not least the country's preparation for EU accession.

The third part provides a short-term forecast for 2002, while the fourth one consists of a statistical appendix enabling the readers to find a wide range of quantitative information about the recent decade of macroeconomic development in Hungary.

*

The first and the third chapter are based upon GKI's recent collective works, the authors are as follows: Judit Adler, László Akar (CEO), Judit Barta, Balázs Benyó, György Csáki, Miklós Hegedűs, Gábor Karsai, Miklós Losoncz, Jenő Malatinszky, László Molnár, Katalin Némethné Pál, Gábor Papanek, Raymund Petz, László Skultéty, Zoltán Sulyok, András Vértes (Chaiman of the Board), Erzsébet Viszt and László Zacher.

The volume has been written by the 18 researchers of GKI Economic Research Co. and compiled and edited by György Csáki, Ph.D. and Gábor Karsai, M. Sc. from the Budapest University of Economics—both Research Directors at GKI. Economic Research Co.

Budapest, October 15, 2001

CHAPTER I
FROM SOCIALISM TO CAPITALISM: THE HUNGARIAN ECONOMY FROM 1990 TO 2000

INTRODUCTION

"...to most European statesman the loss of Hungary was of far greater importance than the establishment of factories in the Orient, and the threat to Vienna more significant than their own challenges at Aden, Goa and Malacca; only governments bordering the Atlantic could, like their late historians, ignore this fact." This quotation is taken from the well-known work of Paul Kennedy,* the famous American historian, and implies that those immersed in day-to-day affairs are often unable to recognize those events that will have a significant influence on the future.

Are the general public, politicians, and writers on contemporary Hungarian society aware of the real directions, and of what is at stake, in the ongoing economic and social transition? Which of the various phenomena do they regard as decisive? The positive phenomena—namely the end of the shortage economy and all that it entailed, unlimited rights to private property and entrepreneurship, the inflow of global technical and cultural innovations, unobstructed personal and economic relations with the rest of the world, and the birth of parliamentary democracy? Or the negative phenomena–the dramatic rise in unemployment, the erosion of state services, the significant fall in overall consumption and the widening gap between rich and poor, the rising crime rate, and the moral crisis in society and politics?

And is not the clarity of vision of foreign politicians, businesspersons, and social scientists—people with a thorough knowledge of the nature of developed market economies and democracies, who look at Hungary from abroad—blurred by distance, by

* Kennedy, Paul: *The Rise and Fall of the Great Powers.* First Vintage Books, New York, 1989 p. 26.

the differences that exist between declarations and actions, the difficulty of seeing beneath the surface, their lack of local knowledge, and the complexities involved in verifying logical assumptions.

It will take several more years before the position of this region within the new world economic order can be evaluated, and before any appraisal can be made of the successes of the various policies put in place by the different countries, on the basis of actual economic performance and the quality of life enjoyed by the general public.

The building of capitalism (which is generally referred to as the "social market economy") has, indisputably, begun in this region. However, success is not guaranteed. The possibility cannot be ruled out that in certain countries the positive phenomena outlined above will be obstructed, while the negative ones become dominant. The signs are, however, that there are countries that *are* capable of closing the gap between themselves and the developed world, and even of beginning to catch up with it. Besides the international conditions, the extent to which a country is able to continue the social and economic reform policies that allow for the flexible adaptability of its economy will be of vital importance in this respect—that is, the extent to which it is capable of turning the process of the collapse of the planned economy into a creative destruction, and of mobilizing its forces in order to create new structures rather than defending the old ones.

Central East European countries are facing the historical opportunity of integrating into a socially and economically more developed part of Europe. Naturally, this in itself will not eliminate the above-mentioned negative phenomena. However, as part of a dynamic development, these negative phenomena can be regarded as inevitable side effects that can be mitigated in the framework of the fulfillment of the transition to a market economy and the realization of EU integration. Regardless of whether or not the social players understand it, their relationship to this process will define those players' roles in shaping the future, that is, to update the terminology of the socialist period, it will define whether they choose to continue the building of capitalism and, after laying its foundations, whether they will regard their main task as the creation of a highly developed Hungarian capitalism ready for EU integration, or—shying away from the serious contradictions and the inevitable tensions inherent in the tasks ahead—whether they will look for some kind of (in reality nonexistent) "third way" that will preserve the, obviously noncompetitive, structures of the economy and society.

This volume comprises analyses and forecasts regarding the process of the Hungarian transition to a market economy between 1990 and 2002, a period which includes three parliamentary cycles. The study begins with the first year of the change of regime in 1990, and ends with 2002, the year by which Hungary has declared it will be ready to join the European Union. The study is based on the data available as of early 2001. Accordingly, it focuses mainly on the economic situation as it existed in 1999 and the economic processes and economic policy that gave rise to that situation. On the other hand, it also deals with expected economic developments up to 2002. The study concentrates on the key aspect of the transition, that is, the structural changes in the economy.

The 1990s in Hungary represent a period of major social and economic transformations. A change in economic system took place, and, as a result, the Hungarian economy, over the last decade, has become a European-style market economy in its essential features. The main effects of this are the following:

- In contrast to the former dominance of state property, domestic and foreign private ownership has become dominant; the proportion of private ownership in the generation of GDP has risen to between 80 and 85 percent, and real owners now have genuine control over the operations of their companies. Hungarian privatization practice has proved unquestionably successful in terms of creating a competitive economy.

- The structural system of the economy has been turned on its head and now resembles that of a market economy. Today, the overwhelming majority of economic players exist in the form of small and medium-sized enterprises, while the number of big corporations is relatively lower.
- Both in terms of exports and imports the economy has opened up towards the world economy. The Hungarian economy—above all as a result of the establishment of multinational companies—has integrated into the world economy, and especially into the EU.
- Prices, employment and wages, investments, and market cooperation are shaped by the autonomous decisions of the economic players.
- The institutional system of the money and capital markets has gradually evolved and has become open to domestic and foreign players.
- Economic competition has become predominant in contrast to shortages.
- The forint has been made convertible.
- In the institutional system of economic policy, frameworks for the rational division of labor have emerged. (The fiscal sphere has been divided into more or less independent subsystems. Its deficit is being financed from the market, and the independence of the Hungarian National Bank is provided by law.)
- The conditions for sustainable growth have been created both in terms of the institutional system of the economy and the real competitiveness of the business sector. Since 1997 the Hungarian economy has produced an annual growth of 4 to 5 percent, while the internal and external balance has been either favorable or, even in the worst years, acceptable.

However, this does not mean that the establishment of a market economy has been completed. On the one hand, it is often the case that the actual operations of the newly created institutions do not entirely follow the practice of developed European market economies. On the other hand, the transformation of the institutional and service systems related to public finances is only in its initial phase.

The attitudes and performance of enterprises have significantly changed. The transitional period in the entrepreneurial sphere has come to an end, but the process of transformation continues. The degree of structural change is remarkably varied:

- Within the Hungarian economy it is largely those sectors in which multinational companies have appeared (for example the machine industry, telecommunications, the financial sector) that have begun to develop. Within the region as a whole, foreign capital has achieved its best position in Hungary. However, growth is increasingly spreading in the economy and affecting more and more sectors. Besides exports, domestic demand has begun to increase.
- The weakest points in the competitiveness of domestic companies are reliability and knowledge of the markets. The attitude of enterprises is increasingly characterized by market orientation. However, they still have a tendency to look for the roots of their problems in external factors. Small and medium-sized companies tend to be weak and capital poor, although some of them are competitive and, by the end of the 1990s, were set on the path towards development.
- The output of the, often consolidated or reorganized, companies and banks that survived the crisis has improved significantly. Since 1994 the profit rate in industry and the national economy as a whole has been positive and is increasing. Partly as a result of this, and partly because of large-scale foreign investments, the capital reserves of enterprises are increasing even in real terms.
- The influence of the state on economic activities remains more significant than in developed European countries. However, this

is not so much due to its continuing position of ownership as to the frequent changes in regulations. Illusions as to the usefulness of the state's limiting of market processes are still alive and occasionally gain strength. However, the state's actual room for maneuver is much narrower than is sometimes declared rhetorically.

- Willingness to invest on the part of the majority of companies is improving, but is still weak. Besides the lack of resources, insecurity and lack of confidence in the state play a part in this. Multinational companies, however, reinvest in the Hungarian economy a significant part of the profits produced in Hungary, while investments made by domestically owned companies are also increasing. Although capital exports by Hungarian companies are not yet significant they do exist, predominantly in the form of investments in some of Hungary's neighboring ex-socialist states.
- The upsurge in the number of small enterprises following the change of regime has been followed by a process of centralization and concentration. Some of the companies have access to significant capital and are capable of Central European and even global cooperation, while others are still vegetating on the borderline between existence and nonexistence. The activities and circle of ownership of companies is changing more rapidly than in an "established" market economy. The redistribution of markets is ongoing (but now without the participation of the state).

The development of a market economy (whether in Hungary or elsewhere) provides no automatic protection against certain unfavorable phenomena. Thus in Hungary:

- Serious macro-imbalances have emerged and are likely to emerge in the future.
- Monopolistic positions have arisen, and abuses of power and improper market behaviors are frequent.

- Due to the amount of tax and especially of social security contributions, as well as to the existence of greed in a period of capital accumulation, and to newly imposed customs duties, the use of semi-legal and illegal practices is widespread, that is a relatively large "black economy" does always exist in Hungary.
- Due to unreliable information it is difficult to see clearly certain important features of the macroeconomic situation and of the micro-sphere.

Both as a result of historical tradition and the difficulties of the transformation, the Hungarian economy has a strong tendency to encourage unfavorable market-economic processes.

The change of regime and the laying of the foundations of capitalism brought with them serious social-economic and individual-family tensions. For the moment—if we look, for instance, at individual consumption—the process has more losers than winners. It must not be forgotten that the country's income (GDP) was, even in 1999, less than in 1989 (it has just reached and surpassed this level in 2000). It is also an undeniable fact that the winners have mostly been successful due to their individual achievements: the state has helped them only occasionally and to a limited extent. On the other hand, these "achievements" have often involved subterfuge and deception, or even the open flouting of the law. The greatest "achievement" of society as a whole has been its endurance. Although public consumption in 1998/1999 increased significantly, exceeding 4 percent per year, and although the situation of almost every stratum improved, the measure of this improvement still falls far behind the recession that preceded it.

Crisis situations have also arisen. In autumn 1990 the taxi drivers' strike, which took place a few months after the first free elections, can be seen as one example. Amid general public sympathy, taxi and lorry drivers, in response to the drastic and unannounced raising of petrol prices by the state (then still in control of petrol supplies), brought traffic to a standstill almost throughout the entire country. Society was then faced with the fact that the economic transition would be accompanied by much suffering and that the change of regime would not automatically bring about welfare and transparency.

The escalation of the "Postabank panic" in 1997, when confidence in the second largest retail bank was shaken and its deposit and account holders "besieged" the bank, could easily have led to a profound financial and political crisis. Two other situations within the political sphere also threatened to have serious consequences: a) during the 1990 to 1994 government, the emergence and growing domination of a pronounced far-right platform; and b) at the beginning of the 1994 to 1998 period, the government's inward-looking detachment (i.e., its postponement of unpopular measures in order to maintain solvency) that resulted in its inability to act. Another difficult situation arose when, immediately after Hungary's admission to NATO membership in the late spring of 1998, the country was forced to support NATO action against neighboring Yugoslavia, a country with a significant Hungarian minority population. In the case of the government in power since 1998, there are signs of occasional tacit cooperation with the radical Right.

In the above situations, a section of the dominant economic and intellectual opinion makers acted quietly but with determination in the interests of mitigating tensions and through commitment to the market economy and democracy, so contributing to the solution of such problems. At the same time, the majority of society—probably as a result of their past experience—preferred to remain detached.

Despite the ultimate success of the transformation, there are still crisis points. Throughout the decade the country's traditionally underdeveloped eastern and northeastern regions found themselves increasingly lagging behind. In certain sectors (e.g., in most areas of agriculture, in railroad transports, and in the majority of the public services, especially the health service) there are no signs of movement from the low point that has been reached.

Market-economic reforms and continuing modernization are vital for the effective exploitation of the economy's existing resources, since certain resources are still scarce.

In many respects the planned economy financed itself at the expense of the future: examples of this behavior include the postponement of renewal and refurbishment; the over-exploitation of infrastructure; and the accumulation of foreign debts. On the other hand, the structure of production, which had never been governed by the criteria of international competitiveness, was devalued to a great extent due to changes in the world economy that had taken place in the meantime. According to expert estimates, at least 30 to 40 percent of the economy's capital reserves in 1990 have since proved to be of no value. This means that the modernization process continuously demands large amounts of domestic savings and the inflow of foreign capital. As a result of their relative cheapness, human resources represent a significant potential for exploitation. In recent years, however, the land itself has had only a theoretical importance. In the absence of market conditions, its real value is impossible to estimate.

At the same time, a favorable feature is the fact that a high level of working capital inflow can be counted on in the long term. As part of AGENDA 2000, the European Union's budget for 2000 to 2006, EU subsidies have begun to be granted on a larger scale.

Finally, the Hungarian economy had set itself on a new course by 1997. On the basis of significant achievements in terms of stabilization and modernization, economic growth has accelerated to an annual average of 4 to 5 percent, which, even in international terms, is remarkable. For decades the Hungarian economy did not have the kind of opportunity it has now to approach, slowly and gradually, the average level of European development. Based on the experiences of the past decades, the key issues and conditions with respect to economic development can be outlined as follows:

- The continuing deep-seated reform of public services and administration is a basic necessity. The main aim is more effective functioning, but, in the meantime, the ratio of redistribution and state debt compared to GDP needs to be further decreased.
- Accordingly, the sustainable growth of the economy must be export- and investment oriented. The volume of investments and exports will need to increase at least twice as rapidly as public consumption. In this sense, growth cannot be consumption lead, although real public incomes, following a halt of over approximately two decades, can show a marked increase.
- Due to the focusing of internal domestic demand in the direction of quality products (or, in certain cases, in the direction of extremely cheap products) and to a natural demand for modern technology, the economy's import demand will significantly increase. This is a natural phenomenon which accompanies the Hungarian economy's export-oriented growth: it increases competitiveness and improves the availability of consumer goods.
- With the completion of basic economic reorganization inflation was in the one digit area during certain months of 1999, and by 2000 turned out at a yearly 9.8 percent average.
- According to international experience, the beginnings of economic growth alone can produce only a slight increase in employment. However, the rapid growth of the Hungarian economy in recent years has had a beneficial effect on employment. Unemployment in Hungary, according to ILO methodology, is already lower than the EU average. In addition, it is important to focus on "whitening" the economy by bringing to the surface previously underground economic activities.
- As a result of the above, the already established significant international—as well as the improving domestic—business and public confidence in the Hungarian economy can further increase. This is a precondition for the increasing of invest-

ments, the slowing down of inflation, and the appropriate treatment of the social tensions that will continue to be inevitable.

The present study aims to show how, in the last decade, Hungary has become a European market economy in its main aspects, and how it is increasingly becoming part of the European integration processes. The creation of the institutional and legal system necessary for EU membership; the approximation, and long-term adherence, to the Maastricht criteria; and the clarification of the state's role and mode of functioning (areas undergoing changes even within EU countries), even in a favorable case, might well become the program of an entire decade in Hungary. In the meantime, Hungary must adjust to the permanent changes in the world economy while maintaining the economy's competitiveness and ability to attract capital. The key issue is adaptability, since a small country in an increasingly globalized world in fact has little alternative. Such adaptability, of course, is only in contradiction to efforts to preserve traditions and circumstances, not to the country's ability to make use of them. In the socialist period Hungary was fairly successful in making itself the West of the Eastern bloc. Now, with its new capabilities, it needs cleverly to exploit the prospect of becoming the "East of the West", not by any delusionary national politics but by full integration in the European Union. This, however, is not in contradiction to the opportunity for the country to benefit from the economic-geographical capacities resulting from its location on the less-developed eastern fringe of the EU. Although these capacities tend to be in the form of disadvantages, they can also be of use in attracting foreign capital and building economic bridges. (The reality is that the majority of Hungary's neighbors, even in favorable conditions, will become members of the EU well after Hungary.) The utilization of these capabilities, integration, and the gaining of ground would seem to be the decisive processes in the forthcoming decades.

Unlike the first two freely elected governments in Hungary (which came to power in 1990 and 1994), the present government, elected in 1998, does not have to deal with crisis management. However, if this makes it complacent and leaves it too much ground for its populist policies, that is—returning to the words of Paul Kennedy quoted earlier—if it is not capable of recognizing those events that will have a decisive impact on the future, then Hungarian society will once again have to pay a great price.

I. FOCAL POINTS IN THE TRANSITION TO A MARKET ECONOMY

By the end of the 1980s and the early 1990s, in every Central and Eastern European country a serious economic and (a partly related) political crisis arose. The roots of this lay in the general crisis of the planned economies, which manifested itself in crises in the areas of internal and external macroeconomic balances, growth, macroeconomic structure, institutions, and modernization. This led to a general change in the political system, although the speed and depth of this change differed in the various countries and regions.

In contrast with popular misconceptions, the change in economic system was accompanied by serious economic recession. An extremely grave recession, lasting even to the present day, took place in the majority of the former Soviet states and of the post-socialist countries of the Balkans, where the limited change in the political system—often accompanied by political chaos, tensions, and the potential for civil war—made it impossible, or at least extremely difficult, to carry out meaningful economic reforms or, in some cases, even to begin such reforms.

The Visegrád countries were also affected by a highly significant recession–although less significant than that described above. Countries that were not burdened by debt at the beginning of the transition (Czechoslovakia, and later the Czech Republic and Slovakia) saw as important a fall in GDP as those which had previously been in debt (Poland and Hungary). Recession was experienced in countries in which there had been no reforms prior to the political changeover (Czechoslovakia), but also in those in which there had been several years of reform (Hungary and Poland).

There is no difference with respect to whether the ideology of the economic politicians openly favored “shock therapy” (Poland) or “gradual transition” (Hungary). Recession was closely related to the collapse of COMECON—and the subsequent loss of export markets—and the inevitable opening up of the domestic markets. However, this did not simply reflect mere quantitative problems but an overall structural crisis.

For this reason, the handling of the economic crisis—above all the preservation of solvency in the individual countries, the relief of internal and external balance tensions, and the maintenance of low inflation levels—must have not been be limited to stabilization measures but, at the same time, must have been characterized by modernization. This means modernization in the classical, sociological sense, which implies assimilation to the most developed Western economic and social organizational systems. In the absence of this, the conditions for sustainable growth following the recession will not be created. However, from this it follows, *inter alia*, that the change of regime, the building of a market economy, and the establishment of conditions for sustainable growth constitute a lengthy process, which—since it is accompanied by significant social conflicts—yields results only after halts and digressions, and in the context of a unique learning experience.

Change in GDP, 1990 to 2000

(1989 = 100)

	Hungary	Czech Rep.	Slovakia	Poland
1990	96.7		99.6	88.4
1993	81.8	79.2	76.7	86.9
1996	86.6	88.5	91.5	103.9
1999	99.3	85.5	103.7	121.0
2000	104.6	90.7	105.8	127.5

Source: CESTAT Statistical Bulletin

The development of each of the so-called Visegrád countries (Hungary, Czech Republic, Slovakia and Poland) has been characterized by the fact that in the 1990s—unlike the overwhelming majority of post-socialist countries—they achieved significant success in the transition towards a market economy. They were transformed into parliamentary democracies and have established an institutional system capable of handling social conflicts. They have abolished the shortage economy, created the fundamental institutions for a market economy, and, by means of radical liberalization and by limiting incomes more drastically than ever before, they have put money back into the "driving seat" of the economy. Lasting hyperinflation has not occurred in any of the countries (hyperinflation in Poland lasted for just two years), foreign trade has been successfully channeled to Western markets, and, in the majority of the countries, the rapidly increasing unemployment rates ultimately differ little from Western European tendencies. Without exception they have preserved or regained their solvency. At the same time, the permanent recession in those Eastern European countries that have delayed stabilization and market reforms indicates in itself that the economic crisis is not the result of the change of regime but vice versa—that is, the change of regime became inevitable due to the crisis.

However, the development of the Visegrád countries has not been without setbacks. The fact that the growth which followed the recession, both in the Czech Republic and in Hungary, had to be followed by new stabilization and reform packages (the same task lies ahead for Slovakia), and that these did not take place simultaneously, reveals that fluctuations in the growth rate do not primarily depend on world economic trends but on domestic circumstances. (The development of Poland since 1992 appears to be without setbacks. However, the presence of a crisis which had begun much earlier, and which was therefore all the more profound, plays a role in this, as does the waiving of debts. Meanwhile, the significantly deteriorating external balance and internal structural tensions make it probable that the current slowing down of growth is due, among other things, to domestic reasons.)

The repeated emergence of balance problems in every Visegrád country (in Hungary in 1995, in the Czech Republic in 1996, in Slovakia in 1998, and in Poland in 1999/2000) implies that the conditions for long-term growth and the creation of a new macroeconomic structure that meets the requirements of the world economy can only be achieved by means of "creative destruction". This conflict-producing destruction is inevitable, although governments, in order to avoid the creation of social tensions, attempt to postpone it. However, such delay leads only to the spreading of tensions; to the worsening of the internal and external balance, which seriously affects the entire economy; and to inflation. Nevertheless, for the ex-socialist countries the main opportunity to overcome crisis and create lasting growth lies in changing the institutional system and in carrying out market-economic reforms. This involves privatization, the creation of competitiveness and a market environment in the business sector, and the transformation of the state budget. This is a precondition for the effective allocation of resources and, in the event of this, for the inflow of foreign capital, the domestic accumulation of capital, and the modernization of post-socialist economies. The key issue, therefore, is to improve the ability of the economy to utilize, attract, and accumulate capital, all of which are closely related.

It is only after the gradual fulfillment of these capacities that resources will be available to devote to creation after the destruction has taken place, and that such creation is likely to be "real". At the same time, this is a lengthy process which cannot take place overnight. Both society and the governments in power will have to show patience and consistency. Hurrying the process (for instance by easing the restrictions on domestic demand before creating suitable conditions through the harmonization of supply, and especially by artificially generating demand) and postponing painful reform measures (for example the postponement of the application of bankruptcy laws, the postponement of real privatization, or the postponement of state budget reforms) can obstruct the stabilization/modernization process (as happened in the Visegrád countries). At the same time, economic pressures can stimulate the carrying out of reforms. The opportunities available to certain post-socialist countries are obviously limited by world political considerations. Their room for maneuver, however, both in positive and negative terms, is considerable. Hungary's success in attracting foreign capital, and Slovakia's exclusion from the first countries invited to take part in EU accession negotiations, are good illustrations of this. An investigation of certain important characteristics of the development of the Hungarian economy reveals distinctive fluctuations.

The years in question can readily be divided into distinct periods. These periods are characterized above all either by improvement or deterioration in the current balance of payments, and by various changes in GDP. Behind these factors, however, changes in the other economic processes and in the direction of economic policy can also be pointed out.

Thus, in the first period, between 1990 and 1992, despite the extremely pronounced economic recession which manifested itself in the production and use of GDP and in rising unemployment, the foreign trade and financial balance were both favorable and had improved significantly compared to the previous levels. However, in the second period, between 1992 and 1994, the balance worsened significantly once again, while a slight growth (but, within this, dynamic domestic consumption) began. The financial balance in the third period, between 1995 and 1996, improved significantly, while the rate of growth decreased (and domestic consumption fell temporarily). Dynamic growth began in the fourth period starting in 1997, which, in the first quarter of 2001, appears to be definitely

Volume indexes of GDP production and use, 1990 to 2000
(previous year = 100)

	1990	1991	1992	1993	1994	1995	1996	1997	1998	1999	2000
GDP production	96.7	88.1	96.9	99.4	102.9	101.5	101.3	104.6	104.9	104.5	105.3
Industry	92.4	82.2	93.3	104.4	105.9	107.0	103.3	111.2	108.3	108.2	118.3
Agriculture	95.4	91.9	83.4	92.1	99.6	102.7	104.2	99.5	98.5	98.7	100.0
Private consumption	96.4	94.4	100.0	101.9	99.8	92.9	96.9	102.0	104.9	104.6	
Investment	92.9	89.6	97.4	102.0	112.5	95.7	106.3	108.8	113.3	106.6	106.5
Domestic use	96.9	90.9	96.4	109.9	102.2	96.9	100.8	103.7	107.8	104.2	
Exports	95.9	95.1	102.1	89.9	113.7	113.4	107.4	126.4	116.7	113.2	130.0
Imports	94.8	105.5	100.2	120.2	108.8	99.3	105.7	125.5	122.8	112.3	132.5

Source: Central Statistical Office

Balance-related data for the Hungarian economy, 1990 to 2000

	1990	1991	1992	1993	1994	1995	1996	1997	1998	1999	2000
Consumer price index (previous year = 100)	128.9	135.0	123.0	122.5	118.8	128.2	123.6	118.3	114.3	110.0	109.8
Foreign trade balance (USD billion)	0.9	-1.2	-0.4	-3.6	-3.9	-2.6	-2.4	-2.1	-2.7	-3.0	-4.3
Convertible current balance of payments (USD billion)	0.1	0.3	0.3	-3.5	-3.9	-2.5	-1.7	-1.0	-2.3	-2.1	-1.9
Number of registered unemployed persons at end of year (1,000 persons)	80	406	660	632	520	496	478	464	404	405	
Balance of the state budget excluding privatization income, as a percentage of GDP	0.3	-2.9	-7.0	-5.6	-8.4	-6.8	-3.1	-4.6	-4.9*	-3.9	
Net foreign debt, with owners' credits (USD billion)	15.9	14.6	13.0	14.9	18.9	16.8	14.3	11.8	12.9	11.3	

* Excluding special consolidation expenses.

Source: Central Statistical Office, Ministry of Finance, Hungarian National Bank

sustainable, while on the whole the balance is favorable. This suggests that the cyclical nature of the Hungarian economy was significantly reduced during the last decade, when a decisive role was played by the establishment of the market economy, and within this the reform of the institutional system (the significant reduction of the state's opportunities for voluntarist interventions), the strengthening of competitiveness and flexibility in the entrepreneurial sphere, and the integration of the Hungarian economy within the world economy.

In the coming years leading up to the elections in 2002, domestic consumption is likely to exceed the growth in GDP, while the financial balance will slightly worsen. However, on the one hand, due to Hungarian export capacities, which have strengthened remarkably in recent years, and to the lower levels of debt, this does not imply a danger similar to that which existed in the mid-1990s. On the other hand, the kind of fluctuations generated by elections are characteristic of developed market economies as well, and Hungarian budget commitments, even before the elections of 1998, displayed this kind of tendency.

In the following we will analyze the important economic developments in the various periods.

1. The economic crisis and attempts at financial stabilization (1990 to 1992)

The Hungarian planned economy was characterized by the strengthening and abatement of waves of reform. These had various outcomes—above all the quality of life of the Hungarian population was better than in other socialist countries—but ultimately, for political reasons, the scope of the reforms was limited and, as a result, repeated setbacks prevented the Hungarian economy from becoming really effective. Increasing demand, coupled with worsening competitiveness, led time and again to the rapid accumulation of foreign debts. While in the 1970s debt ultimately financed growth, in the 1980s it was only sufficient to bring about stagnation.

Thus Hungary ended the 1980s with a stagnating economy (GDP in 1988 fell by 0.1 percent and in 1989 rose by only 0.7 percent compared with the previous year); with an enormous balance of payments deficit compared with exports (the deficit of USD 0.8 billion in 1988 rose to USD 1.4 billion in 1989); and with decreasing foreign currency reserves (the USD 2 billion convertible hard-currency reserves of 1998 had fallen to USD 1.7 billion by 1989, and to USD 1.1 billion by 1990). By the fall of 1989 the Hungarian economy found itself in a critical financial situation.

In order to avoid an external debt crisis, the last government of the socialist period put in place a stabilization program. Among other things they raised taxes, reduced budget expenditure, introduced a stricter monetary policy, devalued the forint, and lowered the amount of foreign currency that those traveling abroad were permitted to take out of the country. A three-year stabilization program (1990 to 1992) was elaborated, which included overall reform steps such as the continuation of the liberalization and deregulation that was already taking place, and the establishment of a legal and institutional system for privatization.

The new government, led by the Hungarian Democratic Forum(MDF, for short in Hungarian), which was formed in May 1990 following free elections, promised to create a social market economy. The unfavorable effects of the uncertainties of the first months, and of the approach to economic processes on the basis of narrowly interpreted political and power considerations—for example the re-election to their former positions of the managers of state-owned companies and the centralization and deceleration of the privatization process—were mitigated by the fact that the fiscal and monetary policy were in practice following the previous government's stabilization decisions.

Changes in GDP and the current balance of payments, 1988 to 1992

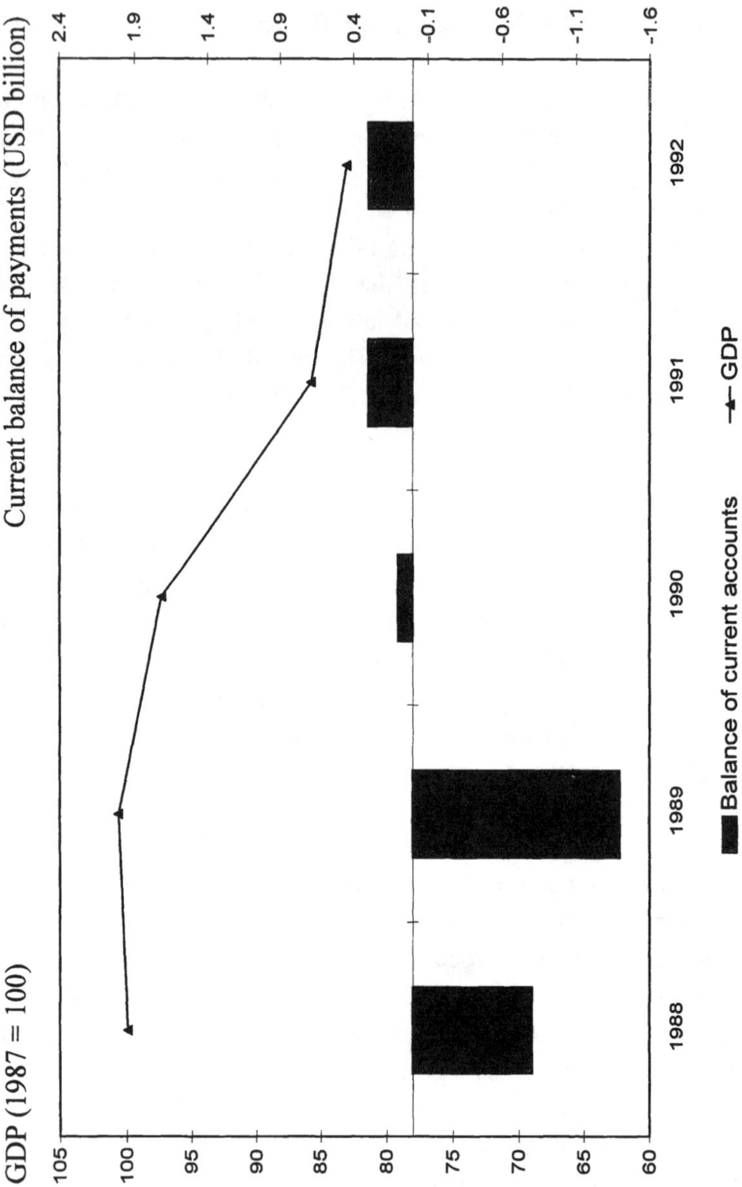

Source: Central Statistical Office

At the same time a drastic, although economically justified, rise in petrol prices—which, both in terms of method and implementation, shattered the illusions cherished by society (illusions that the government had, until then, done nothing to dispel)—was followed by a domestic political crisis: the so-called taxi-drivers' strike. Paradoxically, an economically sensible solution, that is, the liberalization of prices, emerged as a result. Although in Hungary the economic politicians—mostly relying on the results of the Hungarian reforms that had been going on for decades—regarded shock therapy as unnecessary, the collapse of COMECON and the resulting shrinkage of the domestic market represented a real shock to the Hungarian economy. In 1991 the government approved a four-year economic program, "Stabilization and Convertibility", which contained, *inter alia*, radical reforms.

Strict budgetary and monetary policies were introduced. The state budget deficit, which in 1989 amounted to more than 4 percent of GDP, became a surplus in 1990, while the 1991 deficit was balanced by a rapid increase in domestic financial savings. The growth rate of domestic net assets in 1990/91 (7 to 9 percent) fell a long way behind the nominal GDP, and although the expansion of the money supply in the wide sense slightly surpassed the growth rate of the GDP, taking into account the historic transformation of the institutional system, the growth in transactions demand, the relative fall in the need for queuing, the liberalization of hard-currency accounts held by the public, and the rapid growth in household demand, the conclusion can be drawn that monetary policy in 1990 was perhaps slightly restrictive, while in 1991 it was neutral.

As a result of the strict budgetary and monetary policy, the balance of current accounts, compared to the outstandingly high deficit in 1989, showed a slight surplus in 1990 and 1991, and by the summer of 1992 a surplus of more than USD 0.5 billion. However, this surplus was not the result of increased exports—the volume of exports fell by 4 percent in 1990 and by 5 percent in

1991, and even in 1992 increased by only 1 percent—but of the fall in imports which, over the three years, amounted to 7 percent, and of the increase in so-called invisible items. As a result of the beginning of direct foreign capital investments—the sum of which was approximately USD 1.5 billion in both 1991 and 1992—the country's total net foreign debts fell, while foreign currency reserves normalized.

Public savings showed an important increase. This was largely due to the fact that many people seized the opportunity to pay off housing credits, which had been provided at very low interest rates, so avoiding increased nominal interest. Furthermore, the high nominal interest rates that resulted from galloping inflation created the illusion of money, which also stimulated savings. Due to high inflation, unprecedented in the socialist period, and a sudden rise in unemployment—while the quality of consumer goods availability improved significantly—the public's sense of existential security was shaken, resulting in cautious expenditure on investment.

The growth in savings played a significant role in the fact that inflation, although rising steeply, could be kept in hand. Following a maximum level of 38.6 percent in June 1991, a year later it was only 20.1 percent (as a percentage of the same month during the previous year). Despite negative expectations, confidence in the Hungarian forint could be re-established and even strengthened. The difference between the forint's official and black-market rates did not only stop increasing but, by the summer of 1991, the difference had practically been eliminated.

Besides macroeconomic stabilization, further main tasks were the "laying of the foundations of capitalism", the creation of an institutional and legal system for the market economy, and the creation of the necessary conditions for its operation. This required, on the one hand, privatization, and, on the other hand, the creation of the institutions and legislation necessary for establishing the norms of civilized market attitudes and behaviors.

The Hungarian privatization process was basically market oriented and "created" real owners. Throughout the process, however, a demand for increased state control and a preference for certain groups of domestic buyers arose periodically, which—due to the subsequent privatization slowdown and resulting fall in privatization income—were followed by renewed bursts of privatization. Thus the 1990 centralized privatization program lost steam, and was followed in 1991/1992 by methods relying more heavily on decentralization and involving foreign capital.

The spread of civilized market behaviors demanded, above all, a serious restriction on company budgets. This meant, *inter alia*, a radical reduction in subsidies, the strict application of the bankruptcy laws, and the creation of modern accounting regulations. (This last, by means of a compulsory allowance for deficits and the regulation of amortization, effectively prevented companies from declaring nonexistent profits.) However, laws related to the financial intermediary system, competition, and consumer protection were also included here.

At the same time, due to the structural changes accompanying the transition to a market economy, the collapse of COMECON and its effect on the domestic markets, the significant liberalization of imports, the recession in the world economy, and the inevitable recession in domestic demand, production fell significantly. Industrial production fell by almost 10 percent in 1990, by 20 percent in 1991, and in 1992 by a further 10 percent; while in the same years the volume of agricultural products bought up fell by 10, 15, and a 13 percent respectively, that is, by altogether almost 40 percent. This was shortly followed by rapidly rising unemployment, which, between 1990 and 1992, grew from an insignificant level to 13 or 14 percent.

Significant structural changes in the micro-sphere were brought about by the re-launching of privatization in 1991; the strict Bankruptcy Act of 1 January 1992, which was in force until mid-1993 and which included provision for compulsory self-declared bankruptcy; and a modern act governing financial institutions and accounting. Above all, this meant the elimination of non-profitable production, the modernization of company structures, and the inevitable mobilization of resources. However, the crisis in sales that took place at the same time resulted in the collapse of capacities that could perhaps have been saved in part. Due to lack of capital and high interest rates—which were only slightly alleviated by the inflow of foreign working capital, outstanding in Hungary compared with the rest of the region—only a limited number of new investments took place. While GDP fell, the investment rate remained at about 20 percent, and a relatively low reduction in consumption was made possible by the drastic reduction of stocks.

2. Attempts at growth accompanied by serious balance tensions, 1993 to 1994

Although at the cost of major sacrifices, the first period of the transition to the market economy, which ended in 1992, produced major achievements in stabilization. The external balances were stabilized, and inflation markedly decreased. For many, this produced the illusory hope of the beginnings of growth, although the consumption/GDP ratio and the low rate of investments became an obstacle to growth; a significant part of the surviving business sector financed itself by using up assets (e.g., by transferring amortization funds to current expenditure) and by various methods of concealing income; and the unfinished, or unstarted, market economy reforms threatened to result in the wasting of existing resources. Despite such illusory hopes, the balance deteriorated dramatically in 1993 while no growth took place. Then, in 1994, the beginnings of growth were accompanied by an unsustainable annual balance deficit of USD 3.5 to 4 billion.

From the late summer of 1992, the current balance of payments displayed a gradually weakening performance, and in the second half-year, particularly in the last quarter, it produced a significant deficit. The dynamics of exports to developed market economies were also interrupted in the summer of 1992, and the annual foreign trade balance closed with a deficit. The unfavorable current balance of payments was, of course, related to domestic financial processes. Individual consumption did not fall even in 1992, and in 1993 rose by almost 2 percent. The growth rate of net household savings slowed from fall 1992, and growth had almost stopped by 1993. Community consumption began to increase dynamically. In parallel with this, the state budget deficit rose from 2.9 percent of GDP in 1991 to 7 percent in 1992, and in 1994 reached 8.4 percent (excluding privatization revenue).

The fall in inflation also slowed down at the end of 1992, and the slight fall in 1993 was already the result of an overestimation of the effective rate, which was a significant component in the deterioration of the foreign trade balance. Another important reason for the latter was the abandonment of the restrictive monetary policy. The deterioration was manifested in the growth of the state budget deficit, and in the monetary policy that was aimed at lowering interest rates artificially. Despite this, investments increased by only 15 percent in 1993/1994, which represents a modest rate compared to the very low levels of earlier. Growing domestic demand, coupled with non-competitive domestic production, reduced the pressure to export and generated a hunger for imports.

The delayed effects of the disappearance of markets in previous years probably played a role in the fact that exports lost steam in 1992 and 1993. Initially some companies, driven by a strong survival instinct, were willing to produce, at almost any price, goods that could be sold in the developed market economies, using capacities originally created to serve other markets. This, however—due to regular inefficiency and to the recession in the West—was not sustainable.

The turning point in the summer/fall of 1992 was manifested not only in the worsening of the macroeconomic indicators, but also in the change of declared economic policy. It was at this time that the government approved its new working program. Not only were several elements of the previous program abandoned (e.g., the reform of public finances was not even begun), but monetary and fiscal policies were eased as described above, and the state, rather than market measures, was more often expected to solve conflicts. The relaxation of the Bankruptcy Act, the methods of credit and bank consolidation, the reorganization that was to be extended to an increasing number of companies, the growing dominance of biased privatization techniques, and ambivalent attitudes towards foreign capital not only worsened the position of the budget but relaxed the budget constraints on the banks as well as on state and private companies. Interest rates, which had diverged from inflation expectations, had an unfavorable impact on household savings.

Behind the economic-political turnaround lay a number of political factors. It was at this time that the ruling governing party began to be fragmented into various platforms, and a pronouncedly far-right group gained an almost dominant position. Following a lengthy hesitation, and pressured by various economic power groups, the party's center sacrificed its former economic policy (and some of its key figures).

One of the most significant actions of the period following the credit consolidation of 1992/1993 was the bank consolidation that took place in 1993/1994. Credit consolidation meant, above all, buying from the banks, in return for credit consolidation bonds, the credit of companies of "national economic importance" that had fallen on hard times (for 90 to 100 percent of their face value), which amounted to HUF 60 billion. Despite this, the sum of the banks' problematic loans in 1993 was still more than HUF 400 billion (according to the newly introduced credit rating regulations). Since the losses not only endangered the banks' stock capital but also a significant percentage of deposits, the government decided to begin bank consolidation in 1993. Unlike credit consolidation, this was not carried out by clearing the banks' portfolios but by state capitalization. In order to achieve this, special long-term state bonds were issued. The interest of net HUF 300 billion on the credit and bank consolidation bonds was a serious burden on the state budget, amounting to 1.2 percent of GDP in 1994, and to 1.6 percent of GDP in 1995.

Several factors played a role in the accumulation of the banks' problematic credits, such as the poor credit portfolio inherited from the period of the one-tier banking system and subsequently permanently perpetuated; the normal risk entailed by granting new credits, which, at the time of the crisis that accompanied the transition to the market economy, became far higher; the irresponsible (and occasionally, as a result of political pressure or corruption, consciously irrational) granting of credits by banks, which, in practice, were not under the control of a real owner; and the system of accounting regulations, which made it possible to conceal anomalies. The consolidation of state-owned banks that had experienced a loss of capital was unavoidable. However, the method employed was marked by the same arbitrariness that had made consolidation necessary in the first place. This resulted in significant additional expenses and was not accompanied by a clear-cut bank privatization strategy—in certain cases, only the transformation of the banks' structure and management took place (and in some cases not even that). Thus, despite the promises, several tasks in the consolidation of the banking sector were left until the second half of the 1990s. However, the fact remains that, from 1995, the privatization of the banks was given huge impetus, which could not have happened had some kind of consolidation not taken place earlier.

Changes in GDP and the net foreign debt position, 1992 to 1994

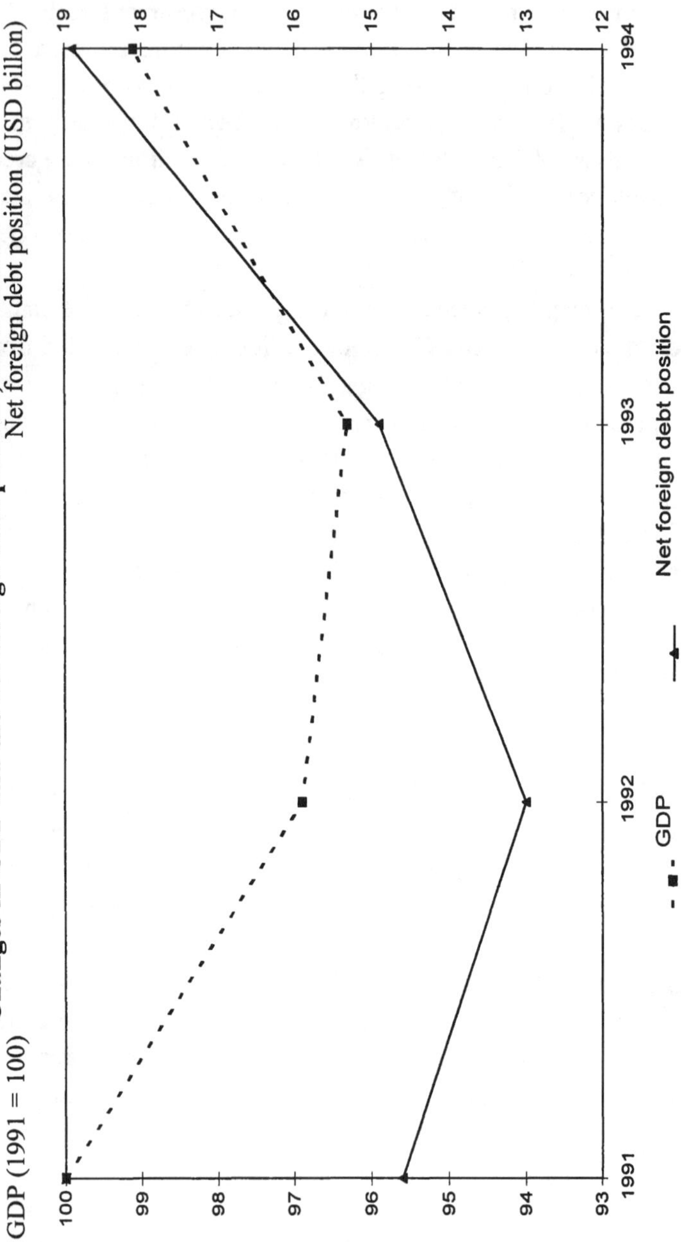

Source: Central Statistical Office

The economic program outlined above, which slowed down, or even put a stop to, economic reforms and market-based privatization while experimenting with the artificial stimulation of demand, further increased the already existing structural tensions in the economy, resulting in the renewed upsetting of balances without producing rapid growth. Political considerations played a role in this economic policy: with the approaching elections it became an important goal of the government to increase consumption and to give the public a share in state assets on favorable terms. This economic policy was made temporarily feasible by the improvement in the external balance in the early 1990s.

Sensing the tensions in the balance, the Hungarian National Bank was forced to tighten its monetary policy slightly—and as it turned out ineffectively—as early as mid-1993. Although the Hungarian National Bank had no alternative but to act in spite of the absence of any modification in the budget policy, this line of action proved extremely problematic. It could not suppress demand or improve the current balance of payments as a result of, among other reasons, the low level of confidence in the monetary policy, the delay between the raising of interest rates by the central bank and the commercial banks, and the fact that creditworthy enterprises were turning towards foreign credit providers. Furthermore, additional structural tensions emerged in the economy: a strong differentiation occurred within the financial system according to who was capable of participating in the rapidly expanding area of hard-currency financing, and who was not.

The central bank was mistaken in artificially reducing interest rates, thus for a long time it inspired no confidence when raising interest rates. Although the strict monetary policy and the lenient budget policy eventually led to a significant increase in real interest rates, this nevertheless meant a serious burden on the state budget and domestic enterprises that had no access to foreign-currency loans. In the election year the amount of foreign working capital inflow into Hungary temporarily fell, although in terms of the region it remained outstanding. In 1994 foreign debt greatly increased.

3. The stabilization process without economic recession, 1995 to 1996

In the summer of 1994 the newly formed socialist and liberal coalition government led by the Hungarian Socialist Party (MSZP), recognizing the dramatic deterioration in the balance of payments, declared crisis management as a key task of its economic policy. In practice, however, a political (and personal) struggle took place that lasted for almost half a year. During this struggle the government's economic policy became stricter, but not sufficiently so. The postponement of devaluation and of increases in energy prices (as well as the level of these increases) reflected this ambivalence towards the whole of the 1994 supplementary budget. During the debating of the privatization act, privatization almost came to a standstill, and in the course of preparations for a social-economic agreement between the government and the trade unions the real meaning of such an agreement, that is, agreement on prices and wages—due to the unacceptability of the significant reduction in real wages—was pushed into the background while the trade unions increased their activities in an attempt to influence the government's economic policy as a whole. A modernization program (which meant, in practice, an alternative economic policy) was taking shape, independently from the tasks connected with stabilization and, above all, in an attempt to project an attractive image of the future.

A good illustration of the situation is the fact that, while the IMF proposed forcing down the state budget deficit to GDP ratio from the 8 to 9 percent expected for 1994 (in reality 8.4 percent) to 3 percent by 1995, the government decided on a ratio of 5.5 percent. However, the minister of finance, after the passing of the

Budget Act in late 1994, declared that only the acceptance of a supplementary budget could ensure even this latter figure. In early 1995 the Hungarian National Bank, which at the time was functioning without a president, wrote to the prime minister demanding measures in order to reduce to a level of USD 2.5 billion the current balance of payments deficit, which threatened to reach USD 4 billion once again in 1995, and insisting on the inevitability of a stricter monetary policy.

Only after a dramatic increase in balance tensions—which meant not only a lasting deterioration in the balance of current accounts but also, in conjunction with the financial crisis in Mexico in early 1995, the shaking of international confidence in Hungarian economic policy—did the government finally launch a tough, consistent, short-term stabilization program. (This was widely known as the "Bokros Package", after one of its creators, the minister of finance.) In the course of 1995 this brought about a real change in monetary policy and, by means of a supplementary budget, made the budget much stricter.

The stabilization package included the immediate and continuing reduction of the budget deficit. The main means of achieving this were the introduction of an 8 percent surtax, an important one-off devaluation of the forint followed by a declared monthly devaluation, and a strict wages policy. Certain additional tax increases (for instance tax on cars) were also imposed. Cuts in social expenditure were also planned (most of which were later postponed or proved to be unconstitutional). The package aimed to achieve significant structural changes in the state budget and set out an ambitious privatization program that included the sale of the energy sector and of the commercial banks.

The turnaround in economic policy resulted in a dramatic improvement in the internal and external balance of the Hungarian economy. The balance of payments deficit decreased from the USD 3.9 billion level of 1994 to USD 2.5 billion in 1995, and to USD 1.7

billion in 1996. In 1995 the FDI inflow—partly due to the privatization of the energy sector—was a remarkable USD 4.5 billion, but even in 1996 exceeded (by approximately USD 200 million) the current account balance of payments deficit. This, in addition to initial portfolio investments, led to an improvement in the net foreign debt position and the increasing of foreign currency resources. Hungary's net foreign currency debt position improved from the USD 18.9 billion level of late 1994 to USD 16.8 billion in late 1995, and to USD 14.3 billion by late 1996. The balance of foreign trade deficit improved from the USD 3.9 billion level of 1994 to USD 2.6 billion, while in 1996 it remained at this level.

The fact that the state budget's consolidated deficit (not taking into account privatization revenues) compared to GDP decreased from the 8.4 percent level of 1994 to 6.8 percent in 1995 and 3.1 percent in 1996, represented an important achievement. In relation to this, the ratio of income redistributed by the state budget to GDP had fallen from 61 percent in 1994 to 50/51 percent by 1996.

Also favorable was the fact that the significant improvement in the financial balance was not accompanied by a fall in GDP. The growth in exports was able to balance the fall in domestic demand, thus GDP improved by 1.5 percent in 1995, and by 1.3 percent in 1996. Since 1994 the profits in the corporate sector have been positive in the national economy as a whole, as well as in industry. (Pre-tax profit, projected against owners' capital, was, in the national economy as a whole, -4.3 percent in 1993, rising to 0.1 percent in 1994 and to 5.6 percent in 1996.) An unfavorable fact was that investments stagnated or increased only slightly.

The declaration of the convertibility of the Hungarian forint in early 1996 was an indication of what had been achieved. The credit agreement made with the IMF in spring 1996 (which, due to the more rapid than expected success of stabilization, was not put into practice) was an acknowledgment of stabilization, as was Hungary's acceptance into the OECD and the general improvement in the country's rating among international credit institutions. By the end of 1996 Hungary was listed among the countries recommended to investors.

GDP and the state budget deficit compared to GDP, 1994 to 1996

Percentage

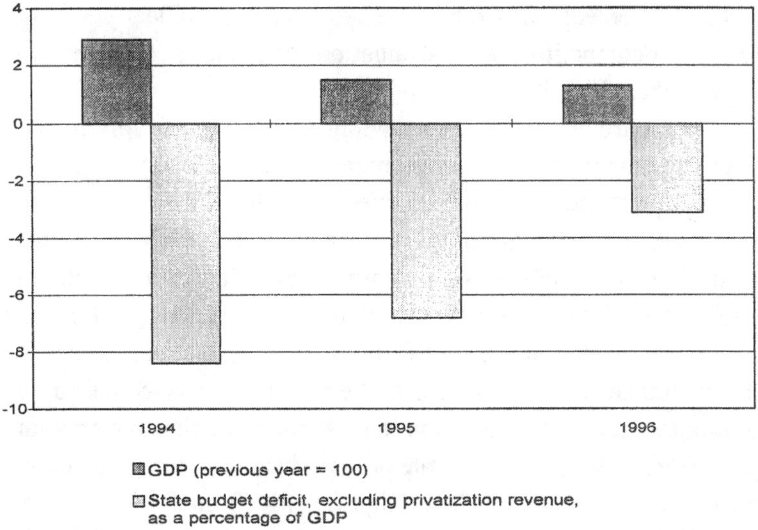

Source: Central Statistical Office

One of the central elements of the economic-political package introduced in March 1995 was the changing of the exchange rate policy. The one-off 9 percent devaluation of the forint took place as part of this package: it was designed to produce a significant improvement in the Hungarian economy's external competitiveness and, furthermore, with additional stimulation given by the introduction of the customs surtax, to create an important reduction in the demand for imports.

At the same time, following the important one-off devaluation, the so-called crawling peg devaluation system was put in place. In this system, instead of the whole amount of a revaluation or devaluation taking place at once, it is spread in small percentages over a number of months. Thus, in the remaining part of the first half-year of 1995, a monthly 1.9 percent devaluation took place, and in the second half-year a monthly devaluation of 1.3 percent. In 1996 this figure was 1.2 percent; in 1997 the rate of the monthly devaluation fell to 1.1 percent, and from August to 1.0 percent. Clearly, in order to protect competitiveness, devaluation took place at a much slower pace than the fall in inflation.

The introduction of the crawling peg did not simply mean a new rate policy, but also commitment to the kind of economic policy that provided a so-called monetary anchor for the budget and for wages and incomes policy. According to this, the sole, ultimate goal of monetary policy is the reduction of inflation, to which only one intermediate goal belongs, that is, the nominal rate. (The amount of money in the system is determined internally, since, if the central bank wishes to protect the rate, it can change the supply of money only in subordination to it. At the same time the crawling peg means a stricter interest rate policy, since in this system domestic interest rates cannot differ significantly from foreign interest rates, from the declared devaluation, or from the level justified by the country's risk assessment rating.)

The experience of the operation of the crawling peg system has been favorable. The acceleration of inflation stopped in mid-1995, and the inflation rate, although at a much slower pace than the government had expected, began to show a continuous fall. (Inflation was 31 percent in July 1995 and 19.8 percent in December 1996, compared to the same months in the previous year, while annual average inflation in 1995 was 28.2 percent, and 23.6 percent in 1996.) In accordance with this, there was also a change in interest rate trends. In discount treasury bill tenders the permanent increase in yield came to an end, and at the end of the summer of 1995 a fall began which, by early 1996 and later in the same year, had become extremely significant. Demand for longer-term government securities rose significantly. The National Bank of Hungary continuously decreased the repo-interest rate. This, among other things, following the measures taken in March, made it possible for the inflow of foreign currency to increase and become continuous. On the other hand, the fall in interest rates on longer-term securities reflected the easing of inflation expectations. Whereas previously devaluation expectations had arisen from time to time, from March 1995 (apart from the short period following the Russian financial crisis of late summer 1998) there were no such expectations.

The improvement in the balance of payments and in the balance of the state budget, as well as confidence in the rate system and, above all, the strong inflow of foreign capital, which was related to the acceleration of privatization in late 1995, altogether created an opportunity in 1996 for the nominal interest rate to fall more rapidly than inflation, thus the difference between forint and foreign currency interest decreased significantly by 8 to 10 percent in one year, to reach 4 percent. This, taking into account the exchange rate risk—did not represent a significant difference between the two, thus the inflow of speculative foreign currency decreased.

During 1995/1996 the Hungarian economy as whole made important progress in the stabilization process. The internal and external financial deficit fell to a manageable level. The state budget deficit of 3.1 percent of the GDP in 1996 (excluding privatization revenues) was far more favorable than the 4.5 percent average among EU countries, while the surplus of the primary balance (4.4 percent of the GDP)—excluding interest rate expenditure—was among the highest in Europe. The increase in exports since 1994 has been in double figures. Hungary's foreign balance of payments deficit is continuously and significantly decreasing and is conveniently covered by the inflow of foreign capital and other sources. Thus the country's net and gross debt has significantly decreased and the country's international monetary standing has dramatically improved.

Stabilization has not been completed by 1997: in particular, inflation still remained high. Temporary measures—such as unsustainable reductions in certain budget expenditures, the introduction of the surtax, and privatization revenues—played a significant role in forcing down the state budget deficit. The transformation of structures, mechanisms, and institutions progressed very slowly, the few exceptions being the creation of the Treasury, and in 1997 the approval of old-age pension reforms. (For example, the number of hospital beds was reduced by 10,000, giving rise to serious conflicts. However, due to the compromises reached—the government refrained from closing hospital buildings which would have resulted in substantial savings—the savings actually achieved were minimal.)

Stabilization naturally came at a price. Due to the upsurge in inflation in mid-1995 and the restrictive budget and incomes policy, living standards in 1995/1996 fell by almost 10 percent, with the middle classes in particular ending up as losers. Incomes were realigned, to the disadvantage of the general public and the state budget, and to the advantage of enterprises and foreigners. During the correction of the balance, economic growth inevitably came to a standstill and investments slowed down.

Stabilization gave rise to certain illusions. Neither hopes for a rapid fall in inflation, nor the idea that the resources newly made available to enterprises would be spent automatically on investments, were substantiated. Too high inflation and too little investment slows down economic growth. Thus although certain conditions for sustainable growth were created (financeable deficits, international confidence), others (an environment able to stimulate investments, the reform of the state budget) were not, or only emerged in part. At the same time, the recovery that began during the last months of 1996, became more marked in 1997.

GKI Co.'s economic activity index and its components, 1996 to 2000

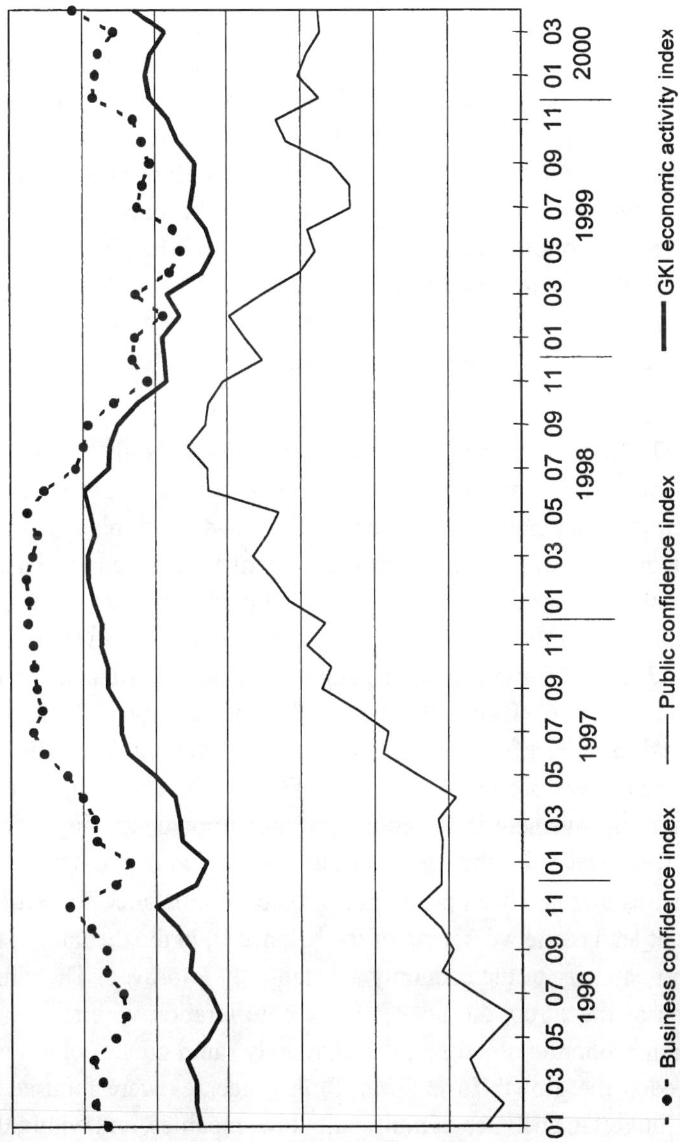

Source: GKI Co. surveys

The following graph shows that in 1998, due to the approaching elections, public confidence showed a marked increase, then fell rapidly. Following the shock caused by the stabilization measures introduced in spring 1995, both the business and the public confidence indexes showed a tendency to improve in 1996 (while the significant fluctuations were partly due to seasonal factors). In 1998/1999, with the deterioration in the world economic situation, business and public expectations were lowered; then, in the second half of 1999, an improvement began.

4. On course for sustainable growth, 1997 to 1999

In 1997 the Hungarian economy unquestionably shifted from the low point it had reached. Following earlier structural changes and a radical correction, substantial economic growth took place without any worsening of the external balance—which in fact showed a significant and general improvement. The internal monetary position was not as positive as this: the pace at which inflation was falling slowed down, while the state budget balance was practically the same as in 1996. (Due to the time differences in financial accounting and to corrections for the changing constructions, the deficit in both years was around 4 percent of GDP.) There was significant further improvement in the country's international standing.

It proved to be the case that the elimination of the temporary measures that had been put in place to achieve balance corrections did not lead to the worsening of the balance if, in the meantime, the export capacity of the economy substantially improved. The elimination of the surtax did not lead to a deterioration with respect to foreign economic processes: the extremely rapid growth of exports exceeded the growth in imports. Both processes were focused on the Hungarian affiliates of multinational companies, and within this group onmanufacturing. Experience showed that, in the event of there being competitive supply—and the presence of conditions facilitating, as well as forcing, this situation—there was no necessary contradiction between growth and equilibrium. The growth rate of the Hungarian economy in 1997 reached that of the region and slightly surpassed that of the EU.

Annual average inflation significantly decreased (from 23.6 percent in 1996 to 18.3 percent in the next year). This, however, was mostly due to the impact of the previous year, which is clearly illustrated in the fact that the price index of December 1997 (18.4 percent) was scarcely lower than in December 1996 (19.8 percent). In addition to the level of energy prices and insecurity on the Hungarian stock exchange brought about by the Southeast Asian crisis, the rapid outflow of nominal wages played a role in this.

In 1998 rapid growth took place in the Hungarian economy, accompanied by the marked deceleration of inflation. However, domestic demand (use) increased more dynamically than production, and the central budget deficit was high. This latter situation was largely related to the ambitious budgetary projects elaborated in the election year. Due to the Russian financial crisis and uncertainties on the international money and capital markets, the external economic balance worsened. However, the current account deficit was acceptable and financeable.

As a result of a growth in exports of approximately 21 percent and a growth in imports of about 24 percent, the deficit in the foreign economic balance grew by USD 600 million to reach USD 2.7 billion. Partly due to this, but mainly due to the significant increase in income and profit outflow, the current balance of payments produced a deficit of USD 2.3 billion, exceeding the 1997 deficit by USD 1.3 billion, which represents a dangerously rapid deterioration. The level of FDI inflow fell, and even with portfolio investments did not reach the amount of the balance of payments deficit. Including owners' credits, net debt rose by USD 1.2 billion, while excluding owners' credits it fell by USD 0.4 billion.

GDP and its domestic use, 1990 to 2000

(comparative amounts, 1989 = 100)

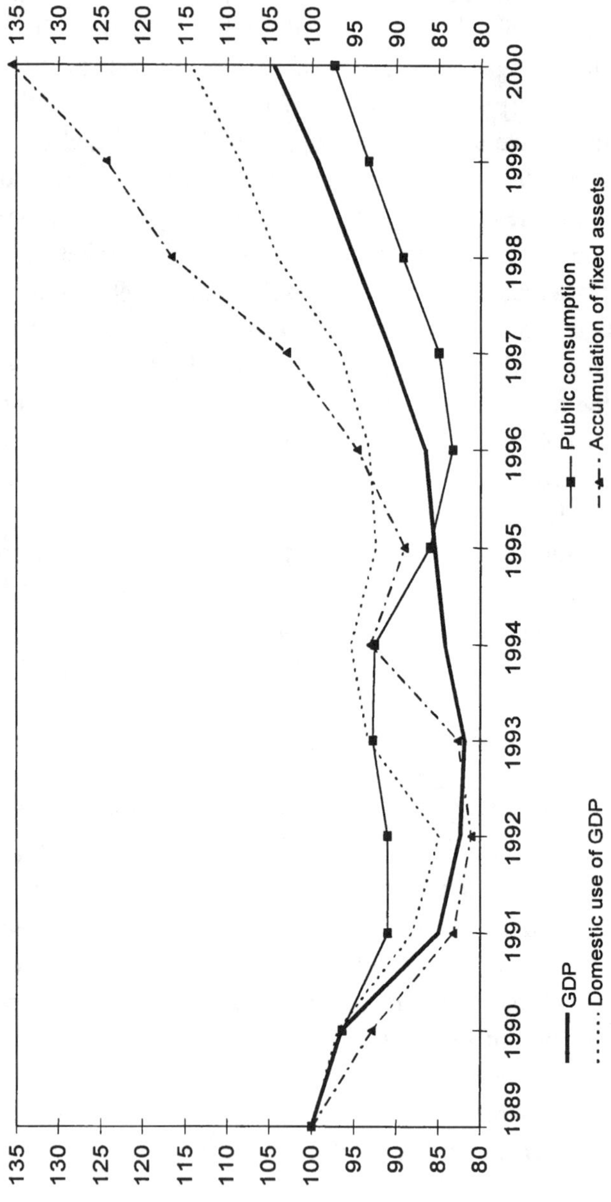

Source: Central Statistical Office. 1999 to 2000: GKI Co. forecast

However, inflation fell more rapidly than in previous years and more rapidly than expected. Very low world-market energy and food prices played a role in this, as did significant over-supply on the domestic market. Expectations were also significantly lower. The annual price index was 14.3 percent, and in December was 10.3 percent. The former was 4 percent lower than the previous year, while the latter was lower by 8 percent.

Monetary policy in 1998 adjusted itself well to the situation brought about by the international and domestic crisis in the fall of that year. It maintained confidence in its rate policy and allowed for the necessary increase in real interest.

On the whole, 1999 was a good year for the Hungarian economy. It became apparent that the business sector was able to develop and adapt more readily than had been expected. It was fortunate that the unfavorable world-economic impact was less serious than expected and that the European boom took place more rapidly and strongly than experts had predicted.

There was a slightly slower increase in GDP (4.5 percent) than in the previous two years (4.6 and 4.9 percent). Even by international standards this is a remarkable rate, representing about twice the average growth of EU countries (which, from 2.7 percent in 1998, fell to 2 percent in 1999). The terms of trade worsened, and GDP, corrected accordingly, increased only by approximately 3.5 percent. The majority of balance figures were relatively favorable. The state budget deficit in terms of GDP was 3.9 percent, that is, lower than the 1998 figure of 4.9 percent. The current balance of payments deficit was USD 2.1 billion, somewhat smaller than in 1998. The country's net total outstanding debt, including owners' credits, fell by about USD 1.5 billion, and excluding owners' credits by USD 1 billion. Average annual inflation fell significantly, from 14.3 percent in 1998 to 10 percent.

However, tensions emerged with respect to GDP use, where the growth rates of 1999 proved unsustainable. Consumption increased slightly more rapidly than GDP (by 4.6 percent), while investments rose more slowly than in the previous year (when the figure was 13.3 percent) and, at 6.6 percent, more slowly than the pace required for modernization. Inflation accelerated in the second half of the year.

The Hungarian economy has already become integrated to a significant extent in the world economy, and predominantly in the EU. Even between fall 1998 and spring 1999—a period which saw a marked decline in European prosperity—Hungarian industry proved capable of producing extremely dynamic growth even by international standards. This resulted from the fact that foreign investments had produced a significant improvement in the competitiveness of domestic industry. The growth was almost entirely due to exports by Hungarian-based multinational companies. As a result, the manufacturing industry, and especially the machine industry, proved more capable of improving production and exports, and less dependent on European prosperity, than had been expected. At the same time, the Hungarian business sector, and above all industry, was able to profit from improvements in European prosperity, and in the second half of 1999 exports significantly accelerated. As a result of this, and also of the rise in domestic consumption, domestic industrial sales also increased in the second half of the year.

The smallness of the increase in the foreign trade deficit, while the terms of trade worsened, can also be explained by the Hungarian economy's better than expected export capacity, since imports increased dynamically by 14 percent.

In the business sector, as in earlier years, there was significant competition and differentiation. The changes in branch, subbranch, and product structure, which are one of the most important indicators of modernization, continued in line with international tendencies. For example, between 1997 and 1999 GDP increased by exactly 15 percent, even while the energy consumption of the business sector increased slightly. Machine industry exports in 1999 already exceeded imports. The surplus in the turnover of goods between Hungary and EU countries, and between Hungary and Germany in particular, further increased. The most important exception was the still stagnating agricultural sphere, where natural disasters, as well as the political debates surrounding subsidies, diverted attention from the basic issues: the unsettled question of the use of land and the related lack of ability to attract capital; the absence of an institutional system for market coordination; and the resulting low levels of profitability. The weight of food exports fell back to 6 percent from the 10 percent level of the previous year. There are also many problems in the area of public services, where little happened to improve the situation in 1999. Furthermore, the fact that during 1999 there was no strengthening of the legal security of the economy, the constitutionality of the economy, or the general willingness to abide by the law, remains a fundamental problem. Likewise, the spread of innovation has been insufficiently rapid.

Investments of the corporate sector were relatively high. At the same time, as a tacit means of budget correction, cutbacks in budget expenditure (for example expenditure on the construction of motorways and subsidies for the building of apartments) meant that the very goals that were supposed to be given preference from 2000 onwards were pushed into the background in 1999. Other developments in the areas of infrastructure (railroads and local transports, city bypasses, etc.) and environmental protection were also postponed, which was unfavorable from the point of view of EU accession.

According to the most reliable information, the number of those in work rose slightly, by 1.5 percent, while the number of unemployed remained practically unchanged.

The growth in consumption was based on the dynamic increase in real incomes and a marked fall in the savings rate. The larger than expected burden of personal income tax and inflation prevented real incomes from rising. In terms of consumption, the public began to compensate for earlier postponement. The increase in net household financial assets slowed considerably (in 1997 the figure was HUF 870 billion, and in 1999 HUF 760 billion). A major contributing factor was the decrease in nominal interest—even while inflation was rising.

The state budgetary deficit of 3.9 percent compared to GDP (despite the extremely high level of expenditure) was in keeping with the provisions of the Budget Act. This—alongside the outflow of wages, which was more dynamic than expected, and the increase in consumption that generated tax revenue—was mostly the result of the "silent", non-declared mid-year measures to cut expenditure and generate income. Certain of these measures—above all the cut-back in expenditure on investment by the state—represented real savings. Others, however, only resulted in one-off improvements, while in some cases savings were merely achieved by means of peculiar accounting techniques. Examples of the latter include the new financing method for medicine subsidies (the delaying of the transfer of subsidies by a month); and accounting various privatization and concession revenues as current income. Taking all this into account, the state budget deficit in 1999 was about 5 percent of GDP, that is, the fiscal balance was similar to that of the previous year. Within the state budget there are tendencies towards centralization.

The balance of payments deficit turned out to be much lower than had been predicted during the year. In the second half-year, exports, which surpassed expectations, were undeniably an important factor in this success. It is worth mentioning, however, that the strengthening of the dollar against the euro also had a part to play in the improvement. Calculating the deficit in euros would produce a result roughly equaling that of 1998 (which was also favorable). In 1999 the balance of "non-debt-generating" capital (FDI and portfolio investments) was higher than the balance of payments deficit. Within this, however, the net total of direct working capital investments involving real long-term financing was EUR 1.3 billion, that is, much lower than the deficit. It seems that from now on we must calculate with a total of EUR 800 to 900 million annual open (that is, declared in the relevant column of the balance of payments) —and about the same amount of hidden—outflow of profit, since the total of profits taken out of the country was similar in both 1998 and 1999. Compared to the total inflow of foreign capital (approx. EUR 22 billion), and by international standards, this figure is not particularly high.

Calculating according to referential returns over one year, and according to inflation for the same period, real interest fell from 5.7 percent (too high) at the end of March 1999, to 4.6 percent at the end of June, to 3 percent by the end of September, and to 1 percent (too low) at the end of December. Since in the first half-year external assessments of the Hungarian economy were not favorable, and since fiscal policy (at least in the eyes of the outside world) was changing only slowly, monetary strictness was very pronounced in this period. By the end of the year, and in early 2000—as a result of fiscal improvement and the regaining of international confidence—monetary policy became "soft" and, under pressure, "compliant".

A marked tension emerged between inflation, interest rates, the exchange rate, and savings. Portfolio investments grew from EUR 0.5 billion in 1998 to EUR 1.1 billion in 1999. This increase was, on the whole, favorable, and partly reflected improving confidence. However, it included a significant amount of "hot money". The rising inflow of money was partly the result of the large yield available to foreigners on government securities. High interest rates in countries in a position similar to that of Hungary are natural and inevitable, but in this particular case they were also due to the over-reduction of the crawling peg. Because of improving productivity—apart from in certain areas, especially in medium-sized companies exporting in euros—this did not cause major problems for exporters. From the point of view of the budget, the high interest rates helped to reduce inflation. However, due to decreasing keenness to save—partly due to the fall in real interest—the costs of tying down inflowing money were also damaging. By the end of 1999 expectations with respect to the upvaluation of the forint became the basis of speculations.

The reducing of the monthly devaluation rate was exaggerated, primarily compared to inflation trends. The annual average consumer price index fell significantly in 1999, by 4.3 percent, although the December to December index was almost 1 percent higher (11.2 percent) than in the previous year. In December 1999 domestic retail prices in the manufacturing industry already exceeded the December 1998 levels by 13.1 percent (although in the first quarter of the year they were only 3.8 percent higher than in the first quarter of 1998.) Although this acceleration was largely related to energy prices, it was extremely significant. Thus, if we look at the mid-year tendencies, inflation in Hungary in 1999, rather than slowing down, in fact stagnated or even increased in its most important aspects. Inflation pressure (especially on the cost, but also on the demand, side) certainly increased. In such conditions the reductions in the devaluation rate, which took place on several occasions, should not have been carried out so hastily.

In 1999 no substantial reforms were introduced or planned. The failure to introduce the tax reforms that had been much discussed in the spring did not represent a great problem: there would have been no way to reduce burdens significantly, and, without that, declaring the reform would only have led to raising unsubstantiated expectations or to upsetting the stability required in the business sector. However, postponing health reforms and putting public administration onto a regional basis worsened the economy's longer-term perspectives. Another serious problem was that not even the outlines of the much-needed agricultural reforms were elaborated.

The peak of the business cycle has taken place in fiscal 2000: the yearly growth of GDP has equaled to 5.3 percent – although the growth of income, corrected by the deterioration of the terms of trade was not actually higher than 4 percent. The Hungarian business cycle has followed closely the European cycle: the growth rate was 6 percent in the first half of 2000 while it was 4.5 percent in the second half of the year, that meant a 2 percent higher growth performance than in the European Union.

This dynamic growth performance was pretty unequal according to different branches: the industry and telecommunications realized a double digit growth while the performance of the construction sector was equal to about 6 percent and the agricultural production has even stagnated.

Employment grew by 1 percent, in consequence unemployment rated declined to less than 6.5 percent.

The less impressive figure and fact for fiscal 2000 lies in the fact that inflation seems to be stabilized around 10 percent. This performance is not too much encouraging, it was the consequence of three separate causes: the important increase in world market raw material prices, especially crude oil and natural gas prices; the fort strengthening of US dollar against the euro caused severe inflationary pressure (the exchange rate of forint is 100 percent linked to the euro); and—last but not least—food prices increase in an important manner—which was the direct consequence of the previously really very low food prices.

A "hidden budgetary correction" has also taken place in fiscal 2000: since inflation turned out to much higher than it had been planned in the budget (at least 9.8 percent instead of 6-7 percent), plus the unchanged personal income taxes and the higher than expected imports made tax incomes also higher than expected. Therefore, higher than expected budgetary incomes allowed the government to realize an important overexpenditure policy. According to the GFS system, the over-all budgetary deficit—excluding local governments—was equal to 3.2 percent—which meant on the one hand, an important improvement compared to the previous years but, on the other hand the deficit is to high if we take into account that it turned out at the peak of the business cycle. In case of such a high growth performance, even a slight budgetary sufficit would be normal.

The above mentioned fiscal correction, alongside with the mere 2 percent high increase in real wages and an even lower, that is 1 percent increase in the real value of pensions, monetary policy had the possibility to be eased. real interest rates were on decline in the whole year, their value varied between 0.5-1.5 which is much too low. These nominally low interest rates are unfavorable for domestic savings and is, at the same time, too high for external speculation. Exchange rate policy had been based on a 'too optimistic' inflationary forecast by the government, therefore, the Hungarian currency has actually evaluated by about 7 percent against the euro, its monetary anchor. Due to the extremely favorable external conjuncture, this evaluation of the real effective exchange rate of the Hungarian forint did not lead to important difficulties.

The most unfavorable 'development' has actually taken place on the capital markets: both the turnover and the prices have fallen decisively. The performance of the two Hungarian stock exchanged deteriorated significantly – mostly because of the unfavorable government decisions and interference into gas and medicine prices.

The balance of foreign trade has also deteriorated significantly, since it grew from Euro 2.7 billion in the previous year to Euro 4.3 billion in fiscal 2000. Because of the important increase in incomes from tourism, the balance of payment deficit has not increased and equaled to Euro 1.9 billion. FDI inflows declined a bit to Euro 1.8 billion, but capital outflows increase more significantly, therefore, FDI inflows were able to finance no more than half of the current account deficit. While the gross hard currency indebtedness of the country grew to Euro 26.9 billion (it represented an Euro 2.5 billion increase), net foreign indebtedness—without owners' loans—decreased from Euro 6.9 to 6.3 billion. The state has no more direct indebtedness: only the corporate sector has external debts.

Although fiscal 2000 can be seen as successful, in the second half of the year some relatively very unfavorable tendencies have taken place: growth performance has declined and at the same time wages started to increase at a higher rate, inflation increased and both foreign trade and current account balances have been deteriorated.

Main economic indicators in fiscal 2000

	1999	2000[a]
GDP volume index (pc)	104.5	105.3
Industrial production index	110.4	118.3
Construction industry production index	106.4	105.8
Agricultural production index	98.0	100.0
Investment index	106.6	106.5
Export index (at current prices, euro, pc)	113.7	130.0
Import index (at current prices, euro, pc)	114.5	132.5
Trade deficit (in billion euro)	2.9	4.3
Current account deficit (in billion euro)	2.0	1.9
Consumer price inflation (pc)	110.0	109.8

Sourece: Central Statistical ffice, National Bank of Hungary, Ministry of Economy – compiled by GKI Co.

[a] GKI Co.'s preliminary figures, compiled as of March 31, 2000

5. Conclusions and perspectives

While in the 1970s Hungary's external debts on the whole financed growth, in the 1980s they were sufficient only to bring about stagnation. In the 1990s, however, when a further increase in the country's foreign indebtedness was no longer sustainable, a large-scale deterioration in the macroeconomic performance of the economy took place. This reflects the general incompetitiveness of the Hungarian economic and social system as it had emerged under the planned economy, and the discrediting of that structure on the world markets. Almost everyone agreed and agrees with this evaluation, which has become something of a commonplace. However, it is only as a result of the lengthy transformation crisis that society is having to face up to the real scope of the problem.

Planned economies, by definition, mean a structure that is not based on market demands, the inflexibility and anachronism of which have been made abundantly clear in the new era of the world economy. Opening towards the West, which worked more or less as a substitute measure for reform, also functioned according to the logic of the shortage economy, thus leading to permanent indebtedness. In the end, therefore, the Hungarian economy, like all planned economies, found itself in a general modernization crisis, which meant that the world markets (on which it was directly dependent in terms of imports, and, in reality, in terms of exports as well) devalued not only its production structure but its whole corporate structure, investment structure, development strategy, social organization practice, distribution practice, and system of values.

The foregoing meant that financial tensions, increasing debts, the growing and potentially unfinanceable current balance of payments deficit, and the rapid rise in inflation were only the tip of the iceberg. Thus, reducing shortages—although it required great sacrifice—did not represent a permanent solution, since without overall structural changes financial tensions were reproduced. A change of regime was required—even if this was not clear at the time.

It seems that, in the early 1990s, Hungarian society—the political/ideological sphere, the econo-political decision-making elite, and the business sector—failed to gauge the extent of the modernization tasks that faced it, as well as the length of time required to carry them out. It underestimated the scope, extent, and cost of the inevitable destruction of old structures and the creation of new ones, as well as the time that would be needed.

In the transformation period, serious economic losses occurred. These came partly from the devalued structures of the planned economy, partly from the recession that inevitably accompanies transformation, and partly from the mistakes that were made.

The loss of markets—the collapse of COMECON and its impact on the domestic market—is usually cited as one of the major reasons for the recession in the Hungarian economy. However, this is only half the story. It does not take account of the fact that this was not a cyclical recession, since the collapse of COMECON was part of the collapse of the planned economy as a system: the demand produced by COMECON and the domestic markets under the planned economy would never return, and in the future these markets would have to face international competition. Hungarian economic policy reacted adequately to this situation in the short term: both the liberalization of imports and the strict bankruptcy laws were fundamentally correct moves. With hindsight it can be argued that, by means of a more gradual liberalization and of less strict bankruptcy laws, declaring bankrupt those enterprises with what were, in fact, merely short-term problems could have been avoided. However, in the given circumstances there was scarcely any other road that could have been followed in order to acknowledge market realities and bring about a radical transformation in corporate attitudes.

What was a mistake, however, was that for a long time the real devaluation of Hungarian economic performance and assets was not acknowledged. This was partly expressed in the fact that the fall in consumption in the early 1990s did not follow the fall in GDP: consumption as a percentage of GDP rose from 72 percent in 1990 to 88 percent in 1993. (Due to the stabilization measures, the weight of consumption fell to below 80 percent in 1995, then further decreased to reach 62 percent in 1999.) On the other hand, there were permanent illusions as to the effects of the change of regime. According to these illusions the political transformation would be brief, and, following temporary economic recession, would bring about a lasting economic boom. The political decision-making elite repeatedly promised such a rapid change-around while handing over the "task" itself to the economic experts.

A further issue is the question of whom the state had to protect (or ought to have protected), as well as when and to what extent, during this process. It was undeniably right (and unavoidable) to establish a system to tackle unemployment. Although it is hard to make an objective judgment about it, it was probably also right for the state, in the form of various public bonds and by undertaking various obligations, to assume some of the consequences of the loss of capital. The widespread introduction of early retirement was a much more questionable practice. Of course the cost of this had, and has to be met by the taxpayers.

Economic assets that had been accumulated in the previous decades obviously depreciated. However, the extent of this depreciation is very difficult to calculate in the absence of reliable data. Bearing in mind that the real value of owners' capital in joint ventures (deflated by the consumer price index) fell by approximately 28 percent between 1992 and 1996, it cannot be far wrong to say that the capital which had been accumulated in the Hungarian economy depreciated by at least 30 to 40 percent in real market terms (since, in the meantime, over USD 10 billion in foreign capital flowed into the country).

There were other long-term losses as well. While in the corporate sector, or more largely in the entrepreneurial sphere the elimination of non-economic activities and the improvement of productivity were positive factors, the other side of the process—the dramatic deterioration in the ratio of employed persons to dependents—was not: the number of dependents per one hundred employees increased by approximately 80 percent between 1990 and 1996. This aspect of the transformation process in itself required the reform of the state budget and the promotion of self-help, since in the face of such a serious burden there was hardly any way to create new capital. (On the other hand, the increasing of employment was a basic requirement.)

Since, due to the counter interests of both receivers of state benefits and employees, even the first meaningful step in the reform of the state budget (that is, the reform of old-age pensions) was carried out only slowly and after a long delay, in practice the deteriorating quality of state services (especially and most dramatically in the area of health) and the depreciation of benefits were a dominant factor. This was all the more problematic since the unchanging structure was becoming less and less financeable. Within the income expenditure of the economy, the increase in the ratio of investments had, in practice, been continuous for years. However, within the total decrease in consumption, the expansion of the principle of self-help and the marketization and monetarization of public consumption made slow progress.

The creation of the basic institutions of the market economy and the accomplishment of privatization do not lead immediately to rapid market adaptability. It takes time. For companies to be able to establish a strategy a certain amount of "clearing" has to take place in the market as a whole, and relations—in terms of the market and opportunities for capital gain—must become more transparent. Changing the foreign suppliers of the dynamically developing multinational companies into Hungarian suppliers can only take place gradually, since for the multinationals market reliability is even more important than cost. Besides, guaranteeing suitable and steady quality and being able to keep to deadlines unconditionally were not the chief characteristics of the business culture that took shape under the planned economy. Internal integration has begun, however, which was the most important thing. Suppliers are often themselves the Hungarian concerns of foreign companies, while for the moment Hungarian-owned companies are mostly at the bottom of the "suppliers pyramid" that is gradually taking shape.

While market-based privatization in Hungary made a significant contribution to the establishment of a competitive structure, it also went along with social tensions.

Some domestic entrepreneurs and part of the population are reluctant to acknowledge the dynamic activity of foreign capital and often blame foreigners for losses resulting from the economic transformation. The situation was further complicated by the fact that foreign financial muscle occasionally limited the room for maneuver of otherwise viable Hungarian enterprises.

At the same time, in the eyes of the public the domestic entrepreneurial stratum had often earned its wealth by legally murky or morally doubtful means. However, when it comes to functioning in the market economy, those who are capable only of getting hold of assets but incapable of managing them effectively, will, sooner or later, be pushed out of the market or dispossessed of their assets. A similar process occurs in the case of employees' assets.

According to the logic of the market, owners who did not acquire their assets by market means are nevertheless forced to adopt market attitudes. If they prove incapable of doing so, they are forced aside. While this still does not satisfy society's sense of justice, nevertheless, from the point of view of the development of the economy, the functioning of this selective market mechanism is what is most important.

In 1995/1996 the Hungarian economy performed a successful stabilization turnaround. The threat of a critical financial imbalance disappeared, conditions for sustained and balanced economic growth were created, and there is even a chance that growth will continue to be rapid. This, however, depends on further conditions which are currently lacking, or which only exist in part.

- In part of the national economy there is a great shortage of capital, and the conditions which gave rise formerly to losses and the using up of assets are still firmly in existence. At the same time, within the economy there are already organizations that possess significant capital and potential for providing credit. Thus the only obstacles to accessing money are the lack of really competitive projects and of the kind of guarantees required by investors.
- No socially acceptable and financeable state redistribution system has been created, and there is widespread dissatisfaction with the social (welfare-) services provided by the state.
- The economic environment does not stimulate legal activity, the making of profit, or the reinvestment of revenues.
- Economic actors have little confidence in one another, their own interest-representation organizations, the state, and justice, all of which hinders business life. The social acceptance of market economic behavior is also low.
- In several branches (e.g., in the agricultural sector and in certain services) the conditions for market coordination and competition are still not in place.

In the Hungarian economy differences are at the moment more pronounced than is usual in market economies. The competitiveness of products and production is remarkably diverse. As a result of this, enterprises will go bankrupt, and new ones will be created, *en masse*. Contrary to the illusions of many, national assets have not been redistributed for the last time. The less talented, or the less fortunate, will lose their property.

In the forthcoming years Hungarian economic policy will have to bear in mind the demands of EU accession and must try to achieve as favorable conditions as possible for accession. In order to do so:

- The institutional and legal system of the Hungarian economy must be adjusted even more precisely to that of the EU.
- There needs to be clarification as to which of the derogations—that is, the EU regulations that will come into effect only after accession—are important from the point of view of the Hungarian economy, and the achievement of these should be aimed for during negotiations with the EU.
- The economic development programs required in order to obtain grants before or after accession need to be worked out (thus creating an administrative system that meets EU requirements).
- There must be an awareness that, following accession (which will take place after 2002 and hopefully before 2005) the need to fulfill the so-called Maastricht criteria will become pressing. Although the fulfillment of these criteria is not a condition for accession, progress in that direction will almost certainly be expected.

II. THE CREATION OF THE MARKET ECONOMY

1. The political system in Hungary

As a result of Acts approved by the Parliament between 1989 and 1991, the country's form of state changed from a socialist state structure to a democratic state structure. The foundations for this change were laid by amendments to the constitution in 1989 and 1990. The change therefore took place during the last years of the socialist system and were endorsed in the course of negotiations held with the opposition. In contrast, in establishing the institutional system for a market economy there was a much greater degree of continuity. The introduction of market features and economic infrastructure in Hungary had begun much earlier than 1989 or 1990. Ever since the conception of the "new economic mechanism" in 1966 and its introduction in 1968, a continuous reform of the planned economy, although with halts and reverses, had been taking place. The last phase of this, which took place in the second half of the 1980s, comprised tax reform, the creation of the two-tier banking system, and the passing of the Companies Act.

With the removal in 1989/1990 of the political barriers to social-economic development, the opportunity arose to make market relations the general and dominant form of relations. This required practical efforts in the areas of liberalization, deregulation, and legislation, since new regulations were needed in order to abolish former prohibitions, to establish new, market-oriented institutions and attitudes, and to carry out privatization. Thus from 1989 to 1991 the various laws required for the creation of the market economy emerged one by one.

a) The democratic state

According to the constitution, the basic institution of legislative power is the Parliament. The Parliament is formed as a result of democratic elections held every four years. Electoral rights and the election of parliamentary representatives (MPs) are regulated by Act XXXIV of 1989. The foundations for the multiparty system were laid down by Act II of 1989 on the Right of Association, and Act XXXIII of 1989 on Political Parties.

Since the change of regime in 1990 there have been three free elections—in 1990, 1994, and 1998. In the first two cases the elected parties held office for the full length of their four-year mandate (the next parliamentary elections will take place in April 2002), and on all three occasions a different political platform won. Thus the political system in Hungary has proved to be stable. The head of state, that is, the president of the republic, is elected by the Parliament for five years. The Hungarian president is a so-called ceremonial head of state, since Hungary is not a presidential, but a parliamentary, democracy. Parliament's legislative power is counterbalanced by the Constitutional Court, which investigates the constitutionality of the laws and abolishes those that are contrary to the constitution. The judges of the Constitutional Court are elected by Parliament for nine years.

The handling of public funds is controlled by the State Audit Office (Act XXXVIII of 1989), the president of which is elected by Parliament for twelve years.

Act LIX of 1993 created the institution of the ombudsman, common in Scandinavian countries. These representatives of citizens' rights were given wide powers to protect the legal interests of citizens against the public administration.

The constitution ensures the human rights of all citizens, and especially civil rights (including economic, social, and cultural rights), some of which—for example the right to assembly—are governed by a special law, that is, Act III of 1989. Special state organizations to ensure these rights were created in connection with the Parliament.

In Hungary, the office of public prosecutor is directly linked to the Parliament, and the prosecutor general is elected by Parliament for six years. The public prosecutor is responsible for the legal supervision of police investigations and represents the prosecution in court proceedings, but also has wide influence in civil and public administration matters.

Finally, in order to guarantee the right to freedom in the area of mass communication, Act I of 1996 (the Media Act) created the National Radio and Television Commission, which is directly connected to the Parliament. Its task is to ensure the broadcasting of balanced and objective information.

Executive power is held by the government, and the central administration is organized in the form of ministries and public administrative organizations with national authority. In terms of its structure, the government follows the so-called chancellor system that exists in Germany: the government is, in practice, the government of the prime minister, which can only be overthrown by the Parliament by means of a constructive vote of no confidence in the prime minister. Since 1990 all governments have been coalition governments, therefore ministers have been appointed by the prime minister on the basis of political coalition agreements. The legal status and responsibilities of ministers and undersecretaries of state are governed by Act LXXIX of 1997.

A separate act enumerates the various ministries, which change according to the government. The number of ministers is around fifteen, and the institution of the minister without portfolio also exists. Also following the German model, since 1998 the Prime Minister's Office, as the central organization of the government, has been headed by a minister. Legal and political control is exercised over the army by the civilian minister of defense, and over the police by the minister of internal affairs. The political supervision of the secret service is carried out by a minister without portfolio. Most branches of the public administration are governed by laws—for instance the Water Act, the Environmental Protection Act, etc.

There are special governmental organizations which, due to their specialized tasks, enjoy a certain independence from the government, and their heads are appointed by the president. These include the Hungarian National Bank as the country's central bank (Act XV of 1991), which is responsible to the Parliament, and the Office of Economic Competition (Act LVII of 1996).

Elected local self-governments, which are independent of the government, play an important role in the public administration of the country. The local self-governments are organized on two levels: territorial self-governments, meaning self-governments on the county level; and settlement, town, or village self-governments.

The territory of the country—excluding Budapest—is divided into nineteen counties, and in addition to these there are certain towns and cities with county rights. Due to the approaching date for EU accession, since the late 1990s the organization of the seven regions that exist for statistical and planning purposes has become particularly significant.

The representatives of the local self-governments and the mayors of the towns and settlements are elected by the population for four years. The head of the public administration of the self-government is the mayor and/or the notary. The legal status and powers of the self-governments are regulated by Act LXV of 1990 and Act XX of 1991. In order to ensure the rights of minorities living in Hungary there are minority self-governments (such as Romani/Gypsy, German, Slovak, Croatian, etc.).

In order to maintain contact with the local self-governments, the government operates county public administration offices, which mostly fulfill second-level functions.

The independent state organ of the administration of justice is the independent judiciary. An overall reform of the administration of justice in Hungary began in the second half of the 1990s. Court-related administrative functions were moved from under the aegis of the Ministry of Justice to the newly created National Judiciary Council, presided over by the president of the Supreme Court (Act LXVI of 1997). The president of the Supreme Court is elected by the Parliament for six years. The courts are organized according to the territorial divisions of the country, and the creation of boards of justice began at the end of the 1990s following the Austrian model.

In the past ten years the infrastructure of the administration of justice has been established, basically in the form of professional chambers which are independent of the state. These are the chambers of lawyers (Act XI of 1998), of public notaries (Act XLI of 1991), and of judicial experts (Act CXIV of 1995).

Within the state structure, independent public bodies play an important role not only in the judicature but in other areas too. The Hungarian Academy of Science and the economic chambers are examples of such bodies. The independent functioning of the churches is ensured by a separate law (Act IV of 1990). (This act was approved by Parliament in its session on 24 January 1990, and came into force on 12 February 1990.)

By the end of the 1990s the legal and administrative structure of the democracy had been consolidated. Only fine adjustments and minor modernization measures can be expected from now on.

b) The institutional system of the market economy

The transition from the planned economy, which was based on socialist public ownership, to a market economy system of private ownership, was carried out in Hungary by means of intensive economic legislation. The creation of the most significant laws took place between 1988 and 1992. The most fundamental of them, Act

VI of (October) 1988 on Business Organizations, was created before the change of regime.

In terms of the economy the constitution provides for private property, the right to economic entrepreneurship, and free competition. On the basis of the constitution the Civil Code underwent an overall modification.

At the foundations of the market economy are enterprises. In Hungary there is no trade code, thus a number of separate acts regulate individual and joint enterprises.

The individual enterprise is regulated by Act V of 1990, which was approved by Parliament on 26 January and came into force on 13 February 1990. This makes the establishment of enterprises conditional on the possession of an entrepreneur's permit, which can be obtained from the Chamber of Trade or on registration as a company at the Court of Registration.

The operation of business organizations that are created by registering with the Court of Registration was formerly regulated by Act VI of 1988, and has more recently been regulated by Act CXLIV of 1997. Hungarian company law basically and traditionally follows German company law. In Hungary, five types of company can be established in order to carry out business-oriented economic activities: the general partnership; the limited partnership; the joint enterprise; the limited liability company; and the joint stock company. The Hungarian Companies Act recognizes extensive concern rights, following German rights in the case of private limited companies, and American takeover regulations in the case of public companies.

The transformation of state-owned corporations into business organizations was effected by Acts LIII and LIV of 1992, although, naturally, foreign investors and Hungarian entrepreneurs can create joint stock companies.

In Hungary, farming, marketing, purchasing, consumers', and other cooperatives play a significant role. The operation of the cooperatives is currently regulated by Act I of 1992.

The stock exchange in Budapest was re-established in 1990. The commodity exchange was institutionalized by Act XXXIX of 1994. Following Act VI of 1990 (which was approveed on 25 January 1990 and came into force on 13 February 1990), the issuing of securities and investment activities are currently regulated by Act CXI of 1996.

As a general rule, credit institutions (commercial banks, etc.) and insurance institutions can only operate in the form of joint stock companies, and apart from these there are two banks serving specific economic goals (one of which is the State Development Bank). These are in private (mostly foreign) ownership. Credit institutions are regulated by Act CXII of 1996, and insurance institutions by Act CXVI of 1995.

Business competition is indispensable in a market economy. Hungarian competition law was first drawn up in 1990, and Act LVII of 1996 is currently in force. This act forbids unfair competition, horizontal (cartel) agreements, and abuses of economic power (monopolistic positions). The act regulates the legal status of the Office of Economic Competition, the permission of which is required for company mergers and for the creation of concerns.

Consumer protection is ensured by a separate law—Act CLV of 1997.

Trade relations between enterprises are regulated by the section on contracts in the Civil Code. There is general contractual freedom and no obligation to use standard forms of contract. Hungarian law makes it widely possible for the contracting parties to choose courts of arbitration (Act LXXI of 1994) instead of state courts, and in the case of foreign contracting parties a foreign court of arbitration is allowed.

Besides creating winners, economic competition inevitably has its losers as well. Since 1991 Hungarian law has included an insolvency law (Act IL of 1991) which includes regulations governing final settlements and the liquidation process.

A logical obstacle to economic competition in ex-socialist countries was the huge state sector, which needed to be privatized. The first privatization laws in Hungary were created in as early as 1989/1990. Following the forced transformation of state-owned companies into business organizations (between 1992 and 1995), mass privatization took place, on the basis of Act XXXIX of 1995, by selling the stocks of state-owned companies. Privatization was carried out by the Hungarian Privatization and State Holding Company (ÁPV Rt.) in the form of a government one-person joint stock company, which was established in the wake of several legal predecessors.

The non-profit sector complements the business-oriented economy. Its basic institutions are governed by the amended Civil Code. Belonging within this circle are mergers of various legal entities, as well as associations, civil corporations, foundations and public foundations, and public service corporations. According to the so-called Non-Profit Act (Act CLVI of 1997), the state assists the functioning of these organizations by tax and other benefits.

Finally, the institutional system of the labor market has been established. Collective and individual labor laws are regulated by Act XXII of 1992. According to Act II of 1989, employers' interest representation bodies and trade unions are social organizations. Trade union rights and the institution of the works council are also governed by the Labor Code, as is the institution of the collective agreement, which is very popular in Hungary. The right to strike is regulated by Act VII of 1989. The care of the unemployed is regulated by the Social Security Act (Act III of 1993).

2. The functioning of the legal and institutional system

As far as the legal environment is concerned, Hungary is a market economy, and all the significant features of the European economic legal system have been established and are more or less operational.

In spite of this, there are several legal and institutional problems that hinder the effective operation of Hungarian enterprises. Certain laws and modifications (for example the reform of the real-estate law and the contract law) are still lacking. Conceptually, the majority of the existing economic regulations are not sufficiently developed and include a number of internal contradictions as well as contradictions with other laws. They have not been sufficiently revised: they contain a number of problematic rulings and are full of technical, structural, wording-related, and codification errors.

For example, until the end of the 1990s the annually approved tax laws regularly had to be modified, often just one or two months after they had come into force. The first version of the Insolvency Act proved to be too strict and threatened with insolvency companies with merely temporary liquidity problems. However, after being made more lenient in this respect, creditors were provided with inadequate protection against non-payment.

The Insolvency Act, which was approved in 1991 and which came into force on 1 January 1992, was by far the most strict within the region and, furthermore, until being made more lenient in September 1993, it actually worked—unlike similar laws in other ex-socialist countries. According to the law, company directors were criminally liable for the initiation of bankruptcy proceedings against their own companies if they were not able to pay their debts within ninety days. The act led to an enormous wave of bankruptcy petitions: company directors initiated 5,000 bankruptcy proceedings, and creditors 16,000 such proceedings, between January 1992 and September 1993. Modifications to the law in 1993 included the abolition of compulsory self-declared bankruptcy; the reduction of creditors' demands from 100 percent to two-thirds; and the making of the previously compulsory automatic ninety-day overdue payment moratorium dependent on the creditors' agreement. Following this, the number of bankruptcy petitions fell to a fraction of the former figure. Apart from the easing of the bankruptcy regulations, the bank and credit consolidation program of late 1993 probably played a part in this. The modification of the bankruptcy proceedings was aimed at creating greater interest in petitioning for bankruptcy, while the modification of the liquidation process—by making stricter the conditions for petitioning and by reducing interest in the survival of the company—attempted to accelerate the liquidation process, since, during the former liquidation period lasting two years, the majority of assets often disappeared and creditors remained unsatisfied. One important change was that the Mortgage Loan Act modified the execution rules so that, out of the income from execution by public sale, mortgage-based demands were given priority over other public loans.

Legal harmonization with the EU will generate further significant tasks for the future. The ultimate goal of the government's so-called legal harmonization program, approved in 1998, is EU accession. The aim is to adopt the EU's legal regulations, as laid down by the European Commission, prior to the signing of the accession agreement. The adoption of the EU's legal regulations takes place according to the outcome of the lustration negotiations, which are held with the relevant organizational units of the European Commission. With a few exceptions legal harmonization can be completed before 1 January 2002. The exceptions are related, on the one hand, to the fact that, for economic reasons, Hungary needs more time to adopt certain regulations (e.g., in the area of environmental protection). On the other hand, the deadline for the adoption into the national legal system of certain recently issued directives (e.g. the gas directive) will expire, even in the case of EU member states, only after 2002. The fact that Hungary's EU accession will almost certainly take place later than had been hoped (i.e. later than 2002) might delay the legal harmonization process, or, more exactly, the acceptance of those regulations that are regarded by the government as having negative effects.

The most serious problems in terms of the legal system will not arise with respect to the creation of laws, but rather with respect to their application, with law enformcement. The serious problems in this area are partly due to the fact that, probably unavoidably, the creation of laws in the recent past—as a result of the change of the political system—was of a "proactive" character, that is, new institutions were often introduced in the absence of the proper personal or material conditions. For example, at a time when the courts of registration were barely functional, the authority of the court of registration was required over all companies; a Western-style accountancy law (which allowed for greater liberty in interpretation while, at the same time, demanding greater responsibilities) was introduced, in spite of the lack of qualified auditors; and a stock exchange law was created in spite of the absence of the appropriate market players. This resulted in a permanent conflict between the law and everyday practice. The situation was aggravated by the fact that, capitalizing on the uncertain and unprecedented situation, certain interest groups, keen to make money quickly, acted unethically or illegally. Nor were they subsequently punished (at first because of a lack of preparation, and later because of a lack of power). Tax avoidance became a widespread practice; the breaching of contracts, VAT fraud, and false bankruptcy petitions became pardonable offenses. The situation is clearly illustrated by a survey carried out by Tárki Rt.: in 1998 some 80 percent of those surveyed agreed that, in order to get by, it was necessary to break the rules.

The inaccurate and out-dated real-estate register; the slow process of company registration; lengthy court proceedings; and frequent delays in the pronouncing of verdicts (which are, as a result, often impossible to execute), also further decrease confidence in the legal system (since in cases of the infringement of rights the injured party cannot hope for compensatory damages, while the person committing the offense does not have to worry about penalties).

In the 1990s, as a result of the privatization and compensation process, the poorly computerized Hungarian real-estate registers faced demands for the production and modification of information that were beyond their capacities. Throughout the boom in company creation, company registration faced the same challenge. Thus there is no up-to-date company data with respect to the assets and financial position of market players. The problems caused by overloading, as well as by the widening circle of corruption and other abuses, only make matters worse. The situation has somewhat improved in recent years, and the latest developments in information technology give further hope that the problems can be eased.

The criminal prosecution organizations were at first almost entirely powerless in the face of the spread of economic criminality. Subsequently, they made a number of theatrical (although professionally dubious) moves in cases that they regarded as serious, but suffered catastrophic defeats in the courts. Raising the professional standards of the economic prosecution organizations is vital.

The capacity of the civil law courts is not satisfactory. The management of proceedings, in the opinion of both domestic and foreign clients, is intolerably slow from the point of view of economic practice, which means that illegal moves by certain companies have led many other companies into bankruptcy.

The execution of court verdicts was not really modernized by the Execution Act of 1994. Experience so far indicates that proceedings have become scarcely any shorter. The only substantial change has been the increased costs of, and payments to, private executors who are assigned the task of execution.

The institutional system that lies behind the functioning of the market economy has developed significantly over recent years. However, this has happened at a different pace in different areas. The Hungarian Competition Office operates successfully. The financial institutional system has been entirely transformed: the banking system has been transformed into a two-tier system; there is competition in the commercial bank and insurance sectors; and there are a large number of consulting firms, representative offices, and brokerage firms. Efforts to find solutions have undeniably been made. However, there has been little success in the transformation of the system of agricultural, health, and public education institutions.

The slow development of interest-protection organizations is at the root of a number of problems. For example, the widespread "network" of chambers of commerce could be seen as a positive development. However, these organizations and their functions lack transparency; the distribution of work among them is unclear; and certain institutions are over-financed while others are short of resources. Following the end of compulsory chamber of commerce membership for enterprises, the number of members is likely to fall dramatically. Smaller companies in particular will be unable to see the benefits of membership. Consumer-protection organizations are developing even more slowly (partly as a result of financing problems). There is insufficient emphasis on marketing standards: breaches of marketing regulations are regularly discovered and penalties are ineffective. The proportion of illegal markets, counterfeit goods, undocumented deliveries, abuses of monopolistic positions, and corruption is still significant. At the same time, in 1998/1999 the rise in incomes and the spreading of large business chains significantly reduced illegal street and market trading. This fact is confirmed by sociological and market research surveys.

Research carried out by GKI Economic Research Co. has, time and again, highlighted the malfunctions of the market economy that have been pointed out above. Entrepreneurs, and in particular small-scale entrepreneurs, often regard as insufficient the available information on resources (especially financial resources), on market opportunities, and, above all, on the preparations necessary for EU accession. They are critical of the underdevelopment of the consultative, management, and support network that exists to help small and medium-sized companies gain access to the market and undertake modernization, as well as of the regularly poor-quality performance of this network.

Opportunities for capital redeployment (especially for the rapid and cheap release of invested capital) are very limited. The stock exchange, in this relatively uncertain transitional period, cannot fulfill its task of collecting small amounts of capital and transmitting them to medium-sized companies. Due to the excessive risks resulting from legal insecurity and the weakness of interest protection, small firms are barely eligible for credit, while recently established firms are practically ineligible. However, due to surviving or newly created monopolies, and the frequent shortages of capital among weaker competitors, the number of existing opportunities for market access is often justifiably criticized. This situation is often exacerbated by the unpredictable attitude of the state. Another issue is the fact that behind these unpredictable state attitudes there is a reluctance to carry out unavoidable restrictive measures. This is underlined by the fact that, among the factors hindering their expansion, companies surveyed by GKI Co. attribute only minimal importance to their own lack of competitiveness, suggesting that they overestimate external factors.

The establishment of the legal/institutional system of the market economy took place with remarkable speed and consistency compared with the rest of the region, which, at the same time, has made the process the focus of wide criticism. The essence of the criticism is that "over-liberalization" has only increased the already grave economic problems. The postponement of regulations, the forcing of financial transparency between the government and the banking system, and the insistence on financial discipline within the business sector would probably have involved less destruction. However, this would also have led to less "creation", since, in the absence of such factors, far less foreign capital would have flowed into the country and the existing resources would have been utilized less effectively.

Today there is keen competition among individual countries as to which can provide more favorable conditions for capital investments, including the stimulation of the investment of foreign and domestic savings. The IMDC, the prestigious Swiss International Management Development Center, compiles an annual report on the conditions provided for the business sector by various countries. According to their spring 1998 report, Hungary had moved up eight places in one year, and with its ranking of twenty-eighth in the world is not only the best placed among the ex-socialist countries, but is more favorably placed than Portugal or Italy, which come below it in the table. This reflects the fact that the stabilization policy of recent years was much more "entrepreneur-friendly" than was felt amidst the restrictions.

Domestic entrepreneurs tend to be unhappy with the categories mentioned by the IMDC as constituting the "domestic economy" (production, consumption, cost of living, and investment). Their criticisms of the restriction of growth, and especially of domestic demand, are justified by the IMDC's assessment, since, ranked according to the "domestic economy" criteria, Hungary has for years been almost last out of the forty-six national economies examined.

However, these criteria, so much emphasized by domestic enterprises, represent only one of the eight groups of criteria regarded as equally important by the IMDC. In recent years Hungary has made significant progress, jumping to between twentieth and twenty-seventh place in the "infrastructure", "economic openness", and "scientific/technical innovation" rankings. In the past year Hungary's position in terms of "government activity" (budget policy, the depth of state intervention in the economy, and legality) and "financial issues" (opportunities for accessing capital, the dynamism of the capital markets, and the efficiency of the banking sector) has dramatically improved, by thirteen and eight places respectively. At the same time, "management" (productivity, the efficiency of managers, entrepreneurial structures) and "human resources" (unemployment, the educational structure, the composition of the population and public values) are characterized by only slow improvement and continued stagnation.

At the same time, Hungary's position fell slightly in Transparency International's corruption rankings, although this is a tendency that is characteristic for the region as a whole.

In order to accelerate development, to improve companies' willingness to undertake entrepreneurial activity and investments, and to stabilize the inflow of foreign working capital, legal and information security are essential. Companies must be certain of the reliability of land and trade registers, accounts, statistics, and information on the financial standing of the banks. Economic players need realistic opportunities in order to safeguard their interests efficiently and to cover their losses if their business partners fail to fulfill their contractual obligations. Entrepreneurs should permanently feel that legal sanctions, the institutionalized protection of interests, as well as society's moral judgments, will keep their partners from breaking the law (by abuses of monopolistic positions, advantages gained as a result of the evasion of common public dues or corruption, and false bankruptcy petitions). Only thus can business risks be reduced to the levels normal in the developed part of the world economy.

3. The tax system

In Hungary, the reform of the tax system took place as early as 1988, before the change of regime. The main elements of the system are value added tax, consumption tax, personal income tax, municipal taxes, corporate income tax, and social security contributions, which function as a quasi tax. As in the majority of socialist states, most of the state's income had previously come from the taxation of companies, which included numerous exemptions, and from a complex turnover tax operating according to several taxation rates, while the taxation of individuals resulted in very little income. On switching to the new tax system the old taxes were abolished.

From the early 1990s the main emphasis in the modification of tax policy was on reducing the amount of direct taxes. This can be measured by the changes in the tax income structure. The weight of indirect taxes (VAT, consumption tax, customs and import tax) in relation to GDP is now significantly greater than that of direct taxes (personal income tax, corporate income tax). In 1999 the consumption-related taxes (VAT and consumption tax) produced 43.5 percent of the income of the central budget. (In 1995 this proportion was 34.5 percent.) On the other hand, as a result of the temporary surtax introduced in 1995 as part of the stabilization package, the income from duties was extremely high in 1995 (representing 13.8 percent of budget income). This figure subsequently gradually decreased, and in 1999 represented only 4.3 percent of budget revenue.

By international standards, and compared to GDP and total taxation revenues, the proportion of social security contributions, which are intended to provide the resources for health- and pension-related expenditure, is extremely high. (Social security contributions represent one-third of total tax income. However, this figure fell slightly in 1999.) This is not only true compared to averages for OECD or EU member states, but also compared to the similar figures for Japan and Ireland, two countries that can be described as catching up successfully with the world economy (although in different periods and under different conditions). At the same time, it should be borne in mind that international comparisons are the most unreliable in terms of social security contributions: besides differences in incomes, the various types of contribution and the content of the related services vary significantly.

In Hungary, a significant proportion of income (e.g. pensions, family allowance) is non-taxable. This is the main explanation for the fact that, despite the high tax content of the income forming the basis of personal income tax, the weight of indirect taxes is low by international standards. On the other hand—due to the transitional character of the domestic economy—the taxation structure was significantly influenced by the fact that the various governments supported several econo-political goals by tax policy measures (for example, by reducing corporate income tax in order to stimulate enterprises and new investments, or by exemptions from personal income tax, which were often unjustified).

Income-tax rates are only low in the case of corporate income tax. The low weight of income tax (direct taxes) by international standards is not down to the tax rates but to the high proportion of exemptions (especially in the case of personal income tax). Although within indirect taxes the VAT rate is very high (25 percent), an excessively wide circle of products and services enjoy a preferential rate of 12 percent, which is lower than the minimum set down by the EU for its member states.

Within the tax system work-related tax and social security burdens are high, while enterprise-related burdens are lower. Due to this, and to opportunities for operational accounting, the practice of paying wages as sub-contractors' fees is widespread in Hungary. (This explains the large number of enterprises created solely for taxation purposes.)

The figures for the period under examination show a reduction in the total tax burdens. State asset centralization, the extent of which, up to 1994, was more than 50 percent of GDP, was around 40 percent by 1999. This is in keeping with the average for OECD European countries, and is perhaps lower than the amount typical for the EU. However, it is higher than the taxation level of less developed European countries that are nearer to Hungary in terms of development. In any case, the current level of Hungarian taxation does not bear out the opinion that a significant decrease would be justified and/or possible. Naturally, this does not mean that by broadening the tax and taxation base certain rates could not be reduced.

Taking domestic and international experiences into account, the most important tasks in the development of the tax system are as follows:

- Further restriction of the various exemptions, rebates, and allowances, while broadening the tax base (social security contributions' base).
- Spreading common public charges in such a way that incomes, regardless of how they are produced (whether by private persons or companies), are burdened with roughly the same amount of tax.
- In parallel with the broadening of the personal income tax base, pushing up the tax bands much more strongly than valorization, and further decreasing tax rates.
- In terms of corporate income tax, preferring (in particular long-term) accumulation, as opposed to the personal (consumption-related) utilization, of assets.
- The more homogeneous handling of savings; the introduction of a standardized withholding tax on the various capital revenues (dividends, exchange-rate gains, and income from the sale of real estate).
- Closing the gap between the two VAT rates and adjusting them to the EU average.
- In relation to the reform of the old-age pension system, the grossing up and taxation of pensions.
- Further decreasing the rate of social security contributions (in parallel with the reform of the state budget).
- Widening local taxation.
- The significant strengthening of tax management and the improvement of tax collection.

4. The entrepreneurial sphere

One of the most important elements in the economic transition was the multiplication of economic organizations, the radical change in their character and structure, the dramatic reduction in their size, the loss of ground among state-owned corporations, the weakening of cooperatives, the increasing dominance of privately owned companies, and the dynamic spread of foreign ownership. In parallel with this, the black and gray (hidden) economies became so widespread that, projecting from calculations made by GKI Co. in 1994, at present they account for approximately 30 percent of the GDP.

The majority of these topics are discussed in a separate chapter, in Part 2. Here, we will look in detail at the changes in the number and attitudes of corporations.

The period before the change of regime was characterized by the over-concentration and over-centralization of production.

The majority of big corporations were created by artificial mergers; they were autarchic, and, because of their domestic monopolistic position, complacent. In the 1980s, although the number of state-owned corporations and cooperatives was less than five thousand, they accounted for more than 90 percent of the GDP. The proportion of small and medium-sized companies was far below the proportion typical of developed countries. There were scarcely more than 100,000 craftsmen, who employed approximately 20,000 employees. This was one of the reasons why the economy was unable to meet consumers' demands for good quality products and services, and to respond flexibly to new demands. Furthermore, the large corporations are not supported by an appropriate range of suppliers.

The significant increase in the number of economic organizations and enterprises began as early as the beginning of the 1980s, with the legalization of small enterprises. However, from 1989 it acquired new impetus. The source of growth was predominantly newly founded private enterprises, but the division of formerly state-owned companies into smaller units and the dissolution of cooperatives also played a role.

Between early 1990 and late 1996 the total number of officially registered economic organizations almost tripled (from 391,000 to 1.1 million), and stood at 1.1 million at the end of 1999. However, some of the officially registered enterprises do not carry out real activities (either they have stopped functioning but have not canceled their entry in the company register, or may never have begun operations at all). The Central Statistical Office has recorded the number of actually functioning organizations since 1995: at the end of 1997 the figures was 750,000; and at the end of 1999 it was around 800,000.

In Hungary, the proportion of functioning enterprises in terms of the population (7.5 enterprises per 100 persons) is today roughly equal to the West European average.

A significant majority of these enterprises were founded for taxation purposes or as an escape from unemployment, thus they are characterized by employee-like attitudes rather than by a willingness to take risks.

The rise in the number of new enterprises is logically accompanied by a fall in the average size of enterprises. Today, the structure of enterprises is much healthier than the strongly centralized structure that existed under the socialist period, which repressed individual and medium-sized companies. Nevertheless, the transition created many small-scale, and in the long term non-viable, companies, or companies created only for taxation purposes. (It should be borne in mind, however, that in developed countries the majority of newly founded small enterprises go out of business within two or three years.)

The transition from the shortage economy to a market economy was accompanied by a change of attitude among companies: rather than consumers having to adjust themselves to producers,

producers had to respond to consumer demand. At the same time, limitations on the supply side had previously made it complicated, or impossible, for producers to make adjustments in terms of their output. Surveys carried out by GKI Co. reflect, among other things, the subsequent shifts in attitude that have taken place among Hungarian companies.

As early as the beginning of the 1990s, lack of resources was cited to a decreasing extent as one of the factors hindering production; instead, more and more references were being made to lack of demand, especially domestic demand, and to problems with respect to financing. With the liberalization of imports the limitations on resources disappeared, while the abolition of central control over wages meant that shortages in the workforce were transformed into unemployment. On the other hand, the increasing emphasis on competition, as well as financial factors, forced companies to adapt to the market.

According to international practices, companies working in market-economy conditions regard high-quality customer service, and—with some reservations—profit, as their main goals (or "mission"). In surveys carried out by GKI Co., Hungarian responses typically also include mention of increased profits (or increased income and reduced costs, which is closely related) as their "ultimate" goal. In the case of majority foreign-owned companies the importance of the profit criterion is even higher than average. Thus those who responded to the surveys displayed a "rational" attitude regarding their general intentions. (In general the "socialist" companies declared that increased employee incomes were just as important as profitability. Since the shortage-economy practice of the preceding decades proved that this—at first sight—sympathetic attitude stands in direct opposition to the interests of consumers and of the company, its modification must be regarded as favorable.)

In most companies significant changes occurred in relation to strategic goals. The corporate strategy of the majority of companies (following a practice of extensive expansion over several decades) has, for the last few years, been focused on improving the quality of their marketing activities.

According to GKI Co.'s surveys, in certain groups of Hungarian companies it can be shown that globalization and the joining of world-wide networks has improved productivity. Among the companies that compete successfully—or at least in the hope of success—against imports on the domestic market, and prove their competitiveness by significant exports on world markets, large numbers are partly, or entirely, in foreign ownership and/or have intensive international contacts. These successful companies do not only include the daughter companies of multinationals: many middle-sized,or even small,companies—among them Hungarian companies and even, exceptionally, a few (well-managed) state-owned companies—have undeniably become competitive (in terms of exports).

Although nowadays the significance of human resources is equal or even higher to that of capital, the handling of human resources remains a weak element in corporate strategy. The difference between a company's registered capital and its stock exchange (market) value is largely down to the know-how embodied by the company, and its intellectual capital. This partly includes the intellectual capital represented by individual workers, and partly the internal structure characteristic of the given company, which provides for the optimal utilization of that capital. By better utilization of human resources it would be possible to increase significantly the productivity and competitiveness of the economy. However, in past years only companies in certain sectors (for example companies in the manufacturing industry that were acquired by foreign owners) have managed to improve the ways in which they utilize their employees' capacities. In the state sector these "resources" have remained practically unchanged.

In certain groups of Hungarian companies it can be shown that globalization has improved productivity. According to their attitudes, companies can be classified according to three major groups.

In the Hungarian economy there are increasing numbers of companies, which, by significant exports and by their successes on the domestic market, have proved their competitiveness on the world markets. The majority of these are companies that are now partly, or entirely, in foreign ownership, or companies that were created in the form of greenfield investments. However, among domestic companies it can by shown that those that cultivate intensive international contacts are more successful. (This is partly because the development of an international system of contacts is often an element in their ambitious strategy.)

Intensive international cooperation has emerged predominantly in the following areas:

- In certain Hungarian branches, predominantly in the textile industry, simple production cooperation, such as occasional subcontracting, was frequent before the beginning of privatization. It made it possible for many companies—at the cost of part of their corporate independence—to exploit more or less competitive production capacities and to finance production or investment where this would not otherwise have been possible. After 1990, previously successful contract-work cooperation often became the basis for a foreign partner's acquisition of title. However, in other sectors—for example in the chemical, and especially in the pharmaceutical, industry and in certain machine-industrial branches—foreign acquisition of title served as the basis for wider-ranging cooperation, which included contract work.
- In recent years, with the broadening of international relations, R&D cooperation, and especially the technology transfer, has accelerated in several Hungarian companies. This has occasionally helped to create competitiveness in the company in question

and was especially successful if the transfer was accompanied by regular international research cooperation. Companies that gave information about such cooperation in GKI's surveys also reported enhanced competitiveness and improved dynamism.

- International marketing experience has been utilized by many Hungarian companies. Cooperation aimed at the adoption of modern market strategies has proved to be outstandingly successful, which, in the recent past (due to the rapid reduction of the former deficit in terms of the quality of Hungarian marketing activity), has done most to improve the competitiveness of domestic companies.
- With increasing frequency Hungarian companies are establishing international financial cooperation aimed at the modernization of the productive sphere and at the financing of this modernization. In a company under foreign ownership, international financial relations naturally exist within the company itself. Inter-company financial relations, including mainly those between large Hungarian companies and foreign banks, are common. Today, foreign capital investment by Hungarian companies is no longer an exception.
- Multinational companies build organically into their structures the Hungarian branches acquired via privatization or greenfield investments.

The second distinctive group of domestic companies is formed by those that keep contact with international markets predominantly by means of foreign trade. In order to be successful they must make significant efforts to ensure that the quality of their products, delivery deadlines, and the levels of after-sales service, reach world-market requirements. The ISO standards, which are being introduced in a growing number of companies in order to increase marketability, have occasionally fundamentally reshaped company operations. In many enterprises there has been an undeniable improvement in the quality of the management.

The third and largest class of Hungarian companies is (mostly, but not exclusively) made up of small companies that focus on transient opportunities without undertaking serious development. The majority of these companies are predominantly domestically oriented, lack significant international contacts, and have no strategy for improving their typically low level of competitiveness. It would be naive to expect improvements in competitiveness on the part of companies that were created only with tax evasion in mind.

The economic crisis and the transition to a market economy had a significant impact on R&D activity, as well as on the functioning and financing of organizations dealing with this activity, the number of employees engaged in it, and the areas of research chosen. In the planned economy, R&D activity—like the proportion of investments compared to GDP—could be regarded in many respects as excessive. Research findings, and especially those that were utilizable, and utilized, in practice—again like the results of investments—were very modest. As in other areas of the economy a creative destruction is needed here, and, logically, destruction inevitably precedes creation. It should be regarded as entirely natural that companies in crisis, as well as the state budget in the course of the stabilization process, attempted to make savings in terms of R&D expenditure. As long as the conditions for utilizing such expenditure more effectively are not in place, this cannot be regarded as a one-sidedly narrow-minded policy.

With the closure of a significant number of big corporations, R&D groups were disbanded and some privatized companies ceased direct R&D activity altogether. The majority of newly formed enterprises are small and they have too little capital to enable them to carry out their own, or commissioned, research and development. The material resources available to be spent on research and development have continuously become more restricted. The lack of commissions and the fall, in real terms, in state subsidies, have significantly weakened research institutes and other research centers.

The real value of R&D expenditure in 1996 was only 35 percent of what it had been six years earlier. Expenditure on R&D as a proportion of GDP stood at 1.61 percent in 1990, and by 1996, as a result of a continuous decline, had fallen to 0.68 percent. The level remained the same remained 1999. Within this, expenditure on basic and applied research increased, while the proportion of experimental development decreased. Between 1990 and 1996 expenditure in real terms on basic research fell by 30 percent, on applied research by 57 percent, and on experimental development by 78 percent. This runs counter to the latest trends in OECD countries, where more emphasis is being given to applied research and technological developments. This is expressed by support for technological innovation that ensures competitiveness and economic growth. In Hungary, at least until 1996 and the beginning of the economic upturn, the tendency has been rather the reverse. Since 1996, however—partly due to the beginnings of economic growth and in particular to the Hungarian-based R&D activity of certain multinational companies—there have been some favorable changes. The proportion of experimental development is increasing more rapidly and in 1999 approached 40 percent.

Surveys carried out by GKI Co. in fall 1999 support the above statements. According to these surveys, in the recent past more than a quarter of all companies have developed, and almost 60 percent have introduced onto the market, products that can be regarded as genuinely new. (The respective proportions in terms of foreign-owned companies are 42 and 68 percent.) More than 40 percent of companies have introduced genuinely new technology.

5. State budget reform

In the years prior to the change of regime, and especially in the second half of the 1980s, it became increasingly obvious that the tension between the low output of the Hungarian economy by European standards, and high expenditure, could not be maintained. With respect to social security provision under the previous system, the following important criticisms have been made:

- Resources were used inefficiently and wastefully.
- It permanently created demand, the growing budget implications of which were increasingly beyond the economy's capacities.
- Some benefits were socially unjustified and could only be obtained by certain strata of society as a result of their better bargaining position.
- The system as a whole reduced citizens' sense of responsibility for their own fate.

State budget expenditure, that is, revenue redistributed through the budget, stood at 60 percent of GDP before the change of regime. The level of consolidated gross state budget expenditure, even in certain years in the first half of the 1990s, still reached 60 percent—in other words, it was significantly higher, by at least 15 percent, than the 40 to 45 percent typical of developed market economies. In particular, it was higher than the 35 percent typical of countries with a similar level of development to Hungary. Thus the Hungarian state budget represented an excessive burden on the economy.

In the early 1990s the state budget deficit increased at an accelerating pace compared to the falling GDP. It became clear that, given the high level of expenditure and despite the high tax burdens on those who were not able to avoid paying taxes, state budget expenditure could not be financed. The high level of deficit hindered the development possibilities of enterprises, thus obstructing economic growth, and also played an important role in keeping inflation at a high level and in the growth of external debt. As a result of the high level of state debt the proportion of debt servicing increased, which significantly restricted the budget policy's room for maneuver. This was manifested in the tendency for accrued expenses to decrease—a tendency that had otherwise been there since the early 1980s—which, in conjunction with the relative underdevelopment of the domestic infrastructure, also hindered economic growth.

Despite the recognized problems, no state budget reform that included both the revenue and expenditure structure and that was carried out according to consistent principles, took place following the change of regime. Reform-like changes were made in a number of areas at various different times. These included:

- The creation of the State Audit Office (1989).
- The removal of social security from the state budget (1989).
- The creation of local self-governments (1990).
- The placing of social security on a self-government level (1991), followed by its "nationalization" (1998).
- The passing of the Central Bank Act (1992).
- The passing of the State Budget Act (1992).
- The establishment of the Government Securities Issuing Administration Office (the legal predecessor of the Government Debt Management Agency) (1993).
- The removal of non-insurance-based benefits from social security and the introduction of performance-related financing in the health service (1994).
- The passing of the Public Procurement Act (1995).
- The creation of the Treasury (1996).
- The radical decreasing of the number of separate state funds (1996).
- The introduction of tuition fees in higher education (1996) and their subsequent abolition.
- The transformation of family allowances, child-care allowances, and child-care pay (1996), and later their re-establishment (1998).
- The raising of the retirement age (1996).
- The insertion of so-called zero debts into the budget (1997).

- The reform of the pension system (1997).
- The introduction of tax benefits for parents with children (1999).

Although the individual measures were not free of contradictions, in total they indicated a tendency towards the withdrawal of the state from over-involvement. However, as the above list reveals, the government which came to power in 1998 has not only failed to continue the reforms, it has rescinded several of the reforms introduced earlier, or, as in the case of the old-age pension reform, frozen them. (In the latter case, despite the amounts previously promised, the government has not increased the proportion of contributions that can be paid into private pension funds.)

In 1996 consolidated expenses compared to GDP barely exceeded 50 percent (excluding interest expenditure the proportion was around 40 percent), while in 1998/1999 the level was about 45 percent. Four sub-systems have emerged within the state budget. Besides the already existing central budget and separate state funds, local and social security self-governments, independent of the state administration, have been established.

However, the transformation has proven to be controversial. The tendency towards economic autonomy was not in harmony with the transformation of the decision-making system. This was mostly because the autonomy of the self-governments was not a result of their natural economic role. The financing of the local and social security self-governments, which appeared as two new sub-systems of the state budget, is therefore the responsibility of the central budget. As long as the decision-making authority of the self-governments is not in harmony with their financing and deficit management their activity cannot be effective. However, the self-governments are more interested in maintaining the existing conditions, which are convenient for them, than in facing conflicts that may arise as a result of further reforms.

Putting social security on a self-government basis gave decision-making rights to the social security self-governments, and responsibilities to the government and Parliament. Social security thereby created favorable conditions for its own budget, a fact which revealed itself over the years in the difference between the planned and actual deficit in the social security budget. On the other hand, the Finance Ministry continued voluntarist planning. The structure of the social security self-governments ultimately resulted in the one-sided representation of employees' interests. Therefore, from among the measures introduced in 1998 the "nationalization" of social security was directed against a system that was undeniably malfunctioning. The extent to which the conditions for better functioning were created is another issue. The real problem is that, between 1990 and 1998, approximately 1.5 million contribution payers "disappeared" (for example they were made unemployed, retired, or became homemakers), while on the expenditure side little adjustment can be made in response without deep reforms.

The change of regime created widespread autonomy for local self-governments. In practice, however, their autonomy is limited in the economic sense, since their revenues are generally low while being strongly differentiated. Although local taxes have become broader, significant revenues are only generated (in developing areas) by the industrial tax. The role of assigned taxes is much debated and changes unpredictably. Thus in the current financing system—due to the absence of a clear definition of state and self-government powers—there is an over-dependence on the state, due both to the size of the resources and to frequent changes in the subsidy rules. It cannot be regarded as positive—although it is something that happens frequently—for current expenditure to necessitate the using up of assets. (In relation to privatization, huge differentiation emerged here.)

Already in previous decades the creation of separate state funds provided opportunities for various branch interest groups to distribute public monies in a way that was virtually outside the control of Parliament. These funds were predominantly the means by which ministries could strengthen their position in the process of state redistribution. Although according to the State Budget Act of 1992 only those funds were allowed that were legally created by Parliament, even in 1995 there were twenty-nine funds in operation and only in 1996 could the vast majority of the funds be integrated into various chapters of the budget. Five separate funds remained (the Road Fund, the Water Fund, the Labor-Force Fund, the National Cultural Fund, and the Environment Protection Fund), which had a say in 4 to 5 percent of the total expenditure of the state budget.

Funds that are separated from the central budget are justified in two cases: on the one hand, if the provision of separate financing is based on a social consensus; on the other, if the sources of the fund are independent of the budget, or if, in order to broaden the sources of the financing of the activity, sponsorship and business capital is required that necessitates a "fund-like operation".

The changes to the central budget initially meant a greater degree of publicness and transparency. Parliament's opportunities to make decisions and exercise control significantly increased. The State Audit Office's investigations and opinions on the budget, and its revision of the balance sheets, are of enormous help in this. (According to the State Budget Act the period between the submission of a draft act and the coming into effect of the approved act is to be at least three months. The State Budget Act also clarified the duties and responsibilities of those participating in the preparation of acts and the making of decisions.) The passing of the Central Bank Act, then the transferring of the so-called zero interest rate debts into the budget, placed on a market basis the credit drawn by the fiscal sphere, and initially limited, then abolished, the direct central bank financing of the budget. The interest burdens of the state debt, which are accumulating because of the deficit, today appear in the very place where they were created. The creation of the Government Debt Management Agency and the Treasury made the handling of state debts and the financing of the state budget more transparent, cheaper, and plannable. The Public Procurement Act has the same function (although it contains many contradictions).

While with respect to the principles and goals related to the furthering of the reform of the state budget there is an apparent consensus, every future task generates professional and political clashes of interests. Without aiming at giving an exhaustive list, the more important goals are as follows: the further rationalization of the state's involvement; the widening of the system of local and personal autonomy; the harmonization of the principles of shouldering common public charges and equality of opportunity with the concepts of interest, efficiency, and balance; and the more efficient operation of social distribution systems. Compared to previous years a significant new element is that the reform requires neither the reduction of the real value of primary state budget expenditure (excluding interest expenditure), nor an increase of primary assets. Thus there is no longer any need for petty "cuts" which, in previous periods, inevitably accompanied reform moves and which further worsened the already unfavorable response of society.

A further source of conflict are the clashes of interests produced by the reshaping of the former distribution structure. On the one hand, such reshaping damages the interests of those who, in the role of decision makers, have actual power and who stand to lose that power in a decentralized, partly market-based system. On the other hand, it damages the interests of those who realized significant additional profits as a result of the monopolistic positions they held in the former "free", although not free of charge for users, low to mediocre-level social, health, education, and cultural services.

Finally, there is an undeniable danger that in the event of the implementation of an ill-considered reform, in the new, to a certain extent market-based, system certain less well-off but needy strata would not have access to the services they require, or would only have limited access to them. At the same time it is obvious that in the absence of reform the medium- and high-income strata will gradually abandon the public social and health systems and create structures to meet their demands. Thus the state budget would lose its most wealthy contributors.

From the foregoing it follows that there is a strong public resistance to reform of the state budget, and much depends on the level of professional preparations for it. In terms of future reforms the tasks facing the state can be considered as belonging to the following areas:

- The state should guarantee universal and free basic and medium-level health, public education and social services. In addition, it must guarantee the reformed and rationalized tasks of administration, justice, defense, and public order. The performance of these tasks should be independent of the economic conditions.
- The state should finance only in part the tasks of higher education, specialist health services, scientific research, culture, sport, environmental protection, regional and settlement development, infrastructure development, and community services. In the carrying out and financing of these tasks it should share responsibility with the users of the services. The extent of sharing and the list of tasks mostly depend on the capacity of the economy.
- The state should stop, or leave to demand in the market sector, the financing of economic and public authority services along with the individual tasks and institutions. The budget organizations working in this area should be transformed into business organizations or non-profit organizations.

In the course of the reforms certain general principles should be adhered to. It should be decided to what extent welfare policy in the future will uphold the principle of neediness, that is, the extent to which social politics (taking into account the principles of performance-relatedness and self-care) will provide protection and guaranteed security for the middle classes.

In terms of the state and the public administration, the principles of decentralization and deregulation should be followed, bringing about the abolition of the existing parallel institutions that perform overlapping tasks. The existing public administration system cannot realistically be maintained after EU accession. Instead of the county system it should be built on economic, social regions.

The relationship between the state budget and the economy, instead of being based on individual subsidies and tailor-made preferences, should be based on normative grounds.

The main areas in the furthering of the state budget reforms are as follows:

- Performance-related financing and efficient cost control in the area of state services. Within the social/welfare system, the transformation of health insurance and the social provision system.
- Restricting the amount of tax and contribution evasion and narrowing the circle of the black economy.
- The reform of fiscal relations and subsidies in the real economy, with special emphasis on the rationalization of agricultural, export, and public utility subsidies. The modernization of the tasks and financing of infrastructure development and the state development policy.
- The overall reform of the public administration.
- The reform of the tasks and financing of the local and regional self-governments.
- The reform of justice and the armed forces.

III. THE DEVELOPMENT OF THE REAL SECTOR

1. Industry and the construction industry

In all the ex-socialist countries the extensive development of industry and its divergent course from the main trends of world economic development represent one of the most important reasons leading to economic/political crisis. It is for this reason that, for all participating countries, the collapse of COMECON was not only a tragic, but also an inevitable, event, which led to a fall in industrial production almost comparable to that caused by the war. However, it is important not to confuse cause with effect: the inability of the existing industrial structures to develop and the lack of international competitiveness played the most important role in the decline in cooperation, rather than vice versa. It is for this reason that, following the changes, there was no period of restoration giving rise to rapid and general growth. The relatively rapid growth that did begin in certain areas cannot be regarded as reconstruction, but must be seen as accompanying the onset of a new course of development and therefore as part of the structural transformation.

Substantial changes took place in industry following the change of regime. Its main characteristics at the beginning of the decade can be summarized as follows:

- The proportion of mining and raw material production was relatively high, bearing in mind the fact that Hungary has hardly any industrially utilizable mineral resources. (The most significant are its bauxite deposits, which are nevertheless more expensive to extract than elsewhere in the world.)

- The weight of the chemical industry was significant and showed a tendency to increase in the years preceding the change of regime. Besides certain pharmaceutical factories, this mostly comprised petrochemical plants, again without a domestic raw-material base.
- Production was also relatively high in the food industry, where mass goods were produced from the low-quality materials provided by the large socialist producers for export to COMECON countries that were struggling with supply problems (especially the USSR).
- The technical standards of industrial production were uneven. Apart from a few islands of high technology, goods were largely produced using outdated equipment. Manufacturing processes were labor intensive, and human and material resources were utilized with low efficiency.
- Exports were made up mostly of medium-quality mass products, and between 60 and 70 percent of exported goods were absorbed by COMECON. Remaining exports comprised mostly food, raw materials, and minimally processed products.
- Productivity and organizational standards in the companies were low, and company managers had no real business experience.
- Company structure could be described as an inverted pyramid. Apart from a few small and medium-sized companies the structure was dominated by big corporations. Both industrial centralization and concentration were strong tendencies.

For Hungarian industry, the greatest shock brought about by the change of regime was the fact that its markets disappeared practically overnight. At the same time, the prices of raw materials and fuel, which had previously been kept artificially low, rose to world market levels. The fall in exports of processed goods led to a decline in domestic cooperation, while domestic demand also

Changes in industrial production and sales, 1990 to 1999

1989 = 100 %

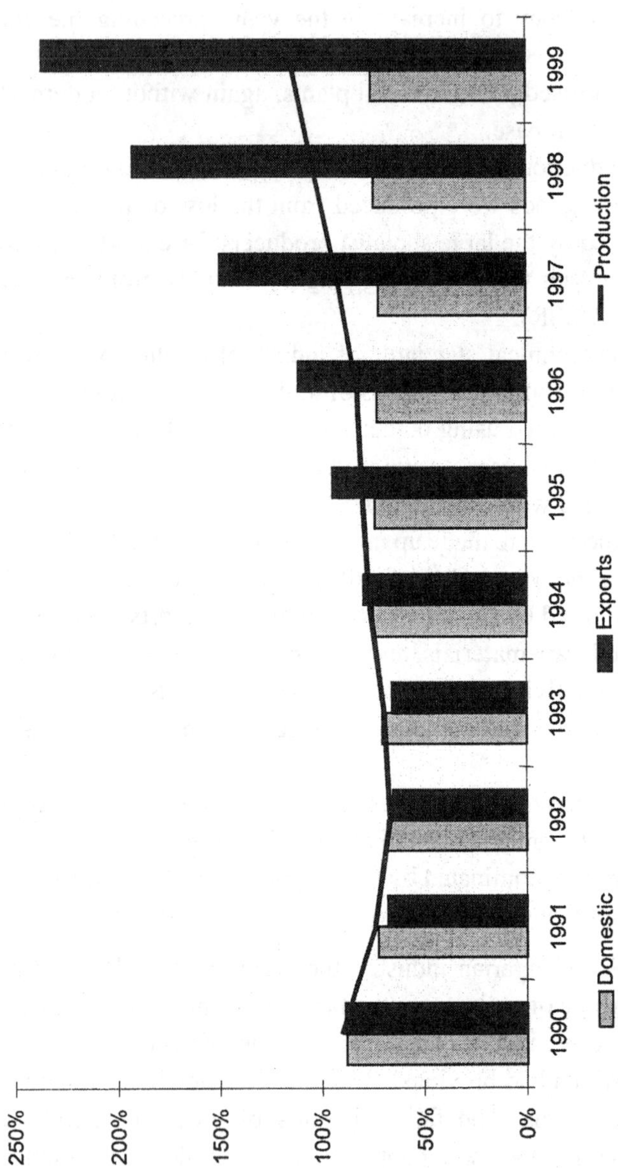

Source: Central Statistical Office

decreased as a result of falling real incomes and the competition created by the rapid liberalization of imports. During the same period this was accompanied by a recession in the main West European export markets.

Thus the change of regime was accompanied by a very profound industrial recession. For a few years problems could be concealed by selling off stocks at depressed prices and by using up resources, but by 1992/1993 the existence of the crisis became obvious. Reputable Hungarian firms and even whole industrial branches disappeared from the economy or were forced out of their previously decisive roles. The decline of oversized and uneconomic corporations was inevitable. At the lowest point of the crisis (in 1992) industrial sales were 32 to 33 percent lower than 1989 levels. The question that then had to be asked was whether or not competitive activities had really gained ground—that is, whether the destruction had indeed been creative.

Hungary, like every other country in the region, had to face up to the loss of industrial markets. The collapse of COMECON also brought about a fall in internal demand, and in addition to this the most important Western European export markets were also facing recession in the early 1990s.

Apart from the period between 1993 and 1994, domestic sales within Hungarian industry steadily decreased. Lasting growth was only produced with the beginnings of an increase in exports which followed the lowest point of the crisis. However, the industrial development of even an open national economy cannot be based entirely on export markets. An important role in the increasing of exports was played by Hungary's participation in the international division of labor to a greater extent than earlier. In addition to the fall in external and domestic demand, further losses were caused by the fact that most sectors lost ground on the shrinking domestic market in the face of increasing competition from imports.

The most significant loss of markets occurred in the most dynamically developing branches. One reason for this was that the structure of production changed in a direction which meant that growth did not adjust to domestic consumption but to the demand of foreign, and especially Western European, markets. In several areas imports rapidly drove out domestic products in the course of keen competition. Moreover, the increasing proportion of imports was a natural consequence of the transformation of the production structure that accompanied participation in the international division of labor.

Changes in the market share of Hungarian industry on the domestic market, 1992 to 1998

(domestic sales/imports + domestic sales, percentages)

Branch	1992	1995	1998
Mining products	24.9	15.4	12.1
Food industrial products	90.6	87.5	83.8
Textile industrial products	37.3	25.6	19.5
Wood, paper, and printing industrial products	64.3	60.2	53.4
Chemical industrial products	61.2	50.3	44.5
Non-metallic mineral products	76.9	70.4	60.3
Metallurgy and metal industrial products	58.3	52.2	40.4
Machine industrial products	31.6	28.9	14.3
Other manufacturing industrial products	49.6	39.6	35.3
Electricity, gas, heating, and water	96.9	98.1	97.8
Total industrial products	61.3	54.4	41.7

Source: Central Statistical Office

In the Hungarian manufacturing industry—and this is of key importance in terms of economic development—the huge decline in 1991 was followed by stabilization in 1992/1993, after which, from 1994 onwards, rapid and lasting growth based on structural transformation began.

Changes in industrial composition on the basis of production value, 1985 to 1999
(percentages)

	1985	1990	1995	1999
Mining	2.0	1.8	1.1	0.6
Food and tobacco industry	20.7	22.2	23.6	15.2
Textile and clothing industry	8.1	6.3	4.6	3.9
Wood, paper and printing industry	3.5	4.3	5.4	4.8
Chemical industry	21.5	21.9	20.0	13.9
Production of non-metallic mineral products	3.2	3.4	3.2	2.6
Metallurgy and metal-working	11.3	11.0	9.7	7.2
Machine industry	17.0	15.3	17.9	40.4
Other manufacturing industry	1.7	1.6	1.3	1.1
Electricity, gas, heating and water supply	11.0	13.2	13.2	10.3
Total	100.0	100.0	100.0	100.0

Source: Central Statistical Office

Undeniably, it was manufacturing, and mostly the machine production industry that survived the crisis most successfully. In this branch a really creative destruction took place. Although the machine industry suffered the second largest recession after metallurgy and metal-working, in the second half of the 1990s it became the driving force of growth within the manufacturing industry. This was brought about by a radical structural transformation. While in 1992, at the lowest point of the crisis, plant manufacturing (the production of machine tools, agricultural machinery, and textile industrial equipment, etc.) represented 39 percent of production within the branch, this proportion had fallen to 24 percent by 1996. By this time the leading position had been taken over by road vehicle manufacturing, the proportion of which rose from 22 percent in 1992 to 32 percent. This is a remarkable development, bearing in mind that before 1991 car manufacturing did not exist in Hungary: the assembly of Opel cars was only just beginning in Szentgotthárd, and the manufacturing of Suzukis would only start in the following year in Esztergom. However, the most important factor was not the opening of the car plants themselves but the fact that, in their wake, the great spare-parts manufacturers also opened factories one after the other, from where they delivered their products not only to the domestic car plants but to their entire European networks. In 1996, however, the seeds of another structural change were sown: in the fall of that year the IBM hard-disk factory opened in Székesfehérvár. Two years later, computer manufacturing—that is, mostly the manufacturing of electronic units and spare parts—had become the largest machine industrial sub-branch. By 1999 information technology, which in the meantime had also begun to grow at an amazing rate, had already surpassed the computer industry, and in this sub-branch it is the manufacturing of consumer products rather than the production of spare parts that is the more significant area.

The increase of production of manufacturing industry was accompanied by an increase in exports. Export-orientation in the various sub-branches can clearly be seen to be much more marked in those areas where foreign capital had a significant presence. However, since the Hungarian market is very small, one cannot exclude the possibility that the correlation was reversed and that areas with good export potential in fact attracted foreign capital. In the period of world economic stagnation in 1998/1999, the advantages of belonging to international networks rose markedly to the surface. In this period Hungary was the only country in Central and Eastern Europe which was able to increase its exports and sustain growth with respect to other performance indicators, although at a slightly slower rate than in previous years. Industrial exports, for example, only increased in the customs free zones in 1999.

The division of industrial production by branch, based on current price, 1990 to 1999

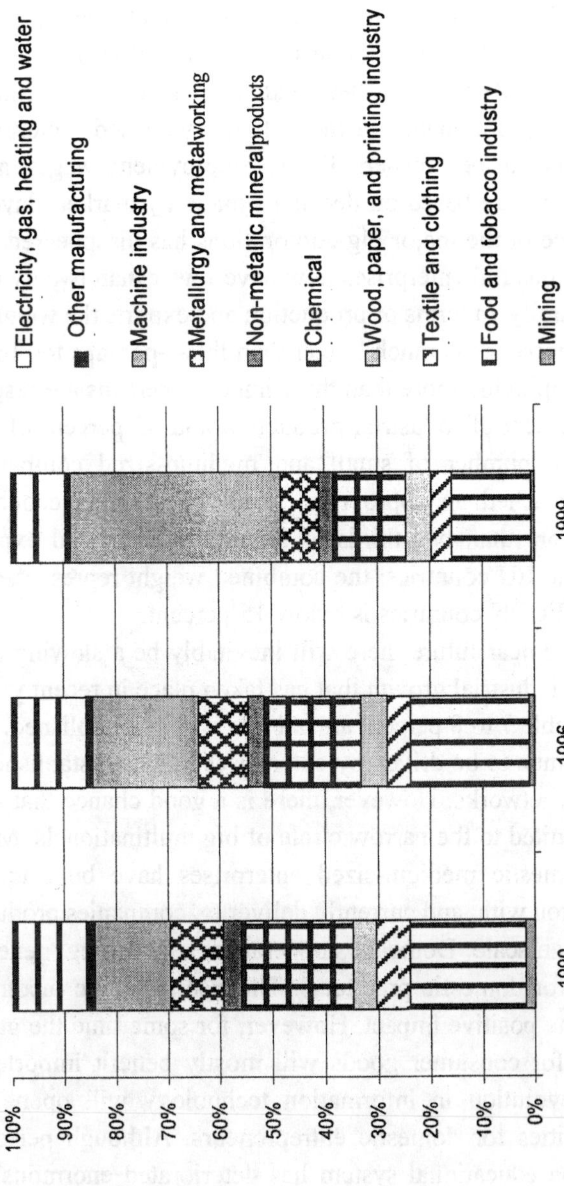

Source: Central Statistical Office

At the end of the decade Hungarian industry presents an entirely different picture from that which had characterized it at the beginning. Modern production facilities have become not merely sporadic islands but are widespread and play a decisive role in production. The dominance of the state has vanished. Enterprises are in the hands of real owners. Prices, employment, wages, and market relations are based on decisions made by market players. The dominance of the major big corporations has disappeared: 94 percent of industrial enterprises now have fewer than twenty employees. Naturally, in terms of production and exports the weight of the larger companies is much bigger than this—perhaps too big: companies employing more than three hundred persons are responsible for 73 percent of industrial production and 82 percent of exports. While the number of small and medium-sized companies has already reached an appropriate level they remain economically weak. More than two-thirds of Hungarian industrial exports are directed to EU countries: the combined weight represented by the ex-COMECON countries is below 15 percent.

In the near future there will inevitably be a slowing down of the rapid industrial growth that has taken place in recent years, and a sustainable 7 to 8 percent annual rate will be established. Growth will continue to be driven by enterprises that are established within global networks. However, there is a good chance that this will not be limited to the narrow circle of big multinationals. More and more domestic medium-sized enterprises have built up lasting cooperation with, and currently deliver to, companies producing on a European scale. Domestic cooperation is widening, generating a demand for domestic producers. The rise in public incomes may have some positive impact. However, for some time the growth in demand for consumer goods will mostly benefit importers. The recent revolution in information technology will open up new opportunities for domestic entrepreneurs. Although performance within the educational system has deteriorated enormously since the change of regime, the traditionally high standard of mathematics and physics teaching mean that the Hungarian labor force has a solid foundation from which to acquire the skills necessary for participation in information technology. It is no coincidence that electronics companies are establishing their development centers in Hungary one after the other. If the prediction that in ten years' time more than half of all economic activity will be related to information technology in one way or another is realized, then it is also likely that Hungarian enterprises will be important and respected players in the new economic order.

Performance in the construction industry can be divided into three cycles. The first began with the dramatic decline in production in the early 1990s: it was at this time that the branch had to face the narrowing of its markets due to the significant restructuring of customer and investor bases. As a result of the reduction in available resources, along with political uncertainty during the change of regime, central and local budget organizations cut back their demand for construction. At this time, most participants in the economic sphere were concentrating on survival rather than on commissioning large-scale constructions. Accelerating inflation and the re-evaluation of the role of the state led to the collapse of the apartment financing system: demand for the construction of apartments fell to a fraction of the previous levels. Subsequently, in 1992/1993, output in the branch increased slightly (by an average of 2 percent). In 1994, due, in particular, to the rapid increase in infrastructural investments, output then increased by more than 12 percent. The second cycle began in 1995 when, mostly as a result of cutbacks in the central budget and in local self-government construction investments, there was an almost 18 percent drop in the output of the construction industry. While 1996 can be regarded as a year of stagnation, in the following three years (1997 to 1999) there was a dynamic increase in output of altogether almost 30 percent.

The development of this branch is, to a great extent, dictated by developments in the domestic market, since the construction industry is predominantly not export oriented. Hungary's Euro-Atlantic integration will be unable to change this substantially. Two-thirds of construction orders come from the economic sphere, almost 30 percent from budget organizations, and 5 percent from the public. These proportions have been characteristic of the past four or five years and in this respect no radical restructuring can be expected in the near future, although an increase in the proportion of government financing is likely. (And not before time: the Hungarian figures are well below the EU average.)

Two important areas within the construction industry that experienced contrasting courses of development in the 1990s are the apartment and office markets.

In the early 1990s there was a steep drop in the construction of apartments. This was fundamentally due to the deteriorating economic situation: the public, the local self-governments, and the state budget had no resources available for such activity. The privatization of apartments also diverted resources from construction: the buying and selling of real estate became a more dynamic process, thus creating smaller demand for new construction while solving the housing problem for some families. The fall in the size of the population also reduced demand, since real estate appeared on the market as a result. Smaller families increased the demand for smaller apartments. After 1994, as a result of new social benefits, the construction of apartments saw a temporary upsurge. However, to a great extent this was due to the more "cunning" claimants, whose sole aim was to exploit the available social benefits by using one lot of building materials to "build" two or more apartments. Following the tightening of the rules in 1996 there was no fall in the number of apartments built: this was due not only to the improving economic situation but also to the increasing dynamism of the apartment market (especially in terms of purchases by foreigners).

The steady improvement came to an end in 1998 when the number of apartments that were constructed fell back to 1994 levels.

This took place despite the fact that, in the meantime, new constructions were being carried out and the interest rates on housing credits had begun to fall. The building societies did not live up to expectations, since the amount of the loans they were able to provide was very low compared to recent construction costs. Although between 1997 and 1999 mortgage lending became more dynamic, this represents a solution only for those on high incomes since it is generally they who are able to meet the banks' risk criteria and who own high-value real estate. Due to the rapid increase in additional costs (that is, contract fees and the investigation of creditworthiness) the reduction in credit burdens was smaller than the reduction in credit interest rates. The situation of those commissioning construction work has been further complicated by the fact that the costs of construction have risen dramatically and the price of building land has also increased at a rate well above inflation. For the majority of the population construction is not an available option, although in 2000 the government's new system for housing construction subsidies improved the situation somewhat.

On the other hand, there has been a dramatic development in the office market. The days are slowly being forgotten when the local representative branches of even some famous companies were obliged to work in offices that had been transformed from apartments. Effective demand brought about the construction of new office buildings initially in the downtown area, then, after 1995, to an increasing degree on the outskirts of Budapest. As in business life, the dominance of the capital city is undeniable in terms of the construction of office buildings, too. Over a short space of time the area of office space available for rent multiplied, while at the same time rental fees were reduced. By mid-1999 the luxurious downtown office buildings were already struggling to stay in business—while supply rapidly increased, the number of those renting office space fell, since, due to high rental fees, it was worthwhile for them to build their own offices. The offices that were vacated as a result further increased the supply surplus.

In total, office rental fees have decreased by 30 percent since 1991, while even the German mark weakened. Thus today, rental fees have fallen to around DEM 25 to 30 per square meter per month, which, in the longer term, still makes it a lucrative investment for the constructor (since in the meantime the interest on credit has decreased and construction sites on the outskirts of the city have become cheaper).

Conditions necessary for the development of the construction industry on the supply side are mostly in place. This branch is one of the most competitive sectors in the Hungarian economy. At the same time it is characterized by numerous problems. In the second half of the 1990s concentration processes began that are likely to continue in the near future. Unfair competition is a major problem in the Hungarian construction industry, as is the frequency of construction errors. According to estimates, about 20 percent of all constructions, and almost 50 percent of apartment constructions, are carried out using black-market labor, which quite clearly represents a high proportion. Of particular cause for concern is the fact that in the recent period these phenomena are increasing, rather than decreasing. Due to the deterioration of the system of construction controls, and the excessively wide scope of construction licenses, the proportion of technical errors and complaints about incompetence is between 20 and 40 percent. In this respect there have been some positive changes in recent years, although their impact has not been significant as yet.

2. The agriculture

Hungary's ecological capacities in terms of agricultural production are very favorable both by international and EU standards. In Hungary, the area of land per inhabitant that can be utilized for agricultural production (0.6 hectares) is 1.5 times the EU average, while the area of arable land is more than twice the EU average. Despite such advantages and the relatively favorable production potential that existed before the change of regime, agriculture has undeniably been one of the greatest losers change of regime in Hungary.

Over recent years the weight of the agriculture within the national economy has fallen continuously and significantly. The number of active wage earners working in agriculture and the contribution of the branch to exports and to GDP have fallen radically. (The 7.8 percent share in the GDP represented by agriculture in 1992 has now fallen to 4.7 percent, and the 26 percent share in exports has fallen to 8 percent.) This decrease will continue in the medium term. The fall in the weight of the agriculture within the national economy is, on the one hand, an international tendency that accompanies economic development everywhere in the developed world: on the other hand, it can be seen as a domestic peculiarity since the Hungarian agricultural sphere performs poorly even in terms of the opportunities available to it.

The major reasons for the drastic decline include the fall in domestic demand; the collapse of the COMECON markets; the reduction in subsidies; and increasing competition from imports. However, agricultural privatization, which was carried out without any economic rationale, along with uncertainty in terms of ownership, should not merely be listed among the reasons for the decline but must be seen as the main contributing factors to the lasting agricultural crisis. The missing, or poorly functioning, institutions of agricultural market coordination also "contribute" to the ongoing

The volume of gross production value in crop and livestock farming
(1989 = 100)

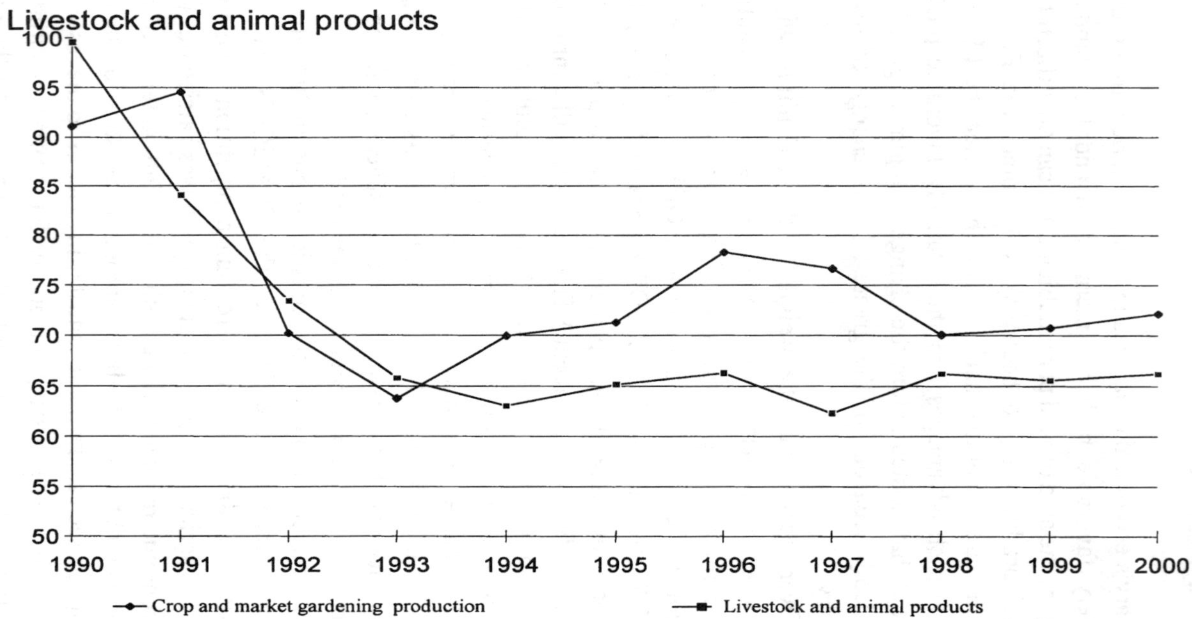

Source: Central Statistical Office

problems of agriculture (which go much deeper than in other areas of the economy).

One of the well-known and general features of agricultural production is the fact that inertia here is greater than in other branches of the economy, and it is less able to react to market changes. However, in recent years reactions have been even slower in the case of Hungarian agriculture. In Hungary, the radical fall in production in the early 1990s was not accompanied by a radical change of the system. In Hungarian agriculture, grain and meat production will probably remain decisive in the medium term too. The growth in the proportion of crop farming within total agricultural production (as compared to livestock farming) will continue only at a rather slow pace. Within crop farming the weight of market gardening (fruit and vegetables) may well increase. (However, this will not be of significant volume.)

The greatest blow to Hungarian agriculture was undeniably the compensation law. As a result of this law many owners appeared in the agricultural sphere who regarded their property only as an investment and who were thus unwilling to invest capital in order to modernize techniques and technology. Many new owners appeared who, as a result of their age, attitudes, and wealth, were incapable of participating in agricultural production. This is how the distorted landholding structure arose, in which the number of non-viable estates (that is, landholdings below five hectares) is outstandingly high, while in the EU landholdings of even fifty hectares are regarded as small.

Changes in the volume of agriculture and GDP (previous year = 100)
The proportion of agriculture within the GDP (percentage) **1990 to 2000**

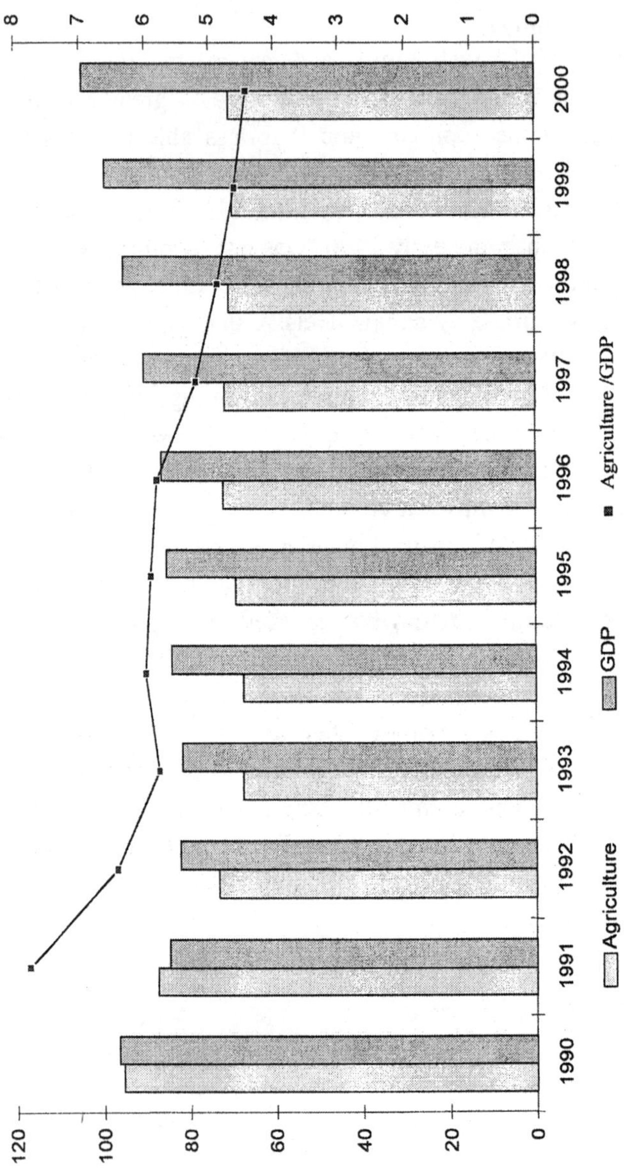

Source: Central Statistical Office. 1999: GKI Co. estimate; 2000: GKI Co. forecast.

The spread of small landholdings was accompanied by a drop in crop yields. Due to farming practices that were not always efficient, and to the increasingly serious shortage of capital, the importance of quality production was pushed into the background. Farming cooperatives were transformed compulsorily and in theory became cooperatives of smallholders. At the same time external owners appeared, who are able to represent their interests in only a limited way in this new type of cooperative. To obtain a cost-effective amount of land the cooperatives have to rent further land, since the law does not allow the purchase of landholdings of over 300 hectares. Apart from one or two special cases, foreigners are not allowed to acquire land ownership. This represents a significant obstacle to the inflow of capital, while the majority of domestic producers have neither sufficient capital nor mortgageable assets. Thus agricultural credits predominantly flow to the major producers (cooperatives and processors).

Currently almost 300,000 people make a living on agriculture, and another few hundred thousand keep livestock or cultivate land as a part-time activity. Concentration is beginning, although slowly, among them. There is a relatively small number of owners of medium-sized estates (of around fifty hectares) who already have sufficient capital to obtain further land and agricultural machinery, partly due to their creditworthiness, partly to their political connections, and partly to their real economic activity. They are helped in such purchases by state guaranteed credits and the production subsidy system. It is they who are most interested in keeping land prices low and therefore they object to cooperatives and foreigners obtaining land. At the same time, it is they who demand further state subsidies while making little contribution to common public charges.

The division of arable land according to size of estate and economic form, 1998

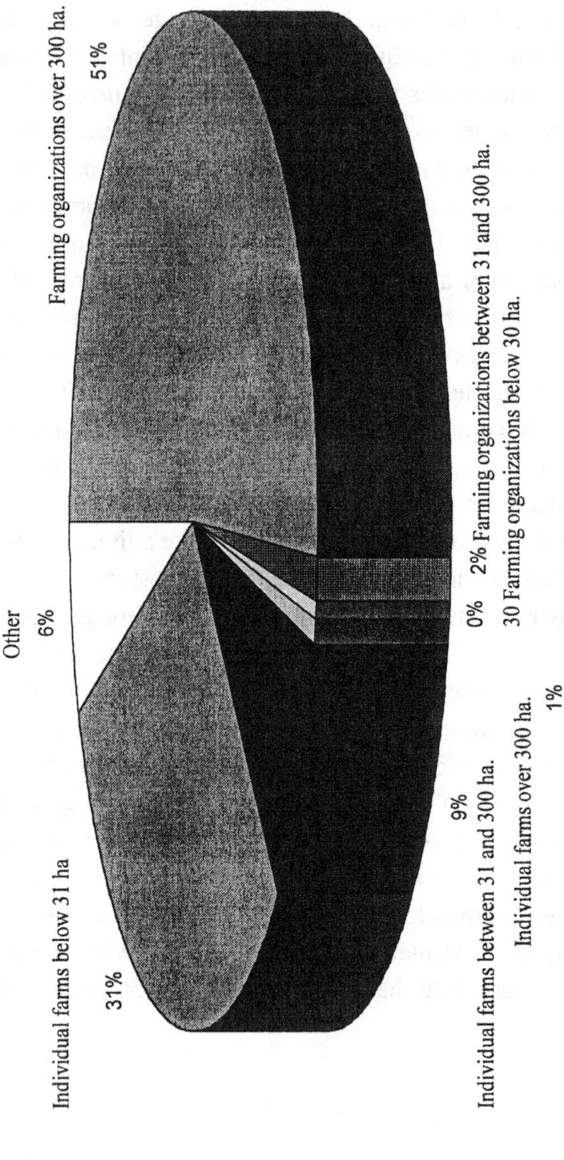

Source: Central Statistical Office

Bearing the current situation in mind (a practically dysfunctional land market and non-negotiable land ownership), economically rational estate sizes and estate structures cannot be expected to gain ground before 2002. Within the branch, a "secondary" change of ownership, which will concentrate well-operating estates and assets into relatively few hands, is yet to take place. This situation is accompanied by a lasting uncertainty in structure and ownership in Hungarian agriculture. Due to the limits on land acquisition and to low profitability the branch will continue to be avoided by capital, and lack of resources will remain a general problem. Small-sized farms that lack capital will not be competitive in the EU.

In the medium term three types of farm will be characteristic in the agricultural sector. The major source of production in the medium term will continue to be the large estates and farms.

In order to avoid misunderstanding it should be pointed out that there is no such thing as an optimal farm size, therefore the presentation given below of the emerging sizes and types of production does not express any particular preference. It is our opinion that different sizes of farm are suited to different types of production. Activities requiring manual labor, such as the majority of market gardening production, can be very effective even in the case of smaller-sized farms of as little as ten hectares. On the other hand, activities requiring less manual labor (such as crop farming), which are still strongly present in Hungarian agriculture, are only effective on larger farms of eighty hectares or above.

In the medium term (that is, for a period reaching beyond 2002), large-scale businesses and large estates (economic associations, cooperatives, enterprises) will inevitably be the decisive organizational forms in the agriculture. These farms, which will continue to own 45 to 50 percent of arable land, have been/will be created partly as the successor organizations of the former state farms and cooperatives, and partly as the farms of new private, individual farmers.

Use of land according to economic form, 1990 to 1998

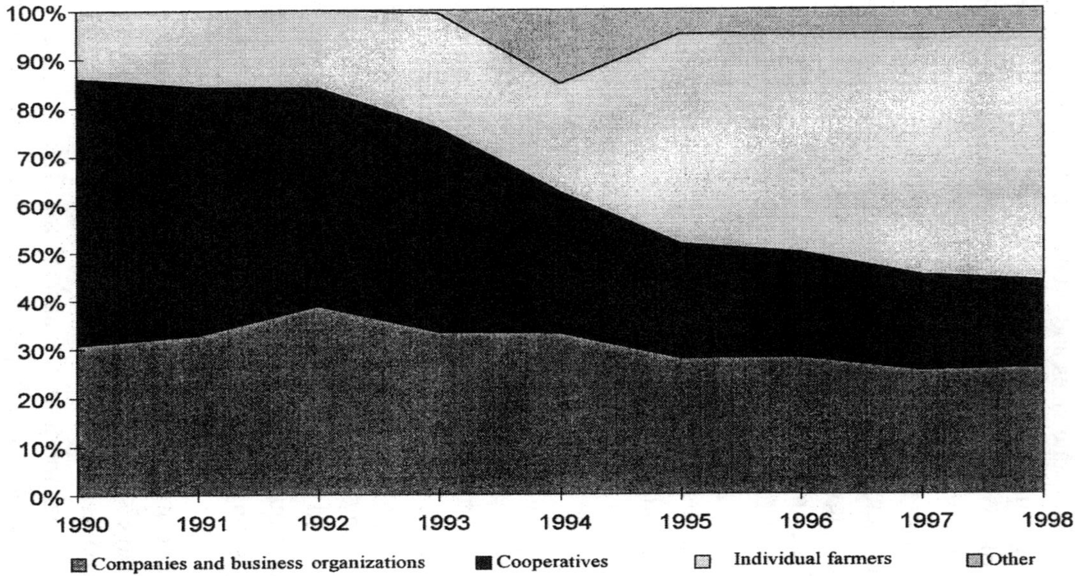

Source: Central Statistical Office

Medium-sized farms of between 15 and 50 hectares, based on family ownership and predominantly on family labor force, might come to represent 30 percent of arable land. A more significant growth in medium-sized farms, which are characteristic of the production structure of agriculture in Western Europe, would take place in Hungary only in the event of stronger government support. However, this would be very expensive and would cause a significant temporary drop in efficiency.

Nevertheless (not only in the medium term but also in the long term), small producers and part-time farmers must still be taken into consideration. It is possible that the approximately one million small producers might join the Hungarian market successfully, mainly in the production of fruits and vegetables and the raising of small livestock. In other respects they will be less and less capable of participating competitively on the markets. However, even in the long term the majority will only produce enough to be self-sufficient. Alternatively, they will be forced to become entrepreneurs, although the profitability of such enterprises will be low and it will be difficult for them to make a living. Solving the problems of agricultural wage laborers and unemployment in the villages is naturally not the task of agricultural policy, but rather a social issue. Of course, it is possible that agricultural subsidies might serve social purposes as well in the short term, but successful agricultural policy cannot be built on this.

At present, the structure of production is characterized by inertia, under the pressure of the need to exploit existing resources, rather than by conformity to the market—that is, in many cases farmers are not producing what can be sold but are trying to sell what has been produced.

One of the key issues for the success of agriculture continues to be how quickly the institutions of agricultural market coordination—that are either missing at present or not in conformity with the EU—can be established. Of fundamental importance is the establishment of a technical advice and information system that can help farmers and agricultural entrepreneurs in their decision making. The current Hungarian practice of frequently avoiding both tax and registration may turn out to be one of the most critical points in negotiations with the EU. Significant progress is needed before 2002 in the area of agricultural coordination and in the agricultural registration system.

Medium-term opportunities in the agriculture will be determined to a significant extent by loss of income and the depletion of assets that has been going on for years. In the medium-term period examined here, producers' prices—compared to the extremely depressed levels of previous years—will rise. Agricultural producers, however, with their extremely weak bargaining position (small-scale, scattered producers and divided interest-representation bodies), will remain unable to realize their—according to them—justified claims for higher prices. Nevertheless, a further reduction in the gap in earnings can be expected in the medium term. (The "price" of this will of course be a further reduction in costs.)

In the majority of farms the renewal of basic fixed assets has not taken place. General technical standards are very low. The mechanization of farms has occurred at very different levels: wealthier agricultural entrepreneurs have modernized their farms with the addition of new machinery. However, the main branches of domestic agronomy and livestock rearing will fall further behind EU levels.

The slow capital recovery and relatively low profitability (wherever these exist) continue to be unfavorable from the point of view of agricultural financing. Subsidies in the agriculture will only bring forth changes for the better if transparent, well-structured relations emerge in the agricultural sector. Without this, subsidies will continue to be "poured away". The most desirable situation would be for the state to take a role in promoting the acceleration of landholding concentration, the coordination and control of markets, the integration of producers (into cooperatives, etc.), and the improvement of efficiency, rather than preserving recent production and market structures that further hinder the agricultural transition by serving social and political goals. Although there are still plenty of question marks in terms of EU accession, it is already clear that Hungary will have to be prepared for less subsidized agriculture under the EU.

Based on the present and foreseeable future situation there is no chance that agricultural production will approach 1990 levels by the end of the medium-term period: production levels will remain around 25 percent lower. The conditions required for a more rapid expansion are not in place: such conditions would most importantly include fixed ownership and organizational relationships, the stable use of land, a functioning land market, rational farm structure, market-based cooperation among agricultural producers, machinery pools, and the strong representation of agricultural interests. Also—in order to supply these missing conditions—the clear and predictable involvement of the state is essential.

The extremely unbalanced agricultural prices and the almost predictable market malfunctions are not mere coincidences but are a consequence of the existing "system". According to surveys carried out by GKI Co., the unpredictability of the state's control is criticized every year by a larger percentage of producers in the agricultural sphere than in industrial or trade companies.

An important condition for the boosting and success of Hungarian agriculture would be the stabilization of land ownership and the promotion of the sale and concentration of land. Agriculture needs fresh capital, whether from domestic enterprises of from abroad.

As long as the circle of potential landowners and land buyers does not include capital-rich consumers, and as long as the ban on selling land purchased with compensation vouchers is not lifted and the profitability of agriculture fails to improve, the domestic land markets will not move and land prices will remain unrealistically low. Low land prices are of course favorable in the case of those who purchase land for speculative purposes rather than for utilization and cultivation. They are, however, contrary to the interests of agricultural entrepreneurs and real farmers, since land "without value" cannot function appropriately as collateral for credit. As long as land prices are so low the Land Credit and Mortgage Bank will be unable to make available sufficient credit. Of course, higher land prices would push food prices higher, but this will be unavoidable sooner or later in any case.

Following accession to the EU foreigners cannot simply be excluded from opportunities to purchase land. However, within domestic regulations restrictions can be introduced that connect the purchase of land with certain conditions (residence in Hungary, an undertaking to cultivate the land). However, such conditions cannot be limited to foreigners. As a temporary measure, restrictions should be imposed not on investments of foreign capital in Hungarian agriculture but on the extraction of capital (in this way foreigners cannot own land directly).

It is clear today that agriculture has been one of the main losers in the Hungarian transformation processes, since practically no fresh capital—either domestic or foreign—has flowed into this sector. Slow capital recovery and the lasting insecurity of ownership have kept away both domestic and (legal) foreign investors from agriculture.

The following basic dilemma exists: to which common agricultural policy and EU institutional system (that is, the current or the foreseeable reformed ones) should Hungarian agriculture adjust? Hungary will unquestionably have to adjust to Europe. However, during the accession negotiations it should aim to achieve more favorable positions.

3. The service industry

a) Transports and telecommunications

In the past decade development in the areas of transports and telecommunications has seen entirely contradictory tendencies. Output in terms of transports fell more significantly than the decline in the economy as a whole, while the development of telecommunications is progressing at a significant rate even by international standards.

So far, in terms of transports output within the national economy, the negative impacts of the transformation, the collapse of the Eastern markets, and the Yugoslav war have proven to be decisive. Domestic demand for transports capacity, which was developed to satisfy mostly quantitative requirements, has fallen even more rapidly than production as a whole, partly due to the strengthening of foreign competition and partly to changes in the production structure—that is, the shrinking of energy-consuming production activity, the fall in energy consumption, and the fall in the production of mass products requiring transports. The fall in solvency among the general public, the drastic decline in employment, and the spread of vehicle ownership has played an important role in the decline in passenger transports. Freight transports productivity, measured in terms of GDP, is not currently as high as the levels reached in the late 1980s, due mainly to the almost 50 percent drop in railroad freight transports. However, road and pipeline transports does approach 1990 GDP levels, while air transports significantly exceeds them.

Transports infrastructure is still very backward. Hungarian railroads are among the slowest in Europe, there are permanent speed limits in place, and the quality of passenger transports is not always adequate, although the introduction of new rolling stock has improved the situation. Apart from the building of motorways,

Changes in freight and passenger transports, 1990 to 2000
(in millions of tons and passenger/kilometers)

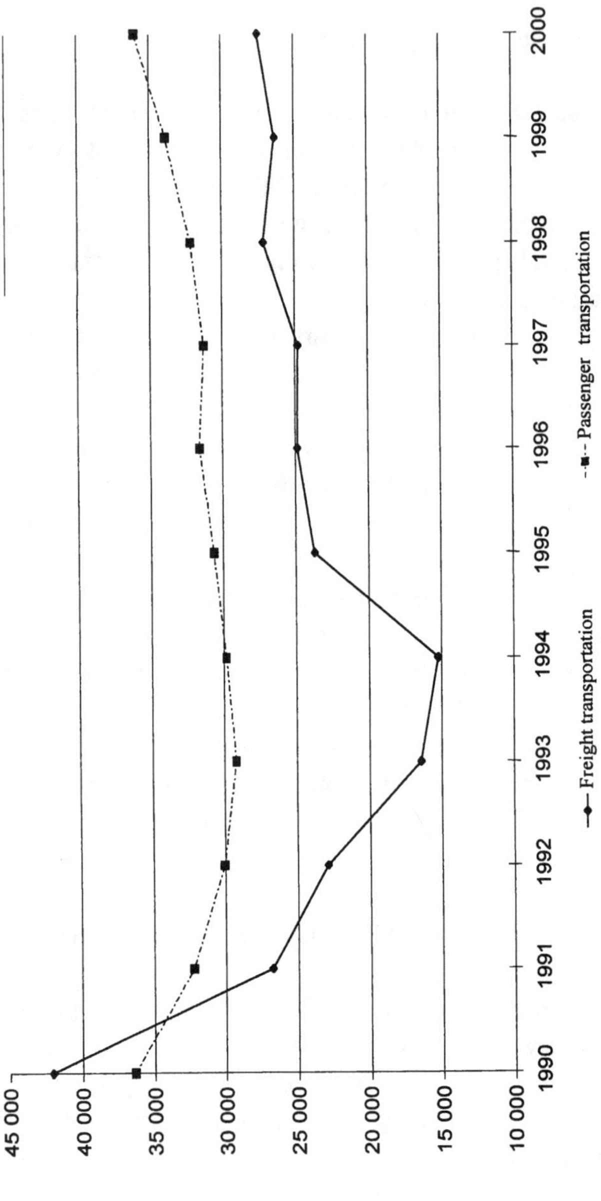

Source: Central Statistical Office. 2000: GKI Co. forecast

public roads have been increasingly neglected and in 1998/1999—despite the declaration of ambitious plans—highway and motorway development came to a stop.

In terms of freight transports, output decreased up to 1993 and has since increased steadily, apart from a setback in 1997. The same can be said of passenger transports, although in this case the setback was much more drastic. This is reflected in the fact that output in freight transports is expected to reach 1990 levels in 2000, while passenger transports will be around two-thirds of the 1990 levels.

This, however, can only partly be blamed on the quality of railroad passenger transports, since, in the meantime, the number of cars has significantly increased while commuting has practically stopped (at least to locations further away). The impact of this probably played a more significant role in the fall in output.

Within the decade the continuous decline of railroads within freight transports can be observed. This was partly a consequence of the above-mentioned infrastructural shortcomings (although dramatic developments also took place—in order to extend Ro-La and Ro-Ro delivery, for example). However, it was also partly a consequence of circumstances, since the Balkan War and the economic boycotting of Yugoslavia automatically reduced traffic. The crisis in Hungarian heavy industry and agriculture also significantly decreased demand for transports, while the developing motorway network gave road transports an advantage. The fact that waterway transports practically disappeared is down to practically the same reasons. Following a rapid decline at the beginning of the decade, output in terms of pipeline transports subsequently stabilized.

Since the beginning of motorway construction in the 1990s, a total of 180 kilometers of new motorway have been built (although in the meantime 31 kilometers of highway have been lost). Alongside the motorways a vivid economic life has sprung up, proving that motorways are a necessary (although not the only) condition for the economic boom. According to government forecasts almost 100 kilometers of highway are to be built in the next few years. The source of financing for this remains unclear as yet. With the exception of the M5 motorway, the government has eliminated the financing method that prevailed between 1990 and 1998, when roads were built by concessionary companies who collected tolls from users in return. Thus the using of roads became somewhat cheaper in 1999: however, when the section of motorway between Budapest and Győr was made into a toll road any benefit was canceled out. While former prices included the costs of development, the new tolls cover only maintenance and running costs, thus the entire burden of construction costs must be met by the budget, and therefore by taxpayers. One of the greatest disadvantages of this is that foreign users are not paying for the costs of construction; on the other hand, non-users have to contribute to running costs. This is contrary to the EU directive according to which users should pay a proportionate price for using motorways.

Telecommunications ran an entirely different course of development. In the first part of the 1990s this was the only sector in the Hungarian national economy to produce an increase in output. Following the change of regime, and especially the introduction of new legislation and the privatization of MATÁV, dynamic investment and development programs began. Although output in telecommunications had already increased in the early 1990s, the real breakthrough took place in 1996: the number of telephone lines and the value of output in terms of telecommunications services doubled compared to 1990, the number of those waiting for a telephone line fell to a minimal level, and mobile phones became part of everyday life. In telecommunications, not only has output risen by an annual 10 percent, but a marked modernization and increase in capacity has taken place.

Length of motorways and highways (km), 1990 to 2000

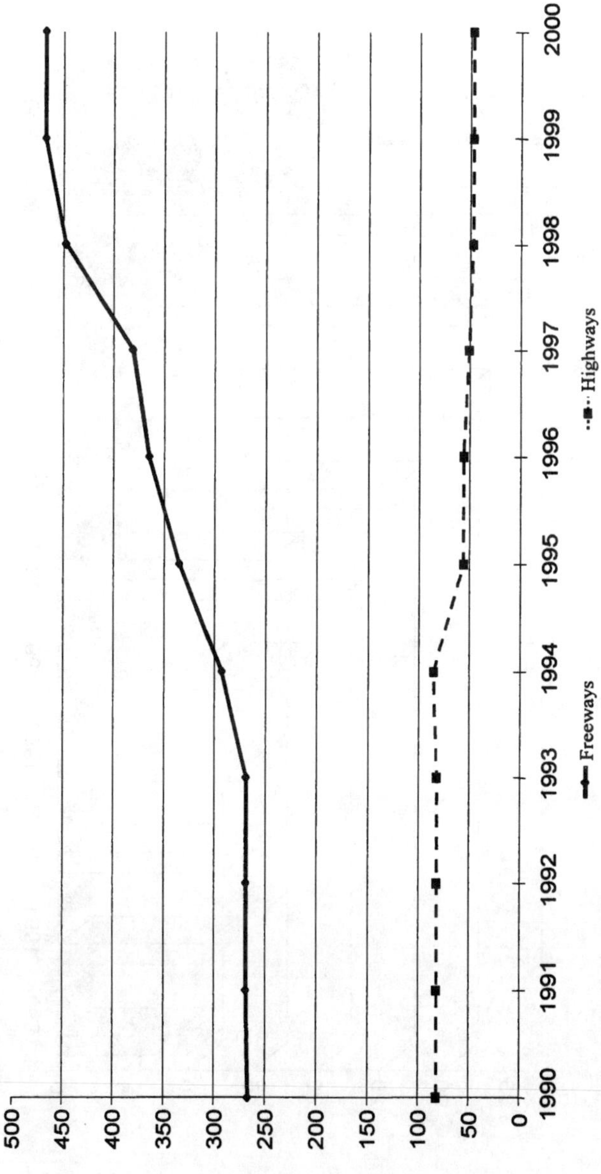

Source: Central Statistical Office. 1999: GKI Co. estimate, 2000: GKI Co. forecast

Number of cable-TV subscribers, telephone lines, and mobile telephone subscribers (per 100 persons), **1990 to 2000**

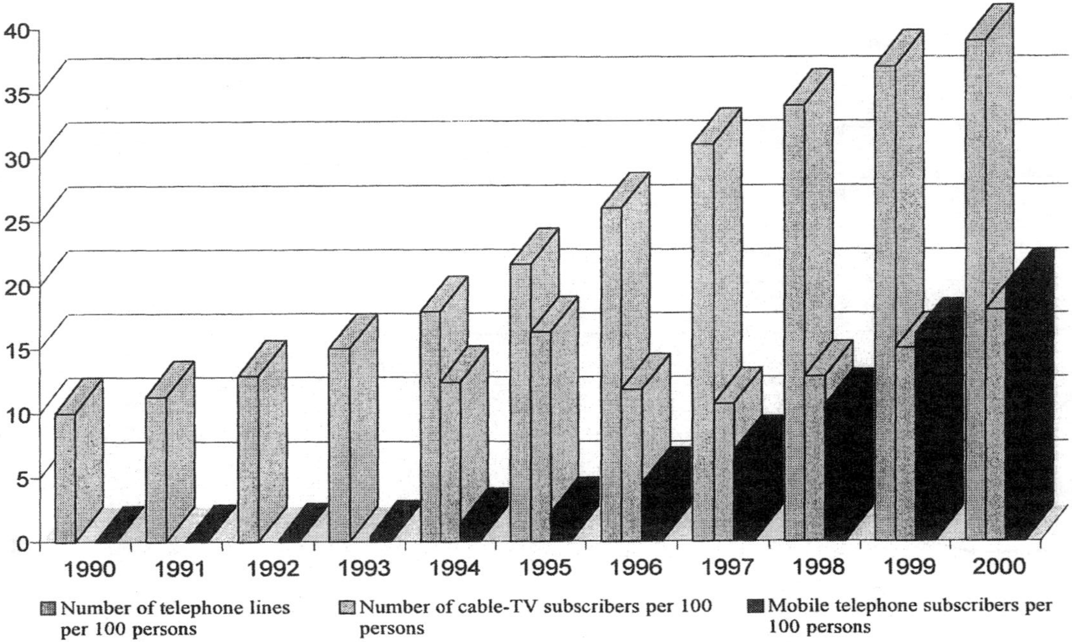

Source: Central Statistical Office. 1999: GKI Co. estimate, 2000: GKI Co. forecast

The telephone network has developed significantly in terms of both quantity and quality. On the one hand, approximately three-quarters of households have a telephone; on the other hand, shared-service lines have practically disappeared. Traditional analog cables have been replaced by optical cables capable of digital data transmission, thus the elimination of Hungary's disadvantage in terms of informatics has become a realistic possibility. The number of Internet users will rise steeply and the number of mobile phones (which in 1999 already stood at sixteen subscribers per 100 persons) is high even by EU standards. This will enable the use of banking services entirely from home to become accessible and will also result in an increase in the weight of e-shopping in the area of retail trade.

The Telecommunications Act currently under preparation for amendment adopts the recent market regulations in force in EU countries and will have a major impact on the widening and dynamization of competition and the further increase in investments and in various services. The rapid spread of mobile phones has decreased MATÁV's monopolistic position, and a fall in the level of mobile phone charges will further this process. Potential providers who already have main-line networks without concessions are keen to break into MATÁV's markets, something which is today hindered by the concession rights enjoyed by MATÁV, which were granted in its privatization contract. Developments in technology are expected to create competition among local telephone and cable television networks. There is already keen competition among Internet providers. The conditions for liberalization will be regulated by the Telecommunications Act currently in preparation. Since the adjusting of interests is a complicated task it is unlikely that the act will come into effect before the expiration of the current concessions (2001/2002), but even so competition will be free from 2002, which will result in the lowering of prices and improvements in quality and service.

In the area of postal services there have recently been signs of improvement and transformation. However, the unclear division of labor between the state and the business sector hinders the development of investments, while state resources are not sufficient to trigger a dynamic transformation.

b) Trade and tourism

In the absence of properly comparable figures there is little opportunity to analyze precisely the changes in consumer-goods trade, whether in relation to entrepreneurs and businesses or to retail trade.

According to data issued by the Central Statistical Office, between 1990 and 1996 the number of retail outlets more than doubled, while the volume of retail turnover fell by 30 percent—that is, turnover per shop (based on comparative prices) was barely one-third of the turnover in 1990. This—even though the increase in the previously low number of small outlets in the early 1990s was a daily experience in Hungary—was scarcely believable. Especially in terms of retail turnover it was likely that the level of private trade, with the spread of small shops and black trading, had been underestimated. Likewise, the rapidly increasing retail trade turnover in the second half of 1998 was probably partly the result of improvements in statistical sampling and partly a result of the growth in large retail units which are forced to declare their turnover in greater detail.

At the same time, due to the statistical system in use the number of shops was significantly overestimated. Until 1997 statistics for the retail trade network showed the number of shops and catering establishments, and within this the number of shops run by individual entrepreneurs, according to type of business and geographical distribution. These figures, however, included a great deal of duplication, since the statistics were based on licenses granted by the local self-governments. It was frequently the case that the same shop encompassed several lines of trade, which necessitated the holding of several licenses, thus the number of licenses was significantly higher than the number of shops. As a result, since 1997 the Central Statistical Office has applied a detailed statistical system which eliminates this duplication. The Central Statistical Office's methodological comments relating to the publication of data include the remark that the statistics of 1997, with respect to retail outlets, "can be compared to those of previous years only to a limited extent".

This means that, while in 1996 a total of 180,000 shops were registered, in 1997 there were only 125,000 registered, and by the end of 1999 there were around 150,000 shops in the country (in all cases excluding catering establishments and pharmacies). According to the—relatively reliable—statistics for 1990, the number of shops was 76,000, that is, growth has been very dynamic: almost 100 percent over eight years. (However, numbers did not double in the space of four years, as had been suggested by earlier statistics.) At the same time there is no possibility of analyzing the process over time.

In the first half of the 1990s, following the significant growth in the levels of price differentials, a change also took place in the proportions of those price differentials. Earlier, price mark-ups on everyday items were much higher than in the case of high-value consumer durables, although this situation was later reversed. The lowest price mark-ups are now to be found among products with a rapid circulation. Low prices are useful for attracting customers. The capital-rich multinationals are involved in very keen price bargaining—especially with the food industry—and occasionally lower their own price margins to such an extent that, in the case of certain products, they even risk losses.

In 1990 the approximately 150,000 shops were run by around 100,000 business organizations. More than 80 percent of enterprises had only one shop; 18,000 enterprises had between two and five shops; less than 600 enterprises had between six and ten shops; 250 enterprises had between eleven and twenty shops; and 200 more than twenty-one shops. In many cases the appearance of large hypermarkets and shopping centers has increased and even dynamized competition. It is obviously also for this reason that, compared to the statistics for late 1997, there is clear evidence of centralization. The number of one-shop organizations has fallen by 10 percent while the number of two- to five-shop organizations has risen by 30 percent; the number of six- to ten-shop organizations has risen by 50 percent; and the number of organizations with over ten shops has risen by 10 percent. Among the conditions for competition this is a fact to be welcomed, in that there are business groups capable of spreading and of utilizing the advantages of size.

An increasing amount of capital is being invested in this sector. New trade outlets are being built, while the old network can only become competitive at the cost of significant modernization and technical development. Competition is very broad, which generates rivalry in the application of increasingly modern solutions—solutions that are unavoidable today but very expensive in the first, technical, phase of investment. Logistics; purchase, storing and retailing tasks; and the related security technology have required serious computer-based developments. It is almost unprecedented, even in international terms, for so many large multinationals with the same or overlapping profiles to appear on the same market. The process of buy-outs has thus already begun among them.

Indicative of the change of structure is the fact that, according to Central Statistical Office's figures, both in 1998 and 1999 the majority of new shops operated in shopping malls, while the number of food and general stores decreased by more than a thousand. This is supported by research carried out by GFK Hungária, according to which hypermarkets increased their share in the turnover of everyday items from 0 to 8 percent between 1998 and

1999, against small general stores and semi-legal street trade. At the same time supermarkets have also lost position. According to a survey carried out by A.C. Nielsen, half the turnover in food products was carried out in 5 percent of the shops. It is clear that hypermarkets and shopping centers represent a major challenge, in the case of other groups of products also, to traditional shops and the wholesalers serving them.

According to the Association of Hungarian Shopping Centers, in late 2000 there are around fifty shopping centers operating in and around Budapest, and another fifty in the provinces—especially in the county towns. The shopping centers' share in the retail industry reached around 10 percent in 1999. (By 2002 this may well increase to around 14 to 15 percent.) There are currently 49 square meters of shopping mall space per one thousand inhabitants in Hungary, which is less than a third of the average in Western European countries. These indicators suggest that the building of shopping centers still has great potential. At the same time, retailers in Hungary compete for much lower levels of consumer power than in the West, while construction costs are scarcely any lower than in Western countries. Thus shops operating in malls have to produce a relatively larger turnover than in Western Europe. It is this factor that, in many cases, leads to losses and the inability to lease existing retail outlets, and that, in the medium term, might limit the creation of new retail space. It is likely that, in spite of this, enterprises are counting on dynamic growth, a lasting increase in consumer power, and the favorable impact of EU accession.

Domestic Internet-based (electronic) trade still stands on very weak foundations. The absence of legal guarantees for electronic signatures is only one of the reasons for this. Equally important are limitations related to the spread of the Internet. As a result of the Sulinet (Schoolnet, later Írisz) and university programs, many high-school and university students are in daily contact with the world of the Internet. However, access to modern technology is often limited.

Furthermore, the Írisz program reaches far fewer schools than was originally planned, and its functions in the aiding of tuition have also decreased. Telehouses could also be of great help, but functioning here is also hindered by lack of funding. High telecommunications and cable television tariffs limit the spread of modem and cable-based Internet use. At the same time, it should not be forgotten that for the overwhelming majority of society virtual reality is an alien concept, and even the majority of users only access the Net for the purposes of "chatting" and e-mailing. At the same time, the relatively low cost of computer hardware in theory favors the rapid spread of Internet use. The younger generation just leaving school, who have already come across the Internet during their school years, will sooner or later create a demand as regular users of the Internet, thus the potential e-commerce market will grow steadily year by year.

No reliable figures are available for the volume of domestic Internet trade. Estimates change almost weekly, partly as a result of methodological problems. This leaves room for ungrounded speculations and for forecasts that change annually by several decimal places.

In the development of enterprises in the catering and hospitality sector there are similar structural processes at work as in trade. In recent years the number of small enterprises in the sector has increased dynamically, since there was/is a real demand for small-sized premises and guest-houses. The large hotel companies have developed dynamically (with a centralization process also taking place among them), while in terms of catering, the largely multinational fast-food franchise networks have seen outstandingly rapid development. With the increase in domestic demand there are good prospects for increasing turnover in both areas. Despite this, bankruptcies are also to be expected among non-competitive enterprises.

The tourist industry is one of the most dynamically developing sectors of the national economy. This sector was being developed even before the change of regime. The large number of foreign visitors to Hungary was related to the fact that Hungary was the most open of the socialist countries: this attracted tourists and business persons from both East and West, as well as from the Hungarian minorities in neighboring countries, although it also provided opportunities for smuggling. Hungarian tourism-related revenues and assets increased dynamically in the 1990s, the former rising to USD 3.5 billion by 1997/ 1999, and the latter to between USD 2.2 and 2.5 billion. During the years of economic recession, tourism among Hungarian citizens understandably decreased. However, it has recently begun to pick up (in terms of both domestic and foreign destinations).

c) Service-providing businesses and public services

Between 1989 and 1994 the share in the GDP represented by service-providing businesses (excluding trade and transports) increased significantly, largely as a result of the decline in other productive sectors, the inflexibility of public services, and the appearance of market-based services as partly new activities. Since then, this proportion has slightly decreased as a result of the more rapid increase in other sectors, and has recently stagnated at between 38 and 40 percent.

Analyzing the development of service-providing businesses is made more difficult by the fact that in 1989 only the seeds of this sector, which is characteristic of market economies, existed in Hungary. Leaving aside the figures, this development meant the establishment of an institutional system for service-providing businesses, the appearance of new professions, the growing prosperity of formerly unknown activities, and the emergence of a qualitatively different service-providing business branch by the mid-1990s.

The development of the service branches is determined by the interrelated changes in three major groups of factors. The service-providing businesses react very sensitively to changes in the general economic situation. The tasks related to EU accession and the resources that are occasionally provided for them from abroad might stimulate both business-based and public service providers. The speed and depth of state budget reform affects mostly the prospects of the public services, but as a result of the channeling of a part of their activities to the private sector it directly affects business-based service providers as well.

The role of services in employment is somewhat smaller (34 to 35 percent for several years) than their weight in terms of GDP.

The geographical distribution of GDP contribution within the service sector is very uneven. More than half of it is produced in the capital city, and half of the GDP recorded in Budapest is produced in the service branches. Registering companies according to seat rather than according to activity also plays a part in this. While the GDP contribution of public service providers shows only slight regional differences, the difference is much more pronounced in terms of business-based service providers. The minimal presence of business-based service providers in the provinces makes it difficult for backward regions to catch up, while the backwardness of such areas leaves these enterprises unmotivated to carry out an appropriate amount of regional expansion.

The relatively dynamic growth in the number of people working in public administration and social security came to an end in 1999. The organizational system of public administration and social security is gradually transforming as a result of the changeover of the expert personnel. However, the impact of this on the quality of work takes a longer time to show.

Share of the service sectors in GDP, 1991 to 1999
(percentages, calculated according to current base price)

	1991	1994	1999
Financial activities and contributory services	4.4	6.3	4.1
Real estate transactions, leasing, and activities supporting economic activities	10.2	13.4	15.5
Public administration, compulsory social security	6.4	7.4	7.2
Education	4.8	5.7	4.5
Health and social care	4.2	4.8	4.4
Other community services	2.6	4.1	3.0
Total services	32.6	41.7	38.7

Source: Central Statistical Office

In the educational system there is a marked over-supply in terms of quantity (both in terms of the number of teachers and the number of institutions), while there are several qualitative demands which neither the state nor the private education system is able to meet. Within the branch there is a significant internal restructuring in progress. Due to the permanent decline in the numbers of children there will be demand for fewer and fewer elementary school teachers, while increasing specialization within middle and higher education requires a significant number of tutors. However, a staff capable of transmitting new knowledge is lacking at every level, therefore a knowledge-based information society will take a longer time to establish.

The situation with respect to health reform is still uncertain. The main aim of the state budget is to reduce the rate of cost increases. However, a systematic analysis of the work of the sector would be a huge and complex task even if the various competing interest groups did not behave in such a way as to make a task of this kind near impossible.

With respect to health, not even the directions of change have crystallized. The resources and mechanisms required to improve the standards of provision remain unclear. For the population, it is not only the case that the financial burdens relating to the health service—above all the cost of medicines—have increased: using the services has also become more complicated. The impact of practice privatization, which was suddenly introduced within the sphere of basic services in early 2000, still remains to be felt.

The aging of the population and its generally poor state of health create significant demand for health and social services. In order to obtain such services the population occasionally spends beyond its capacities. The increasing number of private clinics as well as the creation of voluntary health insurance funds are signs of the channeling of the health service onto market or semi-market paths, although the services provided are not full scale. For the present, the voluntary health insurance funds have only around 10,000 members.

Among the business-based service providers, economic strength is rather varied. Financial service providers have unquestionably experienced a favorable course of development in the last one or two years. However, the market is still unsettled. Every year there are one or two dramatic bankruptcies or quiet withdrawals from the market, and this segment of the national economy, like many others, has not been able to rid itself of unfair business practices.

In the case of other business-based service providers the picture is varied. The situation of providers dealing with computer technology and services supporting economic activities appears undeniably promising. The market opportunities for business-based service providers have been improved by the relatively significant levels of spending among the population and the boom in the real estate market. Higher than average increases in the cost of services suggests that providers are trying to capitalize in the short term on the significant demand that exists.

The non-financial business-based services are very sensitive to the state of the economy, and due to the insignificant level of foreign interest they attract they are extremely dependent on the domestic market. The number of enterprises, the volume of net revenues, and the number of employees in the area of computer technology are permanently increasing. The dynamic spread of small companies is still characteristic in this sub-branch, and employment potential is increasing.

Due to the fragmentation of the various institutions, the number of organizations belonging to the branch of scientific research and experimental development rose between 1990 and 1998. Every other indicator, in spite of some degree of fluctuation, reveals a significant decline. The real value of money spent on research and experimental development in 1999 was approximately one-third of the amount spent in 1990.

The real estate market has been extremely vivid for several years. The significant rise in prices in terms of the residential housing market has reached a level that will become an obstacle to further increase in turnover—and prices are likely to continue to rise. In the market for office space and industrial real estate the turnover continues to be significant. The supply of office space available for rent in Budapest will continue to increase, although the utilization of such space is even now below full capacity. There is a serious shortage in the market for quality storage space and logistic centers. In these areas serious developments are expected to take place in the near future.

4. Foreign economic relations

Between 1989 and 1992 the Hungarian economy faced a deep crisis that was characterized by the collapse of the COMECON market and the difficulties of adapting to new markets. There was an extremely steep drop in exports: the approximately 20 percent fall far exceeded the level of domestic sales. However, since the level of domestic sales also fell, exports provided Hungarian enterprises with an opportunity for growth, manifested in 1993 by growth more rapid than that of the GDP. Since 1996 the increase in exports has been continuously high, that is, in double figures (this dynamism was not interrupted even by the slight economic recession in the main export market, the EU, in 1998/1999).

During the 1990s the geographical structure of exports suddenly changed, although the fall in importance of ex-socialist and developing countries and the increasing role of developed market economies had already slowly begun in the 1980s. This process accelerated in 1990, and in parallel with the collapse of the COMECON market and the drastic breakaway from the Soviet Union in 1991, traditional trade relations were restored with developed countries, mostly in Western Europe. The adhesion to the Europe Agreement in 1991, along with the establishment of CEFTA in 1993 and its subsequent enlargement, resulted in a marked impact on the geographical structure of foreign trade. While in 1990 only one-third of exports were directed towards the EU, in 1994 the proportion was three-quarters, since when the level has remained this high. Within the EU Hungarian exports are strongly concentrated: half of all exports go to Germany, followed by Austria, Italy and France, although Holland and Belgium, despite their small size, also fulfill an increasingly important role in Hungarian exports. As far as developed countries outside Europe are concerned, exports to the USA increased significantly, while in terms of the developed Far Eastern markets no ground has been gained.

Changes in exports and imports, 1985 to 1999
(1980 = 100)

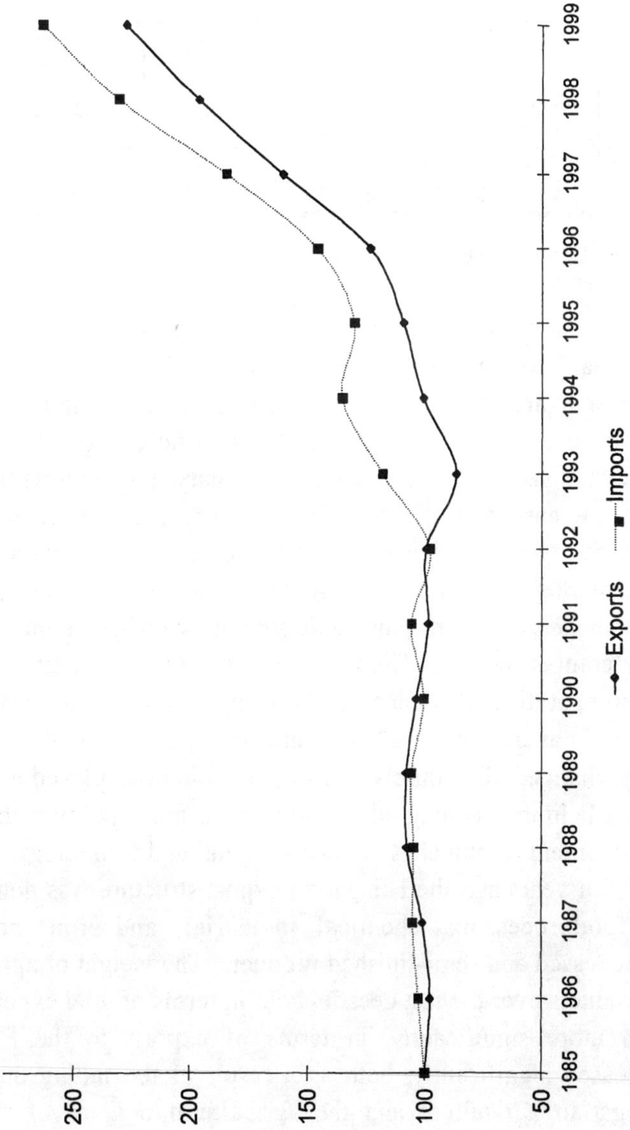

Source: Central Statistical Office

Division of exports and imports - to developed and East European countries, 1989 to 1999 (percentage)

	Developed countries		EU countries		East European countries	
	Exports	Imports	Exports	Imports	Exports	Imports
1989	44.2	49.7	24.8	29	45.2	42.8
1994	72.0	70.6	51.0	45	22.1	22.8
1999	83.8	74.6	76.5	64	12.4	14.3

Source: Central Statistical Office

As a result of this process, in Hungary, as in other Central East European countries, the specialization of exports has largely increased, and within trade relations between Central and East European countries and the EU the significance of trade within individual sectors is increasing. In Hungary, for example, it is not only the case that the machine industry, a sector representing advanced technology, has gained space in exports towards developed market economies, but also that an increasingly large number of branches of the machine industry are capable of maintaining their competitiveness. The previously existing situation, in which the comparative advantages of the Hungarian economy were manifested in areas that were labor- and energy-intensive, has substantially changed. The inflow of foreign capital has played a significant role in this: among other things it has made possible the rapid development of branches requiring capital and technology.

Ten years ago the Hungarian export structure was dominated by foodprocessing, chemical industrial, and iron industrial unprocessed and semi-finished products. The weight of agricultural products over the last decade, both in terms of total exports and, even more significantly, in terms of exports to the EU, has decreased significantly, both as a result of the falling output of Hungarian agriculture and the agricultural policies of the EU. Machine industrial spare parts and processed products have become dominant within exports.

The TOP 10 commodity groups in Hungarian exports

1990 Commodity group	%	1999 Commodity group	%
Meat industrial products	10.1	Office appliances	13.2
Chemical industrial semi-finished products	8.6	Power-generating machinery	11.6
Iron and steel - semi-finished products	7.1	Electrical appliances	11.2
Clothing	6.8	Road vehicles	9.0
Means of transports	4.8	Communication technology	7.9
Metallurgical raw materials	4.2	Clothing	5.3
Preserved fruits and vegetables	3.3	Metal products	2.5
Chemical raw materials	3.2	General machinery	2.4
Iron- and metal-industrial semi-finished products	2.3	Meat and meat products	2.2
Pharmaceuticals	1.7	Furniture	2.1
TOTAL	52.1	TOTAL	67.4

Source: Foreign Trade Statistical Yearbook, 1990 and Ministry of Economics, Brief Review of Foreign Trade Turnover, January to December 1999.

There has been a marked increase in the role of the machine industry within exports: in 1993 machine industrial commodity groups represented only 15 percent of exports, while in 1999 they represented 46 percent. Out of the top ten export and import commodity groups, six belong to the machine industry—an indication that in Hungarian trade, as is usual in foreign trade in developed countries, intra-industrial development has now become characteristic. The marked changes in structure are clearly displayed by the import contribution margin, that is, the proportions of exports and imports. This indicator clearly shows that in the area of computers (and office appliances), for example, Hungary has gone from being largely an importer to being largely an exporter. In the case of road vehicles, levels of exports and imports have become balanced, amid a large increase in turnover, by the construction of significant machine industrial capacities.

Since changes of a similar nature are taking place in terms of the foreign trade of several Central and Eastern European countries (in Poland, the manufacturing of electrical appliances, communication technology, medical appliances, and vehicles; in the Czech Republic the manufacturing of electrical appliances, means of transports, and communication technology; and in Slovenia the manufacturing of machines and machine equipment, electrical appliances, and office equipment and computers are becoming increasingly important branches of exports towards the EU), the competitiveness of these countries is increasing in several areas of the machine industry on EU markets. In the five CEFTA countries the presence of foreign companies is decisive in the manufacturing of road vehicles, in the rubber and plastics industry, in the production of electrical appliances, and in communication technology, and within all these branches there is strong intra-industrial trade, while in the export structure of countries that are likely to be included in the next wave of EU accession—the Baltic States, Bulgaria, and Romania—the proportion of traditional branches is higher.

TOP 10 commodity groups in Hungarian imports

1990		1999	
Commodity group	%	Commodity group	%
Energy sources	12.5	Electrical appliances	12.3
Chemical semi-finished products	12.0	Road vehicles	8.6
Other machine industrial products	6.3	Office appliances	6.8
Clothing	3.5	General machinery	6.2
Vehicles	3.0	Communications technology	6.1
Chemical industrial raw materials	2.7	Power-generating machinery	6.1
Raw materials from plant sources	2.5	Various processed products	5.2
Metallurgical raw materials	2.4	Metal products	3.4
Iron- and metal-industrial semi-finished products	2.3	Mineral oil and mineral oil products	3.2
Precision engineering products	2.2	Natural and artificial gas	2.2
TOTAL	49.4	TOTAL	60.1

Source: Foreign Trade Statistic Yearbook 1990 and Ministry of Economics Brief Review of Foreign Trade Turnover, January to December 1999.

5. Employment and unemployment

The quantitative changes in employment in the past ten years can be divided into three periods: between 1990 and 1995 employment fell steadily, although at different rates: between 1996 and 1997 there was near stagnation; while since 1998 there has been an increase of 1.5 percent. In total, employment in the period between 1990 and 1999 fell radically: according to estimates 1.2 million workplaces closed and employment fell by almost 24 percent. The lowest point, in the middle of the decade, saw the disappearance of 1.5 million jobs and a 30 percent fall in employment.

The labor force began to be selected from the point of view of quality. Those with low, or no, qualifications, or those who did not have marketable skills—that is, those unable to adjust to the new market economic conditions—were pushed out of the labor-force market. The fall in employment—with the exception of trade and commerce—affected all sectors of the national economy, although not to the same extent: in sectors belonging to the competitive sphere the number of those employed fell much more dynamically than in the budget sphere, which, although offering lower levels of income, provided employment in order to preserve social harmony. Productivity, at the level of the national economy, continuously improved—although with some fluctuation—predominantly due to the extraordinarily dynamic growth of industrial productivity.

According to a more detailed analysis, including surveys of workplaces with over twenty employees, between 1993 and 1998 only two sectors (the machine industry, and services supporting the real estate business and economic activities) were able to achieve an increase in the number of employees. Examining the sub-branches in further depth it can be seen that in branches using advanced technology, with high levels of exports and with high levels of foreign capital, besides productivity being extremely high employment has increased significantly.

At the same time, sub-branches of a low and medium technological level, employing high numbers of workers, were also important from the point of view of employment, since the increase in production was provided by increasing the number of employees. The major sub-branches which were losing employees were characterized by their low percentage of exports, the low presence of foreign working capital, low productivity, and low wage increases.

Employment in the service sector ran a different course. Economic organizations employing over twenty persons were not capable of absorbing the labor force formerly employed in the productive branches.

The rise in employment gradually extended to a growing number of branches of the national economy, although at a different pace, while the motors of development will remain those branches that currently drive development and those which receive significant investments.

The restructuring of employment shows new characteristics. While employment in companies in the competitive sphere with more than ten employees fell by 16 percent between 1994 and 1997, the fall was only 10 percent in the budget sphere. (In 1998 employment saw stagnation in both sectors.) In the market sphere during the period under examination only the machine industry and health-related enterprises—which started from a very low level—were able to produce an increase in employment (by 12 percent and 9 percent respectively). (The proportion of those present as entrepreneurs in health-related enterprises is very small, at around 3 to 4 percent.) From among the budget sub-branches with a significant number of employees, the number of those employed in the public administration and in compulsory social security fell the least (by 7 percent), while in education the fall was the greatest (by 16 percent).

An indication of the change in the direction of the process is that in 1999 market enterprises with more than five employees achieved a 2.5 percent increase in employees, compared to the 2.8 percent fall in the budget sector. In all but two of the twelve sub-branches of the business sector an increase in the number of employees has been recorded, the two exceptions being agriculture and financial activities. According to the budget system, among economic organizations there is a general decrease, with the exception of transports, warehousing, post, and telecommunications.

Labor-force supply has remained practically unchanged. A fall in the birth rate began in the second half of the 1970s, thus the number of young people now entering the labor market has also fallen. The raising of the retirement age resulted in only a slight pressure on the labor-force market, since approximately half of those reaching retirement age had already retired. For the moment, the reintroduction of child-care allowances has reduced labor-force supply only minimally.

Labor demand is likely to see significant variations. The re-acceleration of the growth in investments and the improvement of the general economic situation will generate employment in the competitive sector, while in the budget sector a fall of the same degree can be expected. Tensions in the labor-force market will slowly increase, and in a growing number of skilled jobs (at the medium and higher levels) there will be shortages. At the same time, due to low mobility in terms of housing in Hungary (despite the small size of the country), the right employers and employees come together only with difficulty.

Geographically, the employment capacity of the Central and Transdanubian regions will continue to increase, and in these regions some of the inactive persons who had retired will become active once again. In the medium term all regions will absorb labor force, but in the eastern parts of the country the dynamics of this process will not be sufficient to compensate for the disadvantages created during the 1990s. The more highly qualified members of the labor force will continue to have better chances to find employment, but employment in the area of manual labor is also likely to see a tendency towards improvement.

The radical fall in employment in Hungary in the first half of the 1990s took place without dramatic social conflicts. This was due partly to the introduction of an initially generous unemployment benefit system, and partly to the fact that the state "turned a blind eye" to the spread of the black economy. The breathtakingly rapid emergence of unemployment in the early 1990s was a new phenomenon in the Hungarian economy and society: practically in the space of three years the number of registered unemployed persons had risen from zero to 700,000 by February 1993. The unemployment rate peaked at 14.1 percent. Following a steady fall, the number of registered unemployed persons was around 400,000 in 1998/1999, that is, 9.6 percent. However, this favorable tendency was not so much due to any improvement in the employment capacities of the economy (this was only true of the process of 1998/1999) as to the increasingly strict regulations within the unemployment benefit system. Unemployment benefit, which could initially be claimed for two years, was reduced to one and a half, and then to one year. Bearing in mind that for benefit to be paid for one year a person needs to have been in work for four years (or a minimum of one year for three months' benefit), those who have once claimed benefit have great difficulty getting back into the unemployment benefit system again.

According to the European Economic Commission's analysis in 1994/1995, in all the Visegrád countries the duration for which unemployment benefit could be claimed decreased. In the Czech Republic and Slovakia it was a maximum of six months; in Slovenia, depending on previous employment, it was up to two years; while in Poland and Hungary it was one year (although in Poland men who had been in work for thirty years and women who had been in work for twenty-five years could claim unemployment benefit for one and a half years). In the third quarter of 1994 the level of unemployment benefit in the Czech Republic was 26 percent of the average wage, and in Slovakia 31 percent of the average wage. In the fourth quarter of 1994 it was 26 percent of the average wage in Hungary, and in Slovenia 46 percent.

For those living in the worst economic conditions, social benefits following the expiration of unemployment benefit were initially granted "for life". However, in mid-1995 these benefits were limited to two years and thereafter made conditional on proof of subsequent re-employment. Those who became ineligible to claim even these social benefits were no longer counted among the registered unemployed. A further restriction in 1996 was the change in the benefits available to those looking for first-time employment. An active employment policy device was introduced whereby these young people were instead offered part-time jobs or retraining programs, which resulted in a marked fall in registered unemployment in this category. (The numbers decreased not only due to the cutting of benefits, but also because those participating in training programs are not registered as unemployed.)

In early 2000, as a result of the re-transformed unemployment system (which has gradually eliminated the institution of social benefits and shortened the duration of unemployment benefit), a further decrease can be expected in the number and rate of registered unemployment. In a few years' time the internationally comparable unemployment rate, calculated according to ILO methodology, will reach a "natural" level of around 5 percent, while, despite rising employment, the numbers of those of working age who are out of work will remain high.

An indirect proof of the more extended scale of real unemployment is the fact that, while the number of registered unemployed persons is falling, so is the number of those in employment, while the number of those of a working age who are out of work is significantly increasing. Some of the women who are out of work have retired to become housewives or belong to the hidden economy, and some of those nearing retirement age have taken early retirement (although the opportunities for doing so have been restricted).

The major problem in terms of Hungarian unemployment is the high proportion of long-term unemployed persons (those out of work for over one year). This is partly due to the economy's weakened employment capacities, but also to the difficulties faced by the unemployed in returning to employment (among the unemployed there is a high proportion of unskilled persons and persons with unmarketable skills). Unemployment shows marked differences in terms of geographical region, while the proportion of unemployed persons among the young is higher than in other age groups.

Since its emergence, the structural characteristics of unemployment have been stable, therefore those with low qualifications, the unskilled, those in poor health, and those with social problems have predominantly disappeared from the labor-force market and have mainly become long-term unemployed. At a lower level, the differences in unemployment in terms of geographical location have also remained stable.

The approximately 1.5 million jobs which disappeared between early 1990 and late 1996 resulted in a transformation of the economy's employment structure.

Naturally, at the beginning of the period production fell more rapidly than employment, further decreasing the already low productivity level. However, from 1992 a significant improvement began. Industrial productivity followed the tendency of the national economy, although the increase was much higher here. A favorable factor was that this tendency continued even in the period of growing employment.

Changes in productivity, 1990 to 1999
(previous year = 100)

	1990	1991	1992	1993	1994	1995	1996	1997	1998	1999
GDP index/ Employment index	98.7	94.4	107.6	107.6	106.9	103.4	102.1	104.6	103.5	102.9
Industrial GDP index/ industrial employment index	-	-	-	107.5	111.5	109.7	109.5	111.3	106.3	107.0

The employed include active wage earners and employed pensioners, based on the figures for the labor-force balance as a mathematical average of the figures for the beginning of the year.
Source: Central Statistical Office and GKI Co. calculations

According to ILO's analysis, between 1989 and 1994 the level of employment in the Visegrád countries fell by the smallest amount in the Czech Republic, that is, by only 11.5 percent. This, however, was coupled with a 7.7 percent fall in productivity. The other extreme is represented by Hungary where, in the same five years, employment fell by 28 percent, and at the same time productivity increased by 8.6 percent.

The level of the fall in employment in the various countries is indicative of the rate of transformation. At the same time, the lower fall means that previously existing companies and workplaces remain that are less productive and competitive and in which the process of transformation has not, or has only just, begun. In places such as Hungary where, on the other hand, employment fell rapidly and was coupled by a rise in productivity, transformation, privatization, and the related structural and organization changes took place more rapidly.

In recent years Hungary's employment structure has changed in the most favorable direction, since the number of those employed in the service sector has increased significantly despite the fact that, due to Hungary's natural capacities and traditions, the role of agriculture is far from negligible. The structure of employment has been modernized to the least extent in Poland, where, due to the fragmentation of agriculture, the large number of poorly mechanized small farms still accounts for a significant labor force, and in many cases this sector provides work for the labor force made redundant in other sectors of the economy.

6. Investment

The restrictions that inevitably followed the halt in the growth that had been experienced in the1970s, which had taken place at the cost of indebtedness, affected investments above all. Between 1980 and 1985 the of investment volume had already fallen by 20 percent, then up to 1990, in spite of fluctuations, there was a slight overall increase.

In the past ten years there have been marked fluctuations in terms of investments. As a result of the economic recession there was first a fall, after which, as a forerunner of the later boom, the volume of accumulation increased in 1993. This dynamism came to an end in 1995, but from 1996 an almost linear growth can be observed. Surprisingly, the "cyclical" movement was not caused by the private sector (as is usual in developed countries), but by the budget sector. This is true even for the upturns in investments, since the upturn in 1993 was caused by accelerated infrastructural developments; then in 1995 budget restrictions resulted in a halt in investment dynamism. Fortunately, the private sector represents an increasing weight in the total accumulation, and as a result the impact of the state will become smaller and smaller.

At the very end of the 1980s projects involving enormous state expenditure (for example the construction of the Bős-Nagymaros dam, as well as the Eocene and Liass programs, and chemical industrial development) were taken off the agenda. The major state-owned companies, in their shaken situation, were unable to compete with increasing imports and were mostly unable to break into Western markets. Thus only a few companies had enough strength to develop using their own resources.

Investments were dynamic mainly in the manufacturing industry and in infrastructure, but significant investments were made in telecommunications and, from 1997, in real estate development. The partial privatization of the electrical power system had a positive effect in that the new owners compensated for the decades-long investment deficit in the space of just a few years. In terms of infrastructure motorway constructions, some new bridges, the development of the high-voltage electricity grid, and the reconstruction of railroads, as well as the further progress of railroad electrification, deserve special mention.

Changes in the volume of accumulated fixed assets, 1990 to 2000
(1980 = 100)

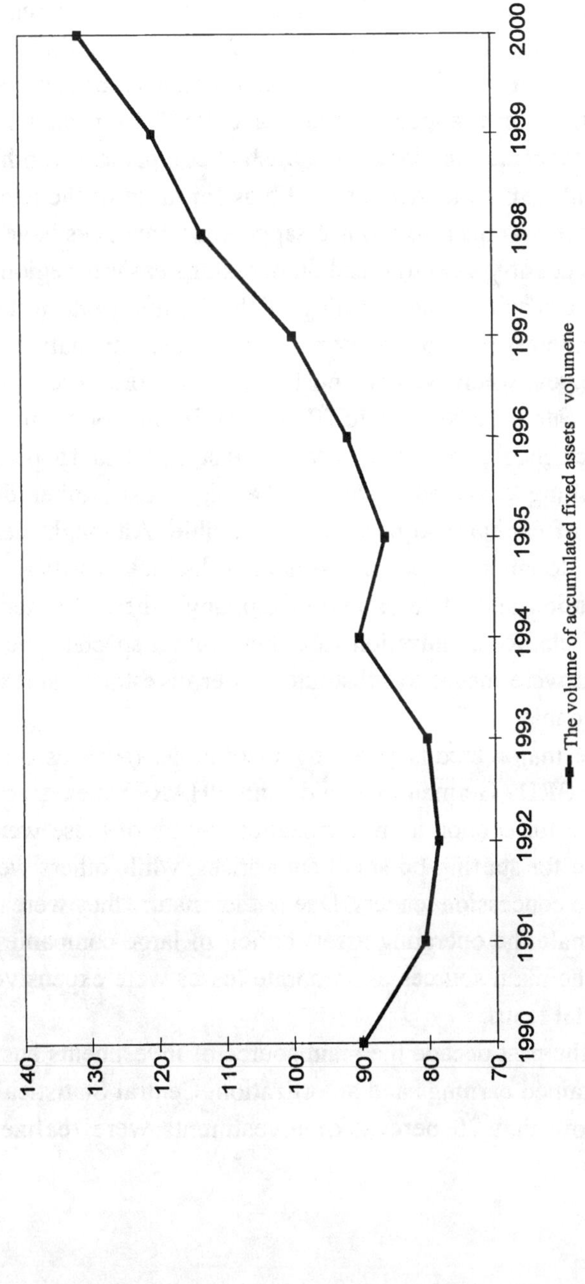

Source: Central Statistical Office; 2000: GKI Co.'s preliminary figure

A significant amount of investments took the form of greenfield investments. This is how the manufacturing of cars and car spare-parts, the computer technology sector, and the majority of synthetic material processing were established. A positive development in recent years is that, besides major investments, smaller subcontractors have appeared who have built their manufacturing plants alongside the already established companies. Another positive trend is that the geographical bias (in favor of the capital city and Western Transdanubia) is disappearing. Investors have discovered the country's central, and on occasions eastern, regions.

As a result of the spiraling of the inflation rate in the early 1990s, interest rates on investment credits rose dramatically: there was one year when even the most reliable debtors were given credits at an interest rate of 35 to 40 percent. In relation to the producers' price index, this meant real interest of 10 to 15 percent for those taking out credit. Due to the high costs, other domestic sources of capital also became inaccessible. Although there were state endowments and investment subsidies (mostly via the Privatization and State Holding Company), these affected only a small circle. Reorganization subsidies were a special type of subsidy that were meant to substitute earlier investment and working capital loans.

The major credits given by institutions (such as the World Bank, EBRD, German coal aid, and PHARE) meant additional resources for economic modernization. Some of these were made available for starting up small enterprises, while others were connected to concession tenders. Due to their nature they were not able to eliminate the operating assets deficit of large companies, while one of the main sources of corporate losses were expensive working capital loans.

In the past decade the main source of investments has largely been retained earnings and amortization. Central Statistical Office data show that 70 percent of investments were realized from

Changes in investment credit portfolios, 1995 to 2000
(HUF billion)

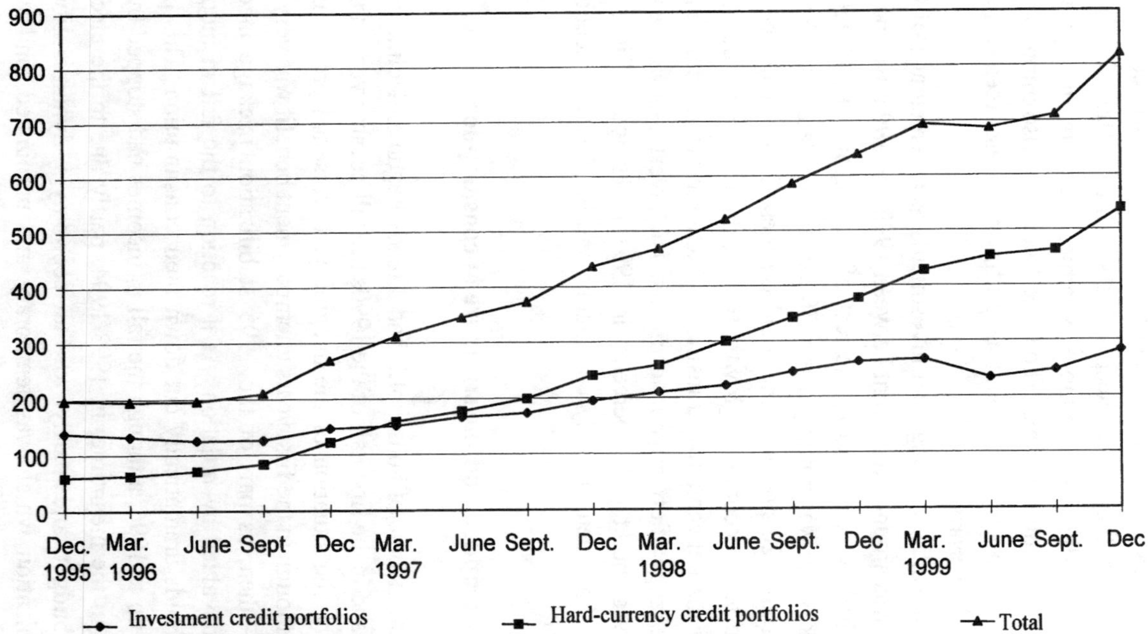

Source: Hungarian National Bank.
Note: part of the hard-currency credit portfolios of over one year are not investment credits, but they cannot be treated separately.

owners' resources up to the mid-1990s (no relevant figures are available for subsequent years). The most important additional resource was hard-currency credits, especially since, compared to HUF credits, they were cheap and abundant. In 1999 the demand for HUF credits was also more dynamic, caused by the significant fall in credit interest rates. The banks' liquidity also improved as a result of bank consolidation, thus putting new resources at the disposal of enterprises.

The value of Hungarian investments as a percentage of GDP, which was around 20 percent between 1990 and 1996, was not particularly low compared to the rest of the region. The Czech and Slovak figure was initially nearer 30 percent, but later, as in Poland, was around 20 percent. The yield on these investments was not manifested in economic growth, that is, the high rate—due to the slower market economic transition—did not at the same time mean a wide range of effective investments. The investment rate reached its lowest point (18.9 percent) in 1993 in Hungary. Since then growth has been virtually continuous and in 1999 it exceeded 24 percent.

7. Consumption and the structure of consumption

The real income of households had already begun to decline before 1990, and in the first half of the 1990s the fall became very marked. Initially, the situation of the unemployed worsened predominantly—although in the first years unemployment benefit was very generous—then, as part of the 1995 stabilization package incomes were devalued by inflation. As a reaction to the fall in incomes, households dramatically cut down their consumption. This phase lasted up to 1996, although the fall in incomes had stopped by this time. (In the meantime, in 1993/1994, partly due to the election-year budget and partly to the economy's dynamization—a dynamization which was temporary and unfounded, and which

Household incomes and consumption
(1990 = 100)

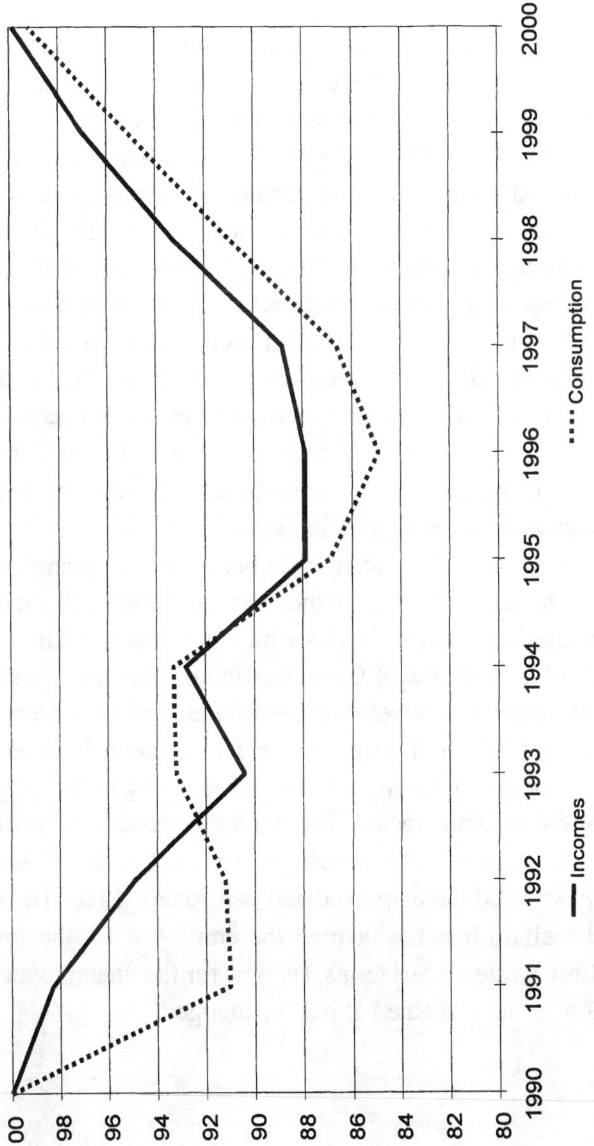

Source: Central Statistical Office

therefore led to unsustainable external indebtedness—public incomes and consumption temporarily increased.) At the lowest point, in 1996, the population was living on incomes that were 10 percent lower than in 1990, while consumption was 15 percent lower than 1990 levels. Public incomes and consumption began to increase again in 1997, and in 1998 the growth accelerated.

The fall in incomes and consumption took place at very different rates. Among those with a stable income the greatest losers were old-age pensioners and those working in the budget sector. Employees in the competitive sector experienced a much smaller fall in real wages, and since then their real income has increased more rapidly. The real losers in the change in political system, however, were the marginalized masses who, after becoming unemployed, did not receive a regular income. In 1997 households received 15 percent less in social benefits in real terms (excluding pensions and sick pay) than in 1990.

Divisions within society thus became more pronounced in the 1990s. Due to the changes in the method of data collection, the time axis in the figure below begins with 1993, therefore the figure does not provide evidence of the dramatic changes that most probably took place in the first years of the decade. The 10 percent of people belonging to the highest income bracket received 4.5 to 5.5 times more income per annum than those belonging to the 10 percent in the lowest income bracket. The dramatic increase in incomes since 1997 has been of little benefit to the least well off, since it has mainly affected the employed and pensioners. Likewise, the rise in social welfare benefits favored the employed (in the form of tax benefits), while, in real terms, support for the unemployed and non-pensioners has remained at best unchanged.

Changes in the real value of the main types of income
(1992 = 100)

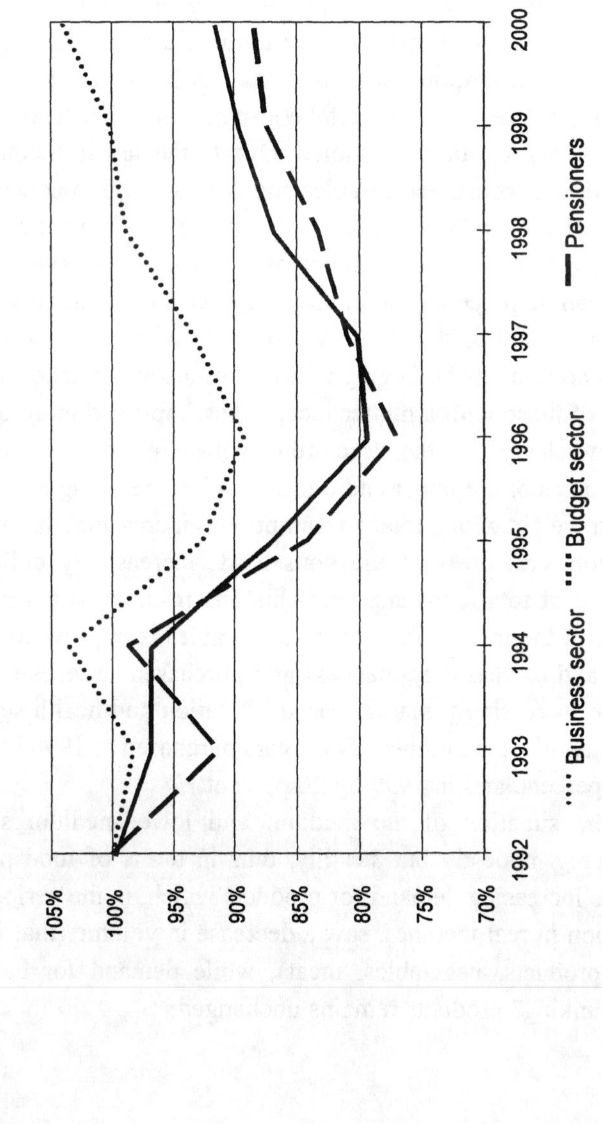

Source: Central Statistical Office

In the 1990s household consumption was significantly restructured. This was due partly to dramatic changes in the price structure and partly to changes in the absolute level of consumption. The redevelopment of state price subsidies, the suppression of the role of administrative prices, and the bringing of energy prices more closely into line with the levels of the world market greatly influenced the consumption structure of households. As a result, for example, the weight within total consumption of household expenditure on energy almost doubled. Due to the fall in incomes, the proportion of consumer durables and clothing within consumption temporarily decreased. As a result of the modernization of the economy and the establishment of a market for services, today more than 42 percent of total consumption is made up of services.

As a result of the strongly differentiated increase in incomes among households belonging to different income brackets (the situation of those with a higher income has improved more quickly) the slow changes in the structure of consumption continue. Since the incomes of the upper and middle deciles are rising more rapidly, their weight within total consumption is increasing, thus the consumption structure of these households increasingly defines the structure of total consumption. This has resulted in a significant growth in the market for consumer durables (cars, furniture, electronic and electrical appliances) and purchased services (tourism, and the increasingly market-based education and health services). (For example, the number of new cars purchased in 1998 increased by 37 percent, and in 1999 by 20 percent.)

The situation of the medium and lower-medium strata is improving modestly but steadily, thus in terms of food products there is increasing demand for products which, in the period of the reduction in real incomes, saw a decrease in volume (that is, fruit, dairy products, vegetables, meat), while demand for basic and "low-ranking" products remains unchanged.

Indicators of income inequalities,1993 to 1998

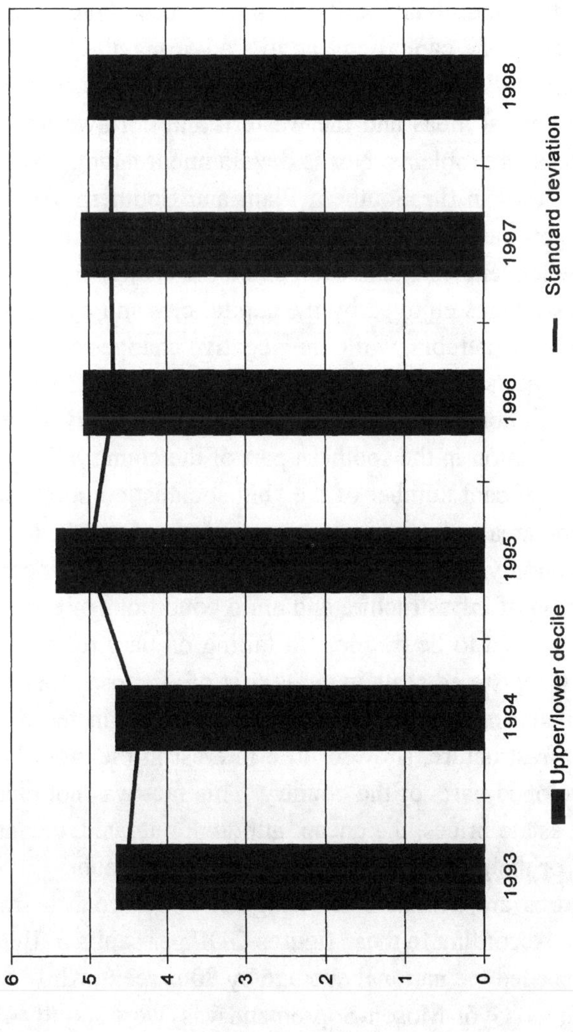

Source: Central Statistical Office and GKI Co.'s own calculations

8. Regional structures

In Hungary, despite the size of the country, there are marked differences in terms of the development of the various regions. Besides the traditional political, social, economic, and cultural dominance of the capital city and its environs, the lagging behind of the country's eastern and northeastern regions in comparison with the central areas and the western and northwestern counties causes serious problems. Nor is development taking place at a satisfactory level in the Southern Plain and Southern Transdanubia. Polarization has increased since the beginning of the 1990s. The favorable tendencies that accompanied the change of regime added to the advantages enjoyed by the capital city and by Northern and Western Transdanubia, while the negative changes exacerbated the disadvantages suffered by the eastern parts of the Great Plain and the northern counties. The crisis in the Balkans served to complicate the situation in the southern part of the country.

A significant number of the "big socialist corporations" operated in the area of heavy industry, which was later devalued in the world economy, and industries established in the provinces without the creation of infrastructure and amid conditions of economic crisis have proved to be fragile. On falling on hard times companies with their registered seats in cities first of all closed their non-economic plants in the provinces. New investors, in the absence of proper infrastructure, showed little interest in the more backward, less-developed parts of the country. This fact was not changed by low real estate prices, the cheap, although outdated, means of production, or the great masses of available cheap labor.

Figures are available showing GDP per county from 1994 onwards. According to these figures GDP per capita in Budapest in 1994 exceeded the national average by 80 percent, while two western counties (Győr-Moson-Sopron and Vas) were slightly above the average. Fejér, Zala, Tolna, and Csongrád counties were slightly below the average, while the traditionally backward Nógrád and Szabolcs-Szatmár-Bereg counties had the lowest GDP per capita. By 1998 the advantage of the capital city and of Győr-Moson-Sopron and Vas counties further increased, while the centrally located Fejér county, which is preferred as a seat by multinational companies, moved into second place. At the same time the disadvantages of the two most underdeveloped counties increased: in both, the GDP per capita fell to 57 percent of the national average.

Thus Central Hungary is the most developed region, followed by Western Transdanubia and Central Transdanubia. The least developed regions are northern Hungary and the Northern Plain, where GDP is 30 percent below the national average. The southern part of the country (Southern Transdanubia and the Southern Plain) are in a more favorable situation: there, GDP per capita is only 20 percent lower than the national average.

In 1999/2000 there were signs that foreign capital was beginning to flow into areas outside the most developed regions. This is mostly due to the fact that in the developed regions there is a structural shortage of labor and real estate prices are becoming increasingly expensive. In the medium term, however, it is unlikely that the recent inequalities will change significantly. By 1998, in the central region of the country GDP per capita, calculated according to consumer power parity, reached 71 percent of the EU average (and in Budapest 89.5 percent). In the most backward northeastern regions it was below one-third of the EU average).

The differences between the regions of the country and the increasing differences between towns and villages (in terms of GDP, income, and unemployment) might logically have resulted in a strengthening of internal migration. However, between 1990 and 1997 the total number of migrations merely fluctuated but showed an overall stagnation. Every year between 210,000 and 224,000 persons move to a different settlement. Approximately half of all the migrations that took place involved migration within a county (typically from town to village and less often from village to town). In terms of migration between counties the role of the capital city is particularly pronounced. Between 1994 and 1997 Budapest was the destination in the case of between 10 and 16 percent of all migrations. Most of the arrivals in the capital were from the agglomeration, as well as Borsod-Abaúj-Zemplén, Szabolcs-Szatmár-Bereg, and Veszprém counties, which were stricken by the economic crisis. Despite this, the population of the capital city decreases by 10,000 persons every year as a result of people moving into the agglomerations.

Per capita GDP by regions, 1998

(HUF 1,000)

Region (per capita GDP)		County
Central Hungary	*(1,474)*	Budapest Pest
Central Transdanubia	*(978)*	Fejér Komárom-Esztergom Veszprém
Western Transdanubia	*(1,102)*	Győr-Moson-Sopron Vas Zala
Southern Transdanubia	*(770)*	Baranya Somogy Tolna
Northern Hungary	*(673)*	Borsod-Abaúj-Zemplén Heves Nógrád
The Northern Plain	*(675)*	Hajdú-Bihar Jász-Nagykun-Szolnok Szabolcs-Szatmár-Bereg
The Southern Plain	*(761)*	Bács-Kiskun Békés Csongrád

In Hungary, regional differences in total migration support the theory that the structural backwardness that was brought to the surface during the decade of transition, and the inequalities in territorial development, generated migration from the backward areas to the dynamically developing areas. It can be observed that between 1994 and 1997, in terms of percentage of the local population, most people left Borsod-Abaúj-Zemplén county, which suffered most severely from the collapse of Hungarian heavy industry, but almost the same number of people left Szabolcs-Szatmár-Bereg and Nógrád counties. Significant migration also took place from the Eastern Plain and from Baranya and Tolna counties. Most people chose the central region of the country and the prosperous Western Transdanubia (Győr-Moson-Sopron county) as their destination, but Fejér and Bács-Kiskun counties also attracted settlers. In Central Hungary there was a marked tendency to move from the capital to Pest county, caused by the upvaluation of the green belt.

The fact that in Hungary territorial mobility did not increase despite the increasing of regional differences is due to the peculiarities of the housing situation. The proportion of rented housing is very low throughout the country: almost 90 percent of households live in privately owned apartments, while 3 percent live with relatives. Thus the proportion of those living in rented accommodation must be at most 7 percent. This accommodation is almost entirely made up of self-government-owned apartments, for which tenants pay an extremely low rent. The apartments are available only to people in a certain social category, and even they must wait until a vacancy is found. The high proportion of privately owned apartments hinders territorial mobility, since the buying and selling of property involves high transaction costs. However, the major obstacle remains the marked differences in real estate prices. In the more backward regions, understandably, real estate prices have fallen and are much lower than in the dynamically developing or developed regions. This is a natural phenomenon that accompanies a property market moved by supply and demand. Thus, moving to a prosperous region represents a serious expense resulting from the difference in value between the apartment being sold and the one to be purchased. Due to the recent increases in property prices the dynamization of internal migration cannot be expected either on the medium term. At the same time, investments today do not only flow to the most developed regions but also to the eastern parts of the country, thus the factors that are at the root of migration will gradually be alleviated. Until this happens, almost 30 percent of workers will travel to their workplaces as commuters.

REFERENCES

Antal, László (1998): "Az átmenet évtizede (Kormányok, programok, gazdasági folyamatok)" [A decade of transition (Governments, programs and economic processes)]. In: Kurtán – Sándor– Vass: *Op. cit.* pp. 57-81.

Bara, Zoltán and Szabó, Katalin (editors): *Gazdasági rendszerek, országok, intézmények. Bevezetés az összehasonlító gazdaságtanba. Összehasonlító gazdaságtan* [Macroeconomic systems, countries and institutions. Comparative economics]. Budapest: Aula Kiadó, 2000.

Csaba, László (2000): "A szovjet modell összeomlása és a rendszerváltozás első két szakasza" [The collapse of the Soviet model and the first two phases of the transition process]. In: Bara – Szabó: *Op. cit.* pp. 327-393.

Kornai, János (1993): "Transzformációs visszaesés" [Transformation crisis], *Közgazdasági Szemle,* No 7-8, pp. 569-599.

Kurtán, Sándor, Sándor, Péter and Vass, László (editors): *Magyarország évtizedkönyve. A rendszerváltás (1988–1998)* [The Book of a decade of Hungary. The change of regime (1990–1998)]. Budapest, 1999.

Pitti, Zoltán (1998): "Bejött, de mit hozott a tőke?" [The capital flew in – but what it carried on?], *Társadalmi Szemle,* No 3, pp. 14-32.

Sárközy, Tamás (2000): "Magyarország államberendezkedése" [State administration in Hungary], *História,* No 2, pp. 16-19.

Tardos, Márton (1999): "A magyar gazdaság helyzetéről" [About the state of the Hungarian economy], *Kritika,* No 1, pp. 3-6.

Vértes, András and Karsai, Gábor: (1998): "Gazdasági átalakulás és gazdaságpolitika" [Economic transformation and economic policy]. In: Kurtán – Sándor – Vass: *Op. cit.* pp. 102-115.

CHAPTER II
SOME CRITICAL ISSUES OF ECONOMIC TRANSITION

I. PRIVATIZATION IN HUNGARY*

1. Transition and privatization

Privatization is one of the most important and crucial elements within the unprecedented process of political and economic transition in Central and Eastern Europe. In the context of a multiparty parliamentary democracy (that is, following the changeover from a single-party political system), the aim of the transition was to replace the centrally planned economy, the dominance of state property and of producers' cooperatives, and the collective autarchy created and maintained within COMECON, with a national economy based on private property organized into individual and group enterprises and integrated, as an individual and equal-ranking partner, into the world economic system based on the free movement of goods and capital. Following four decades of state socialism the population looked to the change of system to bring them the democracy, freedom and welfare for which they hoped.

In Central and Eastern Europe—unlike in Western Europe and Latin America, where the overwhelming majority of national assets had to be privatized within a relatively short time and where, as a result, full-scale privatization was, and is, taking place—a choice had to be made between two possible methods of privatization: distributive and/or market-based privatization. Both methods had, and have, benefits and disadvantages that successive governments have

* This chapter was written by György Csáki, Ph.D. of economics, Resarch Director of GKI Research Co. We would like to express our gratitude to Ákos Macher, managing director of ÁPV Rt., for kindly allowing us to use material contained in the study by György Csáki and Ákos Macher: "A magyarországi privatizáció 10 éve". In: *Magyarország Politikai tízévkönyve*, Budapest, 1999, as well as for providing us with privatization data for 1999 and 2000.

had to take into account when making decisions with respect to privatization strategy.

In distribution-based (voucher) privatization, every member of the population receives securities to an equal value, which can then be converted into part-ownership of a corporation of some kind. In effect, this guarantees each individual a right to a percentage of the national wealth.

The advantages of this method are obvious:

- previously state-owned assets are transferred largely into domestic private hands;
- a large number of shares end up on the stock-exchange market, leading to the rapid development of the stock market;
- the vast majority of citizens have the opportunity to become small-scale shareholders;
- the process can take place very rapidly;
- there is no opportunity for corruption when converting the vouchers into shares, etc.

On the other hand, the disadvantages were also obvious from the very beginning:

- no budget revenue is generated;
- there is no improvement in the balance of payments position;
- it does not attract foreign entrepreneurs (rather, it excludes them in practice from the opportunity for privatization acquisition);
- it does not provide supplementary resources for companies suffering from a serious shortage of capital;
- it does not improve the standard of corporate governance and corporate management;
- it does not inspire the development of an enterprising attitude and skills and does not bring them into line with existing international standards;
- it does not encourage technical development;

- it provides opportunities for maintaining direct state intervention in company management, or may be used to conceal such intervention, etc.

Of course, market-based privatization, in which every—or almost every—state-owned asset is privatized in the form of a market sale, also has significant advantages and disadvantages. The most important advantages are that:

- the former state-owned assets are transferred into the hands of real owners;
- a new model of state management can be established that is suitable for a modern market economy;
- the transparency of the entire process can be ensured and, theoretically, so can complete sector neutrality;
- it attracts foreign entrepreneurs;
- it improves the balance of payments position of the national economy;
- it provides significant budget revenue;
- it means real denationalization, since the state does indeed move out of the corporate sector and the opportunity for state control—even indirect state control—over the privatized corporations ceases.

However, the market-based privatization method also has certain disadvantages:

- it does not support, or more exactly does not favor, the formation of a domestic owner class;
- it does not support maximally the development of the capital market—which also hinders the economic strengthening of the domestic middle class;
- foreign investors "automatically" find themselves in more favorable positions due to their vastly superior financial muscle and credit worthiness;

- it does not create real opportunities either in terms of market protection or export promotion, and it makes preferential treatment for the regions more difficult;
- it cannot be carried out as rapidly as voucher privatization.

We might call the two contrasting methods the Hungarian (market-based) and Czech (voucher) privatization strategies. Of course, between the two basic privatization strategies there have been—and are—certain areas of overlap: compensation and self-government assignment of assets occurred in Hungary, while in the Czech Republic and Poland individual privatization contracts were made with foreign investors.

The choice between the two strategies—or "models"—was, in every country, motivated by the given political and economic situation. Firstly, among the strongest pressures in Hungary for the adoption of the market-based method (which, among other things, generates the maximum amount of revenue) were the country's serious foreign debts, as well as its significant ongoing budget deficit problems.[1] Secondly, there is no doubt that Hungary enjoyed relative advantages due to the more decentralized economic management system, the greater degree of corporational independence and the related corporational knowledge of the market, and generally widespread entrepreneurial attitudes. Thirdly, and as a result of the foregoing, in Hungarian economic political thinking the welcoming of the role of foreign capital—and the freedom of that role—in the privatization process was part of the deeper strategic concept of importing working capital. This was something that had been happening in practice even before the change of system. Fourthly, in the Hungarian privatization process—which had begun in 1988, two years before the change of system, in the form of spontaneous privatization—the creation of "real owners", the formation of modern corporate governance, and the inevitability of corporational reorganization were central ideas from the very beginning.[2]

The burdensome economic heritage, in the context of which the transition—that is, the creation of a modern European market economy—had, and still has, to take place, was determined by the events of earlier economic-historical era(s) and comprises the following three major features.

1. A lack of appropriate corporate governance due to the absence of real owners; old-fashioned and outdated machinery and equipment in most areas of the economy, and the resulting non-competitiveness of the economic structure.

2. Extensive concealed unemployment ("unemployment within the factory gates"), a lack of modern corporate organizational and structural systems, as well as a general lack of modern corporate organizational, marketing, and management know-how.

3. The collapse of COMECON, that is, of collective autarchy, which led to the "liberation" of the affected national economies from the burdens of a technically and structurally restrictive economic system of relations. At the same time, the loss of their largest markets forced these economies to undertake an extremely rapid geographical reorientation of their foreign economic relations.

2. The goals and requirements of the Hungarian privatization process

Following lengthy political and professional debates, and taking into account the experiences of the previous half a decade, the objectives of the Hungarian privatization process were stated in the Privatization Act[3] as follows:

- to establish a market economy based on private property;
- to decrease the state's economic role while at the same time increasing the state's revenues;
- to increase the efficiency of the economy and enhance competition;
- to eliminate the economy's shortage of capital;

- to reduce state expenditure (by cutting subsidies to poorly performing companies);
- to introduce modern technologies and management methods into the Hungarian corporate sector;
- to encourage economic structural transition;
- to multiply the number of domestic market players;
- to develop the domestic capital market and to involve domestic and international capital and multinational companies;
- to maintain the interest of foreign investors in privatization;
- to participate intensively in international specialization of labor;
- to maintain the operability of business organizations;
- to protect and create jobs;
- to utilize privatization revenue for the enhancement of financial stability, the development of technology, reorganization, the alleviation of environmental damage, and the expansion of exports;
- to promote workers' acquisition of property and management buyouts;
- to extend the circle of small investors and to provide proper assets in return for compensation vouchers.

Obviously not all of the objectives outlined above could be realized simultaneously, or to the same degree, in the course of the Hungarian privatization process. In fact, many of the goals and requirements are mutually contradictory. Domestic owners cannot always be the "real" owners of privatized assets due to their lack of capital, their lack of the kind of management abilities and market knowledge required on the world markets, their inability to provide banking support for the successful operation of the privatized asset, etc. Foreign owners, for their part, are often aiming at no more than the acquisition of a market and care little about technology transfer or the spreading of modern management know-how. The aim (or perhaps pressure?) to maximize budget revenue might blur such "quality" goals as the spreading of modern technologies and company management techniques, market protection and the encouragement of exports, etc. Improvements to the balance of payments position might lead to an "unhealthy measure" of support for foreign acquisitions, thus stifling support for domestic ownership, demands for the development of capital markets, market protection, etc. The requirement to protect and create jobs—if this is included in the privatization contract among the conditions for acquisition—decreases the acquisition price and, consequently, the budget revenue.

Even if the privatization process were not permanently beset by clashes of interest, this complex system of requirements could still only have been realized as a result of compromise. It is also obvious that in the course of privatization the degree of importance accorded to the various goals—or requirements—was continually changing and that certain goals were pushed to the forefront to the detriment of others. Between 1993 and 1994, the creation of a stratum of domestic owners was privileged, while in 1995 the strong political desire to maximize revenue and reestablish the confidence of foreign investors resulted in hard-currency privatization revenues of USD 4.5 billion. In 1997, following progress in the moves towards stabilization and successful corporational reorganization, it was capital-market privatization transactions that moved to the forefront. As a result, certain significant high-value stock-exchange flotations took place and, for the first time in the history of the Central and Eastern European transition, the shares of a privatized company, MATÁV, were introduced on the New York Stock Exchange.

3. The creation of a legal and institutional framework for privatization

The beginning of the privatization process—in the period immediately preceding the change of system—was primarily brought about by the amendment of the Constitution of 1989,[4] which contained a declaration of the right to property and to free enterprise, and of the equal legal standing of, and protection for, various forms of property. The economic and legal provisions contained in the amended Constitution were based on the provisions contained in Act VI of 1988[5] "On Business Organizations" and Act XIII of 1989, the so-called Transition Act. It should also be mentioned that Act XXIV of 1989 already provided for the protection of foreign investments (prohibition of nationalization, freedom for exchange movements and for profit repatriation). One of the most important achievements of the Hungarian economic transition was the early and relatively full-scale creation of legal and institutional frameworks and the generation of high interest for foreign capital investments. "The legal obstacles to the development of private property were essentially lifted in 1989–90, creating the opportunity for organic development."[6] Thus privatization—so-called spontaneous privatization—began in Hungary well before the change of system and without any central/government initiation.

Each year, from 1990 to 1995, parliamentary decrees were passed setting down policy guidelines with respect to assets. In 1990, four important acts defining the process and practice of privatization were passed: Act VII of 1990 "On the State Property Agency (ÁVÜ) and the Administration of Its Assets"; Act VIII of 1990 "On the Protection of State Assets";[7] Act XVI of 1990 "On Concessions; and Act LXXIV of 1990 "On the Privatization of State-Owned Corporations Involved in Retail Trade and the Catering Industry", or, as it was popularly called, the Pre-privatization Act. These acts represented the first wave of privatization-related legislation.

In 1992 the Antall administration published the Government's Ownership and Privatization Strategy. Based on this document the so-called Privatization Acts were passed, mostly in 1992, representing the second wave of privatization legislation.[8]

The government formed by the Hungarian Socialist Party (MSZP) and the Alliance of Free Democrats (SZDSZ), which came to power as a result of the general election in 1994, aimed to realize its privatization strategies within new organizational frameworks and on the basis of standardized legal regulations, while preserving the foundations of the earlier legal frameworks. At the same time, it declared as its goal the completion of mass privatization during the parliamentary term 1994 to 1998. The standardized legal regulations were framed by Act XXXIX of 1995 "On the Sale of State-Owned Entrepreneurial Assets" (the "Privatization Act"). This act, which was submitted to the Parliament in November 1994, already represented the third wave of privatization legislation. It was the task of the Privatization Act "to accelerate privatization. A further aim was to mitigate the shortcomings of the privatization process on the basis of practical experience. The amalgamating of two acts (LIII of 1992 and LIV of 1992) in order to achieve a more clear-cut privatization strategy placed the creation of standardized privatization rules on the parliamentary agenda. The new law aimed to standardize the organization of the privatization process and to reduce the excessive costs of privatization. It preserved the basic categories contained in the previous acts ("entrepreneurial assets", calculation methods for assets remaining in long-term state ownership, etc.) as well as the successful elements of the former acts (e.g., Part V on holding contracts). However, it also introduced significant changes, based partly on the changed economic situation, partly on the new political situation brought about by the 1994 election, and partly on the new government program. In terms of its wording, therefore, the new Privatization Act represents evolution, even if the lack of a firm definition of "entrepreneurial assets", for example, is still somewhat disturbing."[9]

The Privatization Act—as indicated in the quotation above—set forth the goals and requirements of the privatization process and created a standardized privatization and holding organization. It clarified the division of owners' rights and economic tasks between the Hungarian Privatization and State Holding Company (ÁPV Rt.) and the Treasury Property Management Organization representing the Treasury. It provided a precise definition of the circle of companies remaining in long-term state ownership, itemized in a schedule to the act, and it stated the exact percentage of state ownership with respect to each company. Act XXXIX of 1995, as amended on 30 March 1997, remains the legal basis for privatization and state holding up to the present day.

The Center-Right coalition that formed the government in 1998 had not made any amendments to the legal framework for privatization and state trusteeship as of March 2000. However, changes were made to the organization of ÁPV Rt., to the extent that ÁPV Rt. centralized several holding activities that had previously been performed by the Treasury Property Management Organization and the Hungarian Development Bank (MFB), working under the supervision of the Ministry of Finance. (The MFB itself came into the portfolio of ÁPV Rt.) Since 1998, ÁPV has been under the control of a chairman/chief executive officer, and government supervision is no longer carried out by an individual minister without portfolio but by the minister in charge of the Prime Minister's Office. The ownership rights of the state-owned banks—MFB, Postabank—are owned by the Ministry of Finance. All this—along with the organizational restructuring carried out within ÁPV Rt.—represents a definite centralization of privatization and holding.

*

The organizational framework for the privatization process and state property management was dominated by three institutions: the State Property Agency (ÁVÜ, 1990–1995), the State Holding Company (ÁV Rt., 1992–1995), and the Hungarian Privatization and State Holding Company (ÁPV Rt., 1995–).

> ÁVÜ came into being as a result of a number of simultaneous and related political demands. Firstly, there was a need for an organization to coordinate privatization in the name of the state: it controls, coordinates, and records. It was also clear that privatization is a long-term process, requiring an organization that can exercise the state's instrument of title for as long as three or four years. Furthermore, the creation of a special privatization organization was also necessitated by the fact that the legal framework—or rules—for privatization had not yet been set down. The process of privatization had already begun, however, and someone or something had to be authorized to decide what could and could not be done.[10]

Like all the other privatization and/or holding companies, ÁVÜ was forced by circumstances to become a departmentalized organization, officially by the summer of 1992. This was the only way of providing the necessary expertise and experience, and of ensuring harmonious and effective cooperation between experts of particular departments—in this case, between ÁVÜ and the experts of various ministries.

Several privatization programs were devised and initiated by ÁVÜ:

1. The First Privatization Program of September 1990 was aimed at the privatization of 21 companies of entirely different profile and quality. It met with varying degrees of success—for example, the first stock-exchange privatization, that of IBUSZ, had little success; however, Richter Gedeon, which was privatized several years later, is currently one of the high fliers on the Budapest Stock Exchange. At the end of 1994/beginning of 1995, the privatization of HUNGARHOTELS, or rather its failure, was one of the greatest privatization scandals. The privatization of the hotel chain in fact

took place only in 1996. The First Privatization Program went down as a failure in the history of privatization: it started very slowly, dragged on for years, and several companies went bankrupt during the time it was implemented.

2. With the Pre-privatization Act the government intended to promote the widespread creation of small enterprises by simplifying the valuation of businesses available for privatization and by selling these businesses at auction. By the end of 1997 the program was practically complete, and more than 10,000 restaurants, shops, etc. had been sold.

3. The Second Privatization Program, which was launched in January 1991, was designed to include 85 companies with combined assets of HUF 35 billion. These companies had earlier organized themselves into corporations and according to the most ambitious plans were meant to be privatized in three phases. However, the program came to nothing, not even being partly fulfilled.

4. In 1992 the Downtown Office-Building Program was drawn up for the sale of downtown office buildings taken from state-owned companies that no longer needed them—or, more exactly, that were letting them for high rents. The program brought in relatively little revenue for ÁVÜ and the majority of the office buildings in question are still being rented out via the property management company, Belvárosi Irodaház Kft.

5. A program aimed at the privatization of former foreign trade monopolies was launched in 1991: within a relatively short time it led to full-scale privatization in only three instances. Several companies were terminated by liquidation. Two companies—TESCO, which deals with exports of intellectual property, and the fair and exhibition organizer HUNGEXPO—are still in state hands.[11]

6. In addition to the Pre-privatization Program, the Self-Privatization Program was also created by ÁVÜ in order to sell large numbers of companies. The program began in two phases among companies with fewer than 1,000 employees and with assets

or turnover of less than HUF 1 billion. The transformation and privatization of approximately 700 companies was carried out by a consultancy firm appointed by ÁVÜ. The consultancy firm was granted the ownership rights and was remunerated from the sale of the companies. This speeded up the mass privatization of small and medium-sized companies, while allowing ÁVÜ to concentrate on the privatization of medium-sized and large companies. As a result of the program, which was completed by 31 March 1994, a total of 478 companies out of 520 were transformed mostly into limited liability companies. Some 412 of these were sold in full or in part, thus their privatization can be regarded as successful and as fulfilling the expectations of the program. In the case of two-thirds of the sales realized as a result of the program, the buyer was a domestic investor. These sales included a significant number of employee buyouts. Investors were able to use Existence Credit and could also pay with compensation vouchers.

7. In the fall of 1997, ÁVÜ launched an ambitious program primarily for the privatization of palaces, but also of country-houses, large villas, city mansions, mills, hunting lodges, and large inns: the "Palace Program" was eventually limited to 100 historical buildings—resulting in remarkably few sales.

The State Property Agency had to function in response to changing, and mostly contradictory, political requirements, and amid disputes over concepts and struggles for prestige among the various lobbies within the ruling parties. This inevitably led to controversies regarding the functioning of ÁVÜ, and, as a result, the organization came under attack from all sides.

The privatization that had begun before the actual change of system was—understandably—halted in 1990/1991. The new, democratically elected government—and the fact that it was democratically elected is important here—intended to put an end to spontaneous privatization processes and to avoid a spontaneous loss of assets. However, the new programs initiated by the government failed one after the other due to the absence of an adequate organizational framework, to employees' lack of experience, and to the macroeconomic situation, which was much worse than had been believed.

In 1991/1992, the "continuity" of privatization was only maintained by the unbroken interest of foreign investors. The government realized the seriousness of the problem and by 1993 was able to give impetus to the privatization process.

Act LIII of 1992 established the State Holding Company (ÁV Rt.) to manage effectively the most strategically important elements of the state's entrepreneurial assets. According to this law, ÁV Rt. had to utilize the state's instruments of title "in an entrepreneurial and businesslike manner in adapting to the existing market conditions". The State Holding Company functioned as a public limited company with a management board and supervisory board, and its legal supervision was carried out by the minister without portfolio responsible for privatization.

The definitions of tasks contained in the act and in the annual asset-related policy guidelines were over-generalized; there were contradictions in the relationship between ÁV Rt. and ÁVÜ; and tensions and clashes of authority existed between ÁV Rt. and the related ministries. As a result, the functioning of ÁV Rt. never proved efficient. It was a giant—the total subscriber capital of the 160 corporations of strategic importance that came under its jurisdiction represented one-quarter of the state's entrepreneurial assets—but it was "a giant with feet of clay,"[12] which, in the course of its rather ambiguous self-definition and activities, characteristic both of a commercial enterprise and a state organization, was incapable of creating the kind of lasting balance between various elements of the government that would have enabled really efficient state asset management.

"The government formed by the Hungarian Socialist Party (MSZP) and the Alliance of Free Democrats (SZDSZ), which came to power in the summer of 1994, had clear-cut views regarding privatization. There was no doubt that the parallel functioning of ÁV Rt. and ÁVÜ would be halted. On the other hand, the government intended to create the legal conditions for the privatization of the large public utility companies and trade banks. It also became obvious that the privatization of smaller companies had to be accelerated."[13]

It took the government a surprisingly long time to pass a new privatization act: the parliamentary debate began on 31 January 1995 and lasted 11 session days. The law was passed on 9 May. The foundation of ÁPV Rt.—and the simultaneous appointment of the members of the management board and supervisory board and of the leading functionaries—took place on 17 June 1995. In legal terms, ÁPV Rt. came into being simply as a result of ÁV Rt. changing its name, but in reality an entirely new organization had to be created and set in motion.

The Hungarian Privatization and State Holding Company was created as a public limited company, primarily for practical reasons. "Privatization is the type of activity for which neither the public limited company nor the state budget organization is an entirely appropriate form. It is no coincidence that several features of ÁVÜ's organization and functioning did not conform to the general rules for budget organizations: ÁVÜ was headed by a board of directors and had a managing director; employees' wages were similar to those received by bank employees, etc. Unlike the public limited company, the main aim of privatization is not to realize business profits; at the same time, the financial conduct [of a privatization agency] is entirely different from that of the budget organization, since its assets are permanently decreasing. In other words, both the budget organization and the business organization are inadequate, each form of organization having disadvantages as well as advantages. However, there can be no other option without a willingness to cause further disruption within the legal system by creating a new sui generis legal entity."[14]

The Hungarian Privatization and State Holding Company is, in reality, an asset-management holding company whose task is the management of assets remaining in long-term state ownership and the selling of all other assets as quickly and efficiently as possible. The owners' functions within the one-person public limited company are performed by the minister without portfolio responsible for privatization as the "minister exercising shareholder's rights". The company's decision-making organ is the Board of Directors, whose authority cannot be withdrawn by the supervising minister without portfolio. The functioning of ÁPV Rt. is supervised by the State Audit Office (ÁSZ). The government is obliged to submit an annual report to Parliament regarding the activities of ÁPV Rt., which can only be debated together with the annual report submitted by ÁSZ. In accordance with the provisions of the Law on Business Organizations, the Supervisory Board[15] exercises permanent control over the activities of ÁPV Rt. Like other public limited companies, ÁPV Rt., in accordance with the Law on Business Organizations, appoints a permanent auditor.[16] The Organizational and Operational Rules of ÁPV Rt. are approved by the government.

4. Privatization: facts and figures

The State Property Agency began privatization with 1,859 state- and council-owned economic organizations and socialist enterprises. In the past ten years huge transformations and movements have taken place in the state's entrepreneurial assets. The State Holding Company has transformed the vast majority of socialist enterprises into business organizations (1,300 companies came into its portfolio in this way). The state's entrepreneurial assets were also increased by companies founded by ÁVÜ, as well as by the dissociated subsidiaries of companies owned by ÁVÜ. To date, the number of companies founded and dissociated by the state holding companies exceeds 400.

In the course of the privatization process the various holding companies had, by the end of 1997, handed on, with legal authorization, more than 150 economic organizations to other holding companies. Most typically, companies functioning as enterprises and forming part of the state entrepreneurial assets in the ownership of the state holding companies were privatized through winding-up or liquidation: this was the fate of 485 such enterprises. By early 1998 the portfolio of enterprises was practically exhausted.

In Hungarian privatization practice, enterprises were typically sold following their transformation. The holding companies transformed a total of 1,300 enterprises into companies, of which 231 had undergone liquidation by late 1997.

From among the companies belonging to the state's entrepreneurial assets, 1,125 were sold in their entirety by the holding companies. The company portfolio of ÁPV Rt. currently contains scarcely more than 200 majority and minority ownership stakes waiting to be sold.

a) Privatization revenues

The outstandingly high proportion of cash revenues should be mentioned as one of the characteristics of Hungarian privatization. The cash revenues from privatization over eight years exceeded HUF 1,151 billion. There were, of course, significant variations year by year, but the period as a whole is characterized by large cash revenues. Although revenues varied throughout the eight-year period, it can be said that after the practice of mass privatization was established, the holding companies were able to generate annual revenues of between HUF 150 and 180 billion, without serious effort. The total privatization revenues from 1990 exceeded HUF 1,443 billion. In one year, 1995, they reached HUF 481 billion, almost 95 percent of which was realized in cash, and within that, 87 percent in hard currency. The revenues in 1995 alone exceeded by more than HUF 38 billion the total privatization revenues between 1990 and 1994.

In 1997, in the course of the sale and utilization of the state's entrepreneurial assets, ÁPV Rt. realized outstandingly high revenues. Throughout the eight years of Hungarian privatization only the revenues in 1995 exceeded those realized in 1997. (Privatization in the record-breaking year 1995 mainly comprised the sale of the energy industries.) The sale revenues of HUF 349 billion in 1997 were double the average annual privatization revenues. Approximately 80 percent of the total privatization revenues were realized in the period between 1994 and late 1997.

Privatization revenues of the state holding companies
(1990-1999, HUF billion)

	Sale and utilization of assets	Cash revenues	Of which, hard currency	Total revenue*
1990	0.67	0.67	0.53	0.67
1991	30.43	30.35	24.61	31.36
1992	66.91	65.90	40.98	77.23
1993	164.50	133.63	110.67	169.91
1994	148.87	46.36	10.95	156.67
1995	471.93	437.80	411.48	481.03
1996	162.63	119.46	92.73	176.51
1997	340.61	317.70	208.60	349.86
1998	104.80	98.70	38.62	111.52
1999	114.95	99.23	70.00	132.80
2000	21.13	19.83	-	58.23
Total	1,628.19	1,369.63	970.55	1,745.79

Source: Various publications of ÁPV Rt., Privatization Monitor.
* Dividend revenues and the results of financial operations (for example, interest revenue).

In 1997, as a result of ÁPV Rt.'s significant sales activities, the amount of cash revenues within the sales and utilization revenues exceeded HUF 317 billion. In accordance with the Socialist–Free Democrat government's privatization strategy and its Privatization Act of 1995, tendering became the exclusive practice from 1996, which further increased the already high proportion of cash revenues.

b) Privatization techniques and selling methods

A typical technique employed in the course of the eight years of Hungarian privatization was the selling of company shares by means of tenders. The compulsory and (predominantly) public competition for tenders, as a condition of objective decision making, became part of the decision-making mechanism of privatization with Act LIV of 1992 and the related Rules of Competition, and the prescriptions for tendering procedures.

The following table represents the approximate proportions of the various privatization techniques.

Privatization techniques, 1990-1998

Proportion of the various privatization techniques	(%)
Tenders	42
Issuing of shares	15
Compensation vouchers and title deeds	18
Combination of various techniques	5
Market selling without tender	10
Management or employee buyout	5
Other techniques (leasing, etc.)	5

Source: ÁPV Rt.
Note: In 1999, ÁPV sold 24 companies through a total of 28 transactions. Among these, privatization leasing was applied in only one case, to the value of HUF 20 million. In 1999 the privatization organization called in a total of HUF 870 million worth of compensation vouchers, therefore the above proportions could not change significantly.

In every case the privatization technique was chosen according to the government's economic and sector-related political goals, the characteristics of the given region, and the technical means at the disposal of the holding company. The selling practice used in the Hungarian privatization process was based on invitation-based tendering.

Among the smaller, simpler sales, competitive bidding or offers for management and/or employee buyouts were regarded as the most frequent and most effective solutions. In the case of transactions requiring more complex solutions, commercial sale or the issuing of shares was preferred—in line with international practice.

The proportion of techniques based on the issuing of shares depended on the development of the institutions needed for on- and off-the-floor trading and, of course, on the companies' suitability for flotation. The number of privatizations carried out by stock-exchange flotation increased significantly after 1994.

c) Preferential privatization techniques and financial structures

Since tendering was a typical feature of Hungarian privatization, only those with sufficient capital were able to acquire assets. Domestic entrepreneurs are poor in capital, especially in comparison with foreign competitors, therefore throughout the privatization process various techniques were applied to support domestic investors—with varying degrees of success. In order to support domestic entrepreneurial groups, successive governments encouraged the creation of various preferential structures:

- The Hungarian National Bank created a credit reserve, on which the so-called Existence Credit facility was based.
- The Kisvállalkozói Garancia Alap (Small Entrepreneurs' Guarantee Fund) and Hitelgarancia Rt. (Credit Guarantee) were established.
- The Employees' Share Ownership Program (ESOP) was started.

- Finally, in 1994, the Small Investors' Share Purchase Program was launched.
- In addition to the above, the technique of privatization leasing was also used.

All the above measures were undertaken in order to establish a class of domestic owners (entrepreneurs and part-owners). Compensation vouchers also came into general use, which also helped to increase the purchasing power of domestic investors. After 1994 the amount of assets sold using preferential privatization techniques fell dramatically.

Existence Credit facility was granted only to domestic private persons for the purchase of state-owned assets, arable land, or shares. The maturity period was a maximum of 15 years at 7 percent interest. The proportion of own contributions in the case of credit of up to HUF 5 million was 2 percent of the credit applied for; in the case of higher amounts it was 15 percent. Existence Credit facility could not be used otherwise to cover privatization costs. The credit facility could be applied for several times. In February 1993, as a result of a governmental decree, the conditions for the use of credits became significantly more favorable.[17]

In a circular issued on 9 November 1990, the president of the Hungarian National Bank had ordered the creation of this special credit facility, to be used exclusively for the purchase of state assets belonging to ÁVÜ. The credit could be up to 75 percent of the sale price of the asset, or, in the case of share acquisitions, up to 50 percent. The maturity period was 10 years, with a 2-year grace period. The interest rate was 75 percent of the central bank's loan rate.

The Employees' Share Ownership Program (ESOP)

This program, which was launched on 14 July 1992, was drawn up on the principles of the American ESOP of the 1970s and 80s. The shares of a company or business organization were obtained by its employees, who created an organization for managing the business. Any employee who worked at least half of the legal working hours and who had been employed by the company, or its legal predecessor, for at least 6 months, was entitled to take part in the program.[18]

Following the decision of at least 40 percent of the employees, taken at a general meeting, the ESOP, which had the status of a legal entity with self-government and registered participants, was incorporated and could subsequently act in the name of the employees.

Concessions were given by the state with respect to the purchase. It provided credit with a maturity period of 10 years, with a 2-year grace period, at 7 percent interest. The proportion of own contributions was between 2 and 25 percent, the bands calculated depending on the size of share per person. Ownership of the purchased asset was gradually transferred, to the extent of the credit repayments, to the ESOP and the employees, who acquired voting and dividend-related rights as a result of the shares obtained. Sales carried out as a result of the ESOP reached their peak in 1993, and from 1994 the number rapidly decreased. Today, this form of purchase can be regarded as marginal.

Management Buyouts

Executives, as natural persons, could separately or jointly in business organizations buy shares in, or parts of, a company, and for this they could use credit. A substantial part of the price could be paid using Existence Credit or Privatization Credit facilities, but executives could also use other preferential privatization techniques and financing solutions.

The executives, as employees of the company, could take part in the Employees' Share Ownership Program, could buy employee shares, and were entitled to pay by installments. Management buyouts could be motivated by: existential insecurity at a time of change of ownership; the desire to safeguard jobs; the wish to prevent a buyout by a competitor; emotional attachment; the desire to preserve positions of power; the making of profits; aspirations with respect to the share market, etc. The drawbacks of management buyouts were the same as in other preferential procedures: paybacks came at the cost of the extraction of capital and revenues, which meant that there was insufficient money left for development and for financing current assets.

This technique was applied predominantly in cases where the company's value was based on the knowledge and experience of the executives and employees.

Small Investors' Share Purchase Program

This program served to accelerate the privatization of state assets. Companies that were at least 50 percent owned by professional investors could be part of this program.[19]

The program comprised two sub-systems.

- The installment payment sub-system. A sum of HUF 100,000, to be repaid in installments, was available to all Hungarian adults living in Hungary, with which they could buy a "package" from ÁVÜ. However, this method did not prove effective.
- The "compensation voucher" sub-system. People who been given compensation vouchers in their own right, as well as their heirs, could also join a Small Investors' Share Purchase Program. They were entitled to buy unlimited amounts of shares.

Privatization leasing

The procedure of privatization leasing was developed in order to sell companies that were difficult to market and that had been offered on several occasions but remained unsold. The procedure was governed by Acts LIV and LV of 1992. Like the other techniques, the aim was to involve domestic private persons in obtaining assets by creating favorable opportunities. Although these companies had good long-term potential, their financial situation was not strong enough to support credit repayments. On the other hand, they could support the payment of lease fees. From the investor's point of view this did not demand significant financial resources, only the existence of collateral. Despite this, the method did not become widespread. In 1996 and 1997 only a few companies were sold using this technique.

Simplified Privatization

So-called Simplified Privatization was launched by ÁPV Rt. This technique, at least in theory, removes smaller companies from the lengthy and complex series of centralized procedures, allowing the process to take place with the involvement of the executives most interested in the survival of the corporation.

The state-owned company shares of medium-sized and small economic associations were to be sold in accordance with the provisions contained in sections 38 to 45 of Act XXXIX of 1995, if the equity of the company did not exceed HUF 600 million and if the annual average number of full-time employees did not exceed 500 persons in 1994.

In the three phases of the program, 71, 48, and 19 companies were offered. However, Simplified Privatization failed to live up to expectations. Although in the three phases a total of almost 200 companies were sold, the total revenues scarcely exceeded HUF 5 billion. The apparently simple procedure in reality involved a complex and drawn-out series of moves. Some companies with particular problems—the leather company in Simontornya, for instance[20]—were impossible to sell even for a symbolic sum.

The role of compensation vouchers in Hungarian privatization

Compensation and the use of compensation vouchers in privatization—one of the most peculiar aspects of the Hungarian privatization process, and, at the same time, of the change of system in Hungary—should be included among the preferential privatization techniques.

Compensation itself first made its appearance as a symbolic political gesture. It was intended as compensation for the political and economic discrimination experienced by those who had participated in the 1956 revolution. However, in the turbulent change of system it was extended to people whose properties had been confiscated by the state after 1945. Later on, it also came to include those deprived of their freedom and property during the war, those who had been deported, and POWs, etc. Compensation affected two million people in total, that is, one-third of Hungarian families. However, instead of cash it took the form of securities—"compensation vouchers"—which could be converted into life annuities. The securities could be circulated on the Budapest Stock Exchange and could also be used in the course of privatization.

Land auctions were held in 3,000 Hungarian settlements, in the course of which one-third of cultivated land changed hands in return for compensation vouchers.

Between 1991 and 1997, the privatization organization accepted compensation vouchers as payment in part or in full in the course of 1,338 asset-sale transactions. Compensation vouchers were issued to a total nominal value of HUF 120 billion. With the nominal value increased by state-guaranteed interest they were worth a total of HUF 194 billion. To date, ÁPV Rt. has been unable to take out of circulation all the compensation vouchers issued.[21] At every major share issue, ÁPV Rt. aimed to take a certain proportion of compensation vouchers out of circulation: those who had obtained vouchers in their own right were usually given the first option to buy smaller packages (of a limited quantity per person). In this way, by the end of 1997, compensation vouchers with a total market value of HUF 73 billion had been traded in for newly issued shares. This "revenue" represents 14.8 percent of total privatization revenues and 45.9 percent of total domestic sales.[22]

However noble the aim it pursued, compensation sadly became, in a sense, a "historical hoax"[23]: it offered no compensation for suffering and covered very little in terms of damages. It failed to provide property for domestic investors en masse; it did not have a serious influence on the capital markets; and it muddled property relations and functional structures in agriculture. Apart from barely a dozen financial investors who became familiar with the ways of stock exchange speculation via utilization of the compensation vouchers and who realized substantial profits, almost everyone else remained dissatisfied with the system.

One of the basic characteristics of the Hungarian privatization process—as we have stated several times above—was the outstandingly high level of participation of foreign capital. A similar characteristic was the privatization organization's high levels of activity on the capital markets and the very high proportion of IPO's among privatization sales. The privatization of Hungarian banks is also worth mentioning because of its economic importance, but also for the peculiarities of this area of privatization: successive Hungarian governments put into practice the general concept held by professional financial circles, that is, that the "ideal" bank owner is a foreign strategic investor, that is, a foreign bank. Accordingly, with one exception—although this exception was in fact the largest Hungarian bank, OTP—the privatization organization sold the Hungarian banks to foreign professional investors.

In what follows, we will analyze these three areas in more detail.

5. The role of foreign capital in Hungarian privatization

One of the basic characteristics of the Hungarian privatization process was the outstandingly important role played by foreign capital: in Hungary—because of the logic of market-based privatization—foreigners were very rarely at a disadvantage. Apart from certain cases, such as pre-privatization, or certain individual sales in which the only form of payment accepted was the compensation voucher, preference for domestic owners was exercised only through preferential payment terms such as the use of compensation vouchers, Existence Credit, etc. The foreign applicant could still win in these cases, provided it offered a higher amount in cash than the Hungarian competitor using preferential financial terms, as long as all other application criteria were equal.

Also characteristic in Hungary was the large-scale sale of the public utilities—gas and electricity providers and waterworks—to foreign investors. Similarly, Hungary was the first country ready to privatize its national telecommunications and national oil companies with the involvement of foreign investors.

At this point, we should clear up a widespread misconception: although within privatization revenues the proportion of hard currency was unquestionably substantial, the majority of the total foreign direct investment in flow in Hungary did not flow into the country in the form of privatization revenue. In the process of transforming the economy—as we have pointed out in the previous chapter—foreign investors played an important role: in Hungary, total direct foreign investment as of the end of 1999 approached USD 21.5 billion, of which only USD 8.8 billion was privatization revenue.[24] The following table shows the total number of companies affected by foreign capital, the value of investments, and the division of investors by country from 1999. The table highlights the particularly high proportion of international IPOs and the significant activities of certain major investors in Hungarian privatization. Bearing in mind the general foreign-economic orientation of the Hungarian economy, one should not be surprised at the overwhelming presence of German investors and the large number of Austrian acquisitions—albeit of individually smaller value. Many people are surprised at the relatively large weight of France and Italy, and, at the same time, at the lack of interest shown by British investors.

Companies sold to foreigners, 1990 – 1998*

	Number of companies	Proportion Percent	Contractual value x HUF billion
Germany	107	25.18	292.78
USA	43	13.18	153.19
France	43	8.88	103.25
International Public Offer	33	30.67	356.61
Austria	117	5.17	60.08
The Netherlands	19	3.82	44.38
Italy	28	3.00	34.85
Belgium	10	3.33	38.68
Switzerland	18	1.58	18.39
Great Britain	34	1.72	20.04
CIS	16	0.90	10.46
Sweden	12	0.49	5.73
Israel	3	0.20	2.33
Finland	2	0.54	6.30
Ireland	2	0.48	5.60
Other	36	1.06	12.34
Total	510	100	1,162.68

* From among investments the table contains asset-protection sales and contributions in kind, investments at founding, sales of withdrawn assets, capital increase and the sale of shares and business stakes.

Source: Privatization Monitor, December 1999. ÁPV Rt.

The high proportion of stock-exchange flotations, and within this the high number of foreign flotations, was one of the most important features of privatization in 1997.

The participation of foreign capital in privatization made a significant impact on the national economy as a whole, and particularly on the further importing of working capital: “Foreign companies that participate in the acquisition of state-owned corporations generate and extend other greenfield developments. This effect can unquestionably be perceived in the following:

- Parallel with the appearance of a mother company might appear banks offering account management, credit, or financial services in the investor's country; competitors in the same branch or product; and outside suppliers and support (in the field of informatics, for instance).
- The sum of foreign investments in a given country was largely determined by the method of privatization chosen: the high absolute or relative proportion of foreign investments in itself generates interest.
- The presence of foreign companies in large numbers forces the creation of Western legal financial customs and trade systems, which is important for greenfield investors as well.
- Foreign managers and investors with favorable experiences of the country can encourage other foreign investors to found companies in Hungary."[25]

Foreign participation in the Hungarian economy will not end with the end of the privatization process, since foreigners who have obtained assets and who have realized investments in Hungary are planning and carrying out further investments and developments. In the energy sector in the coming years, approximately USD 2 billion of follow-up investments may be made in accordance with the commitments made by investors during the privatization process.[26] Similarly, foreign strategic investors participating in gas privatization plan investments (e.g. building gas pipelines) to a value exceeding USD 100 million over 5 years. The owners of the telecommunications company MATÁV Rt. made similar commitments at the time of privatization, a significant number of which have been fulfilled.

6. Bank privatization

One of the most debated areas of Hungarian privatization is the privatization of banks, and not only because the banking sector is one of the most sensitive and strategically important areas of the economy. Certainly, one of the decisive elements in the debate surrounding bank privatization is the fact that bank and debt consolidation, which was carried out earlier and which burdened the budget with costs of HUF 350 billion, are related to privatization. The banking sector is the only branch of the economy in which privatization was preceded by full-scale and extremely costly reorganization, which could well give rise to untypical profit-and-loss analyses.[27]

Bank privatization is, naturally, primarily a matter of trust: whoever buys a bank, especially if the buyer is a foreign investor, does not simply trust in the bank itself and in the future of the bank, but in the national economy as a whole. It is no surprise, therefore, that bank privatization did not start immediately after the change of system.[28]

At the same time, bank privatization is typically an area of privatization in which maximizing revenues is not necessarily the only, or main, goal. This was especially true in the early 1990s in Hungary, when the two-tier banking system came into operation not as a result of an organic development, but as an act of state administration. In 1986/7, there were virtually no good options: in Czechoslovakia a combination of regional (a Czech and a Slovak bank in every area) and branch banks; in Poland 9 regional banks; and in Hungary 4 branch trade banks were created from the corresponding former divisions of the central banks.

> The *ownership structure* of the banks was created in a very unfavorable way: the banks were dependent partly on the direct state owner and partly on the strong cor-

porational/branch clientele lobbies. The close interconnection between banks, as creditor-owners, and corporations hindered, right from the start, the creation of prudent banking attitudes, and the effect of this was reinforced by the ingrained attitudes of the inherited technical apparatus. The central government's role as a bank owner held the executives of the banks in a state of such dependency that it was hard to see how bankers' considerations could override political-econopolitical interests.

"The generally weak performance of the management of state-owned banks can be attributed primarily to the owners' bad influence on the banks and to their powerlessness. (…) Bearing in mind the credit regulations of the banks, which formally met the requirements of prudence, it can be said that it was not lack of professionalism but the preferring of individual interests over the bankers' interests that led, in the majority of cases, to the wrong credit decisions being made. The owners, however, played (play) a significant role in the emergence of such individual interests.

The banks' misguided business strategies and their belated attempts to change strategy, which often led to an unjustified increase in costs as well as to low levels of performance, are also mostly due to the lack of suitable owners. The banks' strong territorial expansion and client acquisition efforts, which were often carried out without profit-and-loss analyses, are a good example of this. The deteriorating indexes for personnel efficiency and branch utilization reflect the failure of the type of expansion strategies that would have been halted by a properly motivated owner."[29]

From the very beginning there were debates about the nature of "ideal" bank privatization. Many were against allowing in foreign strategic investors, arguing that such a strategically important sphere, from which the whole of the economy could be controlled and influenced, should only be privatized at the very end of the privatization process at a more advanced phase of transformation. Those who argued against diversified ownership pointed to such potential problems as the lack of a real owner (mostly on the basis of the experience of Czech voucher-based privatization) and the excessive power of the management in the privatization process as well as in future operations. Initially—and with significant professional backing—ÁVÜ did not consider it appropriate to initiate bank privatization in the short term. From 1991/1992, however, the majority of experts were already in favor of quick bank privatization involving foreign strategic investors. Although the Banking Act, which was passed in November 1991, limited the maximum ownership share of non-professional investors—including the state—to 25 percent, it allowed 5 years' grace for the reduction of state-owned assets. The Act treated foreign ownership rather liberally: the only obligation was for investors to make a declaration, even in the case of those with a stake of over 10 percent.

The Antall government accepted a strategy for bank privatization in 1992. According to this strategy, consolidation—the cleaning of the portfolio—had to precede privatization, and in the course of privatization the banks' operations had to be improved by cash-based capital increase. Although this strategy enabled MKB (the Hungarian Trade Bank), for instance, to begin privatization, it was soon subject to modification, and the encouragement of domestic investors became its strategic aim.[30] "The bank privatization strategy of the Boross government, passed in February 1994, returned to the original concept (that had been abandoned in the national interest), according to which professional strategic investors had to be found. At the same time, the concept necessitated a revision of the list of the financial institutions remaining in long-term state ownership."[31]

The draft Privatization Act submitted by the Horn government in 1994 paid no special attention to bank privatization: the Horn cabinet was initially occupied with the follow-up work to credit, bank, and debt consolidation. At the same time, in the schedule to the act, only two banks, MBFB and OTP, were named as remaining in long-term state ownership, with a state stake of 25 percent in each case. Bank privatization therefore could have been accelerated in 1994, at least in theory. However, the dynamization of processes began only in 1995 with the passing of the Privatization Act and the confidential government decree on the privatization of Budapest Bank. In practice, the Horn government accelerated bank privatization only with the so-called Bokros package, a set of general economic measures named after the minister of finance at the time.

Although the revenue produced by the privatization of BB and OTP can be regarded as microscopic within the HUF 475 billion privatization revenues of 1995 (4.5 billion of which was in USD), there is no doubt that in terms of "gaining the trust of foreigners" the significance of bank privatization was comparable with that of the privatization of the energy sector and of MATÁV.[32] The privatization of the Hungarian Foreign Trade Bank (MKB), which was in the best condition of all the state-owned trade banks, not even requiring consolidation, took place in several stages. In June 1994, some 25 percent of the bank's shares were purchased by Bayerische Landesbank, as a strategic investor, at a rate of 125 percent; and 17 percent of shares were acquired by EBRD, acting as a financial investor. Subsequently, the two foreign investors increased the capital in order to provide fresh money for the excellent but under-capitalized bank and, in addition, in order to reduce the state to a minority-ownership position. Since the first privatization step the strategic direction of MKB has been carried out by the Bavarian owner with unchanged management and outstanding results. Since MKB is continually increasing its balance-sheet total and improving its market position, today it is unquestionably the second-largest Hungarian bank with very high rates of profitability. In 1995, Deutsche Entwicklung Gesellschaft bought an 8 percent equity stake in the bank.[33] In May 1996, the foreign owners acquired the bank's state-owned equity stake, worth 24.67 percent, at a rate of 219 percent. With this step MKB was entirely removed from the circle of state assets.

The next significant bank privatization was the partial privatization of OTP in summer 1995. While the privatization of MKB was a prototype for privatization involving a professional investor, that of OTP, as the first transaction of its kind, became the "archetype" of privatization involving financial investors and resulting in a diversified ownership structure.

The privatization of OTP took place in several stages:

1. In 1993/94, some 20 percent of preference and ordinary shares *were traded in for compensation vouchers*.

2. In 1994, *local self-governments* received almost 3 percent of the shares in ÁPV Rt.'s portfolio in return for real estate.

3. In the spring of 1995 the *pension insurance self-government and health insurance self-government* received 10 percent each free from ÁPV Rt.

4. In summer 1995, *in a private sale*, 20 percent of shares got into the hands of foreign institutional investors, 8 percent went to domestic institutional investors and private investors, and 5 percent to the employees and management.

5. In the course of the invitation-based sale the bank's shares were oversubscribed at a period when neither the upcoming markets nor Hungary, nor bank papers in general, were attractive in the eyes of international investment circles. Besides the Budapest Stock Exchange the bank is listed on the Luxembourg Stock Exchange and on the London Stock Exchange Automated Quota-

tion System.[34] The shares were sold at a rate of 120 percent, which meant a rate of 84 percent projected against the equity capital.

In fall 1997, the management of ÁPV Rt. initiated the reduction of the state's share in the largest Hungarian trade bank to one "golden share", which took place in November 1997 as part of a successful international and domestic flotation.[35]

"In the case of OTP, the state was capable of reducing its majority stake without professional investors and realizing revenues of HUF 10 billion. The diversified ownership structure *theoretically* made it possible to eliminate the owner's "non-profit-oriented" interference. Despite potential hazards, the management of OTP is carrying out a successful business policy regardless of the diversified ownership structure, which besides an improvement in the quality of services, has manifested itself in a rapid improvement in the bank's results and in its share prices."[36]

The privatization of Budapest Bank took place on 18 December 1995. This was probably the transaction that caused the biggest controversy. In early 1992 the government intended to sell Budapest Bank, which, even after consolidation, was experiencing liquidity problems and suffering serious loss of capital. From among those seriously interested in purchase, three banks were invited to tender. However, the government's preferred choice from among the three banks was made public. As a result, the Irish bank that had been invited in third place withdrew in protest. Following six weeks of investigations Crédit Suisse declared that it was not looking for a universal bank (a nonsense, since the nature of the bank must have been obvious to them right from the start). Next ING, which had formerly succeeded in purchasing the assets of Dunabank without tendering—including its credit-card business, which, at the time, was leading the market—began its investigations into the bank. The dynamically developing Dutch bank/insurance company eventually declared its loss of interest in a rather peculiar manner: almost the entire management of the Dutch bank traveled to Budapest where, during a business lunch, they heaped praise on the Hungarian economy and Budapest Bank, after which they paid a visit to the prime minister. Despite this, on the evening news program they publicly and quite shockingly made dismissive statements about the state of the Hungarian national economy and of Budapest Bank and declared they were not interested in purchasing the bank.

In the meantime, or rather before the above-mentioned events, the government had provided the bank with credit of HUF 12 billion, with a maturity date of 18 December 1995, with the unusual condition that, in the event of privatization, the money need not be repaid. The only remaining interested party was the consortium made up of GE Capital Services and EBRD. The privatization negotiations—conducted contrary to the Privatization Act, which, in this one case, was overruled by a confidential government decree—were carried out by the Finance Ministry, headed at the time by Lajos Bokros, who had formerly been the CEO of Budapest Bank. The Hungarian negotiating position was extremely weak: on the one hand the purchaser knew that the Ministry was ready to accept virtually any conditions in order to sell the bank; on the other hand, it was obvious that HUF 12 billion was the absolute minimum sum required. The business was settled when the GEC/EBRD consortium paid HUF 12 billion (the net profit amounted to HUF 8,000, derived from the rounding up of figures). The purchaser, as stated in the contract, called the HUF 11 billion of asset guarantees.

It can be said that the state, in addition to the credit and bank consolidation and the conversion of some consolidation bonds into Treasury bills (i.e., their conversion into securities with a fixed redemption date), had sold the country's fourth largest trade bank with an immediate loss of HUF 12 billion. In other words, the state paid HUF 12 billion to the purchaser to take the bank. This privatization transaction cannot be regarded as successful for the additional reason that the bank's operations did not improve as a result of privatization: the last three financial years have been characterized by a reduction in market share, decreasing profitability, and a permanent strategic indecisiveness.[37]

Bank privatization accelerated in 1996 and within a year and a half it had practically been completed. On 1 July 1996, GAZPROMBANK acquired 50 percent of ÁÉB's shares at par value from ÁVÜ and 50 percent from the American Central European Development Corporation, then immediately raised the bank's capital by HUF 4 billion to HUF 5 billion.

The Hungarian Privatization and State Holding Company issued a tender for 89.23 percent of the shares of Magyar Hitelbank (MHB, the Hungarian Credit Bank) in July 1996. A new management came into office on 1 November 1996, and the sale of these shares was its first transaction decision, made on 9 November 1996. Although in the end only two offers arrived rather than the four that had been hoped for earlier, the competition proved to be real, even keen, since the two offers were very good and very competitive. Creditanstalt Bankverein made an offer of 200 percent. However, it demanded certain state guarantees and was only ready to commit itself to a relatively low capital increase. At the same time, the more than four-hundred-year-old ABN-Amro attached to its USD 90 million (222 percent) offer a commitment to a capital increase of USD 100 million without asking any kind of state guarantees.

The sale of MHB was regarded as the most successful Hungarian bank privatization for a long time: the purchaser was a large bank involved in truly global activity, which, on the basis of declarations made by its managers, could be expected to regard its Hungarian daughter-bank as a regional/sub-regional center.[38] The bank's performance in 1997 and developments under the management and control of the new owner seemed to confirm the success of the transaction. Of course, not everything in this story is so rosy: besides the consolidation expenses and the direct guarantee, MHB converted consolidation bonds worth HUF 50 billion into discount Treasury bills, which meant an immediate cash injection in the period immediately preceding privatization... In a peculiar development, ABN-Amro Hungary (the new name of MHB) realized huge losses in 1988/89, bringing into question the wisdom and practicality of the purchaser's strategy.

With respect to the special role of Takarékbank (Savings Bank) in the Hungarian banking system—this financial institution is the "umbrella bank" of 280 Hungarian savings cooperatives—ÁPV Rt. invited five foreign banks[39] that carried out similar activities in their own countries to participate in a private tender. As a result of the lengthy preliminary negotiations two out of the five banks invited, the German Deutsche Genossenschaft Bank (DG Bank) and the Austrian GiroCredit Bank, submitted a valid tender for an equity stake representing 61.89 percent of Takarékbank's capital.[40] The DG Bank won with an offer of HUF 4.4 billion, or 532 percent—against GiroCredit's offer of 494 percent.

The country's third largest trade bank in terms of balance-sheet total, Kereskedelmi és Hitelbank (Trade and Credit Bank), was also sold by an invitation-based but two-round tender. Out of the 35 (!) serious potential purchasers, 6 were invited, and in the second round the Belgian-Irish Kreietbank-Irish Life consortium and the Bank of Ireland Group qualified. In a close competition the Belgian-Irish consortium emerged the winner, paying a record-breaking rate of 567 percent (USD 30 million) for 10 percent of K&H. Subsequently, they increased the capital by USD 60 million at a rate of 105 percent, thus becoming the majority owners of the bank. In the meantime, EBRD converted into shares the loan capital of USD 30 million, as a result of which it became the bank's second largest owner. The employees were able to subscribe to 1.5 percent of the total shares. The government decided on the public stock-exchange launch of the HUF 4.5 billion equity stake that remained in the state's hands and the HUF 3.1 billion equity stake owned by the two social security self-governments. However, this had to be postponed, first in fall 1997 and then in June 1998, on both occasions due to unfavorable stock-exchange conditions.[41] In the meantime—in the financial year of 1999—the bank realized serious losses and as a result initiated a capital increase with conditions that were unacceptable to ÁPV Rt.[42] In February 2000, following the postponement of one general meeting, the suspension of another, and a bitter polemic in the press, the Belgian owner bought out the state's stake at 120 percent, then—in order to cover its losses and to provide appropriate liable equity capital—raised the bank's capital by HUF 10 billion.

In July 1997, ÁPV Rt. issued an invitation to tender for its 88.7 percent shares in Mezőbank. Since Citibank did not in the end submit a tender, the competition was decided between Reiffeisen, Unicbank and BankAustria-GiroCredit. The winner, BankAustria-GiroCredit, offered ATS 320 million (HUF 4.947 billion), or 172 percent. In addition, it committed itself to capital increase of HUF 4 billion at a rate of 133 percent.[43]

With respect to Mezőbank's "troubled past" and its forced merger with Agrobank two years earlier, privatization can be regarded on the one hand as a successful transaction by ÁPV Rt., while on the other it obviously reflects the incredible growth of foreign investors' interest in the Hungarian economy.

At the end of 1997 it seemed that Hungarian bank privatization was practically complete, although ÁPV Rt. was obliged by government decrees to take part in the capitalization of Postabank, thereby acquiring a minimal (HUF 1.7 billion) direct stake in this bank with its problematic history. However, the new government decided to settle the fate of the second-largest retail bank. In September 1998 it came into 100 percent state ownership. Its privatization—in theory, according to official statements—might take place in 2001 or 2002.

"Compared with bank ownership relations characteristic of developed countries and of Europe, that is, of Hungary's immediate economic environment, the bank privatization process in Hungary can be regarded as exceptional—not only because in scarcely ten years the state's stake in the Hungarian banking system had shrunk to 20 percent, but also because, at the same time, by the end of 1997 foreign professional investors had taken on a dominant owner's role."[44]

Hopefully the future will prove right the author we have quoted here: the tendency towards the free movement of capital, which is becoming more and more dominant in the money and capital markets, justifies the Hungarian practice generally followed throughout privatization. It facilitated acquisition in the case of banks with a good standing and a clear vision. "Although the methods followed were governed by necessity (the lack of capital-rich domestic buyers) there is a good chance of creating a virtue out of necessity. The privatization method and liberal granting of permission for the foundation of banks has created a realistic chance that by the time the country joins the European Union the international competitiveness of the Hungarian banking system will have gained strength."[45]

The success of bank privatization cannot ultimately be measured by revenues or share prices but by the performance of the Hungarian banking sector and the privatized Hungarian banks, by the widening of the range of banking services and a significant improvement in their quality, and, generally, by the meeting of international standards in as short a time as possible. Judging by balance-sheet totals in 1999 it is also clear that a capital-rich foreign strategic (professional) owner is no guarantee of profitability. Today, the development of Hungarian banks can be seen as management dependent, or at least largely management dependent: the wave of mergers which has been expected for years on the Hungarian bank market will show for certain which of the owners has chosen a really effective strategy.

7. Privatization and the stock exchange

On the Budapest Stock Exchange (BSE), which re-opened its doors on 21 June 1990 after a break of 42 years, shares have been traded since early 1991. Among the first shares traded on the BSE were those of IBUSZ and Zalakerámia, which were floated by ÁVÜ as part of the privatization process. On 31 December 1997 there were 42 companies listed. The capitalization of BSE is developing very dynamically: in 1995 it was equal to 6 percent of GDP and in 1996 to 13 percent of GDP, but on 31 December 1997 it exceeded HUF 3,000 billion (USD 14.7 billion at the December 1997 rate of exchange), that is, about 35 percent of annual GDP.

The BSE initially developed very modestly, then, in early 1994 the first real boom occurred. The stock exchange index (BUX) doubled in one month from 1,000 points to over 2,000. A real hausse occurred in the period between February 1996 and August 1997 when prices were continually increasing, until in early August the BUX reached 8,400 points. The impact of the international baisse was naturally felt on the BSE as well, and the BUX fell by 3,000 points. By December the Stock Exchange had rallied—largely due to ÁPV Rt.'s major flotations. In March 2000 the BUX stood at around 10,000 points.

In 1996/7, development in the BSE's share section was extremely rapid. This was due in practice to the dynamic increase in prices since the number of listed companies hardly changed and the only real "big investment" was the appearance of TVK's HUF 24 billion worth of papers in this period.[46] On 14 November 1997 the issuing of a 25 percent equity stake in MATÁV[47] immediately increased the capitalization of the BSE by 50 percent. Introduced simultaneously on the New York Stock Exchange and the Budapest Stock Exchange, MATÁV had capital of HUF 103 billion and its shares, which had a nominal value of HUF 100 each, were issued at a price of HUF 730.

Capitalization of the Budapest Stock Exchange
(HUF billion)

	1991	1992	1993	1994	1995	1996	1997
EQUITIES	38.2	47.2	81.7	181.5	327.8	852.5	2,801.3
Government bonds	15.3	82.3	241.7	392.9	454.0	703.4	889.3
Corporate bonds	0.1	0.1	0.3	1.8	1.7	1.3	37.2
Treasury bills	-	54.4	74.0	239.6	376.3	697.2	880.0
Investment funds	-	1.9	5.5	19.3	42.8	41.6	32.2
Compensation vouchers	-	16.0	53.8	48.7	18.7	95.0	134.7
TOTAL	53.6	201.9	457.0	883.8	1,221.3	2,391.0	4,774.7

Source: Budapest Stock Exchange.

When talking in general terms about the development of the BSE, in practice we are talking about the privatization organizations' activities on the capital markets and the role played by the Stock Exchange in privatization: from among the 47 domestic corporate bonds listed in the share section of the BSE, the issuing of 24 was initiated by ÁVÜ, ÁV Rt. and ÁPV Rt. together. These 24 bonds yield 93 percent of the capitalization of the share section, being 99.6 (!) percent of the capitalization of the A category and 10.4 percent of that of the B category.

It can be said that in the A category only the papers issued by ÁPV Rt. and its predecessors can be regarded as significant and that blue chips have so far only been issued by the state privatization institutions. In 1997 ÁPV Rt. was extremely active on the capital market and the flotations of MATÁV, MOL, OTP and Richter redrew the map of the BSE's share section. (This is illustrated in the table.)

In fall 1997 MOL's second, complex, share issue took place with marked success. As a result, the Hungarian state's stake in the national oil companyi was reduced from 55 percent to 36 percent: by selling almost 19 percent of MOL's shares on the capital market, ÁPV Rt. realized revenues of more than USD 300 million.

A few weeks after the second issue of MOL shares, also in May 1997, the second issue of shares in Richter Gedeon Rt. took place. In the course of the transaction domestic and foreign institutional investors were able to subscribe to the 2.6 million shares of Richter, while 200,000 shares in the large and prosperous pharmaceutical company could be bought by domestic small investors in a public flotation.

As a result of the favorable foreign and domestic capital market conditions and the strict pricing policy of the management of ÁPV Rt. the papers could be issued with a minimal discount at a price of HUF 14,500, resulting in revenues of USD 218 million, USD 78 million of which flowed back into the company in the form of a capital increase. While consultants (international sales agencies) spoke of the "aggressive pricing policy of ÁPV Rt.'s CEO", the outstanding economic-financial performance of the pharmaceutical company, which in 1991/2 was on the verge of liquidation, was respected on the markets. In 1998 its share price was consistently over HUF 20,000, and in March 2000 it stood at HUF 19,000 to 20,000.

In 1997 the Central European capital-market sensation was without doubt MATÁV's flotation on the stock exchange—if for no other reason than that the company was launched simultaneously on the Budapest Stock Exchange and on the New York Stock Exchange. These were the first Central European papers to be introduced in New York in normal—not OTC—trading. In keeping with tradition, the head of the floated company, in this case the chief executive of MATÁV, rang the bell on 14 November 1997 to signal the beginning of trading. In the course of the flotation, ÁPV Rt. sold 25.45 percent of the 1,037, 281, 600 series A shares with a par value of HUF 100 and the single series B share with a par value of HUF 10,000. The flotation was able to take place because the management of ÁPV Rt.—after obtaining the consent of MATÁV's foreign strategic owners (Deutsche Telecom and Ameritech) and with the consent and mediation of the minister without portfolio responsible for privatization—recommended to the government that the state should reduce its stake to one single golden share in the national telecommunications company.

In spite of the thorough preparation the flotation took place at a very unfavorable time. The completion of the organization of the launch (the "road-show") took place in the days immediately following the international stock-exchange crash of 23 October 1997, while the pricing took place in the subsequent collapse of 11-13 November 1997. The flotation following the "road-show" could not be postponed: it therefore had to be accepted that the shares could only be issued at the low end of the original price range—which was between HUF 730 and HUF 910—at HUF 730. The launch rate achieved in this way was 731 percent, projected against the subscribed capital, and 397 percent projected against the equity capital.

"In the history of domestic public flotations, never had shares in such quantities and at such prices been issued on the market at one time. The 20,745,000 plus 41,492,000 shares at HUF 100 par value were worth more than HUF 35 billion at market value."[48] By means of the flotation of MATÁV, ÁPV Rt. realized revenues of HUF 140.114 billion (= USD 710 million).

Today, MATÁV alone represents almost 37 percent of the capitalization of the Budapest Stock Exchange. Its shares have done relatively well even in an unfavorable stock-exchange climate, and their price is decreasing at less than the average rate. After fall 1999 a new package was launched simultaneously in New York and Budapest, and in the first quarter of 2000 the price of the BSE's leading stock was consistently around HUF 2,000 to 3,000.

Immediately after the introduction of MATÁV in New York, the second issue, of 25 percent of OTP shares, took place. After this, in 1995, the amended Privatization Act decreased the state's stake in the largest Hungarian bank to one golden share. The still unfavorable stock-exchange climate—the baisse in October and November on Wall Street—had a peculiar impact on the pricing of OTP shares: the usual debate/bargaining between the issuer and the consultant did not take place, since it was obvious that every minute's delay might cause further reductions in price. The representatives of ÁPV Rt. and of Shroders Bank therefore agreed in minutes about the London pricing. The 5.6 million OTP shares were sold at a price of HUF 6,010 (=USD 30.4): 57 percent went to foreign institutional investors, 43 percent to domestic institutional investors and small investors. It is worth noting that between 1995 and 1997, within 28 months, the market price of OTP shares rose from HUF 1,200 to HUF 6,010, which means a spectacular success in terms of the second launch. The popularity of OTP on the stock exchange is well reflected in the long-standing share price of around HUF 14,000 in the first quarter of 2000.

Since mid-1999, that is the entering into power of the new right wing coalition government, privatization has practically been stopped down. Since then, no major privatization transaction has actually taken place. Just the contrary, the newly elected government renationalized the assets previously had been hold by the two Social Security Funds (The National Pension Insurance Fund and the National Health Insurance Fund), and bought back the private—concession holding—motorway companies, 35 percent of MALÉV, the Hungarian Airlines, etc.

In 1999, ÁPV realized about HUF 115 billions of privatization incomes and about HUF 133 billions of total income. Hard currency incomes totaled about HUF 70 billion. Direct privatization incomes were actually generated from three major transactions:

1. The minority stake of Trade & Credit Bank was sold to the majority owner, the Belgian Kredietbank at a 120 percent price;

2. 16 percent of OTP, the largest Hungarian bank was sold on the Wall Street as well as on the Budapest Stock Exchange. This

stake had previously been hold by the two social security funds and the price was not too spectacular—well below 10,000 forints (half year later, OTP's exchange rate was between 14,000–15,000—although the BSE is fairly bearish nowadays;

3. About 25 percent of MATÁV, the Hungarian national telecommunication company (wich is in a legally guaranteed monopolistic situation in voice transmission till the end of the year 2002) were actually sold on a fairly good price—at about 1,400 forint per share. It was the only successful privatization transaction since mid-1998—although it is certainly worth to be mentioned that this very transaction was organized and lead by Deutsche Telekom, MATÁV's majority owner and ÁPV played the role of co-manager of the international transaction …

In fiscal 2000 no major single privatization transaction took place! Since 1990(!) it was the very first year when literally no hard currency income was realized in the Hungarian privatization. HUF 9 billion of incomes were realized by the earlier selling of a minority stake of Trade & Credit Bank, further HUF 2.5 billions were generated by selling on the capital market some negligible minority stakes, as well as from selling real estates and more than HUF 2.1 billion were the results of liquidation of state-owned companies which could not been sold otherwise.

ÁPV's performance in fiscal 2000 was overshadowed by two unfortunate transaction failures. First, 37.5 percent of Antenna Hungária, the state broadcasting and microwave telecommunication company were sold on the Budapest Stock Exchange for about HUF 1.197 billion—this transaction had figured with no less than HUF 14 billion in ÁPV's business plan … Second, and it was a much more shameful failure, ÁPV could not sell MALÉV, the Hungarian national airlines. ÁPV Had intended to sell 10 percent of the company and, at the same time, to invite the buyer for a capital increase in order to obtain 49 percent[49] of the company. The idea was to find a strategic partner for MALÉV, in order to make profitable this small national airlines which badly needs fresh capital, managerial know-how but first and foremost some place under the sun, that is some—even minor—role in a global strategic partnership. The transaction had obviously not been carefully prepared by ÁPV's advisor, Credit Suisse First Boston: four major European airlines bought the tender documentation but non of them put forward a bid. Now, MALÉV's image is fairly damaged, a HUF 15-20 billion worth of capital increase is required (by ÁPV, of course) and even so, the future of Hungarian national airlines is doubtful: or a new privatization attempt will successfully take place, or the state will permanently subsidized it (even after a major trimming of its activities)—or even the liquidation of the Hungarian national airlines could not been excluded.

8. Privatization: results, debates, and perspectives

The Hungarian privatization process fulfilled a historical task when, in a record time of eight to ten years, it eliminated the excessive weight of state ownership. Eight years after the change of system, the state's entrepreneurial assets amounted to less than 20 percent of the total assets of the entrepreneurial sphere, which corresponds to modern West European norms.

Privatization belongs among Hungary's success stories and plays a key role in the process that is taking the Hungarian economy forward into the European Union. Due to the outstanding success of the privatization process in the second half of the decade, the country's economy now has a market-based ownership structure. In the course of the eight-year period, most sectors of the Hungarian economy were entirely or substantially privatized. Today, the private sector operates, entirely or in large part, the Hungarian retail and trade banking system, the insurance sector, the pharmaceutical industry, the chemical industry, the construction industry, the tobacco industry, the brewing industry, the food industry, the leisure and hotel industry, printing, the paper industry, the packaging industry, and the food and general retailing network. In addition, the majority of the public utilities have been privatized, including the national telecommunications company (MATÁV), the national oil and gas company (MOL), and the electricity suppliers and the majority of the electricity production capacity.

Today, important sectors of the economy remaining largely in state ownership have been reduced to the nuclear power industry, the electricity grid, transportation, radio and television broadcasts, the national forests, and 27 agricultural companies.

*

The evaluation of privatization is an especially difficult and complex task. National economic, (certain) branch political, sociological, and geographical viewpoints and considerations can be equally important in terms of their impact, effects, and consequences. At the same time, they might give rise to contradictory evaluations. Throughout the entire privatization process the goals of privatization, even in the narrow sense, involved complex and often contradictory requirements that demanded careful balancing in each individual privatization transaction. Inevitably, no decision was without controversy. Nor have we mentioned the political considerations and requirements, the serious existential interests, and the "one-off" opportunities for outstandingly large profits. The potential gains could very often be utilized only by the first private owner and the wasted opportunities could never be redeemed.

In the globalized world economy, in an era of the increasingly liberalized flow of goods, capital, and labor, competition that transcends national borders is an inescapable reality. It was not privatization that brought about their appearance in Hungary; at best it could enhance their development. In this case, however, it obviously helped the integration of the Hungarian national economy into the world economy and the opportunity to develop socioeconomic modernization of all kinds.

> "Let us look around…in Eastern Europe. Where are the competitors? There is no doubt that we have overtaken everyone in the privatization of the 'hard core'. We are ahead in the field of regulation, we are ahead in transactions, and we are ahead in the consolidation of the new structures. Others have not yet proved that this task can be solved in any better way. We have plenty to be proud of.
>
> Between 1989 and 1997, it was not only property relations that went through a transformation: privatization reshaped relations within companies and, due to the widespread nature of the process, the proportions of income and property among the various social groups were significantly changed. In addition to the newly created large industrialists and owners appeared a stratum of middle management, hundreds of thousands strong. Although wage-earners, their position in terms of income and assets was more favorable, in both absolute and relative terms, than it had been before the change of system. As a result of privatization, there is a similarly large stratum of small entrepreneurs and service providers, which directly serve those sections of the population and the public administration that can afford to pay. All these together appear to be a sufficient foundation for the formation of a middle class. And this had been the goal."[50]

The privatization process, however, was by no means free of errors, and public opinion regarding it is not unanimous.

1. The privatization of the sugar, vegetable oil, and milk industries can hardly be regarded as economically well grounded. The same can be said of the early (that is, occurring in the early stages of privatization and without respect for their vertical integration) sale of the large (mostly food-related) retail chains, which left domestic agricultural producers vulnerable and contributed to the acceleration of the already high inflation in the early 1990s as well as to the increasing of certain social problems. No matter how satisfying it is that the dairy products available in Hungary represent a much better—"European"—quality than in the past, significant price rises, brought about by the oligopolistic market, which, since privatization, has largely been dominated by foreigners, have probably contributed to the fact that per capita milk consumption in Hungary (which had never been particularly high considering the economic development of the country and in comparison with international levels) has permanently been on the decrease since 1990.[51]

2. The selling of certain minority stakes attached to majority rights was a particularly unhappy concept. Not only in the case of the sugar industry, for example, but also in the case of the Hungarian national airlines (MALÉV) and the bus-producer IKARUSZ, this devalued the shareholding that remained in state ownership, making impossible its efficient sale. At the same time, the state, although a majority stakeholder, was unable to enforce its will in the management of the company. In the case of MALÉV, a bank consortium has bought out the 35 percent Italian stake, meaning that a new attempt can be made at the privatization of the national airlines. The sale of IKARUSZ could only take place in return for the assumption of obligations that were to be repaid from sources recovered from the company, since the minority owner with majority rights—the Russian ATEX—vetoed every other solution.

3. Minority stakes remaining in state ownership have proved to be similarly unfavorable, or, more exactly, impossible to handle. Strategic investors could acquire companies in such circumstances since "only half" of the company was for sale. However, the cheaply bought company came entirely under their control, therefore the minority stake could in practice only be used to provide employee shares. The shares that remained in the ownership of ÁPV Rt. could be sold only with a significant discount (usually to the majority stakeholder, who had no interest in paying too much for a further shareholding in a company that it already controlled) or they were included in one of the MFB-ÁPV portfolio swaps.

4. Compensation, made non-transparent, complicated, and bureaucratic by competing political groupings and personalities, failed to satisfy any of the strata or groups that it was intended to compensate. Quite the contrary. "Compensation became a kind of hoax. It seemed to be something other than it was. The process was seen and portrayed in as many different ways as there were social groups."[52] At the risk of sounding cynical, which would be quite out of place in this context, we could say that the only social "group" that benefited from compensation, that is, from the use of compensation vouchers, was that group of brokers and investors who, using compensation vouchers, mastered the rules of share trading and from arbitrage opportunities related to compensation vouchers created the financial basis for their future stock-market activities. "In early 1998 it is clear that the problem of compensation lost its meaning. Resolving the problem is not about increasing the smoothness and efficiency of the basic mechanisms of the economy: the process simply needs to be brought to a conclusion and the problem dealt with once and for all."[53]

5. The asset management ('holding') activities of ÁPV Rt. and its predecessors cannot be regarded as successful either. Lacking clear-cut economic orientation, the understaffed holding organization was in the crossfire of permanent criticism, which was even

aimed at the very meaning of "holding". In addition, the organization was chiefly concerned with the financial and ethical success of privatization transactions and was thus left with neither time nor energy to devote to the task of holding. Although they cannot be measured precisely, significant losses must have resulted from the inefficient operation of the companies in long-term or temporary state ownership and profits must have been reduced by the resulting lower privatization revenues.

6. The realization of "soft"—environmental-protection-related or employment-related—conditions contained in privatization contracts and the penalizing of companies for unfulfilled contractual obligations cannot be regarded as entirely successful.[54] This is true even if these conditions are, by their very nature, difficult to quantify (estimates of the costs of environmental damage prevention are particularly imprecise). Lack of fulfillment of such conditions is also hard to penalize, even on ethical grounds.[55] In the majority of cases, the inclusion of such conditions in the contract resulted in the lowering of the sale price, while controlling the performance of such obligations proved to be imprecise and the imposing of penalties impossible to carry out.

7. The shadow of corruption lay and still lies over the entire privatization process, although the Tocsik scandal was the only privatization-related corruption case that became public and reached the courts. The complexity of the case is obvious from the fact that it lasted for four years from disclosure to the final judgement in March 2000. Since the disclosure of the Tocsik scandal, the press and public opinion (the latter obviously informed but also swayed by the former) have regarded corruption as a permanent—and more or less decisive—feature of the privatization process, or at least an accompanying phenomenon. This, despite the fact that the "Tocsik Affair" did not directly involve privatization, but rather privatization consulting, and that it only involved sums that were to be paid by the privatization organization to the local self-governments in

relation to privatization. There are four obvious points to make regarding corruption:

- The selling of state-owned assets (just like public procurements) anywhere in the world "naturally" goes hand in hand with corruption, nor does it appear that there are more "cases" in Hungary than elsewhere.
- The system of compulsory tendering in Hungary is/was much more effective in excluding the possibility of corruption than was the Czech and Polish method,[56] which was based on individual negotiations. The primacy of cash revenues in the course of privatization transactions in Hungary limited the opportunity for corruption: applicants offering a higher price enjoyed significant advantages and their position was difficult for those offering less to match, even if the latter offered better "soft" conditions—business plans, job preservation guarantees, etc.
- The dominance of hard-currency revenues also strongly limited/limits the possibility for corruption since the position of a capital-rich foreign customer does not necessitate the corrupting of the privatizer (with a proper price offer such customers will win anyway) and their competitors are unable to succeed, therefore they have nothing to pay for. Despite this, privatization was accompanied by suspicions and ÁPV Rt. was unable to defend itself against unproved/unprovable accusations.
- The situation has probably best been described by Ápád Kovács: "...In 1994 the 'Clean Hands Committee' of was set up to investigate privatization affairs that had earlier been exposed in the press and that had been mentioned in various reports of the State Audit Office. The several dozen cases resulted in only three criminal proceedings and even these have not yet been resolved. The government committee

> concluded that although the cases discussed were morally objectionable and not economically rational, the transactions were in fact correct and therefore within the law."[57]

In spite of this, the overall evaluation of privatization can only be positive:

1. The once omnipotent and omnipresent state ownership structure was dismantled in an unprecedentedly short time. Hungary can boast that since the turn of 1997/8, mostly as a result of this unprecedentedly short privatization process, it has moved from being a planned economy to being a market economy. Since this time the proportion of state ownership—both in relation to the total state-owned assets and the contribution to GDP—has not exceeded the average for Western Europe. The British privatization process in the 1980s, which is regarded as the forerunner and archetype of West European privatization, took ten years to privatize 5 percent of the GDP. In Hungary, in eight years, 80 percent of the total corporate assets went from state ownership into private hands.

2. Throughout the process, privatization took place on market foundations and using market methods and the investment concessions, regarded as insufficient by both the political elite and the majority of the public, also remained within the market framework and did not affect the market basis of privatization. Therefore, as a result of the Hungarian privatization process, unlike, for example, in the Czech Republic, the former state assets passed into the hands of real owners. This is clearly reflected in the fact that following a wave of bankruptcies and liquidations in 1992 and 1993, only a very small percentage of privatized companies went bankrupt (and even then they were mostly "victims" of secondary privatization and were not forced to cease their activities).

3. Privatization—to a large extent due to the above factors—has been a fundamental tool and a driving force in the shaping of a modern market economy over the last decade.

4. By means of privatization, working capital worth more than USD 8.8 billion flowed into the country. This capital flow helped in the handling of balance of payment problems and led to a decrease in the country's foreign debts. It was also accompanied by extensive importing of technology and the spreading of modern corporational management know-how. The foreign capital that flowed into the country during the privatization process—forming an important part of Hungarian working capital imports—played a decisive role in the significant improvement of the Hungarian economy's export performance and convinced Hungary's foreign economic partners of the seriousness and credibility of the Hungarian transition. In sum, it was effective in promoting the Hungarian national economy's integration into the world economy.

5. Privatization revenues—predominantly in 1995 and onwards—played a far from negligible role in the realization of the stabilization policy, in restoring macroeconomic balance, and, therefore, in creating, by 1997, the conditions for sustainable growth.

6. The Budapest Stock Exchange "came of age": blue-chips and the corporate bonds making up the Budapest Stock Exchange index, the BUX, passed into stock-exchange circulation in the course of privatization. Without privatization, hundreds of thousands of small investors would have had no way of making profitable investments to augment their savings.

*

Without successful privatization there would have been no successful transition to a market economy. Without successful privatization the macroeconomic stabilization that put an end to the transformation crisis could not have come about. Without successful privatization Hungary could not have become, by spring 1998, a leader of economic transition in the Central and East European region.

II. THE INFLOW OF FOREIGN DIRECT INVESTMENT INTO HUNGARY: ONE OF THE SUCCESS STORIES OF THE TRANSFORMATION*

In terms of world trade, the growth in foreign direct investment has been almost unbroken for four decades. Following stagnation between 1989 and 1991, the increase in foreign direct investment exceeded the expansion of both world production and world trade throughout the 1990s as a whole. In 1998, despite the crises in southeast Asia and Russia and the uncertainties in Latin America, foreign direct investment increased dynamically to approach USD 650 billion. According to preliminary statistics there was no change in this trend in 1999, with total annual foreign direct investment approaching USD 800 billion. The 1990s were dominated by a wave of company buy-outs and company mergers—a tendency in fact so consistent that it can scarcely be called a "wave". The majority of foreign direct investment—between two-thirds and three-quarters of total foreign direct investment exports—are traditionally realized among developed countries. Furthermore, as a result of the recent economic crisis, the developing countries' share fell in 1998 to 25.8 percent, the lowest level for a quarter of a century. In 1999, however, investors' confidence in the developing markets began to return,[58] but it is likely that developing countries will return only very slowly to the 1996–7 figure of 37 percent of the total inflow of foreign direct investment.

The most significant change in the 1990s was the fact that the transforming economies of Central and Eastern Europe managed to "make it onto the map" in terms of the international flow of foreign

* This chapter was written by György Csáki, Ph.D. in economics, Research Director of GKI Economic Research Co.

direct investment. Although the share of the region in terms of total foreign direct investment inflows is still fairly modest—3.5 to 4 percent between 1994 and 1997, and since then less than 3 percent—it can be hoped that, with the integration of these countries into the world economy, these levels will rise dynamically, even in the medium term. As far as capital exports are concerned, the transforming economies of Central and Eastern Europe realize less than 0.5 percent of the total foreign direct capital investments in the world economy. Although it can justifiably be supposed that a very limited number of major national corporations in the region will be able to embark on the path towards transnationalization following the successful privatization process, it seems clear that this region, even in the long term, will play a role in the world economy predominantly as a net capital importer.

In Central and Eastern Europe the wave of company buy-outs was mainly realized through privatization. The most frequent form of company merger is for two foreign-owned daughter companies to be merged in the given transforming economy following the merger of the mother companies.

As regards the attraction of foreign direct investment into the transforming economies of Central and Eastern Europe, the growth in 1998 was only 6 percent, while portfolio investments dramatically fell due to the Asian and Russian crises and, above all, the collapse of the Russian financial system. However, total foreign direct investment of slightly less than USD 24 billion mean that, relatively, the region's capacity to attract foreign capital significantly decreased in 1998. Almost two-thirds of the USD 24 billion total—that is, USD 16.5 billion—flowed into the ten associate members of the European Union. When analyzing the ten EU associate member states' capacity to attract capital, the years 1995 and 1998 can be regarded as particularly significant. In 1995 foreign direct investment inflow by the ten EU associate member states in the region doubled compared to the average over the previous years. Ninety percent of this sudden growth was realized in two counties—

Foreign direct investment inflow in Central and Eastern Europe
(end-of-year balance, USD million)

Country	1990	1991	1992	1993	1994	1995	1996	1997	1998
Czech Republic	72	595	2889	3,423	4,547	7,350	8,572	9,234	13,457
Slovakia	-	-	-	453	762	1,066	1,361	1,558	1,888
Hungary	*569*	*2,107*	*3,435*	*5,585*	*7,095*	*11,926*	*14,668*	*15,882*	*18,255*
Poland	-	-	1,125	2,840	4,715	8,374	12,872	17,780	24,780
Poland	2	115	405	985	1,527	2,659	5,427	8,504	13,633
Slovenia	-	-	-	954	1,325	1,760	2,052	2,285	2,863
Central Europe	-	-	-	*13,255*	*18,444*	*30,476*	*39,525*	*46,739*	*61,243*
Albania	-	-	20	78	131	201	291	339	384
Bulgaria	4	60	101	141	247	337	446	951	1,352
Romania	-	40	117	211	552	971	1,234	2,449	4,480
Croatia	-	-	13	109	222	324	857	1,344	2,217
Macedonia	-	-	-	-	24	33	44	60	177
S-east Europe	-	-	-	539	1,176	1,866	2,872	5,143	8,610
Former USSR	-	-	*187*	*3,105*	*5,360*	*9,833*	*15,865*	*26,824*	*34,541*
Baltic States	-	-	-	836	1,369	1,884	2,662	3,461	5,022
Estonia	-	-	-	419	696	955	1,026	1,148	1,822
Latvia				163	394	577	936	1,272	1,575
Lithuania				254	279	352	700	1,041	1,625
CIS (Europe)			170	1,613	2,434	4,799	7,894	15,032	18,191
Russia				1,211	1,851	3,867	6,346	12,589	14,772
CIS (Asia)			17	656	1,557	3,150	5,309	8,331	11,328
10 EU associate member states				*14,443*	*20,612*	*33,668*	*43,867*	*53,600*	*72,097*
C- and E Europe	-			*16,899*	*24,980*	*42,175*	*58,262*	*78,706*	*104,394*

Source: Foreign Direct Investment in Central and East European Countries and the Former Soviet Union. WIIW-WIFO DATABASE (Vienna) 1999/258/L/2196. September 1999.

Hungary and Poland. In the case of Hungary, privatization revenues represented the largest proportion of the extremely high foreign direct investment inflow totaling USD 4.65 billion. Following a comprehensive rescheduling of debts, 1995 was the first year that Poland—the largest country in the region with a population of almost 40 million, and the only country with geo-strategic significance for Western Europe—became open to investors. Compared to the 1995 peak, the years 1996 and 1997 saw a certain decline; however, the capacity of these two countries to attract capital remained significantly more dynamic than in previous periods. Bearing in mind the fact that privatization in Hungary was apparently almost complete by late 1997 and that macroeconomic growth in Poland was likely to see a significant acceleration, it seemed that a new phase had begun in terms of the region's ability to attract foreign direct investment. According to widely accepted expert analysis, among the transforming economies of Central and Eastern Europe Poland has finally taken the position due to it as a result of its geographical location, its extensive domestic markets, and its highly qualified and enterprise-oriented workforce. However, the figures for 1998–99 show that Poland has not been able to increase its performance in terms of attracting capital as might have been expected after 1996–97.

The "spurt" in Czech foreign direct investment inflow in 1998–99 can be seen as an interesting new development. Up until 1997, and especially before 1995, it had been unclear why so little foreign direct investment was flowing into the Czech Republic; today it is just as difficult to tell what lies behind the improved 1998–99 performance.

In 1998–99, significant restructuring within the region shook Hungary's previously unchallenged leading position. Firstly, Poland's capacity to attract capital increased significantly and appeared to stabilize, following levels of USD 4 to 5 billion in 1996–97, at almost USD 7 billion annual capital imports.[59] The

Czech Republic's capacity to attract capital also rose significantly in 1998–99 compared to the modest performance of previous years: the country that was regarded as the "star pupil" of the region attracted between USD 650 and 900 million in 1993–94, and levels barely exceeded USD 1.4 billion in 1996–97. (The figure only rose to USD 2.5 billion following Skoda-related investments.) In the last two years, Czech capacity to attract foreign direct investment seems to have stabilized at around USD 3 billion.[60]

*

In terms of foreign direct investment inflow, the past decade has been an undeniable success story in Hungary: prior to the stabilization of 1995–96, this was probably the only success story in the Hungarian economy.

It is a success story in the quantitative sense, since out of all the countries of the region the highest level of foreign direct investment flowed into Hungary—per person, as a percentage of the GDP, and compared to domestic fixed capital formation. During the 1990s, foreign direct investment significantly mitigated the economic decline. Hungary's share of the total direct foreign investment in the world economy has been permanently—over the past decade—at least double Hungary's share in world trade (0.8 to 1 percent compared to 0.3 percent).

It is also a success story in terms of quality. The significant transformation of the geographical orientation of foreign trade transactions in an incredibly short period of two to three years; technical developments; the rapid development of the corporate economy; and the general promotion of marketing attitudes—in short, the rapid and successful corporate transformation that has taken place—would have been unthinkable without the appearance and activity of foreign capital. Hungary's export performance has undeniably had, and continues to have, a favorable impact on the

Repatriated profits and foreign direct investment in the world economy

		1991-1997**	1995	1996	1997	1998	1999
World economy	Repatriated profit (RP)*	81,773	98,179	11,894	108,589		
	FDI*	217,962	247,874	282,671	351,530		
	RP/FDI (%)	37.5	35.8	39.6	30.9		
Developed countries	Repatriated profit (RP)	56,572	65,438	74,332	74,627		
	FDI	138,220	181,284	171,902	211,271		
	RP/FDI (%)	40.9	36.1	43.2	35.3		
Developing countries	Repatriated profit (RP)	24,828	32,281	36,970	33,021		
	FDI	73,823	81,698	101,984	129,913		
	RP/FDI (%)	33.6	39.5	36.3	25.4		
Latin America	Repatriated profit (RP)	8,350	8,732	10,781	14,200		
	FDI	28,568	19,784	41,148	60,277		
	RP/FDI (%)	29.2	29.3	26.2	23.6		
Central and Eastern Europe	Repatriated profit (RP)	332	460	592	941		
	FDI	5,919	11,505	8,786	10,347		
	RP/FDI (%)	5.6	4.0	6.7	9.1		
Hungary***	Repatriated profit (RP)			238	421	902	823
	FDI			2,040	2,107	1,946	1,657
	RP/FDI (%)			11.7	20.0	46,4	49,8

* In USD million

** Annual average

*** Author's own estimates based on the Hungarian National Bank's balance of payments figures.

Source: WIR '99, p. 165; and Hungarian National Bank: balance of payments figures

trade balance. At the same time, it provides a primary source for financing the current account balance of payments deficit. The branch distribution of Hungarian foreign direct investment inflow is particularly favorable: the processing industry, and within this sector the machine industry, attracted/attracts the most foreign direct investment in Hungary. At the same time, the proportion of investments in services—telecommunications, financial services, transportation, trade and real estate development—is also extremely high compared with elsewhere in the region.

Before 1997 the level of repatriated profits was insignificant. Although this figure rose sharply in 1997–98, but especially in 1998,[61] it was somewhat lower in 1999: that is, by international standards, an acceptable amount of profit was taken out of the country by foreign investors. According to the preliminary figures of the Central Bank the value of repatriated profits in the balance of payments of the 1999 financial year was USD 883 million.[62]

This amount in itself gives no cause for concern: compared to the total of almost USD 21.5 billion foreign direct investment inflow up to 31 December 1999, it hardly exceeds 4 percent and the rate was not higher in fiscal 2000 either. It is obvious, however, that foreign owners do not extract income from their investments only in the form of profit repatriation.[63] If we suppose, however, that the total income taken out of the country is double the repatriated profit, the total of USD 1.7 to 1.8 billion income extracted, which represents about 8 percent of the total foreign direct investment, cannot be regarded as "tragic". The picture is not so positive if we compare repatriated profits with the annual inflow of foreign direct investment: as Table 3 shows, in 1998–99 this ratio was highly unfavorable, even by international standards.

The problem is obviously not caused by the levels of repatriated profits but by the significant slowdown in the inflow of foreign direct investment in 1998–99. The profit repatriation rate in Hungary, which is particularly high by Central and Eastern

European standards, can be regarded at the same time as indicative of the strength of the Hungarian performance in attracting foreign direct investment. Foreign direct investment in Hungary are sufficiently mature to allow them to be operated and developed without the need to reinvest the entire profits realized in Hungary.

Foreign direct investment inflow in Hungary
(USD million, 1972-1999)

	In cash*	Privatization income	Investment in kind	Total
1972 - 1989	387	-	783	1,170
1990	311	20	589	900
1991	1,459	435	155	1,614
1992	1,471	492	170	1,641
1993	2,339	1,163	142	2,481
1994	1,147	103	173	1,320
1995	4,453	3,370	185	4,570
1996	1,983	618	57	2,040
1997	2,085	1,827	22	2,107
1998	1,935	485	11	1,946
1999	1,651	295	6	1,657
2000**	1.600	-	-	1,600
1972–1999	19,221	8,814	2,197	21,446
*1972–2000***	*20,821*	*8,814*	*2.197*	*23,046*

* "Shares and other forms of ownership".
** Preliminary figures of the National Bank of Hungary and ÁPV Rt. (the State Privatization and Holding Company).
Source: Ministry of Economic Affairs (IKIM - NGKM), Hungarian National Bank (http://www.mnb.hu//index-n.httm), State Privatization and State Holding Company.

At the same time, the current account balance of payments—or, more exactly, the financeability of the current account balance of payments deficit—requires that foreign direct investment flow in annually to an amount equal to the current account balance of payments deficit. In 1996–97 everyone in Hungary was convinced that this condition could be fulfilled relatively easily. However, the experience of the last two years has prompted a reevaluation of such an optimistic expectation.

According to an OECD survey carried out in 1999[64]—which relies mainly on statistics from 1997—two-thirds of the total output in the processing industry is produced by foreign-owned companies. This is much higher than the role played by foreigners in the Czech, Dutch, French, Norwegian, Turkish, and Italian processing industries, but also exceeds the respective rate in Ireland, which had been a leader in foreign direct investment inflow for decades. In terms of employment statistics, only Ireland belongs in the same category—43 percent of Hungarian employees work for foreign-owned companies, which by international standards is extremely high.

1. The place and role of foreign-owned companies in the Hungarian economy

The role played by foreign-owned companies in the Hungarian economy is well illustrated by various statistics drawn from the balance figures and tax declarations of partly or entirely foreign-owned joint enterprises. These figures are taken from the publicly accessible data of APEH (Tax and Financial Control Administration), the Central Statistical Office, and the Court of Registration.

Foreign ownership exceeds the national average of 43.3 percent in industry (especially in the food industry and in the production of machine and car components), in other services (especially real estate services), in trade (by 12.2 percent) and in financial services (by 11.3 percent). However, foreign ownership is below average in agriculture (6.2 percent), in the construction industry, in transportation, and in other services (excluding real estate).

There is a clear tendency for foreign capital investors to aim to achieve complete, or at least majority, ownership: minority foreign ownership is becoming more and more the exception that proves the rule. It is no surprise, therefore, that 86 percent of the total capital of partly or entirely foreign-owned companies is in the hands of foreign owners.

Over 61 percent of employees in the processing industry are employed in companies with foreign interest, and the respective proportion in trade is 14 percent; in the hotel and catering industry the figure is 2.7 percent, and in transportation and telecommunication it is 5.1. (In the last three branches, however, it is mainly foreigners who fill the higher management positions that provide lucrative income.)

In the table above, the row giving figures for the machine industry, set in bold, reflects a typical tendency: between 1996 and 1998 the number of those employed in the machine industry fell from 231,862 to 220,722, while the number of those employed in foreign-owned companies in the machine industry rose from 84,965 to 121,312. This means that the percentage of those working for foreign-owned companies in the machine industry increased from 16.5 percent to 21 percent.

The average wage of employees of foreign companies significantly exceeds the average wage of employees of Hungarian firms: throughout the national economy as a whole the former earned 47.2 percent more in 1997, and 46.98 percent more in 1998.[65] In the machine industry the difference was 18.66 and 15.1 percent., while in trade, the employees of foreign-owned companies in 1997 and 1998 earned 72.4 and 82.1 percent more respectively than the average for the branch.[66] The differences in wages are even more extreme in the "transportation, warehousing, post, and telecommunications" sector, where the difference in wages in 1997 was 88.74 percent, and 80.5 percent in 1998.

Number, equity capital, and foreign capital of enterprises with foreign interest, between 1990 and 1998
(expressed as percentage)

	1990	1991	1992	1993	1994	1995	1996	1997	1998
Number of enterprises									
Organizations entirely in foreign ownership	4.1	13.0	27.0	35.1	39.8	43.9	47.5	5. 36	57.0
Organizations with foreign majority ownership	11.2	22.0	25.0	27.5	29.1	27.9	26.3	24.8	23.6
Organizations with domestic majority ownership	84.7	65.0	48.0	37.4	31.1	28.2	26.2	21.6	19.4
Total	100.0	100.0	100.0	100.0	100.0	100.0	100.0	100.0	100.0
Registered capital									
Organizations entirely in foreign ownership	2.0	8.1	16.6	18.2	24.2	24.5	28.1	30.9	35.3
Organizations with foreign majority ownership	16.6	31.2	38.7	38.3	32.3	36.1	40.2	42.3	48.9
Organizations with domestic majority ownership	81.4	60.7	44.7	43.5	43.5	39.4	31.7	26.8	15.8
Total	100.0	100.0	100.0	100.0	100.0	100.0	100.0	100.0	100.0
Foreign capital									
Organizations entirely in foreign ownership	5.8	17.8	29.4	30.6	40.6	37.2	39.7	41.0	44.3
Organizations with foreign majority ownership	31.7	48.5	50.4	50.1	43.4	42.4	44.1	45.0	49.0
Organizations with domestic majority ownership	62.5	33.7	20.2	19.3	16.0	20.4	16.2	13.9	6.7
Total	100.0	100.0	100.0	100.0	100.0	100.0	100.0	100.0	100.0

Source: *Külföldi működő tőke Magyarországon 1997-1998* (Foreign direct investment in Hungary, 1997-1998). Central Statistical Office, 2000, p. 25.

Numbers and percentages of employees, 1998

Economic branches	Total number of employees	of which: those working in companies with foreign interest	Proportion of employees	of which: those working in companies with foreign interest
	Persons		%	
Agriculture, game and forestry, and fishing	162,107	6,386	7.6	1.1
Mining	10,443	3,104	0.5	0.5
Processing industry	791,573	355,285	37.0	61.4
Food, drinks, tobacco industry	138,149	56,593	6.5	9.8
Textiles, clothing, leather industry	138,076	51,230	6.5	8.9
Wood, paper and printing industry	62,538	17,281	2.9	3.0
Chemical industry	87,862	57,632	4.1	10.0
Non-metallic mineral products	34,681	17,512	1.6	3.0
Smelting and metallurgical industry	81,562	26,465	3.8	4.6
Machine industry	220,722	121,312	10.3	21.0
Other processing industries	27,983	7,260	1.3	1.3
Electricity, gas, heat and water supply	88,844	33,484	3.9	5.8
Construction industry	141,492	14,591	6,6	2.5
Trade, road vehicle maintenance, and maintenance of consumer goods	372,288	81,485	17.7	14.1
Hotel and catering industry	62,289	14,924	2.9	2.6
Transportation, post, telecommunications	231,440	29,772	10.8	5.1
Real estate	206,596	32,296	9.5	5.6
Education	6,932	398	0.3	0.1
Health, social security	20,081	1,491	0.9	0.3
Other services	49,045	5,125	2.3	0.9
Total	2,138,130	578,341	100.0	100.0

Source: *Külföldi működő tőke Magyarországon 1997-1998* (Foreign direct investment in Hungary, 1997-1998). Central Statistical Office, 2000, p. 39.

The Central Statistical Office's 1997–98 figures for the foreign-trade turnover of companies with foreign interest reflect one of the more surprising features specific to Hungarian foreign-trade relations. The turnover of Hungarian companies with foreign interest in terms of foreign trade with developed countries and the EU had virtually a zero balance in 1997 and in 1998 saw a slight surplus, while in relation to Central and Eastern European and "other countries" there was a deficit.

Foreign-trade turnover of companies with foreign interest,
(1997-1998, HUF billion)

Country	Imports	Exports	Imports	Exports
	1997		1998	
Developed countries	2,116.4	2,110.5	3,062.8	3,111.7
of which: EU countries	1,821.8	1,948.1	2,619.1	2,817.5
CEE countries	510.9	454.5	588.3	539.3
Developing countries	213.2	66.6	367.9	133.6
Other countries	40.5	17.4	68.7	21.5
Total:	2,881.0	4,087.7	2,649.0	3,806.1

Source: *Külföldi működő tőke Magyarországon 1997-1998* (Foreign direct investment in Hungary, 1997-1998). Central Statistical Office, 2000, p. 58.

Foreign-trade turnover of companies with foreign interest, according to country, 1997-1998
(HUF billion)

Country	Imports	Exports	Imports	Exports
	1997		1998	
Austria	329.3	298.1	427.8	374.1
USA	109.7	87.6	159.4	194.0
France	133.1	100.3	189.5	137.9
Holland	70.1	75.9	94.9	203.2
Germany	801.5	1,063.4	1,200.2	1,431.9
Italy	183.0	139.6	260.6	196.3
Switzerland	48.8	31.2	66.7	43.8

Source: *Külföldi működő tőke Magyarországon 1997-1998* (Foreign direct investment in Hungary, 1997-1998). Central Statistical Office, 2000, p. 59.

The Central Statistical Office defines as "companies with foreign interest" companies registered on the stock exchange, in which, according to their stock register as of their last annual general meeting, the foreign share in the subscribed capital is at least 10 percent. According to this definition, MOL Rt. is a company with foreign interest, and the entire crude oil and natural gas imports of the country are included in this category.

Foreign-trade product turnover of companies with foreign interest, according to major types of goods, 1997–1998
(HUF billion)

Type of goods	Import		Export	
	1997	1998	1997	1998
CEE countries				
Food, drinks, tobacco	11.6	17.3	103.6	122.6
Raw materials	21.5	24.2	36.2	32.0
Fuels	292.7	288.7	29.3	21.2
Processed products	155.1	201.8	197.1	249.1
Machines and means of transport	30.0	56.3	88.3	114.4
Total:	5,140.9	588.3	454.5	539.3
Developed countries				
Food, drinks, tobacco	53.7	70.3	120.8	146.9
Raw materials	40.3	48.9	37.3	39.3
Fuels	33.5	39.1	45.3	46.7
Processed products	866.3	1,190.6	610.5	839.8
Machines and means of transport	1,122.6	1,713.9	1,296.6	2,039.0
Total:	2,116.4	3,062.8	2,110.5	3,111.7

Source: *Külföldi működő tőke Magyarországon 1997-1998* (foreign direct investment in Hungary, 1997-1998). Central Statistical Office, 2000, p. 61.

The figures given in the table are less misleading when broken down for individual countries. Bearing in mind the fact that a significant proportion of foreign-owned companies established in

Hungary carry out extensive activities on the domestic market (consider, for instance, the partly or entirely foreign-owned companies active in trade, telecommunications, transportation, the financial sector, and real estate transactions and development), the low level of deficit should not be surprising. At the same time, this cross-section also reveals one of the more surprising features of Hungarian foreign trade: a significant export surplus is realized in Hungary's most important and most extensive trade relationship, that is, in Hungarian-German foreign trade.[67]

The explanation is obvious: German capital in Hungary is predominantly export oriented. Exports are primarily to Germany's own EU—and to the extent that this can be interpreted separately—to its own national, markets, and are made up mostly of machine industrial products (Audi, Opel, Ford Motors, etc.).[68] The "spurt" in exports to Holland in 1998 is also a sign of Philips' major investment bearing fruit.

*

The marked concentration of foreign direct investment inflow in certain areas of the country is a commonly recognized problem: the image of the "two Hungaries" divided by the Danube is confirmed by an analysis of the targets of foreign direct investment inflow (in terms of region or county).

Of the 25,244 registered partly or entirely foreign-owned companies, 59.5 percent (14,520 companies) operate in central Hungary, 11.4 percent (2,886 companies) in Western Transdanubia, and 6.6 percent (1,681 companies) in central Transdanubia. The combined share of the three regions out of the total number of foreign-owned companies is therefore 77.5 percent.[69] The concentration is even higher with respect to registered capital, with 65.5 percent (HUF 2,017 billion) of the HUF 3,078 billion total registered capital of foreign-owned companies being concentrated in central Hungary, 6 percent (HUF 186 billion) in central Transdanubia, and

9 percent (HUF 278.5 billion) in Western Transdanubia. Altogether this represents 81.5 percent (HUF 2,481.5 billion) of the total.

Nevertheless, it would be wrong to overemphasize the negative impact of the regional distribution and concentration of foreign direct investment inflow. Foreign direct investors follow the logical principle of, on the one hand, obtaining through privatization the best Hungarian companies, and, on the other hand, establishing themselves "in the place of" those former socialist large corporations that went bankrupt in the whirlwind of the change of system—or, more exactly, in the transformation crisis—and after the collapse of COMECON. In the unparalleled wave of liquidations in 1992–93, a one-off opportunity opened up for a mass of "brownfield" investments: new production equipment, which was often dismantled and moved from another plant, could be set up in existing industrial buildings that had a suitable infrastructure, and operated by the skilled labor force that had formerly worked in those locations. Audi's first plant in Győr and Opel's investment in Szentgotthárd were typical of such moves—both started their operations in the former Rába works using former Rába employees.

The regional characteristics of the establishment of foreign capital simply reflect the process whereby the foreign foreign direct investment that began to flow into the country in 1998 were almost entirely unaffected by any economic-political influence. More exactly, in spite of the inevitable impact of the general economic political liberalization and, what is more, the obvious role it played in turning the country into a popular investment target, it was unable to influence the inflow of capital in terms of either sector or region. The situation—a change of system in politics and a transformation crisis in the economy—is easy to explain and to understand. With hindsight it can also be explained that, in the interests of the acceleration and irreversibility of the economic change of system, the Antall, Boross, and Horn governments deliberately followed Dunning's "non-interventionist scenario".[70]

2. Economic characteristics of companies with foreign interest

In 1997–99 the economic characteristics of companies with foreign interest moved in parallel with those of the national economy, although the rate of increase in performance was significantly more rapid in this sphere. The increase in net sales revenues was about 40 percent, within which the already high export sales showed an approximately 55 percent increase. It is particularly interesting that 88 percent of the total export increase was provided by companies with foreign interest.

It is increasingly important for the future of the Hungarian economy to watch the changes in trend in the gross domestic product (added value). The way the ownership-related characteristics of these behave is especially interesting.

The figures given in the above table suggest that the market results of companies with foreign interest represent a significant force in the country's economic performance. This driving force could be bigger if the domestic enterprises acting as suppliers were better able to meet the requirements of the joint ventures (in relation to deadlines, production capacity, quality, market prices, etc.). The optimum exploitation of this capacity is temporarily hindered by the fact that domestic companies, due to their lack of capital, are unable to keep pace with the development of companies with foreign interest.

The net turnover of all firms operating under company-tax regulations, at current prices, more than doubled from HUF 11.8 trillion in 1995 to HUF 27.7 trillion in 1999. Contributions to this average current-price increase in turnover of 38–40 percent a year came from almost all segments of the economy, although the rates of growth ranged between 15 and 70 percent. The main contributions to the growth in absolute value were made by industry (including manufacturing), trade, transport and telecommunications, and other services. Rates of growth considerably above average occurred in financial services, industry, and transport and telecommunications.

A marked correlation of business results with ownership attributes and stronger concentration can be discerned. Aggregate indicators suggest that the turnover index (at current prices) of firms in majority domestic ownership almost doubled over the period, while that of firms in majority foreign ownership more than tripled. The former just managed to keep ahead of inflation while the later managed a substantial measure of real growth. Deeper analysis shows that a declining number of big companies are capable of determining the overall performance of the economy to an increasing extent.

Firms with foreign ownership perform better than the national average, but industry-level analyses also reveal hectic movements over time and by industries. Upward trends in turnover can be seen in financial services (53.2 percent), other services (46.5 percent), agriculture (43.6 percent), telecommunications, and the industrial categories (including industrial activity in customs-free zones).

The figures for 1995–9 show that the change in added value 'follows' the change in net turnover, where ownership-related attributes can be seen. The aggregate added-value performance of domestic business associations rose by 32–3 percent between 1995 and 1997 and 34–5 percent between 1997 and 1999. Over the same periods, firms with foreign ownership showed an increase of 48–50 percent in the first period (the first two years of an economic stabilization programme) and 36–7 percent in the second.

The difference of performance can also be shown in another way. The per capita value added in 1999 averaged HUF 4.3 million in firms in majority foreign ownership and only HUF 1.6 million in firms wholly in domestic ownership.

The regional distribution of companies with foreign interest is—if possible—even more disproportionate than that of domestic enterprises.[71] The number of enterprises—leaving aside their dominance in the capital—is higher than average in Csongrád, Pest, Győr-Sopron, Bács-Kiskun and Zala counties. The specific value of the registered capital of joint ventures is high in Pest, Győr-Moson-Sopron, Fejér and Vas counties; and Komárom-Esztergom, Borsod-Abaúj-Zemplén, Heves and Hajdú-Bihar counties, as well as Csongrád county, only follow at some significant distance.

Only indirect information can be obtained concerning the motives for foreign investors' preferences in terms of regions and business sites: the proximity of international borders (customs free zones), transportation links (motorways), and the possibility of applying for international grants (from the EU) and regional grants (in Zala county PHARE-CBC grants) all play an important role, although well-equipped industrial parks (as in Győr), successful town promotion (as carried out by Székesfehérvár), or benefits in local taxation (Budaőrs) are also an incentive. Such factors should certainly be emphasized in judging the "appeal" of the various regions, since they can have a telling influence on foreign investors' decisions as to where to establish the site of their operations.

One of the characteristics of companies with foreign interest is that they are alert to opportunities on the domestic and international markets simultaneously. In 1998–99, their performance in Hungary has increased by about 40 percent and on international markets by almost 55 percent, but, more importantly, an increasing proportion of the sales revenues (in 1998 almost one-third) of companies with foreign interest is realized on the international markets. The positive impact of foreign direct investment inflow on foreign trade is clearly illustrated by the fact that in terms of Hungarian processing industry exports between 1990 and 1998, branches requiring high technology[72] rose from 9.73 percent to 35.54 percent, while those requiring medium technology increased from 23.52 percent to 37.12 percent. As a reflection of this, between 1990 and 1998 the weight of branches of the Hungarian processing industry requiring low technology decreased from 66.75 percent to 28.34 percent.[73]

Characteristics of the economic activity of companies with foreign interest and their proportion within the Hungarian economy

(percentages)

	1994	1995	1996	1997	1998	1999
Number of companies	11,2	12,8	10,9	10,6	9,2	9,8
Staff	24,4	25,8	26,8	28,4	27,8	29,2
Net turnover	38,3	63,3	43,2	47,8	48,9	51,7
Out of: exports	*58,8*	*63,3*	*69,4*	*74,0*	*77,2*	*82,0*
Domestic sales	*35,3*	*37,6*	*38,8*	*41,7*	*41,6*	*43,3*
Gross value added	39,4	45,0	47,4	49,6	52,1	52,4
Total costs and fees	38,7	42,3	44,0	47,9	48,2	51,3
Out of: materials	*41,5*	*44,3*	*48,4*	*55,3*	*57,0*	*61,8*
Wages	*32,8*	*35,7*	*39,9*	*41,3*	*42,7*	*44,6*
Social security	-	-	-	*42,9*	*44,3*	*47,5*
Amortization	*49,1*	*51,5*	*50,5*	*53,5*	*53,7*	*56,9*
Investment	81,5	80,2	79,1	75,2	84,6	88,2
Pretax profits	41,5	43,2	53,7	57,1	60,1	52,4
Pre tax losses	-36,1	-41,8	-42,2	-43,9	-49,4	-53,1
Tax in book value	48,8	43,6	53,7	76,4	61,0	62,4
Tax allowances	27,8	92,5	95,6	96,0	95,5	96,4
Corporate tax paid	26,8	36,2	39,0	44,9	45,7	49,1
After tax losses	46,5	44,4	56,2	59,2	63,1	63,9
After tax losses	-36,1	-41,7	-40,1	-42,6	-52,5	-52,9
Dividend paid	64,3	60,7	69,4	73,7	69,2	61,5
Revenues in the balance	36,1	40,1	57,1	59,1	60,5	64,9
Subscribed capital	38,7	40,5	45,2	46,9	46,6	58,0
Out of: foreign	*59,6*	*65,9*	*70,6*	*75,3*	*80,0*	*85,7*
Total equity capital	38,1	41,5	45,8	48,8	50,6	57,8
Share of the increase of equity capital	70,2	69,7	78,5	64,1	62,2	78,7

Source: Zoltán Pitti and GKI Economic Research Co.

Pre-tax profits are fundamentally modified by items—resulting from the goals of actual economic policy—that increase or decrease book income. The assets of business associations have been rising slowly, but steadily in recent years. The pace seems to have increased in the last two or three years, especially in 1999. (This conclusion is supported by the 1999 published-accounts data for retained profits and capital reserves.) The total assets of domestically owned firms in fiscal 1999 remained unchanged, which clearly reflects a difference of corporate behavior. The accumulation of capital was confined to firms with foreign ownership. As a natural consequence of that, the proportion of foreign ownership of assets increased from 38 per cent in 1998 to 49 per cent in 1999. Without exaggeration, 1999 can be said to have brought the biggest increase in the assets of business associations so far, with the aggregate registered capital reaching HUF 1.6 trillion and the asset value rising to HUF 3.2 trillion. Among companies with foreign interest the following profit-reducing items were higher than average:

- Amortization determined as applicable according to the Tax Law.
- Loss carried forward from the previous year and taken into account as a loss in the current year.
- Provisions, that is, amount taken into account as an increasing item in the previous year.
- The sum of dividends and revenues received.
- Reimbursed corporate tax.

In fiscal 1998, the balance of HUF 262.4 billion in the national economy's overall performance resulted from the losses of HUF 732.1 billion produced by enterprises with negative performance and the profits of HUF 994.5 billion produced by enterprises with a positive performance. Items increasing pre-tax profit also reflect the special position of companies with foreign interest, since depreciation accounted for as costs in accordance with the Law on Accounting; loss in value taken into account as expenditure for book purposes; and the costs of non-profit-making activities outside the scope of the enterprise fall below average, thus making the taxation position of companies with foreign interest more favorable overall. On the whole, the improvement in performance exceeds even the rate of change in revenues, and this—at least in the case of profitable enterprises—may lead to an improvement in the profitability of the economy.

The force of the favorable change is weakened by the fact that the total accumulated (accrued) losses during the period of economic crisis did not decrease—in fact, they further increased to the amount of the losses accrued by the performance in 1998 of companies producing a loss. The balance in 1998 of enterprises operating according to the rules of corporate taxation includes altogether HUF 720.4 billion accrued losses (only 45 percent of which are the losses of the "newly created" companies with foreign interest), which, even in the presence of sustainable growth, can only be reduced to a tolerable level in the longer term.

The profitability of companies with foreign interest in Hungary between 1992 and 1994 was higher than the average for Hungarian enterprises. (Domestic enterprises in this period realized negative results.) The difference between the two in the years 1995 to 1997 fell to a minimum (since in this period Hungarian enterprises saw an upturn, while companies with foreign interest were still making large-scale investments). Another turn has been seen in 1998–99, when, with earlier investments bearing fruit, the difference in profitability again seemed to increase. However, the favorable turn overall should not allow us to forget that macroeconomic pointers with respect to profit/capital ratios still fall behind international averages—hence the often-voiced opinion of international advisors, according to which the growth in the inflow of foreign capital into Hungary is rather an expression of confidence than the result of economic judgement. In other words, keeping up the interest of foreign capital in domestic investment opportunities (and turning the profit of companies with foreign interest in Hungary back into the domestic economy) will only be possible in the event of a significant change in the profitability statistics.

The equity capital of companies with foreign interest increased at a rate exceeding the average; HUF 661.3 billion (92.5 percent) out of the total increase of HUF 714.6 billion was realized in this sphere. Companies with foreign interest received additional resources as a result of new investments, and also undertook organizational integration (so improving their specific indicators). Meanwhile, the number of Hungarian-owned companies, or those with domestic majority stakes, increased more rapidly than the value of their own assets, which means that their specific indicators changed drastically for the worse.

The performance of companies with foreign interest is increasing more rapidly than average, and their financial policies are stricter. This, along with the benefits provided by the Hungarian state, means that they perform better. This can be measured by the growth in the enterprises' net worth. Their operating ratios are more favorable than the average for Hungarian enterprises, and due partly to this and partly to their economic background, they have a greater impact on the Hungarian economy than their actual ownership share. Besides the direct impact, companies with foreign interest play an important indirect role through their commissioning of domestic companies, which significantly influences the Hungarian economy's market opportunities.

Comparing firms in total or majority foreign ownership with domestic firms (the figures in brackets), the following could be observed:

1. The average net turnover per foreign firm was HUF 547.7 million (HUF 57.3 million).

2. The value of exports per firm reached HUF 190.7 million (HUF 4.6 million).

3. The GDP figure per firm was HUF 105.6 million (HUF 10.4 million) and the GDP figure per employee HUF 4.3 million (HUF 1.6 million).

4. Although foreign firms receive 96 per cent of the tax concessions provided in the economy, the tax paid per foreign firm was

HUF 4.3 million (HUF 0.5 million), since the pre-tax profit per firm averaged HUF 32.8 million (HUF 1.8 million).

Higher pay: The more efficient and profitable business activity of firms with foreign ownership is also reflected in higher pay to their employees. The average pay level of wholly foreign-owned firms stands at 126.9 per cent of the overall pay level in the corporate sphere. In wholly foreign-owned firms employing 51–1000 persons, the pay level is over 30 per cent higher than average. Here the branch structure is interesting. Firms in total or majority foreign ownership pay particularly well in transport, warehousing, postal services and telecommunications, where they exceed the branch average by 52 per cent and the corporate-sphere average by 80 per cent. Firms in total and majority foreign ownership also pay much more than average in chemicals, commercial services and trade. Foreign-owned firms do not typically employ unregistered labour (or if they do, they conceal the fact well). Furthermore, they pay most of their tax and social-security obligations promptly.

The aggregate relations of business associations with public finance have changed favorably in recent years. There has been a steady decline in the value of the budget subsidies applied for (and received). Meanwhile the direct and indirect payments into the budget have risen fast, against stable levels of taxation. The public-finance relations of firms with foreign ownership present a mixed picture. They do not receive direct subsidies, but they remain the recipients of 96 percent of the tax concessions. Their contribution to tax revenues is rising. GKI Economic Research Co. estimates that 49.5 percent of the corporate taxes (HUF 111 billion out of HUF 225 billion) was paid in fiscal 1999 by firms in majority foreign ownership. The increasing employment that they provide and the higher-than-average earnings of their employees mean that they paid a total of HUF 457 billion into the social security budget in 1999. Foreign owned companies have a further fiscal obligation: they paid in fiscal 1999 HUF 52 billion into the 'Unemployment risk fund'[74] and their employees paid about HUF 243 billion of personal income tax.[75] These items (111 + 457 + 243 + 52) add up to a total contribution to the public-finance system of almost HUF 864 billion forint.

Although the statistics speak for themselves, it is still worthwhile summarizing the main points in relation to the operations in Hungary of companies with foreign interest:

- In every area of the ever more globalized world the role of foreign capital is increasing, and Hungary cannot be an exception to this rule.
- The change of ownership structure has become dramatic; while state ownership decreases, foreign ownership is steadily increasing.
- The improvement in Hungarian enterprises' ability to accumulate has not been able to keep up with the increasing volume of foreign capital, and if no change for the better takes place there may be a further fall in the percentage of domestic ownership.
- The appearance of foreign investors initially mitigated the degree of economic recession, and later on it played an active role in setting the economy on a new track towards development.
- The sensitivity of companies with foreign interest to costs and incomes (and, along with this, their management efficiency) is much keener than that of domestic enterprises.
- The profits of companies with foreign interest—apart from the outstandingly high level of repatriation in 1998 of profits earned in 1997—justifiably remain in Hungary and are used mostly for extending the resources of the economy (which will naturally have an impact on future changes in ownership relations).
- Companies with foreign interest have not so far changed their practice with respect to the distribution of dividends and

stakes in proportion to their performance. Bearing in mind that an ever-increasing number of enterprises belonging in this category are being launched on the stock exchange and that the stock market price is influenced by, among other things, the distribution of dividends, an increased willingness to pay dividends can be expected.

*

According to the assessment of Gábor Hunya and Jan Stankovsky[76] "in the more developed CEE countries, and especially in Hungary, the motivation of the new FDIs has shifted from market takeovers to export-oriented, efficiency-oriented investments". In our opinion this process started much earlier in Hungary and was reflected in the complex multiplier effects of FDIs.[77]

1. It is frequently the case that smaller companies will only take risks abroad, especially in an entirely unfamiliar market, if large corporations known to them have already made investments there.

2. The first investors, paradoxically, inspire their major competitors to invest as well.[78]

3. Major investors very soon attract their regular subcontractors and service providers.[79]

4. The majority of profits from successful investments are reinvested in the country in which the profits were made.

5. Successful operations—resulting from Hungary's favorable (from several points of view) geographical location and the related transportation opportunities—may inspire investors to establish regional or sub-regional production, services, and/or logistic centers.[80]

The consequence of the combined "multiplier effects"[81] is that "investments create investments", and the greatest accolade for the Hungarian economy is the fact that earlier investments have created further investments, producing greater added value, with foreign investors integrating their Hungarian daughter companies more closely into their global network. General Electric's more and more recent developments;[82] Audi's engine assembly plant producing 6 percent domestic added value, as well as their DM 700 million major factory assembling two types of car; the realization of the production in Hungary of increasingly large and complex computer units by IBM, which has become the largest Hungarian processing industry exporter; foreign telecommunications companies investing hundreds of millions of dollars in Hungary every year; Philips, TDK, Sony, Temic, Siemens, etc., which are putting into operation new processing industry plants almost every year—all of these illustrate that whoever has once invested in Hungary will carry on investing, will reinvest profits made in Hungary, and will, in addition, realize new investments. This short list of companies also clearly reflects the fact that multinationals have made an increasing number of strategic investments in Hungary since 1995–96, which undoubtedly indicates a new era of foreign direct investment inflow in Hungary.

*

Privatization represents a distinct area in Hungarian capital imports: Hungary is practically the only country in the region which has not, even in the first period (decade) of the change of system, discriminated against foreign investors. On the contrary, it has continually encouraged foreigners to participate more actively in privatization.

We will not discuss here the relationship between privatization and foreign direct investment in detail, since privatization was the subject of the previous chapter. However, it makes sense at this point to clear up a common misunderstanding. Although approximately 70 percent of privatization revenues were realized in hard currency, and thus foreign capital clearly played a very significant role in privatization in Hungary, it would not be true to say that the majority of Hungarian foreign direct investment inflow flowed into the country as a result of privatization-type company buy-outs. Up to 31 December 1997 almost USD 18 billion of foreign direct investment flowed into Hungary, of which USD 7.058 billion (39.62 percent) was in the form of privatization revenues. It can be said, therefore, that out of the foreign direct investment that flowed into Hungary, approximately 40 percent flowed in via privatization, while the proportion of greenfield investments and of additional investments (including capital increases and reinvested profits) was 30 percent in each case.

One of the interesting consequences of privatization is the phenomenon—often erroneously called "secondary privatization"—whereby the new owner of former state property acquired through privatization is forced to resell, often relatively quickly. The second owner is most often a foreign professional investor who, were we not to give him the benefit of the doubt, might well be supposed to have been behind the first purchaser, who was hired to obtain the financial benefits offered to domestic entrepreneurs. Here we might call to mind the privatization of the vegetable oil producer Martfűi Növényolajipari Vállalat (Martfű vegetable Oil Co.), where the multinational giant that had been excluded from the privatization tender bought, practically on the day the privatization contract was signed, the very division in which it had been interested. The Nagykanizsai Sörgyár (Nagykanizsa Brewery Co.) changed hands three times before finally being closed down by South African Breweries, the owner of the largest brewery in the country covering 40 percent of the market. Also of interest in this connection is the complex transaction between the American MediaOne and Deutsche Telekom, as a result of which 49 percent of both Westel 900 Rt. and Westel Rádiótelefon Kft. got into the hands of Matáv Rt.'s German majority owner, making Matáv the 100 percent owner of the two Westel companies.[83] The total value of the transaction was USD 885 million (!), which makes it the largest company buy-out in Hungarian economic history.[84]

*

The statistics analyzed above, illustrating the place of foreign-owned companies in the Hungarian economy, are, at the same time, indicative of the deteriorating financial position, and above all the vanishing assets, of Hungarian-owned, mostly small and medium-sized, enterprises. The sphere of medium-sized companies is virtually missing from the Hungarian economy—the "subcontracting program", which was supported by three consecutive governments in order to strengthen medium-sized enterprises, is practically defunct and non-existent.

The list of the largest amounts of support for economic developments paid in 1999 illustrates the problem: the ten largest benefiting companies were, without exception, foreign-owned big companies, which received state support for the development of altogether nineteen branch sites.

The largest amounts of support for economic developments paid in 1999

(HUF million)

Benefiting company	Total investment costs	Interest-free loans	Non-refundable support
General Electric (6 factories)	13,507.8	1,464.3	79.7
Philips (4 factories)	7,491.5	648.8	-
Robert Bosch Elektronika	15,666.8	368.0	32.0
Nokia	6,137.8	316.6	83.4
Taurus Mg-i Abroncs (2 factories)	2,201.5	5,000.0	-
Temic Telefunken	1,590.9	387.0	-
Zollner Elektronik	2,311.3	136.2	63.8
Massive Hungária	2,950.7	182.5	17.5
Contitech Hungária	2,108.6	165.7	34.3
Clarion Elektronika	2,179.8	175.4	24.6

Source: Based on the Ministry of Economic Affairs, *Népszabadság*, 7 February 2000, p. 11.

The majority of the companies mentioned in the table are "par excellence subcontractors": Bosch, Temic, Contitech, Zollner and Massive Hungary are subcontractors by definition, but the Hungarian branches of Philips, Nokia, and Clarion also carry out mainly subcontracting activities rather than producing end products in Hungary. In Hungary, the subcontractors of transnational companies are predominantly foreign-owned companies: most frequently the global subcontractors of the big multinationals obtain assets in Hungary so that they can carry out the same activity for the Hungarian daughter company of the multinational in question.

Taking into account the fact that the condition for obtaining tax benefits is the realization of an investment of at least HUF 60 billion, it is obvious that those benefiting—despite the theoretical sector neutrality—can only be foreign investors. On the basis of the total value of the nineteen investments listed in the table, the sum of tax benefits, savings on interest-free loans, and non-refundable state support clearly approaches the HUF 13 billion value that the government spent in 1999 on supporting small and medium-sized companies.

The Ministry of Economic Affairs seems to be determined to support the subcontracting program and to stimulate the sector of medium-sized companies—however, out of the HUF 16 billion at the disposal of the ministry for the financial year 2000 it can hardly be expected to work miracles. On the other hand, foreign investors can likely expect HUF 7.5 billion normative support.[85]

*

The impact of foreign direct investment inflow on domestic Research and development is far from positive. The R&D capacities of the acquired Hungarian companies have mostly disappeared, or, in the better case, have been integrated, losing their independence in the owner's global R&D network.[86] In the first period of the transition—approximately 1995–96—the percentage of GDP spent on R&D fell from the earlier level of 2.3 percent to 0.8 percent, and the real value of R&D expenditure fell by 60 percent over a period of seven years. In companies that came into foreign ownership via privatization, the proportion of employees working in the field of R&D fell by 80 (!) percent. In this category of companies R&D activities were usually limited to product and technological adaptation. The transfer of more developed technical cultures, occasionally involving whole branches, can only be cited in the case of greenfield investments. Even here, the "enclave effect" was common—that is, the advanced technology was isolated from the background of the Hungarian economy.[87] By 1998–99 corporate R&D expenditure—although low—had stabilized, and

> "a small group of both Hungarian and partly or entirely foreign-owned companies emerged that showed an interest in R&D (…). Foreign daughter companies are operating small research groups based on the earlier intellectual capacities of the privatized companies and, besides product development and adaptation, also deal with general technical problems that come within the scope of the given company. Some of these companies have gradually 'realized' that it would be a pity to squander the accumulated technical know-how. In addition—especially in the field of telecommunications and software development—specific R&D investments have recently been made."[88]

Now that they have established their presence and familiarized themselves with the Hungarian environment—as well as the purchased Hungarian company (!)—the innovation capacities of the foreign-owned companies already significantly exceeds that of Hungarian-owned companies (which, of course, is also closely related to latter's notorious lack of capital). According to GKI Economic Research Company's research carried out in 1997–98 and involving surveys of several hundred companies, foreign-owned companies are two or three times more innovative than their Hungarian-owned competitors.[89]

In the processing industry three-quarters of the total R&D expenditure was in the chemical industry—predominantly in the pharmaceutical industry—and the proportion spent in the machine industry remained below 20 percent.[90]

One of the most frequent criticisms in connection with the innovatory and R&D activities of foreign-owned companies is that R&D activities in the Hungarian daughter companies of transnational corporations do not represent an independent domestic initiative but rather R&D "contract production". From among the widely known examples that run counter to this rule, the GE Tungsram Research Institute and the Knorr-Bremse–Budapest Technical University research and development cooperation are always mentioned in first place—and deservedly so.

The two cases are only comparable in terms of their significance and success; otherwise they are of an entirely different nature. General Electric "inherited" Tungsram's famous laboratory with its rich tradition in research, and after a few years of hesitation integrated it into its global R&D system. This was done in such a way—and this is the truly unique feature of the multinational's Hungarian activities—that GE Tungsram became not a "subcontractor" or contract producer, but an independent unit. Knorr-Bremse, on the other hand, based its Hungarian research facility, which today employs more than one hundred engineers, on the vehicles department of the Budapest Technical University (relying predominantly on the department head, Professor László Palkovits). After a few years it had become one of the independent development units of the multinational brake system manufacturer. The GE Tungsram project is probably one of the few examples of the preservation of traditional Hungarian industrial R&D, while the Knorr-Bremse–Technical University cooperation is a rare and successful example of newly created R&D based on a Hungarian university/academic research base.

The 20 biggest spending companies on R&D in Hungary

Company name	R&D expenditure (USD million)	R&D expenditure as a percen-tage of sales revenues
General Motors	4.99	4.9
Ford Motors	3.85	4.1
Siemens	2.75	7.6
IBM	2.62	5.5
Hitachi	2.35	5.9
Toyota	2.11	5.7
Matsushita Electric	2.03	5.7
Daimler-Benz	1.91	4.6
Hewlett-Packard	1.87	7.2
Ericsson Telefon	1.86	14.5
Lucent Technologies	1.84	11.5
Motorola	1.67	9.2
Fujitsu	1.65	7.8
NEC	1.63	7.0
Asea Brown Boveri	1.61	8.5
El Du Pont de Nemours	1.58	5.8
Toshiba	1.55	6.1
Novartis	1.54	11.8
NTT	1.54	3.7
Volkswagen	1.49	3.9

Source: Lilla B. Horváth: "Tudásipar: erősödő multihatás" (Knowledge industry: the intensifying effects of multinationals). In: *Világgazdaság Évkönyv 1999*.

Research and development capacities in the chemical industry are also significant: "The pharmaceutical industry is outstanding in this respect; within it, Sanofi transformed the research institute of the former Chinoin company into one of its research centers, and the Philaxia–Sanofi 'marriage'[91] led to similar developments." The fact remains, however, that these pharmaceutical research projects are directed at specialized areas; they are generally initiated by the mother company's central research laboratory and are carried out under its direct control.

From the point of view of R&D, the domestic software development centers of the great multinational investors are a particularly successful area of Hungarian foreign direct investment. The pioneer in this respect was probably Ericsson Telecommunication Co., the Hungarian affiliate of the Swedish telecommunications multinational. At its software center, which has been under development since 1994, the present workforce of 220—mostly highly qualified—employees is responsible for providing software for all the south and southeastern European investments of the mother company, and for carrying out necessary software adaptations. Established in 1998, the software development institute of the Finnish company Nokia currently employs a workforce of 350; there are plans to increase the number of employees to 500, which is regarded as the optimum figure.[92] Siemens Rt. already employs 550 highly qualified researchers in its R&D units, and the American informatics giant Compaq opened its Budapest research base in January 2000.[93] According to information published by the economic daily *Világgazdaság*, Motorola and Philips also plan to establish Hungarian software development centers. The paper's survey also indicates that about one-third of the 1,500 informaticians who graduate each year find a job in the Hungarian-based affiliate companies of multinational firms. Half of this group of graduates (that is, 250 to 300 persons) find work in the field of R&D, and predominantly in software development.[94]

*

From the point of view of the Hungarian economy's room for maneuver within the world economy, four questions deserve special attention:

- What kind of future growth will take place in the world economy (and within this, predominantly in the EU), and what will be the time span and pace of the accumulation that can be financed in those countries with savings that can be mobilized?
- What kind of competition will there be in the world economy (and within this, in CEE countries) for foreign direct investment, and how successful will the Hungarian economy be in this competition?
- What kind of increase in performance and structural changes will it take for domestic enterprises to be able to provide a secure "production cooperative" background for companies with foreign interest?
- In relation to the above question, and with respect to Hungary's expected accession to the EU in 2004, how long will the Hungarian economy be able to maintain its position as a net capital importer?

These questions can in practice be summarized under one point: What is the most effective way to prevent foreign-owned companies that settle in Hungary from creating export enclaves or from becoming "cathedrals in the desert", whose only contacts with the host national economy take place in the context of the latter's role as a labor-force provider? Looked at from a different angle, the question concerns whether, how, and with what efficiency, the mass presence of transnational companies in Hungary will be able to serve the successful integration of the Hungarian national economy as a whole into the world economy.

Hungary has successfully come through the first quantitative and qualitative phase of the inflow of foreign direct investment.

Today, foreign direct investment does not flow into Hungary in relation to market takeovers. As a result of the multiplier effects of earlier investments, and now that investors have become familiar with the opportunities that exist in the running of Hungarian enterprises and companies, the time has come to make investments that increase efficiency and realize strategic goals.[95] This can be achieved partly by reinvesting profits produced in Hungary, and partly by directing additional resources to the country.

The quantitative decrease over the past two years is, at the same time, a warning sign. The "dream", in which the completion of the privatization process coincided with the official declaration of Hungary's membership of the EU, has not come true. Despite this, efforts to finance the current account balance of payments deficit using the inflow of foreign direct investment cannot be given up. Maintaining the country's capacities for attracting capital must remain one of the fundamental aims of economic policy. The positive image that is painted by international comparisons must not obscure the fundamental tasks that lie ahead for the national economy. Keeping up Hungary's ability to attract capital should also be an integral aspect of the country's accession to the EU—the conclusions are obvious.

If, so far, the Hungarian national economy—for constantly changing reasons—has been able to attract foreign investors without any serious state activity, in the second phase of foreign direct investment inflow it will be essential to carry out goal-oriented state and government activities. However, individual benefits are not primarily what is needed here.[96] In the future, further foreign direct investment should be attracted by the development of the educational and vocational training systems, and by the development of infrastructure, especially transportation infrastructure, so making the country truly accessible.[97] Only on such a basis can investment-supporting projects be built, aimed at the attraction of well-defined groups of investors to specific regions of Hungary.

III. THE ESTABLISHMENT OF THE MONEY- AND CAPITAL MARKET IN THE 1990s*

1. The banking sector

At the moment of the change of regime in 1990 the financial sector in Hungary enjoyed a significant positional advantage compared to the other Visegrád countries. The most important elements of this advantage comprised the establishment of the two-tier banking system in 1987, the approvement of the Securities Act, and the opening of the stock exchange in 1990.

Nevertheless, in terms of international criteria, until the mid-1990s (1995/1996) the Hungarian banking sector, like that of Poland, received only a "B" ranking, while the Czech Republic's banking sector was accorded a higher, "A" ranking. (Naturally, the macroeconomic situation of the country played a part in the judgment, and the Hungarian banks have continuously witnessed an improvement in terms of international ranking since 1996.) At the same time the presence of foreign capital in the banking sector between 1996 and 1999 was at its most extensive in Hungary, while improvement with respect to certain quality indicators was most favorable in this country.

The importance of banking activity within the economy—that is, the monetarization of the economy—is usually described in terms of the balance sheet total of the entire banking system, the broadly defined money supply, and the corporate credit portfolio as a percentage of the GDP.

* The authors of this chapter are Judit Barta and László Molnár, Research Directors at GKI Economic Research Co.

The extent of banking activity within the economy, 1990 to 2000
(percentages)

	1990	1991	1992	1993	1994	1995	1996*	1997	1998	1999	2000
Balance sheet total /GDP	76.5	84.4	72.2	78.0	65.0	63.0	61.0	60.0	62.5	62.0	70.0
M2/GDP	43.8	47.4	51.2	49.6	45.5	42.9	41.5	n.a.	n.a.	n.a.	n.a.
M3/GDP	48.3	54.8	59.4	56.8	52.2	49.9	48.8	n.a.	n.a.	n.a.	n.a.
Corporate credit portfolio /GDP	30.4	30.6	26.1	21.5	22.5	21.5	18.5	19.5	21.0	20.5	n.a.

Source: Hungarian National Bank, Central Statistical Office

According to statistics based on all available indicators, by 1991 the role of the banking sector had already become more extensive than it had been in the 1980s. We now know that this change was only due to the inflationary growth of the year preceding credit consolidation rather than to real growth, and that, following this, the situation deteriorated with respect to every available indicator. The credit position of the entrepreneurial sector became extremely unfavorable, which meant that in the first half of the 1990s the financing of the entrepreneurial sector was excluded from the banking sector.

In 1992 the losses of the Hungarian corporate sector, based on tax returns, were HUF 380 billion, which amounted to 13 percent of GDP. The losses were distributed equally among companies with majority state ownership and other firms. The debts of the loss-making companies totaled HUF 385 billion, which represented almost 60 percent of the corporate credit portfolio. Formerly, companies had based the financing of their working capital on short-term bank loans. Relationships on the financial markets subsequently changed, although only a few companies had the opportunity to change their sources, that is, to change the financing of their operating assets, to their own or alternative capital-market sources. The spiraling interest rates set off by inflation made debts impossible to handle, even among those state-owned companies which, in terms of the market and their technological development, had some chance of staying afloat.

The extent of corporate losses and debts was so great that it became a factor that seriously endangered the stability of the banking system and of the financial system as a whole. Due to the existence of credits that could not be repaid, the majority of commercial banks, which were predominantly domestic and state owned at the time, lost their capital stock, while the loss of the credits that had been paid out was not covered by their own capital but by their customers' money.

The need to maintain a functioning economy made inevitable the stabilization of the financial situation of the strategically important banking sector by means of government intervention. This took the form of credit, bank, and debt consolidation, which was carried out between 1992 and 1995.

Bank consolidation took place in two phases. During the first phase, in 1992/1993, the state bought up bad loans as of late 1991, for 50 percent of their face value, and later credits for 80 percent of their face value, from the banks in question. As a means of payment, twenty-year state bonds were issued. In the second phase, between 1993 and 1994, the most common solution for bank consolidation was the increasing of the banks' equity capital by means of their acquiring stakes in state-issued bonds (called 'consolidation bonds'), then, as a supplementary measure, the offering of subordinated loan capital. Since the problematic assets remained in the banks, and since the representation of the state gained greater weight within the ownership structure, theoretically the state was able more consistently to prescribe and control the supervision and transformation of the banks' organizational, functional, and management system.

The technique used in the consolidation process was, and still is, the subject of major debate. The points of view and the recommendations of both domestic and foreign experts changed several times. Nowadays, perhaps, there is already a consensus that, while bank consolidation in itself was unavoidable, the methods applied were not always optimal, even adequate. According to expert estimates this fact resulted in an extra 10 to 25 percent expenditure.

Of the seven largest commercial banks, three were given a large-scale consolidation-related capital increase. However, the various steps in the credit and bank consolidation involved a total of eighteen banks, to varying degrees. As a result of credit and bank consolidation, in 1994 all the capitalized banks had a positive cash flow and most of them were profitable according to their balance sheets. The capital adequacy of the four entirely capitalized banks—the Hungarian Credit Bank (MHB), the Commercial and Credit Bank (K&H), the Budapest Bank (BB), and the Hungarian Savings Cooperative Bank (MTB)—in 1994/1995 was above 8 percent.[98]

The buy-out of the debts of companies regarded as strategic, and the removal of debts from the banks' portfolios, was obviously aimed at making the financial reorganization of these companies independent of the intentions of the credit-providing banks and at avoiding situations in which the banks carried out only partial debt alleviation.

The fate of those companies whose debts were not bought out, or only partly bought out, by the state, fell into the hands of the banks' decision makers. Of the 13,000 debtors who qualified for participation, only about 24 percent (1,890 debtors) finally applied to take part in the process. From among these, consolidation agreements were made with only 354 enterprises (less than 3 percent of the circle of enterprises originally involved), as a result of which debts totaling HUF 39.9 billion were settled. This involved 27.4 percent of existing bank and state creditors' demands. The debts included in the debt consolidation amounted to 29 percent of the bank debts of the debtors involved, and 60 percent of debts owed to public creditors.

As a result of credit and bank consolidation the HUF 330 billion in consolidation bonds issued up to 31 December 1994 increased the gross state debt. By the end of 1995, as a result of various one-off special offers, the value of the consolidation bonds issued had reached HUF 350 billion. In 1993 the state budget was not yet burdened with the interest on consolidation state bonds. In 1994 the net (following the deduction of interest on loan capital) interest charges with respect to state bonds comprised 1.5 percent of GDP, and 3.5 percent of central budget expenditure. In 1995 the proportions rose to 1.7 percent and 5.4 percent respectively.[99]

At the price of enormous social costs, bank consolidation achieved its main goal: as a result of the process the financial and capital situation of the formerly dominant state banks was stabilized; liability reserves were created to compensate for doubtful and bad debts; progress was made in defining and collecting doubtful and bad credits; and bank management, control, regulation, and risk management activities significantly improved. The example of the Budapest Bank, the Hungarian Credit Bank, and the Commercial Bank proves that, as a result of the foregoing, the consolidated large banks became suitable for privatization. However, the tasks related to the consolidation of the banking sector were completed in their entirety only at the end of the 1990s.

Privatization can be seen as a measure of the success of the consolidation process, because without capital-rich owners consolidation could not be completed since the resources, owners' capital, computer technology/informatics background, and management standards of the banks referred to could hardly keep pace with those of the already privatized banks. This is proved by the loss of markets despite consolidation, by the tendency to be pushed out of the money markets, and, particularly, by the fate of small banks which had neither a large enough market nor sufficient capital reserves to be attractive investment targets. Their fate thus became silent liquidation.

Up to 1993/1994 there was a dynamic increase in the number of organizations; since then there has been a slow decrease which is most likely to be furthered by the wave of mergers that gained strength in 2000.

Number of organizations involved in banking activities, 1987 to 2000

	1988	1989	1990	1991	1992	1993	1994	1995	1996	1997	1998	1999	2000
Commercial banks	8	18	21	31	31	39	40	38	32	32	31	30	29
Specialized banking institutions	14	11	9	7	8	8	6	7	42	n.a.	n.a.	n.a.	n.a.
Investment banks					6	5	6	4	4	4	4	4	4
Savings cooperatives					255	254	254	250	255	270	289	260	260
Credit cooperatives					-	-	4	7	8	8	8	8	8

Sources: Central Statistical Office, National Tax Authority, State Financial Supervisory Authority.
Note: In 1992 a new method of statistical organization was introduced.

The number of Hungarian banks, in terms of recent figures for banking intermediation and compared to recent profitability, is high. A fall in the number of banks is and will be in the near future too, a natural result of market processes. The state could have at best influence this by privatization. The near future will inevitably bring about an increase in asset value per bank, per branch, and per bank employee.

With the change in the number of banks the equity capital naturally increased. However, the banks suffered a loss of capital prior to bank consolidation which, in 1992/1993, amounted to more than HUF 100 billion. On the other hand, the reinvestment of profits and the tightening of the rules of appropriation ultimately targeted the increasing of owners' capital in the banking system, which, by 1995, was 3.3 times higher than in 1990. By 1996, as a result of privatization, reinvested profits, and newly founded banks, owners' capital approached HUF 400 billion. Equity capital, however, remained at 1995 levels.

Between 1990 and 1995 the balance sheet total decreased by 2.4 times (falling behind the nominal GDP). Within a year, by 1996, the balance sheet total had increased by 22 percent. Since 1997, balance sheet total of the Hungarian banking system increased year-by-year and the rate of this increase has been even higher (in each consecutive year) than that of the GDP.

The domestic bank market is oligopolistic. According to its balance sheet total, in 1995 the National Savings Bank (OTP) occupied almost one-third of the banking market, and the six major banks altogether two-thirds of the market. In 1993, however, the latter figure had been 80 percent. As it can bee seen below, this high level of concentration of the Hungarian banking system has diminished in consequence of the successful privatization, but still it is fairly significant. Behind the structural change a twin process was at work. On the one hand, the weight of the large banks which, at the time, were in majority state ownership, was reduced (since they had cleared their portfolios). On the other hand, from 1993 banks in foreign ownership that were founded in the early 1990s, that were unaffected by the banking crisis, and that used cheaper foreign resources, began an intensive expansion, acquiring clients and market share from the formerly market-leading large banks. The majority of larger clients with secure financial backgrounds and with good prospects for development began to change to these banks, further increasing the difficulties faced by the Hungarian-owned large banks. Finally, by the second half of the decade, extremely keen competition had emerged in the banking market.

The high level of concentration in the banking sector was eased by liberalization with respect to the foundation of banks. After this, the concentration according to ownership changed as a result of the privatization process.

The differences between the banking groups are most sharply apparent in terms of changes in the quality indicators. The after-tax profit shows the loss-making effect of the wave of bankruptcies that swept through the economy among Hungarian-owned banks, followed by the improving effect of the subsequent bank and credit consolidation. On the other hand, the favorable position of banks in foreign and mixed ownership reflects the fact that within the same economy could be found groups of companies the financing of which (although only in the event of particular, favorable circumstances) was profitable.

In the case of the Hungarian-owned banks, in the mid-ninetees, that is prior to mass privatization of the Hungarian banking system, negative after-tax profits were accompanied by losses in the balance sheet total and of owners' capital. On the basis of the following figures, it appears obviously that the foreign-owned banks were able to achieve the best specific result indicators.

Between 1992 and 1993 the leverage ratio increased, but in the following two years it already showed a decrease. This can be explained by the rapid increase in own resources, but it also reflects

The distribution of the equity capital of the banking sector, 1993 to 2000
(percentages)

	1993	1994	1995	1996	1997	1998	1999	2000
State/self-government ownership	70	68	42	33	21.7	20.7	19.3	n.a.
Domestic corporate and private ownership	18	15	20	15	15.4	16.0	12.9	n.a.
Foreign ownership	12	16	35	49	60.5	60.6	65.3	n.a.
Cooperative and other ownership	0	1	3	3	2.4	2.7	2.5	n.a.
Total equity capital	100	100	100	100	100.0	100.0	100.0	

Source: National Tax Authority database, Hungarian Banking and Capital Market Supervision

The share of the five largest banks in the assets of the banking system

Year	1989	1990	1991	1992	1993	1994	1995	1996	1997	1998	1999
%	85	80	74	73	70	64	59	60	55	54	54

Source: Hungarian National Bank

the central bank's gradual withdrawal from financing. According to the leverage ratio, banks in mixed ownership use the greatest proportion of external resources, which, in Hungarian practice, usually means resources from private deposits.

According to international practice, (or the BIS capital adequacy requirements) 8 percent capital adequacy is defined by the BIS as the minimum limit required for the safe operation of banks. In Hungary, this 8 percent was achieved in the second phase of bank consolidation (by 1995 almost every bank had achieved this level). Differences in capital adequacy are quite significant, the highest figures usually being produced by foreign banks. However, this also indicates that they cannot, or are not willing to, utilize the available capital appropriately.

Capital adequacy of the banking system, 1992 to 2000
(percentages)

	Capital adequacy
1992	9.03
1993	11.18
1994	15.51
1995	18.24
1996	15.70
1997	16.40
1998	16.79
1999	15.96

Source: Reports by the State Financial Supervisory Authority

In terms of the total assets of the banking system, the proportion of risk-free assets generally increased. In the last one or two years this was predominantly related to the increasing weight of government securities.

The distribution of the banks' qualified loan portfolios, 1992 to 2000
(percentages)

	1992	1993	1994	1995	1996	1997	1998	1999
Problem-free	89.25	70.68	78.67	83.93	89.2	88.5	87.8	88.8
Requiring special attention	10.75	22.53	13.58	9.0	5.0	7.0	7.5	6.6
Below average	2.26	2.94	2.05	1.58	1.0	n.a.	n.a.	n.a.
Doubtful	3.71	6.14	3.41	2.52	1.2	n.a.	n.a.	n.a.
Bad	4.78	13.45	8.12	4.90	2.8	4.5	4.7	4.6
Total	*100.0*	*100.0*	*100.0*	*100.0*	*100.0*	*100.0*	*100.0*	*100.0*
Total (x billion HUF)	1,611	1,828	2,504	2,731	3,818	3,950	3,445	4,076

Source: Reports by the State Financial Supervisory Authority

The extremely rapid development of banking activity can be observed, both in international and domestic practice, in terms of so-called off the balance items. This is where the majority of banking innovations are concentrated. Off the balance operations include the transferring of credits by underwriting, the turning of credits into securities (which will probably turn out to have been the development with the greatest impact in the 1990s), and the rapid increase in money market operations. An analysis of this, however, is impossible without the banks' balance sheets.

The development of the banking sector in the second half of the 1990s was characterized by the application of new financial laws, and by preparations for EU accession and for the introduction of the euro (outside Hungary). The characteristic tendency in the present and near future is and will be a redistribution on the banking market: by the year 2000 the four or five large banks that will continue to define the Hungarian banking sector had been selected as a result of their capital, the diversification of their services, and their profitability. Behind the large banks is emerging a relatively wide and stable stratum of middle-sized banks, comprising six or seven banks; about a dozen small banks specializing in one activity (mostly in vehicle financing); and a stratum which may well consist of several hundred members, having relatively low capital leverage and specializing in one activity, in the form of small banks (savings co-operatives).

The resulting banking structure is, and will be, characterized by the fact the leading banks—apart from the largest, the National Savings Bank (OTP)—are foreign banks. Banks in Hungarian majority ownership survive, and will continue to survive, only to fulfill special, for instance government-backed, development tasks.

In 1996 the amendment of the Banking Act and membership of the OECD created new opportunities for the involvement of foreign capital in the Hungarian banking sector. The Act on the Foundation of Bank Branches, which came into effect on 1 January

1996, made the opening of branches dependent on the same conditions as the founding of banks, thus providing the domestic banks with time to prepare for competition from the new foreign banks.

Besides broadening the banks' sphere of activity, the new legal regulations introduced rules which are, in many respects, stricter than earlier, and which are in harmony with EU principles. The most important of these include the tightening and more accurate interpretation of investment rules. The obtaining of operating licenses was made more difficult, thus the banks' disadvantage in terms of competition with other financial intermediaries will be reduced. The gradual increasing of capital requirements represents a justified tightening of the conditions for entering the market.

As a result of the new regulations the financial institution sector will probably be characterized by greater diversity in terms of type of institution: there will be both banks and special credit institutions, and among these the role of savings banks, and in particular the role of building societies, which are regulated by a special act, will become more important. Among the currently existing commission houses, the largest and strongest in capital—the majority of which are probably operating in affiliation with banks—will be transformed into Western-style investment banks. Banks and other institutions offering insurance-type services (Hitelgarancia Rt., Eximbank) and special mortgage institutions will emerge. In the financial sector, loose conglomerates or groups of institutions working formally as bank holdings (banks, investment banks, insurance companies, building societies, leasing companies, and fund management companies) will become dominant. This institutional structure is already clearly taking shape today, a modern universal banking system is likely to emerge pretty fast.

Between 1998 and 2000 the most rapid and spectacular development took place with respect to retail banking. In the coming three to five years the tendency is likely to continue. The potential size of this market is at least three-times what it is today. In the past five years the proportion of families holding a current account and bank cards has seen a massive increase, as has the number of ATMs and POS terminals. In parallel with this, banks hoping to survive in the retail market are today offering an increasingly comprehensive range of banking services in relation to current accounts. The carrying out of regular and one-off direct debit transactions is becoming a more and more natural service in terms of account keeping, predominantly through the home-banking infrastructure. Besides the appropriate telecommunications infrastructure, which in Hungary is already established, this system depends most heavily on sophisticated services and customer confidence.

In the field of banking/financial innovations, as well as more traditional services, dynamic development and huge medium-term progress can be expected. A wide range of investment and deposit options, insurance products and pension funds, and capital market products and services for the public will emerge. The capital-rich banks with significant branch networks will achieve a dominant position in this market (although computer-network services are also spreading rapidly).

In 1996/1997 the most significant element in the development of the Hungarian banking system was the privatization of the large commercial banks. The main characteristic of the Hungarian banking system—the dominance of foreign ownership—was thus introduced. As a result of the appearance of foreign owners—who were, significantly, real owners—the development of the Hungarian banking system could begin.[100] In recent years a continuing rise in the standard of banking services can be perceived: a viable banking structure has emerged, changes to which can only be determined by the requirements of the market and of efficiency; as a result of the significant rise in capital brought by the new owners, serious investments were made in the banks; and the Hungarian banking system became capable of exploiting the innovations in modern telecommunications and of satisfying the international financial intermediation demands of the Hungarian economy—above all, of the corporate sector.

In the fiscal year 1999 the general economic environment was advantageous for the Hungarian economy. Economic growth accelerated during the year. The annual average growth rate of consumer prices fell by more than 4 percentage points to reach 10 percent. Foreign direct investment and portfolio investment were significant in 1999, and the inflow of capital was strong in each quarter of the year. The central bank reduced its reference rate (two-week deposit rate) during 1999 by 2.5 percentage points to 14.25 percent in December 1999. The short-term lending rate of the banks dropped to 15.4 percent from its starting level of 18.8 percent in December 1998.

During 1999 Hungary's ratings were modified towards more favourable grades. Moody's Investor Service, the S&P, and the F-IBCA raised their ratings by one grade.

The majority of the Hungarian banks suffered losses of varying degrees in 1998 due to the Asian and Russian financial crises. As a result, growth rates and the extent of financial activity were diminished. The banks were planning for recovery in 1999 and wanted to eliminate the losses resulting from banking activity and the losses of the banking sector as a whole. On the other hand, they invested a great deal of money in developing IT and electronic banking. Market competition became extremely strong both in the corporate and retail banking sectors.

The number of fully fledged commercial banks (in possession of a universal banking licence) amounted to 45 in December 1998. A year later the number of such institutions was 43. There had been one liquidation, two mergers had taken place, and one new bank had launched operations.

Based on the aggregate balance sheet of credit institutions the total assets/liabilities grew by 12.9 percent to reach HUF 7,832.2 billion at the end of 1999. This growth rate was 2.9 percentage points higher than annual rate of inflation in 1999, thus the banking sector had achieved growth in real terms, although it was unlikely to increase its share in GDP.

Provisions for loans, securities, financial investments, etc. decreased by 22 percent, which represents a positive development, supposing the banks continue with cautious activity. Provisions for loans and especially for securities decreased markedly, while provisions for financial investments increased significantly. Only minor changes occurred in the structure of liabilities. The deposits of enterprises grew more rapidly than the average growth rate. They now represent one-sixth of the total liabilities of the credit institutions. The highest growth rate occurred in the deposits of small entrepreneurs, where the rate was 25 percent, although this growth represents only HUF 25 billion. Household deposits grew at the same rate as the total liabilities. They represent an increment of more than HUF 300 billion. An important new phenomenon in 1999 was that the banks' domestically issued securities started to increase again.

In the fiscal year 1999 the equity capital of the credit institutions grew by nearly 15 percent, due to the increase in the banks' profits calculated as part of the equity capital. At the end of 1998 many Hungarian banks suffered significant losses due the Asian and Russian crises, and as a result of these losses the equity capital was reduced by HUF 157 billion. This unfavourable situation changed in 1999 and the profit/loss per balance sheet turned positive by the small margin of HUF 32 billion.

By the end of 1999 the profit and loss account of the banking sector had improved significantly compared to the 1998 results, since the losses of Postabank, the Hungarian Development Bank (MFB) and Realbank had been huge and the state had consolidated all of these banks.

With the improvement in Hungary's rating, in 1999 the rating of the Hungarian banks became more favourable. Moody's and

The development of liabilities
(HUF billion)

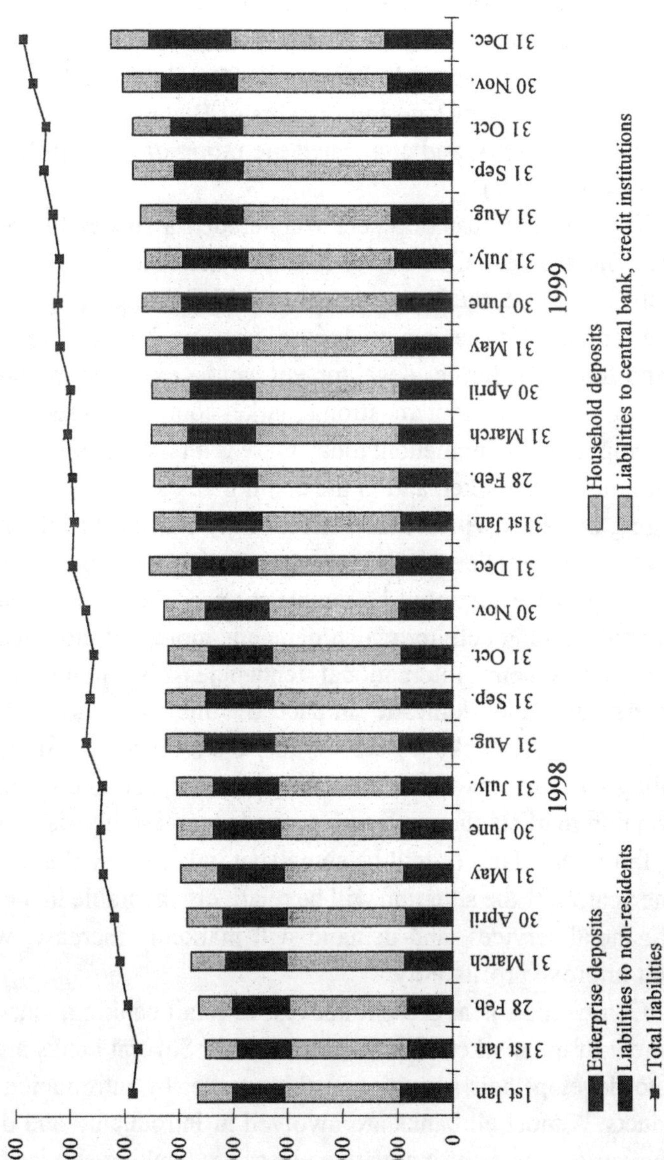

Source: Hungarian National Bank

S&P raised the grades of ABN Amro, and Fitch IBCA put the Hungarian subsidiary of ABN Amro into the same rating category as the mother bank (AA). The ratings of CIB and MKB were modified, being raised several times in 1999. Thomson Bankwatch modified the rating of long-term credits of Budapest Bank in 1999 from BBB- to BBB, and confirmed the rating of the bank's short-term credits (LC-1).

The domestic banking sector concluded a successful year in 2000. The growth of the sector's balance sheet total reached, and slightly surpassed, the increase in nominal GDP, thus bringing to an end a long-existing tendency. According to the banks' own analysis and forecasts, further development can be expected in 2001. In the domestic branch system, strong market competition remains the most important phenomenon: today there is an increasing over-supply on the bank market, and in the coming years the buying up and merging of banks will become increasingly radical. For the medium-sized and smaller banks the only solution will be strong specialization, since they will be unable to meet the requirements of universal banking activity which demands more and more technological investment. International tendencies also point towards mergers, and the domestic impact of this is clearly visible. According to the banks' forecasts, due to strong competition profitability will further worsen, risks may increase, and in the interests of gaining markets they will turn towards increasingly risky areas. The fall in profitability will be somewhat balanced by the fact that in the year 2001 the situation will be relatively favorable in the field of financial services, and demand will markedly increase, which might improve profitability.

Competition is at present keenest in retail banking, since this segment of the market is far from saturated. Several banks are trying to develop their activities in this market by introducing new products. Almost all banks are involved in introducing and developing various types of innovative electronic banking services. The most frequent market-political goal is to consolidate the results achieved on the market and to make progress in one or two specific areas.

The number of bank employees is expected to increase by 1 percent in 2001. In the large banks the tendency today is towards a fall in personnel, while in smaller banks a further slight increase in staff numbers can be expected. Logically, the newly created banks, banks that are significantly widening their activities, and banks opening up new branches, will have an increasing personnel.

Opening new branches is mostly preferred by medium-sized banks that are aiming to become large banks, as well as banks that are moving towards public markets. At present, only two banks have undertaken branch closures, closing one branch each.

In 2001, due to the favorable condition of the economy, the banks are less likely to take branch risks into account, while economic growth and the situation of the international capital markets provides a favorable context for banking activities. Naturally, opening up towards increasingly risky areas in the public and small-entrepreneurial market will increase risks. The expected nominal increase in the credit demand of the state budget will lead to the extensive issuing of state bonds, although market demand is expected to absorb this. In relation to general growth rates the banks are aiming to increase their state budget lending at a much more rapid rate, although this trend was already apparent in 2000. The reduction in compulsory reserve rates will represent significant relief for most banks, while at the same time they can expect a further decrease in the reserve rates and the easing of the regulations governing reserves.

In certain banks the structural shifts in the existing qualified credit portfolio can be estimated from the weighted averages. It can generally be expected that the proportion of non-qualified loans will slightly increase. The distribution of the qualified loan portfolio will shift towards the somewhat better categories, although the proportion of bad credits will remain unchanged.

According to the 1999 reports of the State Financial Supervisory Authority (PSZÁF), in 1998 the capital adequacy indicator for the entire banking system was 16.7 percent, and fell to 14.9 percent in 1999. According to the quarterly PSZÁF reports this reduction in capital adequacy is continuing, although PSZÁF does not see this as a cause for concern. In the case of several banks the worsening of the capital adequacy indicators does not necessarily mean the increasing of the risk level of the portfolio, but rather that the Hungarian-based, mostly foreign-owned commercial banks are utilizing their own resources at an increasing rate and that instead of inter-bank and central bank credits and the buying of state bonds, they are dealing with providing credits in the real economy and with making investments. The crediting boom is likely to continue, mostly in the more risky areas, therefore a further worsening of the capital adequacy indicators is probable. In the large banks, and in medium-sized banks involved in providing credits for entrepreneurs, capital adequacy indicators are lower than in newly founded specialized credit institutions or building societies. In the case of the majority of banks, a small deterioration in capital adequacy indicators is expected, while larger banks can expect a stagnation, or slight increase, in the figure. There are indications that, mostly in the case of small banks with capital adequacy of over 50 to 70 percent, the figure will show a marked decrease.

The deterioration in capital adequacy is influenced by off the balance items: for 90 percent of survey respondents these items made the capital adequacy indicator worse. Changes in the quality of credit portfolios are related to changes in the rate of the qualified portfolio. On this basis, a furtherly continuous improvement can be expected.

a) The development of financial intermediation in the fiscal year 2000

The Hungarian banking system performed fairly well in the fiscal year 2000, while the performances of the individual banks varied considerably.

The National Savings Bank (OTP) continues to head the list of Hungarian banks: OTP has a 22.9 percent market share, while the second largest, the Hungarian Foreign Trade Bank (MKB), has no more than 9.3 percent. The Central European International Bank (CIB) stands in third place with an 8.1 percent market share. The five largest Hungarian banks—these three along with the Trade and Credit Bank (K&H) and ABN Amro Hungary—have a combined market share of 53.1 percent. The total market share of the next six fully fledged commercial banks (universal banks, according to continental traditions) is 23.4 percent.

In terms of assets and profitability, OTP's dominant position is clear: based on its 22.9 percent overall market share, and especially on its 43.3 percent share in retail banking, Hungary's largest bank realized, in the fiscal year 2000, higher pre-tax profits (HUF 39.1 billion) than the four next banks (whose total profits amounted to HUF 36.4 billion).

In 1999/2000, as competition in corporate business became more and more intensive, so more banks turned towards retail banking in order to serve not only greater numbers of private clients, but more small and medium-sized companies as well. This is indicated by the fact that loans to households grew by no less than 40 percent between the end of 1998 and February 2000, and this upward trend has continued. The SME sector currently represents nine-tenths of companies in operation, and two-thirds of the Hungarian labor force at present work for SMEs. However, bankers formerly tended to avoid the sector because of the higher relative costs and the relatively greater risks involved, as well as the dearth

The best-performing Hungarian banks in fiscal 2000[a]

Rank		Assets (x billion HUF)	**Total market share (%)**	Share in corporate lending	Share in retail lending	Pre-tax profits (x billion HUF)
1.	OTP	1,935.382	22.9	10.9	43.3	39.121
2.	MKB	789.929	9.3	11.5	1.6	9.655
3.	CIB	682.679	9.1	9.4	1.5	12.275
4.	K&H	620.386	7.3	10.6	3.9	- 1.515
5.	ABN Amro	469.144	5.5	5.5	2.1	- 1.359
6.	Raiffeisen	350.372	4.1	7.6	1.9	5.921
7.	Budapest Bank*	336.507	4.0	n.a.	n.a.	1.945
8.	Postabank	330.871	3.9	n.a.	n.a.	300
9.	ÁÉB**	329.000	3.9	n.a.	n.a.	7.000
10.	BA/CA***	318.516	3.8	6.1	0.9	7.458

[a] According to the banks' own statements, non-audited figures.
* Owned by General Electric Capital.
** General Crediting Bank, owned by Gazprombank.
*** Bank Austria/Creditanstalt

of credit rating data—that is, the lack of credit records. Car financing represented the first step towards larger retail banking activities. Nevertheless, SME loans still account for only 4 to 5 percent of total private-sector credit. In order to encourage growth in this market the present government and its predecessor both made support for the SME sector a priority, for example by launching cheap SME bank credit schemes. The state-owned Hungarian Development Bank has also been made a conduit for SME lending.[101] In 2000 the international 'merger mania' reached the Hungarian banking industry. In April, Citibank acquired ING Bank's twelve-branch retail banking arm. In this way Citibank doubled its market share in retail banking, although even this doubled share represents no more than 3 percent of the total. After the Bavarian Hypovereinsbank declared its acquisition of Austria's largest commercial bank, BankAustria-Creditanstalt, BA-CA Hungary began to merge with Hypovereinsbank Hungary. This merger will be completed by 1 July 2001.[102] Most recently, Kredietbank (KBC), the Belgian bank insurance group, decided to merge its Hungarian banking activities with ABN Amro's Hungarian affiliate. The deal will mean the full merger of the two banks' local activities: KBC will own 60 percent, and ABN Amro 40 percent, of the new—"Hungarian"—bank. The KBC/ABN Amro merger will create Hungary's second largest commercial bank, which will have a combined market share of 15 percent and which will be the largest bank involved in corporate financing.

In late 2000 a new acquisition attempt overshadowed the recent mergers: ÁPV Rt., the State Privatization and Holding Company, announced that the largest Hungarian Bank, the National Savings Bank (OTP) could begin talks in order to acquire the fully state-owned Postabank. The National Savings Bank is by far the largest and most profitable bank in Hungary: it converted its former state monopoly position on the retail market into very effective and profitable universal banking activity. With its corporate, leasing, real estate development, brokerage, etc. arms it was successful in retaining its dominant market position. Postabank was at one time the fourth largest Hungarian bank and was in second place in terms of retail banking until 1998, when it was nationalized in order to avoid liquidation.

The eventual merger of the two banks could have enhanced OTP's dominant market position, making it both privileged and practically unchallengeable. The deal was immediately heavily criticized due to the lack of transparency surrounding it (ÁPV Rt. avoided an open tender), as well as the unwelcome monopolistic position of OTP. However, ÁPV Rt. eventually refused OTP's bid of HUF 25 billion.[103] The greatest surprise was not simply the refusal: the government declared that Postabank will not in fact be privatized at all and that, in all likelihood, the 100 percent state-owned National Post Offices will "acquire" the bank.[104]

By way of a final assessment, we can share Colin Jones' view that in 2000/2001 the Hungarian banking sector is on the threshold of a new phase of development. "If the establishment of the Hungarian Credit Bank and the K&H Bank [as well as that of Budapest Bank, one might add] in 1987 marks the first phase of the post-communist development of Hungarian banking, and if their financial rehabilitation and the sale to ABN Amro and KBC [along with the sale of Budapest Bank to GE Capital Services, between the end of 1995 and early 1997] marked the second phase, then their merger may be taken as symptomatic of a third phase—namely consolidation."[105]

b) Building societies

By the end of the 1990s the fall in inflation along with massive social demand created the conditions for the operation of building societies. For these building societies 2001 is an extremely important year, since, according to the legal regulations, this is the year in which they can begin paying out their first credits. Accordingly, the societies involved have mentioned as their most important task this year preparations for granting credit, for establishing a suitable process for the rapid judgment of applications, and for the smooth transference of credits. Besides this, naturally, it is an important goal to increase, or at least maintain the level of, market share, the number of paying clients, the total number of deposits, and profits.

In the event of modifications to the recent legislation the societies will consider necessary the creation of new products and product offers and the rethinking of the present range of offers. Although the proposed amendment to the law governing building societies was not accepted in October—something which was welcomed by the building societies—the direction of changes will remain the same, thus the societies regard as vital the ability to adapt rapidly and flexibly to new situations as they arise. For the time being the building societies are hoping for a more favorable proposal: according to them, keeping the state subsidy at the same level and reducing savings periods would be the most beneficial move.

In 2000 the balance sheet total grew by almost 60 percent—by 2001 the societies expect a further 44 percent growth—and currently more than 500,000 clients have building society accounts. However, a condition for the continuation of this positive situation is a more favorable amendment to the law, since, according to the societies, the proposal that has recently been rejected would have meant a drastic reduction in the number of future accounts, while at the same time endangering the liquidity of the societies and their long-term existence.

According to the legal regulations the current four-year savings period will expire for the first account holders in summer 2001, which is when the payment of credits will begin. For the present, two societies are offering a bridging loan, and from mid-2001 a further society will do the same. Despite the uncertainty surrounding changes in the regulations the building societies see developments in the financial climate as favorable and trust in improving results. With the start of credit providing, the capital adequacy indicators will be lower, but even so results of over 100 percent can be counted on.

c) Credit/debit cards in Hungary

The development of credit card business in Hungary and the spread of this means of payment, have been perhaps the most remarkable development in financial intermediation since the change of regime.

In the first three-quarters of 1999 there were 3,613,651 bank/ company cards in Hungary. Of these, 2.2 million were EUROPAY cards, 1.2 million were VISA cards, and most of the remainder had their own logos (e. g., ATM, loyalty cards). The number of AMEX and DINERS cards was only 2,445 and 3,944 respectively.

In 2000, some 91 percent of the HUF 1.049 billion card-related turnover, produced from 4.1 million cards, was made up of simple cash withdrawals, although in the space of one year the number of credit and charge cards had doubled (even so reaching only 205,500). In 2000 the growth in the number of POS terminals appeared to come to a standstill as well: in mid-2000 one could in practice pay by credit/debit card in 22,300 places, the same number as in the previous year.

The total number of cards grew very rapidly. In 1992 there were only 137,000 cards in Hungary. Since then the annual average increase has been nearly 60 percent and the total number of cards has risen by 28 to 29 times. The most rapid increase (99 percent) occurred in 1995 (when it became obligatory for public servants to receive their salaries by bank transfer). In 1999 the growth rate was "only" 33 percent. As a result, almost every Hungarian family had at least one card in 1999 (the penetration rate was around 47 percent if

Number of cards

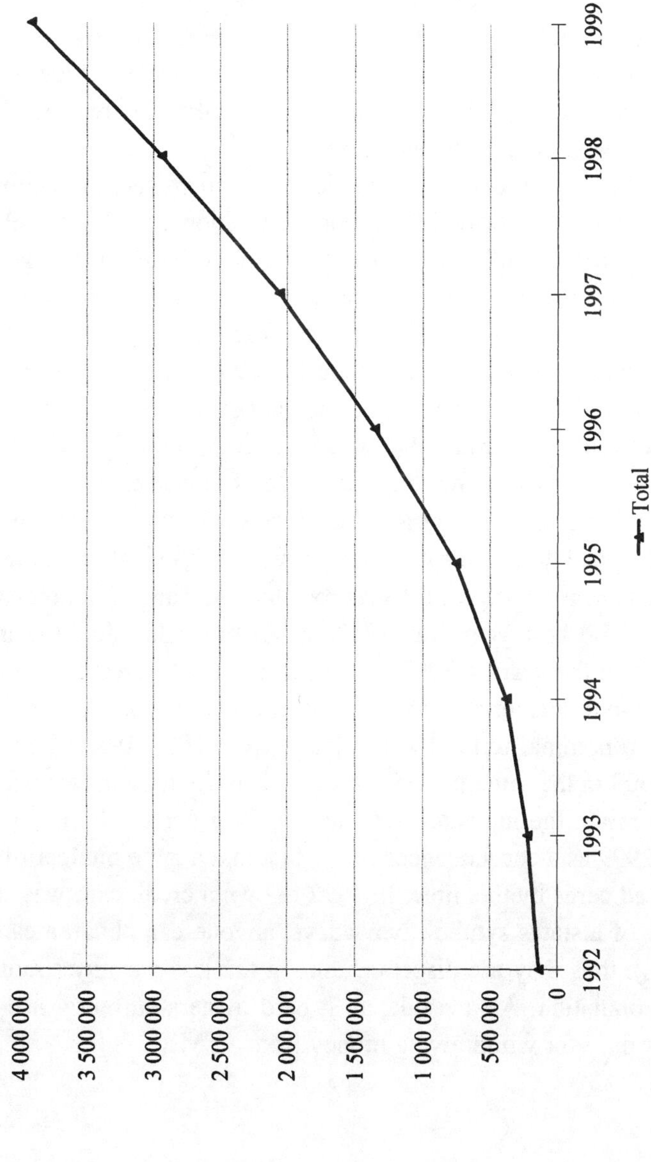

Source: Hungarian National Bank

we leave children under the age of 14 out of the calculation). This rate could be higher, since many older pensioners either do not like using cards or are not interested in holding a card because of the relatively high cost compared to their monthly income. Other explanations might include their fear of card fraud or of losing their card, since there have been some sensational media reports in connection with card fraud and theft.

The number of card transactions has grown very favourably. In 1992 there were only 2.5 million transactions, while in 1999 the figure reached 88.5 million. The growth rate in transactions between 1992 and 1999 is astonishing, with the number multiplying 35.4-fold, or by 1.66 times each year. The highest growth rate was in 1994 (240 percent), while in 1999 it was 25 percent. The annual indicator for the number of transactions per card was 18 to 19 between 1992 and 1994, and 20 to 23 after 1995, which indicates only a slow increase in the usage of these cards.

The value of the transactions rose by 73 times between 1992 and 1999, although this was partly a result of the high inflation rate. In real terms transaction values rose by 18.3 times (50 percent per year). The best year was 1997, when the value doubled in the course of the year. In 1999 the increase was 41 percent (or 55 percent in nominal terms). The value of transactions per card indicator rose in nominal terms by 2.2 times (from HUF 198,500 to HUF 439,000 in the same period). In real terms the growth rate was less favourable: the indicator even fell by 34.5 percent between 1992 and 1999 as a consequences of the fact that a large number of people had cards by this time. In 1992 to own a credit card was something of a status symbol. Nowadays, anyone can obtain a card (or cards), thus they are dispersed among the less wealthy stratum of the population. As a result, most card owners currently use their cards only for withdrawing money from ATMs.

The number of credit/debit card transactions

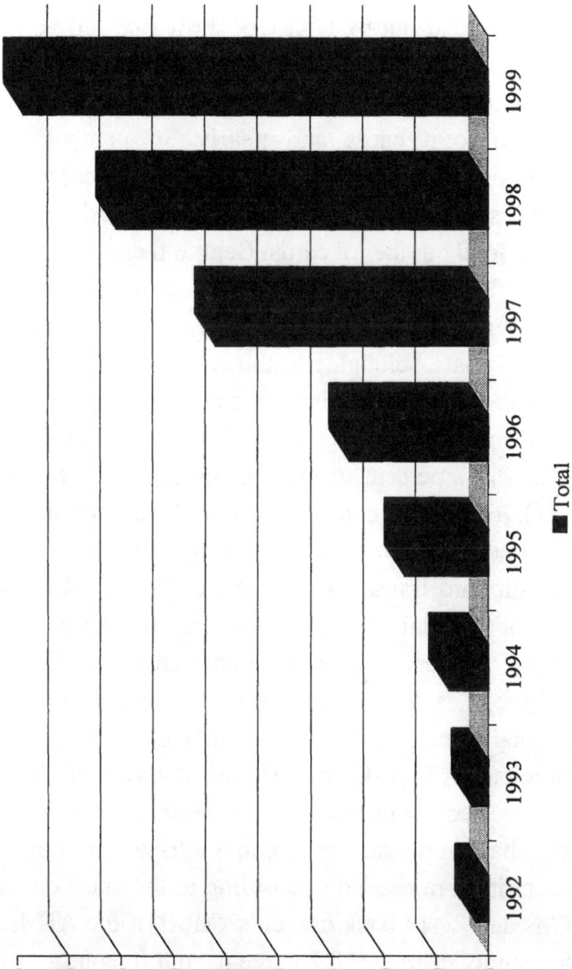

Source: Hungarian National Bank

The overwhelming majority of card holders have such a low monthly income that they are unable to save, thus they withdraw all the money from their account to cover the costs of their everyday lives. Studies carried out by GKI Co. show that only one-third of the population is able to save money on a regular basis.

Of the Hungarian debit/credit cards in use, 45 percent are Cirrus/Maestro joint cards and nearly 30 percent are VISA Electron. Mention should also be made of EC/MC cards, since they have a market share of 12 percent. These three card types cover 87 percent of the total number of cards. Behind these come ATM cards with their own logos, and the VISA classic card. Their market share amounts to 4 and 3.8 percent respectively, with the remaining 5.2 percent market share belonging to the various other issuers.

The number of debit cards stands at 3.5 million (96.6 percent of all cards). In addition, there are 115,000 credit cards and 6,389 charge cards (61.7 percent of them being DINERS cards, and the rest AMEX). The proportion of credit card transactions compared to the total number of transactions stands at 0.7 percent, and the value of credit card transactions amounts to just HUF 6.6 billion (0.6 percent of the total value). The number of charge card transactions is 56,891 (0.1 percent), with a total value of HUF 1.5 billion. EUROPAY credit cards are mainly used for obtaining cash (96 percent of the total value), while VISA credit cards are mainly used for making purchases (71.9 percent of the total value). Charge cards are apparently used for purchasing (72 percent value).

If more banking cards are to come into use in Hungary, more transaction points are needed. According to the latest data there are 2,300 ATMs and 2,414 bank branches. Most of the ATMs are situated in the county centres (60.2 percent), but in contrast, only 23.5 percent of bank branches are located in these settlements.

The division of types of debit/credit cards

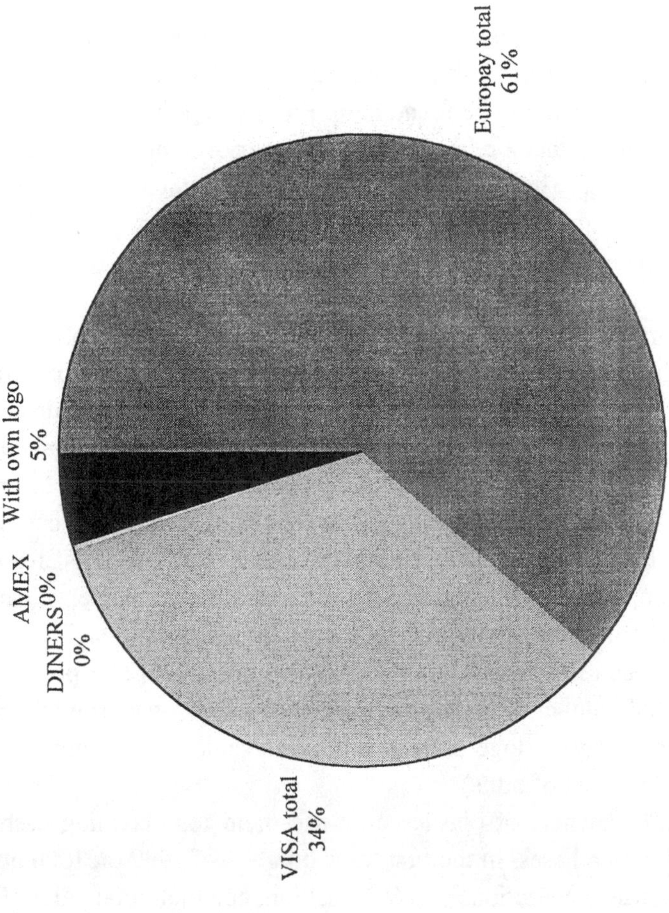

Source: Hungarian National Bank

There is a strong concentration in terms of ATMs and branches. Budapest has 24 percent of ATMs and 9.1 percent of branches. In addition, a further 29.7 percent of ATMs and 15.2 percent of branches are located around the capital (in Pest county). Altogether 53.7 percent of ATMs and 24.3 percent of branches are to be found in or around Budapest. This is partly because the capital city is the financial center of Hungary, and partly because the highest household incomes are to be found here. From this point of view a decisive factor is that a relatively high number of public servants work in Budapest. They receive their salaries into their bank accounts and can obtain cards without any initial charges. Győr-Moson-Sopron county is also over-represented in terms of ATMs (4.8 percent of the total number) and branches (5.2 percent).

In 1999 the number of retail or wholesale units accepting credit/debit cards amounted to 21,963. Most of them have POS terminals (99.5 percent), although in addition they have numerous imprinters (52.5 percent of units). Among the POS terminals only 5,221 units have PIN code control. A reasonable number of trade units accept EUROPAY (64 percent) or VISA (68 percent) cards. In a relatively low number of units consumers can use DINERS (17 percent) or AMEX (29 percent), or even JCB (31 percent), cards. There are a few units which accept own-logo cards. The most numerous of these are Bank Pont, a logo of OTP (23.3 percent of the total number of trade units), the second most widespread being Takarékkártya, a logo of Takarékbank (a savings card with a share of 8.8 percent of units).

The owners of plastic cards use them for obtaining cash or making purchases. In the first three quarters of 1999 the total number of card transactions was 66.4 million, and their total value HUF 1,288,400 million. Foreigners carried out 4.5 million of these transactions to a value of HUF 132 million. Thus Hungarians carried out 93 percent of the total number of transactions representing 89.7 percent of the total value: it is clearly evident that foreigners carried out fewer transactions, with a higher transaction value. Cash withdrawals represent by far the majority of transactions and the highest value as well. The former represent 86 percent and the latter 94.6 percent. As a result, purchasing activities using cards is very poor. The value per transaction in terms of cash withdrawal is HUF 20,500, and only HUF 7,400 for purchases.

The leader in both fields is EUROPAY (its total share is 61 percent of transactions and 66 percent of total transaction value). EUROPAY's share in terms of cash withdrawals is 67 percent, and in terms of trade value 61 percent. With respect to transactions the former represent 61 percent, while the latter represent 61.9 percent. The value per transaction indicator is a little higher than the average (HUF 22,200) for cash withdrawals, but slightly lower for purchases (HUF 7,300). The second biggest issuer is VISA. Its share of total transactions is 33.9 percent, and of total value 29.6 percent. Holders of VISA cards use them more frequently for cash withdrawal (85.7 percent) than for making purchases (14.3 percent), but the value of these transactions is much lower with respect to cash withdrawals (HUF 17,800), and is also lower in terms of purchases (HUF 6,900). Own-logo cards also play a significant role both in terms of number of transactions (2.8 million) and value (HUF 47 billion). The value per transaction indicator is lower than the average with respect to cash withdrawals (HUF 16,800), but much higher with respect to purchases (HUF 14,000). This is because the main issuers are retail or wholesale firms.

Not only do foreigners use cards in Hungary, but Hungarians are also using their cards more frequently abroad. In the first three quarters of 1999 Hungarians used cards 1.1 million times and made purchases of almost HUF 32 billion. The most frequently used card was EUROPAY (605,000 transactions), with VISA in second place (almost half a million transactions). In third place was AMEX (with around 10,000 transactions), with DINERS in fourth place (7,700 transactions). By contrast, if we calculate according to transaction values, then first place goes to VISA (HUF 15.9 billion) with EUROPAY in only second place (HUF 15.3 billion). The value per transaction indicator gives the following values: HUF 25,400 for EUROPAY, HUF 32,200 for VISA, HUF 39,700 for DINERS, and HUF 27,000 for AMEX. The comparison can also be made from another angle. Total transaction value with respect to purchases was HUF 20 billion (63 percent) and HUF 11.8 billion (37 percent) for cash withdrawals. EUROPAY owners used their cards more frequently for making purchases (75 percent of transactions) than VISA holders (74 percent of transactions). At the same time, 97 percent of transactions by DINERS card holders and 96 percent of transactions carried out by AMEX card holders were for making purchases.

Card fraud is a huge problem in Hungary. In the first three quarters of 1999 the number of instances of fraud on the issuers' side was 8,720, with the total damage amounting to HUF 713 million. Most of these were committed by the owners of the cards (30 percent of instances, but representing 70 percent of the total value). The most common situation was when no card was involved in the transaction (49 percent), but the value of the damage was only HUF 41 million (5.7 percent). The number of instances of fraud on the receiving side was 11,408, with the damage amounting to HUF 852 million. If we take into account only the value of the damage, then VISA suffered the highest losses (HUF 476 million, that is, 56 percent). In comparison, EUROPAY suffered losses of only HUF 370 million (43 percent).

2. The development of the insurance sector in the 1990s

The structural renewal of the Hungarian insurance market took place in the first half of the 1990s. The insurance companies had to face a host of problems that had accumulated during the previous decades. Due to social- and production-political reasons Hungarian insurance companies had previously undertaken unrealistic risks. Besides this, they did not produce, or did not produce sufficient, insurance-technical reserves. A further problem was that the insurance-technical reserves and accumulated assets were, time and again, taken over by the budget, while on other occasions they were supplemented from state resources. In the economic management of the insurance companies, there was no classification of insurance-technical reserves, nor was there a practice of classifying according to cost center. These omissions made possible regroupings among certain types of reserves and the cross-financing of certain activities.

With the privatization of the Hungarian insurance companies and with the appearance of smaller competitors it became obvious that the previous system was unsustainable. The Hungarian insurance companies were under-capitalized, their capital shortfall was equal to almost HUF 45 billion. Apart from that, meeting the requirements of European guarantee capital required further capital (HUF 5 to 6 billion).[106]

The consolidation of the insurance sector took place in the period between 1990 and 1993. Consolidation was not carried out by the state, but by the—predominantly foreign—owners. In the period between 1990 and 1993, some 90 percent of the quantitative problems, amounting to HUF 50 billion, could be settled by the new owners.

In 1993, by the end of the last year of consolidation, the economic position of the insurance companies displayed a significant improvement: the degree of loss had significantly decreased, and the real value of the insurance-technical reserves showed growth of almost 5 percent.

By the end of 1992 more than 70 percent of the equity capital and 95 percent of charge-related income of the insurance companies had come into foreign ownership. The foreign owners could not be forced to finance losses or to participate in public supply.

(Besides this, the opportunities for state control became very limited.) Thus the costs of consolidation were largely covered by the clients.

In parallel with this, between 1990 and 1996 the structure of the insurance companies' products went through certain qualitative changes. New forms of insurance (e.g., mixed types of life insurance and compulsory automobile liability insurance that was no longer included in the price of petrol) were created, while others (e.g., group life and accident insurance) disappeared. By the mid-1990s the practice of co-insurance and pool insurance had begun to spread. In the former, the risk is undertaken by two or more insurance companies according to previously agreed rates. The policy is issued by the leading insurance company, which oversees client contact as well.

The changes were also reflected in the modification of the market structure. The proportion of life-insurance-related revenue compared to total revenue was 15 to 16 percent in early 1990, but by the mid-1990s the proportion had risen to over 30 percent. Automobile liability insurance, which remained the last of the sectors controlled directly by the state, made up 32.5 percent of the total revenue of the insurance companies. By the end of 1996 this proportion had fallen below 28 percent (the weight of comprehensive car insurance within charge-related revenues as a whole remained practically unchanged at around 11 to 12 percent).

The insurance market is characterized by increasing competition. In 1990 the market share of the two largest insurance companies still reached 95 percent. However, due to the appearance of new insurance companies on the market, by the mid-1990s the combined market share of the two giants had fallen below 55 percent.

In 1996 there were already sixteen insurance companies on the domestic market, three of which specialized entirely in life insurance. At the end of 1995, some 78 percent of the capital stock (HUF

24.5 billion, that is, USD 196 million) was in foreign ownership, which, in 1996, with the appearance of two new companies, further increased to above 80 percent. (Thus the volume of total foreign capital in the insurance sector increased to USD 212.7 million.)

The concentration of insurance companies' gross charge-related revenues in 1996, in keeping with earlier tendencies, further decreased compared to the previous years. There was a further shift to the benefit of smaller companies, which were able to increase their charge-related revenues far above inflation (even above 200 percent). Of the three companies enjoying the largest charge-related revenues, two lost market share even in 1996 (by 0.7 and 2 percent).

In 1995 six insurance companies produced profits and one had a zero balance (one company even paid some dividend). The results for the remaining seven were still negative. The results of the market-based insurance companies according to their balance were already positive in 1995, however (HUF 2.4 billion), while their post-tax results were HUF 5.1 billion, compared to the HUF –456 million in 1994. The ROA and ROE pre-tax profits of the insurance companies between 1992 and 1996 can be seen in the following table.

The insurance companies' pre-tax ROA and ROE (own capital and equity capital), 1991 to 1996

(percentages)

	1991	1992	1993	1994	1995	1996	1997	1998	1999
ROA	-19.23	-15.01	-1.28	-0.12	2.74	3.89	3.49	3.48	1.19
ROE	-94.82	-62.48	-6.30	-0.57	17.13	19.68	14.72	10.60	5.30

Source: State Insurance Supervision, State Supervision of Financial Institutions.

In 1993 the combined balance sheet total of the insurance companies grew by 25.5 percent, and by over 30 percent in 1994 and 1995 compared to previous years, while the growth in 1996 was 48.4 percent.

In the insurance sector a significant upsurge can be expected. It is predominantly the life insurance sector in which the appearance of further insurance companies is likely. This branch will be very attractive business for the insurance companies since, during the transformation of the social security system, self-help will play a much greater role than before. On the other hand, real incomes, which have now finally begun to rise, will lead to a significant increase in public demand for insurance. In Hungary, compared to the 50 percent average in OECD countries, life insurance charge-related revenues amounted to only 32 percent of total charge-related revenues in 1996.

With economic growth the other insurance sectors will develop. However, in these markets the deficit is not as big as with respect to life insurance.

The insurance companies' charge-related reserves at the end of 1996 were around HUF 100 billion with respect to market-based insurance companies. (This figure is in practice related only to life insurance.) In the future, the rapid growth of these reserves is expected to continue. However, besides the market-based insurance companies, voluntary mutual insurance associations will play an increasing role, which will lead to serious competition on the market.

The foreign presence on the Hungarian markets is very favorable from the point of view of reinsurance. Hungarian insurers enjoy approximately 22 percent of reinsurance protection, which is regarded as good even by international standards. In 1996 the domestic insurers bought passive reinsurance almost entirely from foreign companies. (Total passive reinsurance was more than HUF 43 billion.) The sum paid to foreign insurance companies was almost 43 percent more than in the previous year. The share of the life-insurance and non-life-insurance sectors was almost identical, that is, 47 and 53 percent respectively. Compared to this, the domestic insurance companies' expenditure on active reinsurance was only to the value of HUF 0.5 billion.

The dynamic rise in passive reinsurance is partly the result of increased risk taking by the insurance companies. On the other hand, with the increasing profits of insurance companies, transferring reinsurance fees abroad can be an effective means of exporting capital (profits) from the country.

The insurance companies will continue to invest the majority of their assets and insurance-technical reserves in state bonds. One reason for this is that in 1996/1997 long-term state bonds could be bought with very favorable interest and yield conditions. At the same time, falling inflation largely contributed to the fact that the yield on these investments was above bank interest rates. Thus the weight of state bonds in the portfolios of the insurance companies is expected to stay high (over 60 percent). However, further growth cannot be expected to take place.

With the reduction in inflation the weight of the securities of economic organizations will increase. The 10 to 15 percent dividend on shares, with the permanent reduction of inflation, will make them an increasingly attractive investment. There are serious investment possibilities in the privatization of the energy sector.

With the start of economic growth corporate-issue bonds might also represent an attractive investment. However, their weight in the portfolios of the insurance companies is expected to decrease, since up to the present the companies have owned more than the 5 percent ceiling prescribed in the Insurance Act. Real-estate investment might also become more favorable. In this respect it is predominantly residential real estate (due to increasing individual consumption) and commercial real estate (mainly in the more developed regions or near the country's border) that might represent good investments. Despite this, it is unlikely that real-estate investments will reach (or approach) the 10 percent limit laid down in the law.

Increasing the charges for automobile liability insurance by an average of 29.42 percent in 1996 did not make it possible for the insurance companies to perform this activity profitably. According to the insurance companies the state-decreed increase in charges by an average of 19.85 percent in 1997 was much lower than what was necessary. However, canceling the system of centrally determined prices might make this sector profitable.

In 1995 almost half the insurance companies were profitable. In 1996 around two-thirds of insurance companies were profitable, and post-tax profits in real terms had also slightly increased compared to the previous year, so that by 1996 about one-third of insurance companies were expected to pay out dividends. In 1997 and 1998 the profits of the insurance companies were expected to further increase in real terms as a result of increased interest in insurance activity and the fact that the previous losses of the insurance companies had been written off by the mid-1990s.

By the new millennium, with the creation of conditions for EU accession, a significant growth in the insurance market is expected. The sum spent on insurance in OECD countries is almost twenty times that spent in Hungary. Even calculating with the effect of GDP an average of 3.5 times more is spent on insurance in those countries. The difference in the life-insurance branch is extremely high (almost six times higher), and in the non-life-insurance sector it is only two times higher.[107]

Accordingly, the Hungarian insurance market, with the beginnings of economic growth and in the event of successful preparation for EU accession, has significant growth potential. By 2002 the total gross charge-related revenues are expected to increase by 60 percent in real terms compared to the 1996 level. At the same time a significant shift in proportions will take place towards the life-insurance branch. The share of this branch compared to the 1996 level of 32 percent could reach 45 percent of all charge-related revenues by 2002. As a result, the Hungarian insurance market will approach the OECD average.

After 1994 voluntary mutual insurance associations could be created, and by the end of 1994 there were 72 associations working in the country. By the end of 1996 the number of such associations approached 300, and their total assets amounted to more than HUF 23 billion (more than 0.3 percent of annual GDP). The number of those insured at the end of the year was more than 470,000 persons, which represents 11.8 percent of employees. The average membership of the associations is around 1,800 persons, although the fifteen largest associations concentrate around half of the total members.

For these voluntary mutual insurance associations, the coming years will be devoted to preparations for the old-age pension reforms. The associations are likely to increase their charge-related revenues partly by adding to their already existing insurance schemes and partly by targeting groups of clients.

In parallel with this, there is a process pointing towards concentration. Thus in the future we can expect the merger of associations and the appearance of large market leaders. The growth rate in the number of associations in the future is expected to fall. The growth rate in the number of new members will remain significant, but the new members will join the already existing, reliable associations.

The assets and charge-related reserves of the associations will further increase. The majority of payments, due to tax benefits, will continue to be made up of employers' contributions. The volume of individual payments is expected to increase due to rising incomes and personal income tax benefits.

In parallel with the growth in the insurance associations' assets and charge-related revenues, the associations will become an increasingly significant presence on the securities market. The majority of their investments, as in the case of market-based insurance companies, will be made up of state bonds. With the permanent fall in inflation and interest rates, however, their investments will turn to alternative forms of capital market opportunities.

Following the turn of the millennium—in the most favorable case—the voluntary mutual insurance associations will play an increasingly important role on the insurance market. By the year 2000 their dynamically increasing assets were expected to exceed HUF 200 billion, and their charge-related revenues were expected to approach those of the market-based insurance companies. This was primarily due to the serious tax benefits enjoyed by the associations. On the other hand employers have strong links to the associations and as a result employees will automatically be insured. As a result, the number of members was more than 2 million in 2000, which means 52 to 53 percent of employees.

Due to the stable growth of the economy, payments into the associations also began to increase in real terms in 1997/1998. Thus the assets of the associations are likely to approach HUF 350 billion by 2002 (which is already 2.2 percent of GDP), and the number of members will approach one and half million persons, which will represent 38 percent of employees.

The insurance market continues to expand dynamically—as reflected by the preliminary figures for the fiscal year 2000. In 2000 the insurance companies' charge-related revenues increased by around 30 percent and the total life-insurance-related revenues approached the total non-life-insurance revenues. This proportion reflects an extremely dynamic development in the life insurance branch, since this shift in proportions had been expected by analysts to take place by 2002/2003 at the earliest. The fiscal year 2000 could therefore be extremely successful, since the damage-related payments did not reach the 1999 levels.[108]

Distribution of the insurance market among the main players* (2000)

Company	Market share (%)	Total charge-related revenues (billion HUF)	Life-insurance charge-related revenues (billion HUF)	Non-life-insurance charge-related revenues (billion HUF)	Total damage payments (billion HUF)
Hungária	26.86	103.13	13.44	89.69	64.37
Generali	17.23	66.15	22.70	43.45	28.23
ÁB-Aegon	15.08	57.89	36.01	21.88	28.00
N-N	14.37	55.17	55.17	-	6.75
OTP-Garancia	10.12	38.84	21.24	17.60	14.90
5 largest	83.66	321.18	148.56	176.62	142.25
AXA-Colonia	4.62	17.74	4.65	13.08	7.91
ABN Amro	2.10	8.05	8.05	-	0.43
Ahico	1.85	7.10	3.30	3.80	0.73
Argosz	1.65	6.32	0.04	6.28	3.66
Winterthur	1.52	5.82	4.84	0.98	1.24
10 largest	95.40	366.21	169.44	196.76	156.22

* From among the 22 licensed insurers, including the Hungarian Export Credit Insurance Company.

Source: Preliminary figures of the Association of Hungarian Insurance Companies, and based on statistics provided by the individual insurance companies.

In the Hungarian insurance market there is practically only one company in Hungarian ownership[109]—OTP-Garancia, in the ownership of the largest Hungarian bank, the National Savings Bank (OTP), had 10.12 percent of the total market in 2000. On the basis of the insurance companies' total charge-related revenues, the Hungarian insurance market presents an interesting picture. Generali-Providenzia has integrated itself between the successors of the former state insurance duopoly, Hungária and ÁB-Aegon,[110] which dominated the market for a long time, closely followed by Nationale Nederlanden. (See the table.)

The Hungarian insurance market is still strongly concentrated—however, if we take into account that at the beginning of the decade the duopoly formed by Hungária and AB-Aegon controlled over 95 percent of the market, and today not only has Generali overtaken AB-Aegon, but also the life-insurance specialist Nationale Nederlanden is also set to overake it, then we have to regard as surprising the decline of AB-Aegon, that is, the good performance of Generali and Nationale Nederlanden. The performance of OTP-Garancia is similarly remarkable: in seven years they gained 10 percent of the market, using the branches and infrastructure of the largest Hungarian bank but without any professional background in insurance, and the company's development dynamics look set to continue.

At the same time the market position of the five largest can hardly be shaken, even in the long term, by those behind them.

Generali—after merging its daughter companies working under the names Generali and Providencia—has not only stabilized, but significantly increased, its role as market leader. With respect to AB-Aegon, the fact that it is the only Hungarian insurance company that has been continuously profitable for years will probably balance its steady and significant loss of market share. In the life-insurance market Nationale Nederlanden continues to hold the leading position: neither AB-Aegon nor Generali has been able to decrease its deficit in this field, while in this most lucrative market segment Hungária is unable to improve its position.

3. The development of the Budapest Stock Exchange, 1990–2000

a) The beginnings

The story of the reestablished Budapest Stock Exchange (BSE) can be traced back to 1982. In the early 1980s the first "buzz" was apparent on the then unsettled bond market. In December 1987 a number of Hungarian trade banks signed an agreement to carry out regulated transactions with securities. Act VI of 1990 subsequently created the legal framework for the stock exchange. In summer 1990 the BSE held its founders' meeting with the participation of forty-two banks and brokerage companies.

In the period since its reestablishment, the domestic role of the BSE has significantly increased. The market in Hungary has had one of the best infrastructures in the Eastern European region, and this has played an important role in the fact that most of the region's capital inflow was actually directed to Hungary. The BSE, which in June 1990 began trading only in shares (IBUSZ), now deals in seventy different types of security, although until the end of 1990 trading was unofficial in the case of certain bonds and shares. The market value of all papers at the end of 1990 was no more than HUF 2.9 billion. At the end of 1999, the respective value has been almost HUF 4,145 billion.

b) The development of the BSE between 1990 and 1995

In 1990 only six shares were in circulation on the BSE, but by 30 December 1995 a total of 166 securities were being traded, of which 42 were shares, 36 Investment bills, 34 state bonds, 50 treasury bills, and 3 corporate bonds. In addition, the compensation voucher represented a special type of security.

1. The Capitalization of the BSE

The stock market capitalization
(HUF billion)

	21 June 1990	31 Dec. 1990	31 Dec. 1991	31 Dec. 1992	31 Dec. 1993	31 Dec. 1994	31 Dec. 1995
Capitalization of the BSE	0.5	16.4	53.6	201.9	457.0	883.8	1221.3
of which:							
shares	0.5	16.4	38.2	47.2	81.7	181.5	327.8
state bonds			15.3	82.3	241.7	392.9	454.0
corporate bonds			0.1	0.1	0.3	1.8	1.7
treasury bills				54.4	74.0	239.6	376.3
Investment bills				1.9	5.5	19.3	42.8
Compensation notes				16.0	53.8	48.7	18.7

In terms of capitalization, the period beginning 1992 saw the largest rise, when Compensation notes began to be exchanged for shares. Following the trade-ins, a number of stock exchange launches also took place. In 1994–95 there was outstanding growth in equity capitalization (predominantly due to the papers of MOL and OTP). Government securities were launched on the market in 1992 and immediately had a major and decisive impact.

From 1993 to 1995 the BSE (and therefore its capitalization) was dominated by government securities; however, the weight of shares steadily increased. It can clearly be seen that with the end of the mass compensation process, and with cash privatization coming to the forefront, the role of compensation-voucher capitalization significantly decreased within the capitalization as a whole. Corporate-bond capitalization was practically negligible.

The most significant growth was produced by state bonds (between 1993 and 1995) and shares (mostly in 1995). In 1994–95 the value of corporate bonds showed a marked increase; nevertheless,

The capitalization of the stock exchange according to types of security, between 1990 and 1995 (%)

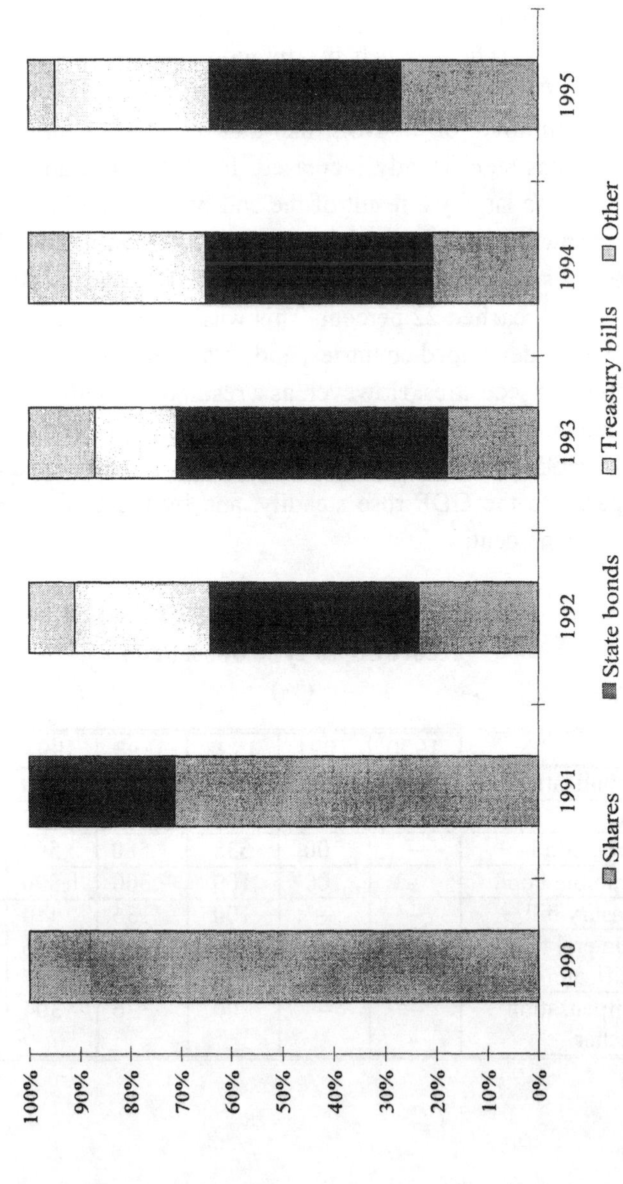

Source: BSE

they still did not represent a significant percentage. Although the growth in the value of discount treasury bills lagged behind, their turnover was already the highest (44.7 percent) in the first year that they were launched, which was predominantly due to their high actual yield.

The turnover of the BSE, like that of other Eastern European markets, has significantly increased. In 1993 the dramatic rise in turnover was largely a result of the end-of-year hausse. Due to the rapid growth rates the weight of the capitalization of the BSE increased significantly compared to the GDP, and by the end of 1995 it had reached 22 percent. This was still low compared to the average for developed countries, and was predominantly due to the government securities. However, as a result of the reduction in budget financing requirements, this pointer concealed a healthier structure in 1995 than in earlier years. The rate of equity capitalization compared to the GDP rose steadily, and by the end of 1995 had reached 6 percent.

Growth in the capitalization of the BSE according to type of security

(%)

	1990	1991	1992	1993	1994	1995
Capitalization	100	327	1,231	2,787	5,389	7,447
Share	100	233	288	498	1,107	1,999
Public bond	--	100	538	1,580	2,568	2,967
Corporate bond	--	100	100	300	1,800	1,700
Treasury bill	--	--	100	136	440	692
Collateral trust certificate	--	--	100	289	1,016	2,253
Compensation voucher	--	--	100	336	304	117

The growth of stock exchange capitalization, according to types of security, between 1990 and 1995 (%)

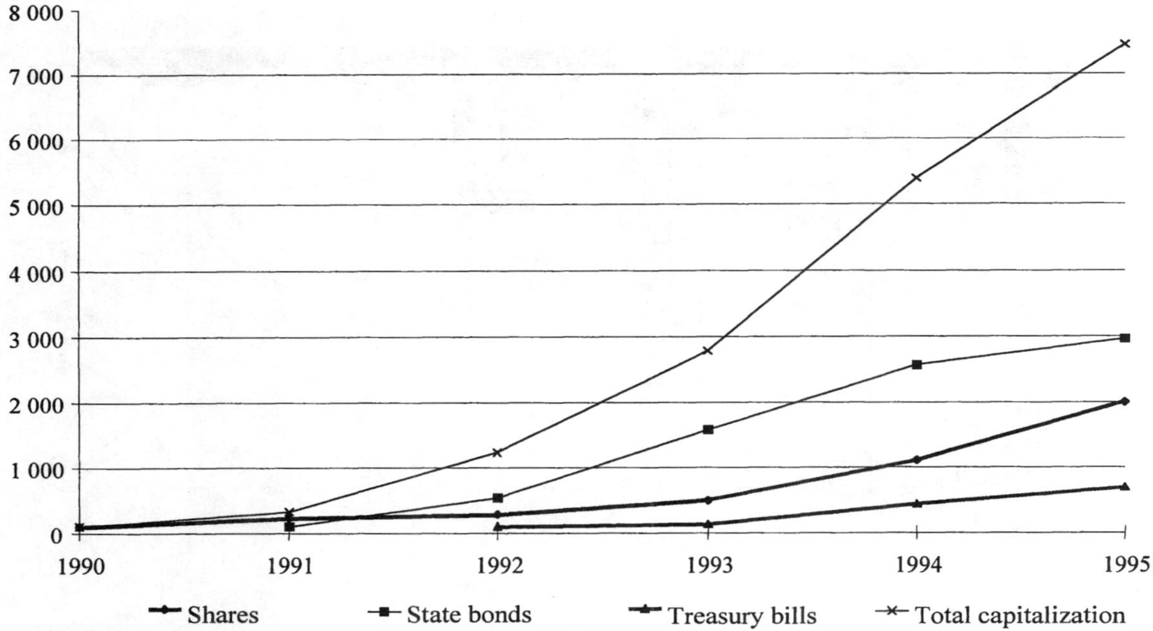

Source: BSE

The rate of capitalization per GDP between 1990 and 1995
(%)

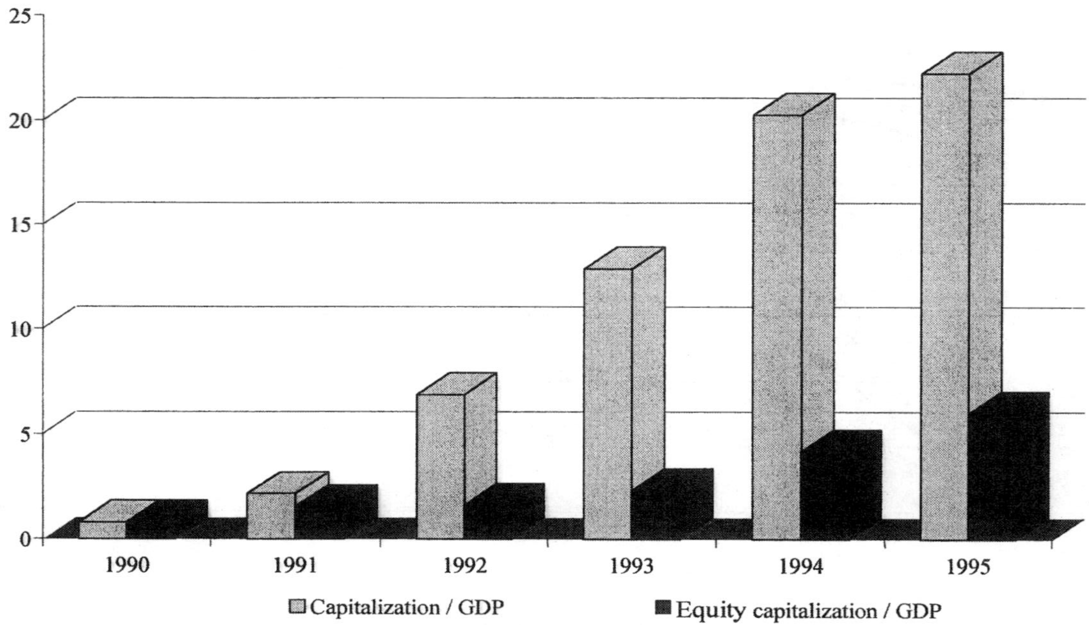

Source: BSE, Central Statistical Office

2. The Turnover of the BSE

Total and security-specific turnover of the BSE
(HUF billion)

	1990	1991	1992	1993	1994	1995
Turnover	6.1	10.1	33.70	185.7	211.2	253.2
of which:						
Equities	6.1	9.8	6.00	18.3	57.1	82.3
state bonds	-	0.3	12.40	73.4	53.9	77.2
Corporate bonds	-	0.0	0.0	0.0	0.01	0.05
Treasury bills	-	-	15.06	85.0	81.2	81.1
Investment bills	-	-	0.03	0.1	0.3	3.4
Compensation notes	-	-	0.21	8.9	18.7	4.2

A more subtle analysis of the turnover was made possible by means of an investigation of the distribution with respect to individual sections. Initially, state bonds appeared in 1991. The majority of the turnover, however, was produced byequities. The proportions were upset in 1992 as a result of the introduction of treasury bills. The 45 percent share in turnover represented by discount treasury bills, and the 37 percent share represented by state bonds, pressed the share represented by shares below 20 percent. The BSE continued to be characterized by the high, although falling, percentage of government securities. The reason for this was the actual yield of between 1.9 percent and 10.4 percent that could be achieved on government securities between 1990 and 1995 (deflator: the consumer price index).

Due to the consistently high actual yield, the proportion of the turnover represented by state-guaranteed state bonds and discount treasury bills remained high in the following years as well. However, as the actual yield became negative, equities increased in value and, as a result, came to represent a more important proportion of the turnover. The following table shows the changes in actual yield.

The turnover of the BSE according to type of security, between 1990 and 1995 (%)

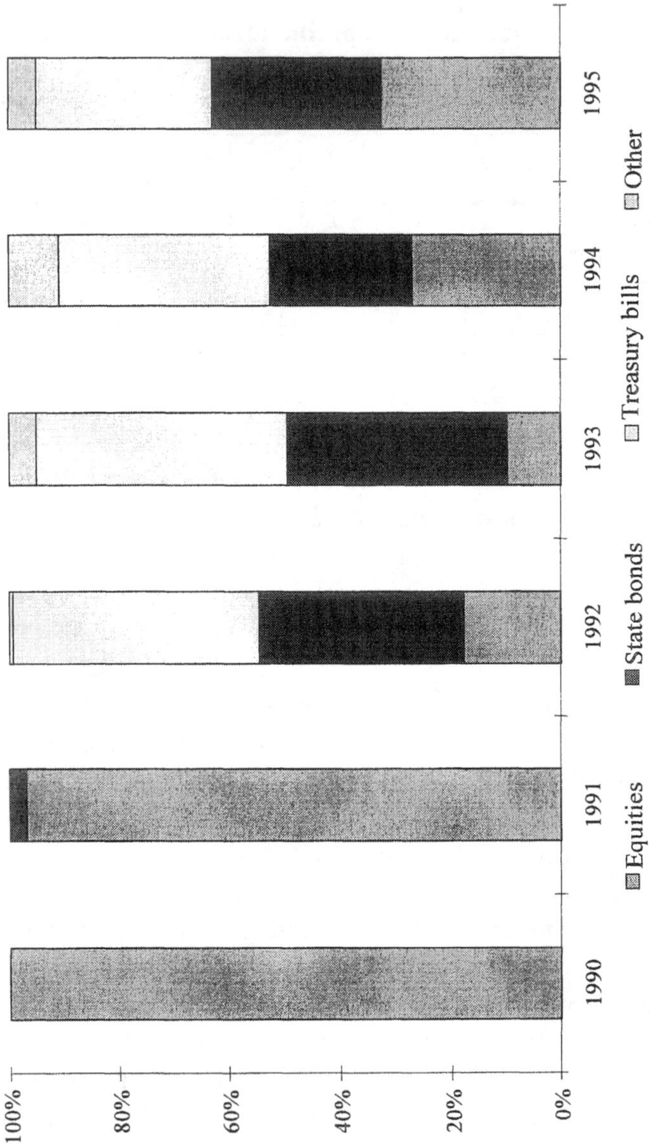

Source: BSE

The impact of the growth in stock-exchange turnover can be measured both by the increasing number of transactions as well as by the increase of the average daily turnover. This latter increased the security of stock exchange investments by ensuring liquidity, thus opening up the path towards further investments. In addition, assessment according to the most important country risk guides, as well the BSE's position as a registered stock exchange, increased investors' confidence in the BSE and in Hungarian stocks. The table below presents the number of transactions and the average turnover.

Turnover of the BSE according to type of security
(%)

	1990	1991	1992	1993	1994	1995
Equities	100	97.0	17.8	9.8	27.0	34.5
State bonds	-	3.0	36.8	39.5	25.6	30.5
Corporate bonds	-	0.0	0.0	0.0	0.0	0.0
Treasury bills	-	-	44.7	45.8	38.4	32.1
Investment bills	-	-	0.1	0.1	0.1	1.3
Compensation notes	-	-	0.6	4.8	8.9	1.6
Turnover	100	100	100	100	100	100

3. The Role of Foreign Investments in the Hungarian Money and Capital Markets

The proportion of foreign investments on the Budapest Stock Exchange has always been high. The growth in the proportion of domestic investment up to the end of 1994 was hindered by the fact that investment-related tax benefits could only be enjoyed if stocks were held onto for at least three years. On the securities markets, foreign investments became most influential in relation to the equity market; according to analysts they represented a weight of 60 to

70 percent on the BSE. Austrian, German, British, French, and American investors were the most influential in the main, and they realized their investments mainly through funds.

Foreign investors on the Hungarian money and capital markets

(HUF billion)

	1993	1994	1995
Non-residents	8	26	60
Residents	409	1,051	1,343
Total	417	1,077	1,403
Proportion of non-residents	2.0%	2.4%	4.3%

At the time of the hausse at around the turn of 1994/95, the proportion of foreign investments suddenly peaked. The table does not reflect the foreign majority on the BSE, since it takes into account all forms of investments (including OTC market investments). The following table offers a more detailed analysis of the 1995 turnover according to the type of security.

Proportion of foreign investors according to type of security, in 1995

(HUF billion)

	Residents	Non-residents	Proportion of non-residents
Shares	67.7	47.4	41.2%
State bonds	343.8	6.1	1.7%
Corporate bonds	20.2	0.4	2.0%
Treasury bills	889.8	6.1	0.7%

In terms of stock-exchange, as well as OTC market turnover, the proportion of foreigners is clearly decisive. Despite their 60 to 70 percent weight on the BSE, the proportion of foreign investors in the equity market as a whole of only 41.2 percent can be explained by the fact that on the OTC market there were only a few—and following the stock exchange launches even fewer—of the high-quality liquid papers that were being demanded by foreigners. In terms of the best of the shares on the market, the fact that these papers were also being traded on the significant foreign stock exchanges must also be seen as a decisive factor. However, with the appearance of the gas and electricity providers, foreign investors temporarily reemerged on the OTC market.

The largest markets trading in Hungarian stocks in this period were Vienna and London. The issuing of ADRs and GDRs in relation to Hungarian shares significantly increased the foreign turnover of these papers. Because of the different prices on the various markets, arbitrage came into play, especially between the Budapest, Vienna, and London markets. On the equity market the weight of domestic institutional investors was relatively small, since until early 1996 the funds and the banks invested in state bonds providing 3 to 5 percent actual real yield.

4. The Derivatives Market

The history of the BSE's derivatives market goes back to 1993: this was the first time that the BSE made an attempt to organize the derivatives market. The real starting point was 31 March 1995, and the following contracts were involved: USD, DEM, ECU, and BUX, as well as three-month discount treasury bills. The beginning of the trade in standardized stock-exchange derivatives was very promising in 1995.

In 1995 the turnover in terms of equity exchange rate values was highest on the three-month discount treasury bills (reaching almost HUF 6 billion, with the number of open contracts reaching 1,800 by the end of the year). In addition, the DEM and USD contracts are worth closer attention (HUF 1.3 to 1.5 billion), although altogether in three months of trading a total turnover of only HUF 10.2 billion was realized.

5. The OTC Market

The over-the-counter market operating alongside the BSE produced an extremely high turnover, especially in terms of state bonds and treasury bills.

Turnover of the OTC market
(HUF billion)

Security	1993*	1994	1995
Equities	10.8	51.0	45.7
State bonds	37.0	145.8	464.2
Corporate bonds	67.9	39.9	70.6
Treasury bills	109.3	586.5	913.5
Other bank launches	9.1	3.8	7.1
Investment bills	0.8	0.3	10.5
Compensation notes	23.4	30.4	18.4
Other	14.9	8.4	16.6
Total	273.2	866.1	1,546.6

* Statistics are calculated by the State Security and Stock Exchange Supervisory Board since 1993.
** Total bonds

The stock exchange hausses in late 1994 and early 1995, as well as at the end of 1995, also had a beneficial impact on the OTC market. In 1995 OTC turnover rose by about 786 percent, while the OTC market turnover of equities in 1995 fell by 10 percent. The trade in state bonds in 1994 almost quadrupled, and in 1995 rose by a further 317 percent on the OTC market. In the case of treasury bills the turnover in 1994 rose 5.4 times, and in 1995 by a further 56 percent.

As can be seen from the table, in the OTC-market turnover the weight of state bonds gradually increased, while after 1994 that of treasury bills gradually decreased. The proportion of government securities in the turnover saw a clear increase: from the 53.5 percent of 1993 it rose first to 84.5 percent and then to 89.1 percent. In other words, the OTC market became, increasingly, a state-securities market. This is even more interesting, bearing in mind that on the BSE an entirely different process was taking place: on the stock exchange, shares were increasingly pushing down the proportion of state securities in the turnover.

Distribution of OTC turnover by factor or on own account, according to the type of security

(%)

Security	1993*	1994	1995
Shares	4.0	5.9	2.9
State bonds	13.5	16.8	30.0
Corporate bonds	24.9	4.6	4.6
Treasury bills	40.0	67.7	59.1
Other bank launches	3.3	0.4	0.5
Investment bills	0.0	0.0	0.7
Compensation notes	8.6	3.5	1.2
Other	5.7	1.1	1.0
Total	100.0	100.0	100.0

* Statistics are calculated by the State Security and Stock Exchange Supervisory Board since 1993.

** Total bonds.

Comparison between stock-exchange turnover and the turnover of the OTC market

(HUF billion, doubled)

Security	1993*		1994*		1995*	
	Stock Exchange	OTC	Stock Exchange	OTC	Stock Exchange	OTC
Shares	18.3	10.7	57.1	51.0	82.3	45.7
State bonds	73.4	37.1	53.9	145.3	77.2	464.4
Corporate bonds	-	67.8	0.0	39.9	0.5	70.6
Treasury bills	85.0	109.3	81.2	586.5	81.1	913.5
Investment bills	0.1	0.9	0.3	0.3	3.4	10.6
Compensation notes	8.9	23.3	18.7	30.5	4.2	18.4
Other	-	24.1	-	12.2	-	23.7
Total	185.7	273.3	211.2	865.6	253.2	1557.6

* Statistics calculated by the State Security and Stock Exchange Supervisors since 1993

The total turnover of the OTC market in 1993 was 1.5 times that of the total turnover of the BSE; in 1994 it was 1.4 times the turnover of the BSE, and in 1995 it was 6.1 times higher than the BSE turnover. This was mostly a result of the huge turnover in government securities. While in 1993 the stock-exchange turnover in terms of government securities exceeded by HUF 12 billion the turnover of the OTC market, from 1994 this ratio was inverted: the OTC market produced a turnover 5.4 times higher in 1994, and 8.7 times higher in 1995. The stock-exchange turnover in terms of shares in each of the three years under examination exceeded the turnover of the OTC market.

The BSE's attempt to direct a part of the OTC turnover towards the stock exchange was unsuccessful, and the stock-exchange free market was condemned to death even at its birth due to the resistance of parties with opposing interests. The stock-exchange infrastructure was predominantly limited to the capital city, although the electronic trading system made it possible to use locations elsewhere. The high stock-exchange fees, supervision costs, and the obligation to publish quarterly reports made launches on the stock exchange extremely costly, thus only large companies were able to afford to go ahead with them. However, the hausse on the stock exchange made it possible for owners to realize significant founders' profits, which compensated for their increased expenses. Besides the evaluation of shares, the rise in capital created opportunities for expansion. On the other hand, it had a beneficial impact on the interest on bank loans. The state owners had other reasons for privatizing via the stock exchange: while on the stock exchange there is a concentrated demand (professional and financial investors are present in equal numbers), far fewer interested parties participate in bidding-type sales, which might force down the prices. In this way, stock-exchange launches made it possible to achieve higher privatization revenues. This was to be all the more true in the subsequent period.

c) Development between 1996 and 1999

The years 1996 to 1999 can be characterized by the fact that the BSE, after a period of emergence, had reached the stage of convergence. Turnover and capitalization had already made it possible for big funds to participate in the trading, and the domestic demand also became livelier. On the other hand, the crises that swept through the developed stock exchanges left deep marks on the BSE. The Hungarian stock exchange proved extremely sensitive to the Southeast Asian, Russian, and Brazilian crises; however, it was able to right itself relatively quickly.

Rates first saw a dramatic rise in 1996, when the first results of the budgetary adjustment policy—as part of the so-called 'Bokros-package—were clearly outlined. Both the foreign and the domestic economic situation dramatically improved, and, as a result, international rating institutions improved Hungary's rating. This increased the willingness of the major region-specific funds to buy, and enabled funds to appear that had previously been kept away by the restrictive Hungarian investment regulations. Altogether in 1996 the value of the BUX rose 2.7 times, and in 1997 a further 80 percent growth took place. As a result of the Russian crisis 1998 produced negative results (a decrease of 17 percent) that were corrected in 1999 by a 40 percent growth. This growth can also be ascribed to the return of foreign confidence in Hungarian economic policy. It is clear that the impact of certain regional financial crises (Southeast Asian, Russian, Brazilian) rapidly disappeared and that there was an increasing convergence between the Budapest Stock Exchange and the stock exchanges of developed countries.

1. The Capitalization of the Stock Exchange

Capitalization of the stock exchange and its distribution
(HUF billion)

	31 Dec. 1996	31 Dec. 1997	31 Dec. 1998	31 Dec. 1999	31 Dec. 2000
Capitalization of the stock exchange	2,391	5,115	5,470	7,306	6,945
of which:					
Equities	852.5	3,058	3,020	4,145	3,393
State bonds	703	952	1,408	2,040	2,607
Corporate bonds	1	37	63	60	56
Treasury bills	697	908	917	968	797
Investment bills	42	34	6	5	5
Compensation notes	95	126	56	69	67

Source: BSE

Despite the fluctuations within each year, the capitalization of the BSE rose steadily between 1996 and 1999, and in the latter year was altogether six times higher compared with the end of 1995. The first spurt took place as early as 1996, and was partly caused by the sudden rise in stock-exchange rates and the new launches. This is clearly reflected in the fact that while the total capitalization almost doubled, the equity capitalization was 2.6 times higher. In 1997 the favorable tendency continued: while the total capitalization was 2.1 times higher, equity capitalization was 3.6 times higher. The Russian crisis struck the East European stock exchanges hard: this is clearly shown by the fact that while equity capitalization stagnated, total capitalization rose by only 9 percent. Although in 1999 the growth rate was rapid, it was much less rapid than earlier, since total capitalization and equity capitalization rose by between 31 and 37 percent.

Growth in the capitalization of the stock exchange, according to type of security
(1995 = 100)

	1996	1997	1998	1999	2000
Total capitalization	196	419	455	598	569
Equities	260	933	921	1,264	1,034
State bonds	155	210	310	449	574
Treasury bills	185	241	244	257	212
Other	221	310	338	242	106

Source: BSE

As a result of the different growth rates the weight of shares within the total capitalization grew significantly (57 percent in 1999, compared to the 27 percent in 1995), while that of the state bonds fell by 9 percent and that of treasury bills by 17.5 percent. This latter figure also reveals that the stock-exchange investors had moved from short-term state bonds to longer-term state bonds, which can be explained by the reduction in inflation expectations.

One of the signs of the development of stock exchanges and the monetarization of the economy is the percentage of stock-exchange capitalization compared to GDP. The years 1996 to 1999 were also outstanding in this respect. While in 1995 this pointer was only 22 percent, in 1999 it was 66 percent. (The fact that this is still far behind the average in developed countries is also due to structural reasons: the Hungarian-based daughter companies of multinational corporations have opted to launch themselves on the stock exchange in insignificant numbers only, while their contribution to the GDP is extremely high.) The equity capitalization/GDP ratio increased from the 6 percent of 1995 to 37 percent by 1999.

The growth rate of the capitalization of the stock exchange between 1996 and 1999
(1995 = 100)

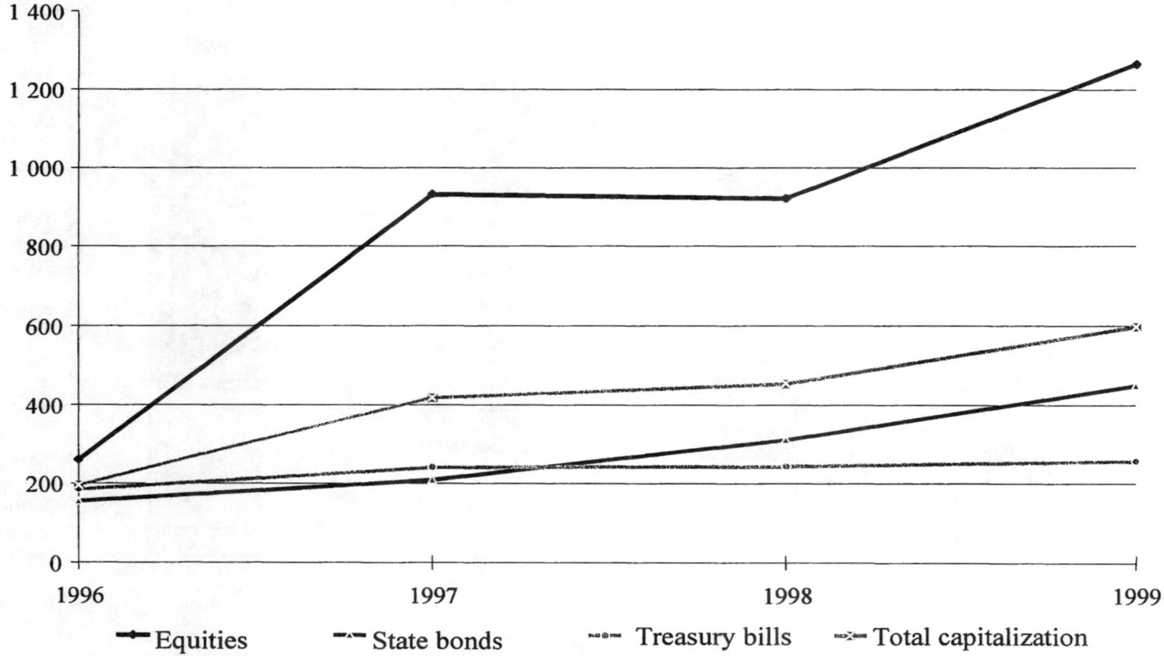

Source: BSE

The distribution of the capitalization of the stock exchange according to type of security, between 1996 and 1999
(%)

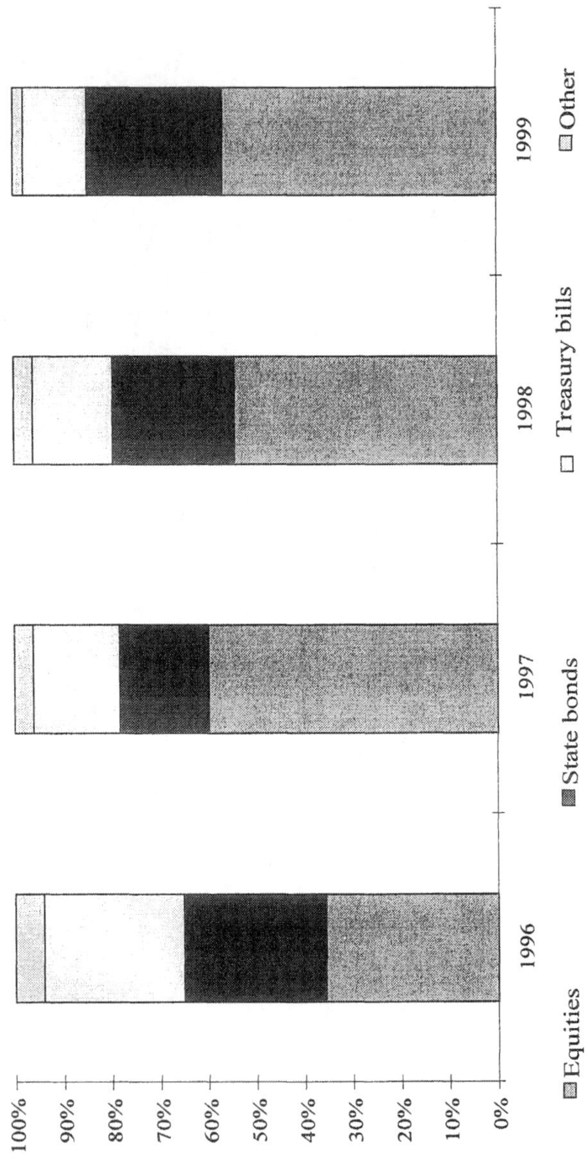

Source: BSE

Stock exchange capitalization compared to the GDP between 1996 and 1999, percent

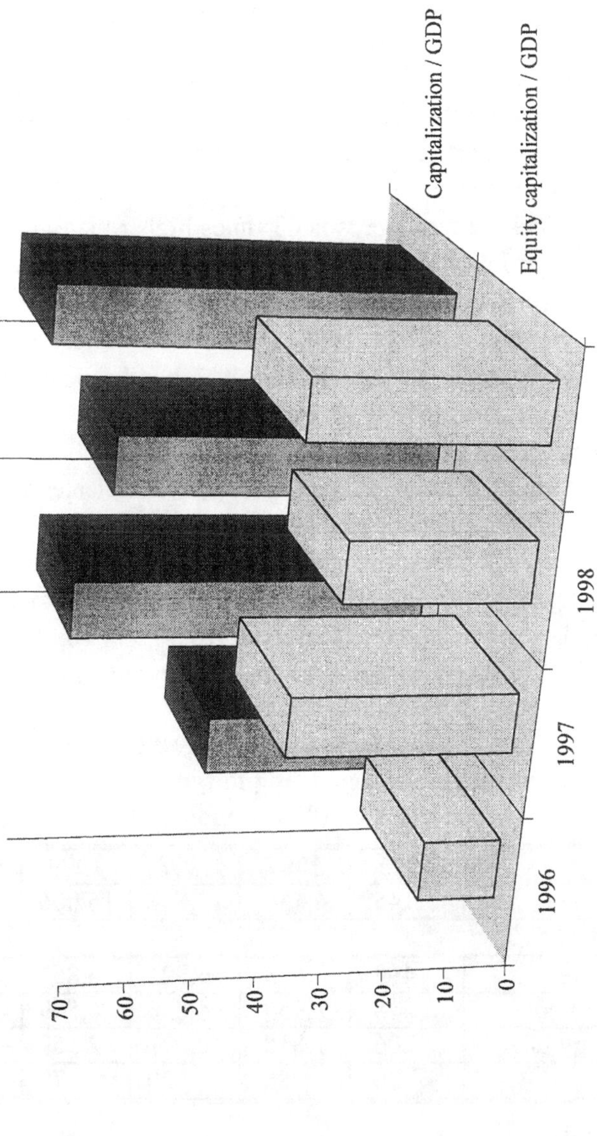

Source: BSE, Central Statistical Office

2. The Turnover of the Stock Exchange

The growth in stock-exchange capitalization ultimately increases turnover, partly because the same number of shares circulate at a higher value, thus increasing the total value; and partly because the rapid growth in rates increases the investors' appetite, generating interest in papers that had previously been less attractive. Thirdly, higher rates attract new companies, which increases capitalization as well as turnover.

By 1999 the turnover was 63 times higher than in 1995. The large foreign Investment bills played a major role in this increase. The turnover was already 4.5 times higher in 1996, and in 1997 it was 6 times higher than in 1996. The turnover almost doubled following lively trade in 1998. Traders who had become used to the dynamic growth rates of the previous years greeted with disappointment the 16 percent growth in 1999.

The capitalization turnover rate, which indicates how many times the securities on the stock exchange change hands on average in one year, is another important pointer. Between 1995 and 1999 the average figure for all securities increased from 21 to 219: within this, the figure for shares increased from 25 to 16; that for state bonds from 17 to 319; while that for treasury bills rose from 22 to 264.

Total turnover on the BSE,
and turnover according to type of security
(HUF billion, doubled)

	1996	1997	1998	1999	2000
Turnover	1,145	6,736	13,848	16,006	8,513
of which:					
Shares	490	2,873	6,921	6,863	6,834
state bonds	418	1,959	4,836	6,509	1,268
treasury bills	206	1,818	2,071	2,559	307
Other	30	86	20	75	104

Source: BSE

In spite of the increase in total turnover, the weight of the various securities within the total turnover hardly changed. The only significant shift took place between treasury bills and state bonds, in favor of the latter. Other securities (corporate bonds, Compensation notes, and the papers of Investment bills) almost entirely disappeared from circulation.

Distribution of the turnover of the stock exchange according to type of security

(%)

	1996	1997	1998	1999	2000
Shares	42.8	42.7	50.0	42.9	80.3
State bonds	36.5	29.1	34.9	40.7	14.9
Treasury bills	18.0	27.0	15.0	16.0	3.6
Other	2.7	1.3	0.1	0.5	1.2
Turnover	100.0	100.0	100.0	100.0	100.0

Source: BSE

The liveliness of the turnover is reflected by the fact that the number of transactions was 25 times higher in 1999 and 22.6 times higher in fiscal year 2000 than in 1995. The average number of daily transactions followed a similar growth rate, while the average daily turnover increased more rapidly, that is, was 64 times higher in 1999 (this value was halved in fiscal 2000). Although the number of trading days did not change, the duration of trade significantly increased after the trading time was extended from 10am to 4.30pm, in contrast to the earlier hours of 10am to 2pm. This in itself reduced turnover, since by the time the Hungarian stock exchange closed the markets of the developed countries were just opening, which limited the extent of daily speculation.

Average daily turnover of the stock exchange

	1996	1997	1998	1999	2000
Number of transactions	170,956	504,879	1,026,646	1,474,083	1,627,033
Average daily transactions	689	2,044	4,140	5,896	6,482
Average daily turnover (HUF billion)	4,619	27,272	55,836	64,023	33,917
Number of trading days	248	247	248	250	251

Source: BSE

The stock-exchange yield in the period under examination was many times higher than risk-free yield. The assets of those entering the market in early 1996 and leaving in late 1999 would be worth 5.2 times more at the end of the four years. Taking the 84 percent inflation rate into account, this meant that the real value was 2.8 times higher by 1999. Those who had invested in treasury bills at the same time would have increased their assets by 94 percent over the four years, which, in real value, would have meant only a 5 percent increase in assets.

Actual yield on 90-day discount treasury bills
(calculated on the bond exchange-rate yield,
expressed as percentage)

	1996	1997	1998	1999	2000
Change in consumer price index* (previous year=100%)	123.6	118.3	114.3	110.0	109.8
Yield on the 90-day discount treasury bill (end of the year)	21.7	19.2	17.2	14.0	n.a.
Actual yield (%)	-1.5	0.7	2.5	3.6	n.a.

* GKI Co's preliminary figure.
Source: CSO, BSE.

Turnover of the stock market, by types of security, between 1996 and 1999 (%)

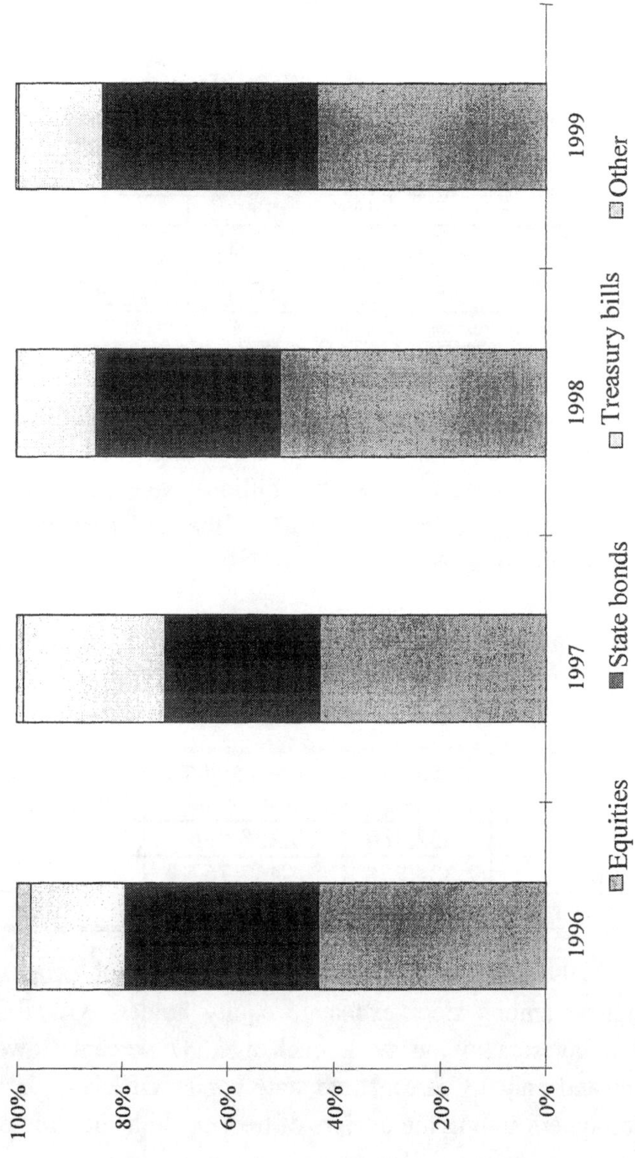

Source: BSE

3. The Role of Foreign Investments in the Hungarian Money and Capital Markets in the late 1990s

Foreign investors on the Hungarian money and capital markets
(HUF billion)

	1996	1997	1998	1999
Non-residents	n. a.	2,130,410	2,403,448	3,705,858
Residents	n. a.	3,720,683	4,327,758	4,556,739
Total	n. a.	5,851,093	6,731,206	8,262,597
Proportion of non-residents	n. a.	36.4	35.7	44.8

Just as in the previous period, between 1996 and 1999 the Hungarian stock exchange depended on foreign investors. On the state bond and equities market a total amount of assets of HUF 3,706 billion (almost USD 15.5 billion) were hold by foreign investors. In 1999 at least 45 percent of the total securities were in foreign ownership.

Proportion of foreign investors according to type of security, in 1999
(HUF billion)

	Residents	Non-residents	Proportion of non-residents
Shares	852,380	3,238,096	79.2
State bonds	2,334,258	467,762	16.7
Treasury bills	1,370,100	0	0

In 1999 one could find an outstandingly high proportion of foreigners among stock-exchange equity holders. Of all foreign capital invested in the stock exchange, 87 percent flowed into shares and only 13 percent into state bonds. Officially there were no foreigners among the owners of treasury bills, but this was due to a peculiarity of the Hungarian regulations, foreigners not being allowed to buy public securities that expire within one year (i.e., treasury bills).

4. The Derivatives Market

The BSE's forward market also showed rapid growth rates: by 1999 it was 129 times higher than it had been in 1995 (although the 1995 figure refers to only a fragment of the year, since trading only began in April). The greatest turnover was in transactions on the BUX Index, producing 87 percent of the forward trade in 1999. Forward trading in hard currencies increased dynamically up to 1998, then in 1999 suddenly dropped to a fraction of what it had been (i.e., from the HUF 974 billion of 1998 to HUF 23 billion). The turnover of the other instruments was insignificant.

5. The OTC Market

As an effect of the stock-exchange launches, the number of OTC shares became smaller and their turnover merely occasional. At the same time, the trade in state bonds saw an upsurge and practically the whole of the OTC market was transformed into a public-bond market. The turnover of investment papers can also be seen as significant on this market.

Turnover of the OTC market

(HUF billion)

Security	1996	1997	1998	1999	2000
Shares	8	259	503	51	
State bonds	474	1,997	9,647	12,716	
Treasury bills	513	1,551	3,595	5,465	
Investment bills	37	1,975	3,565	1,131	
Other	57	11.5	0.3	0	
Total	1,089	5,793	17,310	19,363	

Source: BSE

d) The Budapest Stock Exchange in fiscal year 2000

Fiscal 2000 was a pretty bearish year in the life of the Budapest Stock Exchange: the cash market of the BSE featured HUF 8,513 billion that was slightly more than half of the turnover in the previous year. 80 percent of the turnover in 2000 was realized in equities, the share of government securities declined to 19 percent. The equity turnover was practically equal to that of the previous fiscal year, while turnover of state bonds and T-bills decreased in 2000 by 80 and 88 percent, subsequently. The liquidity rose 10 percent: the average number of daily transactions reached 6,482 in fiscal 2000.[111]

In the fiscal year 2000 the BUX-index declined by 11 percent in forint terms that is 20.6 percent in dollar terms. This fairly poor performance was certainly due to some external reasons too, but on the other hand political wrangling around the price hike of MOL (the Hungarian national oil and gas company) and pharmaceutical societies as well as several unfriendly statements from governmental sources towards foreign investors and capital market speculations has certainly discouraged—mostly foreign—investors.

Because of the important price falls as well as of the 8 delisting (which was not compensated by the one single new listing) the total capitalization of the Budapest Stock Exchange decreased by nearly 5 percent in 2000.

The total derivatives turnover reached HUF 1,353 billion, on December 31, 2000 the number of total open interests was equal to 42,082 contracts—compared to 41,729 a year earlier. The same time, the turnover of the individual equity contracts more than tripled.

The standardized options market started in February 2000 at the Budapest Stock Exchange. The turnover of equity options was 1,231 contracts, while for index options 8,516 contracts were traded. In the second half of the year new maturities were introduced to the individual equity contracts: the two nearest months and September and December. The first Hungarian dematerialized share—that of NABI, the American-owned bus producer—appeared in November 2000.

IV. HUNGARY'S ACCESSION TO THE EUROPEAN UNION: SCHEDULE AND PERSPECTIVES

The aim of this chapter is to provide an overview of the process of Hungary's accession to the European Union, and to analyze Hungary's ability to assume the obligations of membership, as well as some of the foreseeable effects of accession. We regard accession as a process that began in 1999 with the signing of the Europe Agreement between Hungary and the European Community and its member states, and that will end with the signing of the Accession Agreement. Due to considerations of space we have not included every aspect of Hungary's accession to the EU: we have concentrated on those that seem most important with respect to the mid- and long-term development of the Hungarian economy.

1. The history and characteristic features of the relationship between Hungary and the EU

a) The principle phases in the relationship between Hungary and the European Community

Relations between Hungary and the European Community over the past ten years can be divided into three phases. In the first phase, the Agreement on Trade and Commercial and Economic Cooperation was signed in 1998. This agreement resulted in very few material advantages, since it only contained what Hungarian foreign economic diplomacy could not achieve in a multilateral framework following Hungary's joining of GATT. The EC envisaged the elimination of quantitative restrictions in three stages up to 1995. The EC did not grant tariff preferences, nor did it facilitate the market access of Hungarian agricultural products. On these issues it promised mutual negotiations at some undetermined time in the future.

The agreement had no significant direct impact on trade and proved to be irrelevant from a structural political point of view. However, the fact that Hungary diplomatically acknowledged the European Communities did have a political significance.

In order to enhance the transition to democracy and a market economy, in fall 1989, despite the 1988 Agreement on Trade and Commercial and Economic Cooperation, the European Community autonomously abolished the discriminatory quantitative restrictions on Hungarian exports. This was done mostly out of political considerations and was carried out in place of the three-stage schedule that was to have been concluded in 1995. This saw the beginning of the second phase. From 1 January 1990 the EC suspended those quantitative restrictions that did not apply exclusively to the so-called state trade countries. The suspension subsequently had to be renewed annually, that is, the application or suspension of quantitative restrictions still depended on EC decisions.

As of 1 January 1990, the EC expanded the General System of Preferences (GSP) to include Hungary. Under the terms of the GSP, 10 percent of Hungarian textile exports for 1990 were exempted from customs duties. Certain general industrial products were also made customs free. With respect to agricultural products, which made up 26 percent of total Hungarian exports in 1991, the EC granted customs and import levy preferences on a limited group of products. These preferences were granted autonomously by the EC, independent of the activities of Hungarian foreign economic policy.

The beginning of the third phase was marked by the signing of the Europe Agreement on 16 December 1991 in Brussels. This agreement was closely linked to the efforts of Hungarian foreign economic policy and to the transition to parliamentary democracy and a market economy. The Europe Agreement replaced the EC's unilateral General System of Preferences with a contractual commitment to reduce customs duties.

An interim free-trade agreement came into force on 1 March 1992 and remained in effect until the ratification of the contract by the individual nations. On 16 September 1992, the European Parliament approved the Europe Agreement between Hungary and the EU and recommended its parliamentary ratification by the EU member states. The Hungarian Parliament ratified the agreement on 17 November 1992.

The member states of the EU concluded the ratification of the agreement on 15 October 1993, the French Senate being the last to complete the process. The ratification process lasted one year longer than had originally been expected.

The Europe Agreement provided for the full realization of free trade between Hungary and the EU, and for the dismantling of all obstacles (customs duties, quantitative restrictions, etc.) that hindered the movement of goods between Hungary and the EU.

When shaping free trade the parties were guided by a principle of asymmetry. This meant that the EU's various commitments to provide advantages came into force either immediately or within a short delay, while Hungary's similar commitments had to be fulfilled only at a later date. In this transitional period, the Hungarian economy had time to prepare for strong competition from the more developed Common Market producers. In the case of agricultural products, no such free trade agreement was established: instead, the parties proposed favorable conditions for access to each other's markets. The free movement of labor, services, and capital was at best a distant goal. The Europe Agreement provided for the maintenance and mutual development of previous achievements. Finally, the Europe Agreement contained provisions for economic, industrial, scientific, financial, and social cooperation.

There are several differences between the General System of Preferences and the Europe Agreement, in favor of the latter. Most significantly, the GSP was rigid and inflexible, could be withdrawn at any time, and did not include a so-called evolution clause, that is, it did not envisage the institutional realization of free trade in any form. The Europe Agreement replaced the EU's unilateral General System of Preferences with a contractual commitment to reduce customs duties. As a result of the Europe Agreement, Hungarian industrial exports were exempted from customs duties five years after the agreement was signed; textile exports were similarly exempted six years after the signing. Commitments of this kind had not been made by the EU in the framework of the General System of Preferences.

Although preferential quantitative quotas had been increased within the framework of the GSP, this took place only at a very slow pace. On the basis of the Europe Agreement, quotas for Hungarian goods increased while customs duties on goods over the quota were gradually reduced.

In the case of agricultural products, earlier preferences were complemented by new additions. What was envisaged by the Europe Agreement, that is, free trade, could never have been achieved within the framework of the GSP. The Europe Agreement functioned as a stepping stone towards Hungary's European integration.

The EA ensured greater preferences for Hungary than those provided by most favored nation (MFN) status. Since the majority of trade within Western Europe is carried out not on the basis of MFN status but in the framework of preferences, the EA also reduced Hungary's disadvantages when competing in European trading. Compared to the GSP's inflexible system of rules of origin, the rules of origin in the Europe Agreement made possible bilateral cumulation, which was later expanded to Polish-Czech-Slovak cumulation. In comparison with the GSP, the Europe Agreement increased quotas for Hungarian goods while customs duties on goods over the quota were gradually reduced.

As far as the so-called sensitive sectors are concerned, 10 percent of textile exports had formerly taken place in the framework of the GSP. The former Common Market preferences offered by the GSP with respect to textiles were not consolidated. The later preferences that replaced the GSP meant significant advantages compared to the previous conditions.

While the EU's autonomous preferences within the General System of Preferences did not include steel products, the EA abolished quantitative restrictions on such products from 1992 and the customs tariff was reduced from 3.3 to 2.65 percent.

Among general industrial products, the EU's autonomous preferences only envisaged the suspension of non-specific quantitative restrictions that had to be renewed annually. According to the EA, quantitative quotas on general industrial products were entirely eliminated from 1992.

In terms of agricultural products, the EU consolidated, via the Europe Agreement, the 50 percent import levy preferences that had previously been offered autonomously by the General System of Preferences. These preferences were only applicable within certain quantitative quotas (duck and goose meat, salami, and certain pork products), but unlike in the GSP, for five years the quota increased by an annual 10 percent. These quotas only applied to Hungary.

The EU consolidated, on a contractual basis, the preferential customs duties applicable under the GSP (duck and goose liver, horses bred for meat, honey, some fruits and vegetables, horseradish, paprika, raspberries and other berries, and certain jams).

The EU provided customs and import levy preferences for agrarian products, previously treated non-preferentially, that even now play a potentially important role in Hungarian exports. These preferences were calculated according to traditional levels of exports or on the basis of an agreement. The EU agreed with Hungary, Poland, and Czechoslovakia according to the same scheme. In the case of industrial products, and among them sensitive products, the EU, in the majority of cases, provided the same preferences for Poland and Czechoslovakia as for Hungary, and the schedule for the dismantling of customs tariffs was similar. The other chapters of the agreements (on the movement of capital, services, settling, financial and other kinds of cooperation) were in most cases identical in terms of content and structure as well as wording.

The EU followed the same scheme for all three countries in providing preferences for agricultural products. In this respect, Hungary was in a slightly better position in that the initial preferential quotas of 1992 were greater than in the case of Poland and Czechoslovakia and the range of products was, compared to Czechoslovakia, significantly wider.

Although the favorable effects of the EA could be felt in the short term, their benefits predominantly appeared in the long run for Hungarian exporters. In industry and agriculture the agreement resulted in a USD 230 million reduction in the customs duties burden in 1992, and between 1992 and 1996 a reduction of USD 1 billion compared to the previous MFN practice. The additional revenue was divided between Hungarian exporters and importers in the Common Market. By the end of 2000 the signatories to the Europe Agreement, as a result of the reduction in the customs duties burden, will have waived revenues of HUF 400 billion. The EA affected other relations within the Hungarian foreign economic sphere, in as much as it made possible, and even necessary, the working out of agreements similar to the EA. The EU insisted that, on the principle of equal treatment, the goods of EU companies should compete with Hungarian products on the markets of EFTA and of the Central European countries under the same, or very similar conditions, as they did in Hungary.

As for the lowering of customs duties by Hungary, the dismantling of tariffs on about 15 percent of Hungarian imports that arrived from the EU and were subject to duty took place between

1992 and 1994. (The MFN duty had been 8 percent in 1991.) The dismantling of tariffs on 25 percent of exports took place between 1995 and 1997. (The MFN duty had been 7.7 percent based on the 1991 conditions.) Finally, on 60 percent of Hungarian exports the level of MFN duty in 1991 (13 percent) will be abolished between 1995 and 2001.

According to the EA, quantitative restrictions and equivalent measures were to be abolished between 1995 and 2001. Prior to the entire abolition of quantitative restrictions, Hungary has undertaken an annual 10 percent increase in the case of the sub-ceilings of the global quota (an annual 7 percent in the case of the car quota). In the case of consumer demand, the nature of the preferential agreement makes it possible for the corporations of EU countries to get into a more favorable position in the Hungarian market than their competitors. Import-related statistical and customs clearance fees totaling 6 percent have to be abolished between 1995 and 2001.

Although the EA has frequently been criticized from many different angles, in its entirety it can be regarded as favorable from Hungary's point of view. The Europe Agreement between the EU and Hungary inevitably reflects the power relations of the period in question and the existing bargaining position, and, by its very nature, it cannot be regarded as final or perfect. However, compared to the foreign economic diplomatic preliminaries, it inevitably represented a qualitative step ahead and serves the long-term interests of the Hungarian economy.

b) Effects and aspects of the Europe Agreement

As revealed by the above, one of the most important features of the EA between Hungary and the European Community was asymmetry. On the one hand, this meant that the weaker party reciprocated with the dismantling of tariffs and quantitative quotas with an average of four years' delay. On the other hand, it also meant that in the East there was greater opportunity for holding up liberalization (for example, in the case of the EC this affected about 43 percent of industrial imports, and in the case of Hungary, about 60 percent of industrial imports from the EC).

Another ex post device exists, in the form of a clause allowing for the unilateral raising of tariffs, for the benefit of the industries of the weaker party, whether newly created industries or those going through structural transformation. However, in the absence the necessary criteria, identifying such industries appears problematic. The criteria are not detailed either in the EA or explicitly in the European Community's legal documentation. Paradoxically, the agreements between the EC and the Central and East European countries have resulted in a reverse asymmetry.[112]

Presumably, the above-mentioned asymmetries in the scale and timing of the opening of markets have only a limited effect as a counterbalance to the differences in competitiveness and the underlying West European economic power. The greater economic strength of West European exporters probably results in the more dynamic movement of their goods, even through a narrower channel, than the other way around. The less competitive East European exports will probably continue to gain markets more slowly in Western countries.

A significant difference exists in terms of the trade barriers to be dismantled, which is due to differences in tariffs. In Hungary, for instance, the mathematical average of MFN duties is about 13 percent. On top of this come various other duties, in practice surcharges (1 percent licensing fee, 2 percent customs clearance fees, and 3 percent statistical charges). On the Hungarian side, therefore, an 18 to 19 percent import burden has to be eliminated, mostly between 1995 and 2000. On the part of the EC, meanwhile, customs barriers of scarcely 4 percent had to be eliminated by the middle of the decade. Furthermore, in Hungary this will be added to the liberalization measures carried out between 1989 and 1991 when the collapse of the COMECON preferences, the liberalization of foreign trade activity, and the elimination of the general import licensing system within a very short period of time deprived the Hungarian economy of its customary high level of protection.

Free trade only concerns industrial products. The proportion of such goods is different on the two sides in terms of total turnover. At the time the EA was signed, industrial products formed 90 percent of the EC's exports to Hungary, while only 75 percent of Hungarian exports to the Common Market were industrial products. This means that by the last phase of the transitional period (according to the original schedule, between 1997 and 2001) the asymmetrical dismantling of customs duties on industrial products will produce an inverse asymmetry projected onto the entire turnover. At the end of the transitional period the percentage of exports not affected by trade political burdens will be equal to the percentage of exports of industrial products, which is currently approximately 20 percent higher on the part of the EU.

The asymmetry in terms of market share is also worth attention. Out of the total Hungarian exports, those to the EC exceeded 50 percent at the time the EA was signed (at the moment the rate is approximately 75 percent). The Hungarian share of the EC's foreign trade is only 0.8 percent. The liberalization of a marginal market share is qualitatively different from the liberalization of a market share that plays a dominant role in the foreign trade of a national economy.

When applying so-called ex post protective measures, that is, taking steps against market distortion and applying anti-dumping measures, the Western party will doubtless be more efficient. This is suggested partly by the outstandingly well organized interest protection of the entrepreneurial sphere in the West, which is keen to safeguard its markets, by international branch industrial associations and manufacturers' associations, and by the network of chambers of trade; and partly by the application of these measures by government offices, and especially the consistency with which the Brussels Committee carries out the EU's joint trade policy. The EC prefers to cumulate deliberate damages (for instance, in the case of imports of products, coming from various East European countries, in which dumping is suspected), although this is contrary to GATT regulations (in this case, article 6 of the agreement and the related so-called anti-dumping code).

At the time of signing the Europe Agreement, Hungary's strategic goal was a permanent strengthening of EU orientation and, in relation to that, achievement of membership in the EC and the EU. On this question, a consensus was formed between the main interim political players and the economic interest representation groups. The extent of this consensus is illustrated by the fact that the Hungarian Parliament ratified the Europe Agreement with only two votes against and one abstention. In the parliamentary voting there were no votes against the submission of the application for admittance.

The memorandum on the strengthening of integration with the EC and the prospects for accession, which was submitted to the Commission of the European Communities jointly by Hungary, Czechoslovakia and Poland in late August 1992, was aimed at the further gradual economic integration of Hungary with the EU.

In the preamble to the Europe Agreement the EC committed itself only partially to Hungary's integration. Although it acknowledged Hungary's goal of full membership, the agreement did not feature this as a joint aim. The agreement does not mention customs union, which would indicate full integration. Only free trade is mentioned. While a free trade agreement can be made without the goal of integration, there are several elements within the agreement, such as the harmonization of laws, cooperation, etc., which make sense only in terms of this ultimate goal.

The EA reflects a peculiar kind of duality: the envisaged free trade was to be finalized by the year 2000, and its schedule could be accelerated or decelerated by means of the protection clauses. On the other hand, the EA can also be regarded as a frame-like dynamic tool: it is up to the contracting parties what use they make of its provisions.

In the Europe Agreement the EC does not make any promise regarding Hungary's EC and EU membership, but nor does it exclude it. While the EA might prepare the road to full membership, this is not necessarily the end result. Similarly, it does not exclude the possibility that accession might take place before the completion of the agenda set out in the EA. From Hungary's point of view, the agreement has proved a useful framework, but it did not automatically make the country ready for membership.

On 31 March 1994 Hungary submitted its application for membership of the EU. On 18 April 1995 the Council of Ministers decided to implement the procedure set forth in article O of the Maastricht Treaty, which provides for consultation with the Commission. After these preliminaries the document known as the "Commission Opinion on Hungary's Application for Membership of the European Union" was published in the summer of 1997. The document surveyed Hungary's situation from the point of view of the extent to which it was capable of meeting the requirements of membership. The survey gave a very favorable picture of Hungary, much more favorable than that of other candidate countries.

The "AGENDA 2000" document, also published in the summer of 1997, deals with the future of the EU. In this document, when discussing the EU budget, a budget item referring to the CEECs appears only with respect to the year 2002, by which time these countries will have become members.

At the Luxembourg summit of December 1997, a decision was made about the beginning of accession talks with the six countries deemed appropriate by the Commission: the Czech Republic,

Poland, Hungary, Slovenia, Estonia and Cyprus. The talks began in April 1998. The Council of the European Union approved the accession strategy outlined in AGENDA 2000 and endorsed by the Commission.

2. Hungary's ability to assume the obligations of membership

a) The immediate preliminaries to the accession negotiations

Hungary's accession to the EU and the preparations for accession cannot be treated independently from developments during the last decade in foreign economics and foreign economic policy. The most decisive documents relating to the ongoing accession negotiations, on which the strengthening of EU orientation and preparation for membership were based, were built up in various stages.

On the first, basic level were the 1985 White Paper on the homogenization of the internal market of the European Communities, and the subsequent Single European Act (SEA), which was passed in 1987. The SEA targeted the harmonization of the laws of the member states of the European Communities, the reduction or dismantling of physical barriers to financial services, and the reduction or dismantling of technical and fiscal (taxation) barriers. Several statutes (policies or recommendations) were built on the relevant chapter of the SEA.

The second level comprised the White Paper that was passed by the Council at the EU's 1995 summit in Cannes.[113] In the interests of legal harmonization, the EU leadership recommended the Central and Eastern European countries included in the Europe Agreement to accept the Community statutes enumerated in the Cannes White Paper. (Naturally, this only involved principles, since orders or decisions only apply to member states of the Community.) Not all of the Community's statutes have to be accepted by the

CEECs. The statutes in the White Paper are mostly the same as those applying to EU countries (the two sets of legal documents are mostly overlapping, the differences being mostly insignificant and technical), therefore there is no need to make a distinction between the contents of the Cannes White Paper and EU regulations.

The third level is the Europe Agreement made between the member states of the European Communities and Hungary on 16 December 1991. The EA came into force on 1 February 1994, after the European Parliament, the Hungarian Parliament, and the twelve member states of the European Communities completed the ratification process. The EA occasionally allows even more "concessions" than the legal harmonization recommended by the Cannes White Paper. Naturally, the fact cannot be ignored that the EA was born earlier than the Cannes White Paper and contains certain important concessions. (For instance, it gives Hungary a ten-year period of grace in providing freedom of movement in terms of financial services.)

Chapter III of Title 5 of the Europe Agreement ("Approximation of Laws") establishes a link between the Cannes White Paper and the EA. According to this chapter, Hungary's recent and future laws are to be harmonized with EC laws. The government has drawn up, and is carrying out, a so-called legal harmonization program. From the article in the EA on legal harmonization it also follows that Hungary will not only have to adopt the Community's laws mentioned in the White Paper, but also those that will be passed in the future.

Neither the Cannes White Paper nor other Community documents prescribe a set period of time in which those CEECs intending to join the EU have to fulfil the convergence criteria detailed in the Maastricht Treaty.

Adjustment to the Community's laws has been greatly helped by Hungary's participation in the work of various multilateral international institutions (GATT, WTO, etc.) and by Hungary's joining the OECD. Within the framework of these international organizations, Hungary has assumed similar commitments as its adjustment to the Community's laws. Adjustment in these multilateral frameworks, however, took and takes place in the context of a less strict system of conditions than in the case of the Community. The similarities in the features of multilateral and regional (Community) adjustment suggest that the nature of the requirements for Hungary's adjustment to the world economy and its accession to the EU are identical. The differences affect only the scale of adjustment and the fact that accession to the EU involves many areas not regulated by the multilateral frameworks.

Hungary's accession to the EU cannot be seen as restricted merely to the signing of an accession treaty. Joining the EU should be regarded as a process which began on 21 December 1991 with the signing of the EA and which will last until the signing of the accession treaty at some future date, and, in some respects, for several more years.

According to government strategy Hungary should be ready and able to join the EU as of 1 January 2002. The National Program for the Adoption of the Laws and Regulations of the EU, which sums up in 700 pages the schedule and costs of Hungary's adoption of those elements of the Community's laws into its own national legal system that had not already been adopted, was drawn up in accordance with this requirement.

According to the resolutions passed at the 1999 summit of the Council of the European Union in Helsinki, the EU will be ready to accept new member states on 1 January 2003. This is therefore the earliest date on which Hungary will be able to join the EU. Hungary thus has an extra year for its preparations for accession.

b) Hungary's ability to assume the obligations of EU membership, and the main criteria of readiness

In the course of accession talks it is clear that the EU gives a high priority to the candidates' ability to assume the obligations of membership. Besides Western strategic interests, the scale of the intended financial support of the newly joined countries as well as the costs of accession are largely dependent on the readiness of the candidates, Hungary among them, for accession.

The requirements for ability to assume the obligations of membership were defined somewhat loosely at the Copenhagen summit of the Council of the EU in 1993 as: the change of political system, the development of democracy, the establishment of a market economy, and competitiveness.

In itself, membership of the OECD represents an acknowledgement of the fact that Hungary has carried out a transition to a market economy, that it has created a Western-style parliamentary democracy, and has established the legal and institutional framework for a market economy. This was acknowledged by the European Commission's Opinion on Hungary's Application for Membership published in 1997. The only criticism concerned a human rights issue (in relation to the protection of the Roma minority).

Several years before the projected date for EU accession, about 90 percent of Hungarian legislation can be regarded as EC compatible, that is, the overwhelming majority of the principles recommended for adoption by the White Papers have been adopted. Certain steps towards legal harmonization, however, can be carried out only after a number of years, at a time when there is a higher degree of economic development and readiness. This may be true, for instance, in the case of certain laws for environmental protection.

One of the crucial drives behind the EU's eastward expansion is to prevent the destabilization of the Central and Eastern European region and to enhance its stabilization. Contracts made with neighboring states can be regarded as a contribution to the stabilization of Central and Eastern Europe. Between 1990 and 1994 Hungary made such contracts with Ukraine, Croatia and Slovenia, and in 1996 with Slovakia and Romania. Cooperation in the framework of the enlarged CEFTA helps the economic stabilization of the region, the EU-orientation of the CEECs, and their preparations for membership.

Recently, the candidates' ability to assume the obligations of membership has mostly been investigated politically and from the point of view of legal and institutional aspects, somewhat neglecting real economic aspects (structural development, competitiveness in the world economy, and adaptability).[114]

Adjustment in the sphere of the real economy is at least as important as monetary adjustment or the approximation of the Hungarian institutional and legal system to that of the EU. Structural indicators reflect, in a concentrated way, the macro- and microeconomic dimensions of Hungary's ability to assume the obligations of membership. These structural indicators are dynamic and are thus also helpful in prognosis. From among the structural indicators it is worth mentioning that in the case of Hungary, the proportion of the GDP produced by the service sector was permanently increasing during the 1990s and in 1997 reached the highest level in the Central and East European region. The increase in industrial productivity was also outstanding compared to that of other CEECs. The product structure of Hungarian exports has rapidly been modernized: the 1990s saw an increase in the proportion of industrial products, and within that the proportion of machine-industrial products, and within that the proportion of high-technology machines and products requiring a high level of research and development. The proportion of machines and equipment in terms of total Hungarian exports is currently about 60 percent. At the same time, income per one ton of exports has also increased. The transformation of the pattern of goods reflects the concessions of the late 1980s and the 1990s, the improvement of the companies' market activities, as well as the modernizing effect of direct foreign capital investments. On the basis of those indicators of ability to assume the obligations of EU membership relating to economic development and technical and structural transformation, Hungary's situation is the most favorable among the CEE candidates for accession.

3. Challenges, advantages and disadvantages, as well as costs and benefits in relation to EU accession

a) The decision-making system, the first and second "pillars"

Once it has become a member of the EU, Hungary will be obliged to accept the Community's decision-making system. Hungary's role within this system will of course be proportional to the size of its population. According to the present system, this would mean that Hungary would receive twenty-five seats in the European Parliament, and five votes in the Council. With respect to the allocation of rights, the size of a country's population alone is decisive, while in the allocation of financial burdens (contribution to the Community budget) the economic development of the given country, and predominantly the size of its GDP, is decisive.

One of the greatest challenges facing Hungary in relation to EU membership is its joining the third "pillar" of the EU, that is, cooperation in the fields of justice and home affairs. Following accession, Hungary will form the EU's eastern and southeastern border, which will necessitate the application of the Schengen Treaty. Border patrols, the strengthening of border controls, and the fight against organized crime will, for several years, require spending of approximately 0.5 percent of Hungarian GDP.

Joining the EU's second "pillar", that is, common foreign and security policy, will have an effect on the modernization of the Hungarian Armed Forces and on military expenditure. This aspect cannot be separated from Hungary's joining of NATO, although membership of NATO is only marginally related to Hungary's membership of the EU.

b) Foreign Economic Relations and Foreign Economic Policy

As a result of Hungary's accession to the EU, international opinion regarding the country will improve. Major international credit-rating institutions will improve Hungary's risk rating, thereby, on the one hand, improving borrowing conditions (interest rates, maturity periods, etc.)—not so much for the Hungarian National Bank as for the corporate sector. On the other hand, Hungary, as a target of investments, will move out of the category of developing and emerging markets. As a result, not only an increase in foreign working capital investments can be anticipated, but also a rise in portfolio investments.

Following EU accession, Hungary will also adopt the Community's common trade policy, the main elements of which are detailed below.

In foreign trade relations, national competence will be transferred to the European Commission. (In an optimal case, it will take at least five years before Hungary is represented by the Commission.) Following accession, Hungary will no longer be able to make individual international trade and trade political agreements.

The adoption of the Community's trade policy will necessitate Hungary's termination of those earlier trade political agreements that are not in harmony with the common trade policy.

The adoption of the common trade policy will not lead to changes in Hungary's relations with West European and Central European countries. On the basis of preferential agreements made with these partners in recent years, free trade in industrial products will take place by the end of 2000 at the latest. With respect to agricultural products, Hungary and these partners provide significant, although mostly quantitatively limited, concessions to one another.

The adoption of the common trade policy will necessitate the realization of a customs union. The average level of customs duties within the Common Market is significantly (about fifty percent) lower than the Hungarian level, therefore, following accession, the average level of Hungarian customs duties will decrease. Even before the adoption of the Community's customs duties, however, a reduction in the average level of Hungarian customs duties can be expected, partly due to its earlier international commitments, and partly as a result of the Uruguay round of the GATT talks. By 2000, the weighted average of MFN Hungarian customs duties on industrial products will decrease from 9.6 percent to 6.9 percent. It should be mentioned by way of comparison that the average level of customs duties in developed countries is around 3 to 4 percent. In 2000 the expected level of Hungarian customs duties will be approximately double the Community average. In terms of import protection within the agricultural economy, the system of quantitative limitations and licenses will be replaced by protective tariffs, which will be much higher than present duties.

Hungary will have to adopt the EU's preferential trade political contract system ("global Mediterranean" policies, the Lomé Convention, and its legal successor, the UNCTAD general system of preferences [GSP]).

For the adoption of the Community's trade policy, derogations will have to be requested. The technical feasibility of such derogations, however, will be problematic, due to the EU's homogeneous market. These disadvantages will not be neutralized by the application of the Community's protection mechanisms. Actions in the case of dumping, for instance, are problematic, since they take place after the event and are not effective in limiting the increase in imports.

The EU's share of Hungary's foreign trade
(percentage of total exports and total imports)

Year	Exports	Imports
1989	24.8	29.0
1990	32.2	31.0
1991	45.7	41.1
1992	49.8	42.7
1993	46.5	40.1
1994	51.0	45.4
1995	62.7	61.5
1996	62.7	59.8
1997	71.2	62.8
1998	72.9	64.1
1999	76.2	64.4

Source: Central Statistical Office
Note: from 1995 on the EU comprised 15 member states

The indications are that adoption of the common trade policy will not bring about any improvement in the opportunities for Hungarian companies to access markets in the EU. The signing of the Accession Agreement will not therefore affect exports by the Hungarian corporate sphere, since in this respect liberalization has already taken place on the basis of the Europe Agreement.

Hungary's application of the pan-European cumulative provisions, the rules of origin of the European Economic Area, which are also independent of EU membership, will likewise bring about only slight improvement in the conditions for market access for Hungarian goods. Following the adoption of the pan-European cumulative provisions, the system of customs reimbursement has been abolished, which has placed imports from countries outside the European Economic Area at a disadvantage compared with imports from countries within the European Economic Area, with respect to materials incorporated into the exported products.

Common foreign economic policy, and within it, the application of common foreign customs duties, and the adoption of the Community's preferential trade agreements will lead to the further liberalization of the Hungarian economy and to further exposure to foreign competition. This in turn will lead to increasing competition in internal markets.

Efforts on the part of the EU member states to achieve a trade surplus are increasing, regardless of Hungary's accession, since EU member states use their economic relations with the CEECs to balance their trade deficits with respect to the USA and Japan. Such efforts meet with the least resistance in the CEECs.

In the past, Hungarian corporations have participated without restriction in the public acquisition tenders issued by the state and public organizations of EU member states. The liberalization of state and public acquisitions between Hungary and the European Community has taken place independently of accession to the EU. Partly as a result of membership of the European Economic Area, and partly as a result of EU accession, Hungary will have to terminate the overwhelming majority of its present customs-free zones.[115] From among the approximately 130 customs-free zones currently in existence, only about 10 will remain following Hungary's accession to the EU. In Hungary, those companies working in the customs-free zones pay no VAT or customs duties on their imported means of production, while in the EU, means of production coming from outside the EU are not exempt from VAT and customs duties. There is still a debate today surrounding what should be done with means of production already in the country, and whether companies should be burdened with VAT and customs duties retrospectively. Retrospective regulations would lead to uncertainty among investors. Means of production already imported will probably be naturalized in the form of a customs quota with zero percent tax.

Since the benefits of customs-free zones are modest, their termination might at most only produce psychological effects in companies with foreign interests and in relation to the import of foreign working capital.

Meanwhile, the government is looking for interim solutions by which to avoid putting off foreign investors.

c) Use of external resources, migration of labor

In the 1990s Hungary received modest amounts of non-repayable official Community resources. In the framework of the PHARE program, about EURO 100 million have been transferred from the Community each year.

Hungary's accession to the EU will lead to a vast improvement in the conditions for using foreign resources. Following the signing of the Accession Agreement Hungary will have access to the resources of the Community's Structural Funds and Cohesion Fund. At present, the question of how Hungarian agriculture will be affected by the use of these resources can be answered only with large margins of error. The so-called pre-accession programs can be divided into three major groups, as described below.

PHARE's modified conditions provide for the formation of the institutional background necessary for the reception of the resources of the Community's Structural Funds. According to new guidelines, in the period following 1998 the PHARE program was put into the service of preparation for EU accession. In the framework of PHARE, resources of EURO 107 million in 1997, EURO 87 million in 1998, and EURO 110 million in 1999 were awarded to Hungary. In 2000, EURO 97 million support has been awarded to Hungary.

The SAPARD (Special Accession Program for Pre-accession Aid for Agricultural and Rural Development) was created in accordance with the Guidance section of the Community's European

Agricultural Guidance and Guarantee Fund. In the framework of this program Hungary can count on an annual EURO 88 million.

Financial resources have been made available for transportation and environmental protection projects within the ISPA (Instrument for Structural Policies for Accession) program. In this program, resources of an annual EURO 38 million are at Hungary's disposal.

The European Investment Bank has earmarked EURO 8.7 billion for the ten CEE candidates for EU membership between 2000 and 2006. On the basis of previous practice Hungary can expect 10 percent of this, which means an annual EURO 124 million.

Finally, mention should be made of resources coming from non-EU international financial organizations. Of these, the EBRD (European Bank for Reconstruction and Development) intends to make available an annual EURO 500 to 700 million to Central and Eastern Europe. Hungary's share might be 10 percent of this, that is, an annual sum of EURO 50 to 70 million. The World Bank (IBRD) has allocated USD 500 million for the region. If Hungary receives 15 percent of this sum, it will have annual resources of EURO 71 million.[116]

Altogether in the coming years Hungary could receive EURO 470 to 500 million in foreign financing from official sources. The majority of this sum will be non-repayable support from the EU. In the framework of the pre-accession programs there is no opportunity to encourage direct investments by enterprises.

The allocated Community resources naturally constitute only the smaller part of the total resources required. The preparation of agriculture, the police force, customs and border patrols, customs regulations, environmental protection, employment and the social services for EU accession requires a huge amount of investment.

Official non-repayable Community resources available to Hungary prior to EU accession

Sources	million EURO/year
PHARE	97-100
SAPARD	88
ISPA	38
Total	223-226

Source: *Világgazdaság*, 10 March 2000, p. 4.

According to an evaluation based on the Commission's Opinion on Hungary, following its accession to the Community, for which Hungary should be prepared by 1 January 2003 at the earliest, it will have access to the following Community resources:

The expected transfer of Community resources following EU accession

Community support	million EURO
- Market support	250
- Orientation support	300-350
- Direct payments (compensation)	1200
Agricultural total	1750-1800
Structural Funds	1400
Total	3150-3200

Source: Estimates based on EU and other materials

From the agricultural budget, Hungary will receive altogether EURO 1.8 billion. From the Structural Funds, due to the 4 percent ceiling on resources in relation to GDP, it will receive EURO 1.4 billion, which will amount altogether to resources of approximately EURO 3.2 billion. As regards the payment side, like other member states Hungary will pay 1.27 percent of its GDP directly to the Community's budget (which includes customs duties revenue, part of VAT revenue, and the so-called GDP factor), which is currently approximately EURO 550 million.

This means that in the first years after accession (until 2006) the net transfer can be estimated at an annual EURO 2.5 to 2.7 billion. Government policy must therefore take account of the fact that, following EU accession, it will have access to external Community resources as detailed above.

With respect to agriculture, the amount of resources largely depends on how, and to what extent, the Community's agricultural rules apply to the new members. The problematic issues here are mainly compensation payments and the size of such payments. The development of Hungarian companies' business activities in the member states of the EU necessitates the abolition of the Community's present restrictive policy that prevents members of the Hungarian labor force from seeking employment within the EU. The current regulations hinder general contracting activities in EU member states. The indications are that the movement of labor will not be liberalized immediately following Hungary's EU accession.

d) Taxation and tax systems

When making future changes to the tax system, special attention must be paid to the foreign legal harmonization necessitated by accession to the EU.

In terms of direct taxation, European legal harmonization means changes to the guidelines affecting corporate income tax and dividend-withholding tax (mergers, mother- /daughter-company) and, as a result of the agreement on the abolition of double taxation, changes to those guidelines relating to the determination of the profits of affiliated enterprises. The ECOFIN Council's decree on tackling harmful tax competition, which has no political or legal binding force, also has to be kept in mind.

In terms of personal income tax, the main stress must be placed on the application of the principle of equal treatment, and, with respect to the EU's medium-term legislation, on decreasing the burdens on wage earners and on the homogeneous taxation of capital revenue.

With respect to direct taxation, following the necessary preparations and calculations the realization of harmonization will take place in the form of a single significant reform.

According to the Community's Competition Law, tax benefits for investors are regarded as state subsidies and, as such, can be interpreted as prohibited operational grants. If Hungary wishes to maintain such tax benefits it must extend them to all enterprises (regardless of size, sector or location) or it must bring them into harmony with the regulation of competition by a minor modification of the laws. In any case, the benefits must be sector-neutral and transparent. The modifications may not affect existing rights. Companies may retain their present tax benefits until 2011. A reasonable adaptation period must be provided for the introduction of changes. In the EU there are no homogeneous minimal requirements for either personal or corporate income tax rates. Despite this, the 18 percent Hungarian corporate income tax is generally regarded as low. Major foreign corporations will probably declare their profits in Hungary due to the low corporate income tax rates. In this respect, however, Hungary is only exposed to informal pressure since there is no Community regulation according to which this value would need to be changed.

Another potentially controversial area is dividend tax, in the event that a domestic company pays dividends to a foreign mother-company. According to Community regulations, the country in which the daughter company is located has no right to tax such dividends. Dividend tax is only payable in the country in which the mother company is located. The Hungarian budget currently receives annual revenues of HUF 25 billion from the taxation of dividends paid by foreign-owned daughter companies. The government has therefore asked for five years' exemption from the rule. However, it is doubtful whether this exemption will be granted.

e) Derogations

In the course of previous enlargements of the European Union and its legal predecessors, the newly joining countries have usually applied for temporary exemptions in certain areas, known as derogations in Community usage. These derogations have applied to the most diverse areas and periods of time.

Hungary's accession to the EU has generated debates among experts and politicians regarding the necessity for, and the extent of, such derogations. Some experts, partly with reference to the protection of national interests and partly for other reasons, regard application for derogations as necessary. However, the government sees it as desirable to minimize claims for derogations, on the basis that it can thereby keep to a moderate level the derogations claimed by EU member states with respect to the candidate countries, and in order that Hungary can have access to the resources of the Community's Structural Funds at the earliest possible date.

Hungary has thus submitted claims for derogations in certain environmental and agricultural areas. The range of derogation claims is permanently subject to modification. Among the derogation claims the liberalization of the sale of arable lands has created the most controversy. The resistance on the part of the Community is surprising, since in most member states there are significant restrictions on the purchase and sale of arable lands.

f) Hungary and the Economic and Monetary Union

Although Hungary will have to fulfil the convergence criteria detailed in the Maastricht Treaty, fulfillment is not a precondition for EU membership nor will it necessarily have to take place immediately following accession to the EU. First on the agenda is

Hungary's accession to the EU, not to the Economic and Monetary Union (EMU). However, if EU accession is delayed, the timing of membership of the EU and of the EMU will be closer. Under such conditions the requirements for accession to the EU and for joining the EMU cannot be strictly separated. Furthermore, the EU monitors the way in which Hungary fulfils the convergence criteria.

According to the first criterion the budget deficit may not exceed 3 percent of GDP and the national debt may not exceed 60 percent of GDP. In Hungary, the budget deficit (excluding privatization revenues) was 4.8 percent of GDP in 1997; in 1998 it was 4.9 percent; and in 1999 it was 4.6 percent. In an optimal case, the budget deficit in 2000 could be 4 percent; in 2001 it could be 4.5 percent; and in 2002 it could be 4.7 percent of GDP. This suggests that if recent trends continue the convergence criteria laid down in the Maastricht Treaty will not be fulfilled.

The national debt was 60 percent of GDP in 1998. For 2000 and 2001 a figure of 61 to 62 percent can be predicted, and for 2002 around 62 to 63 percent. On the basis of the above figures Hungary will not fulfil the requirements with respect to the national debt.

According to the second convergence criterion, the inflation rate may exceed by 1.5 percent the average of the three best performing EU member states. In 1999 this average was around 0.6 percent (Denmark, France and Sweden), and in 2000 it is likely to be 1 percent (Sweden, France and Finland). Hungary's inflation rate was a long way from the required 2.1 percent (1999) or 2.5 percent (2000), although it was undeniably approaching these figures.

According to the third criterion, long-term interest rates may exceed by a maximum of 2 percent the average of the three best performing EU member states. The fulfillment of this requirement, and Hungary's ability to fulfil it, are closely related to inflation rates. In this respect as well, Hungary's rates are significantly higher than the convergence requirements, although in the medium term further approximation can be expected.

Finally, according to the fourth criterion of the Maastricht Treaty, the normal fluctuation margins (plus or minus 2.25 percent) provided for by the Exchange Rate Mechanism of the European Monetary System had to be observed for at least two years, without devaluing the national currency against the ECU.

Following the establishment of the EMU, the only respect in which this fourth criterion was changed was that rates were no longer pegged to the ECU but to the EURO. According to this criterion, candidate countries for the EMU could not devalue their national currency against the EURO. The requirement for the CEE candidates for EU membership is that the rate of their national currencies may differ by fluctuation margins of plus or minus 15 percent. Hungary has fulfilled this criterion for several years. As of 1 January 2000 the Hungarian National Bank defines the exchange rate of the forint exclusively against the EURO. The intervention band connected to the Hungarian National Bank's parity rate is plus/minus 2.25 percent. The Hungarian National Bank regards as justified the abolition of crawling devaluation, in conjunction with the widening of the intervention band, in the event that inflation is further reduced to below 4 to 5 percent.

It is worth mentioning some of the risks related to the convergence criteria defined in the Maastricht Treaty. In terms of preparation for EU membership, economic growth and wages play a highly significant role. Catching up with the more developed EU member states in economic terms is only possible if the growth rate of Hungarian GDP exceeds the EU average by 2 to 3 percent. In the course of approximation to the EU the economic pressure to raise wages will increase. Firstly, efforts to achieve higher wages by means of wage bargaining will increase, such efforts potentially being prompted by similar wage bargaining in EU countries.

Secondly, if there is a big difference between average Hungarian wage levels and averages in the EU prior to EU accession, then the EU countries will be justified in imposing a temporary restriction on the free movement of Hungarian labor within the EU. At the same time, the present and future medium-term macroeconomic situation does not support the rapid rise in wages required for approximation to EU norms.

Thirdly, there is an EU requirement according to which the minimum wage must be at least 68 percent of average wages. In Hungary this rate is currently around 30 to 35 percent.

If pressure to increase wages grows, there is a danger of a renewed acceleration of inflation, which in turn endangers the fulfillment of the inflation-related convergence criterion.

At this point, mention should be made of the fact that, prior to Hungary's EU accession, the government will adopt and integrate into the Hungarian legal system the Community's guidelines relating to employment, which will result in the further increasing of labor costs.

At present it is hard to define the kind of effect that EU accession will have on wages in the non-competitive sphere, and within this sphere particularly in education and health. It is obvious from the above that the approximation of wages to West European levels will impose one of the most significant challenges in the investment environment.

Due to the different West European employment structure and a limited foreign-language competence among the majority of the Hungarian population (only about 10 percent of the Hungarian population can speak a foreign language) one cannot expect that masses of people will leave the country to find work abroad, even if the accession conditions were to make this possible.

Further measures to increase social security cannot be put in place due to the growing budget deficit, which in turn threatens the fulfillment of the Maastricht Treaty convergence criteria. Reforms in health and education cannot be postponed, although so far the elite of the medical and academic professions have, in the protection of their own interests, undermined substantial reforms.

The fulfillment of the convergence criteria will be hindered by Hungary's accession to the EU and the related access to resources from the Structural Funds. It was mentioned earlier that Hungary will have access to an annual EURO 2.5 to 3.1 billion in Community resources from the Structural Funds. In order to obtain these resources Hungary will have to put forward an equivalent sum, therefore the central budget deficit will be decreased by that amount. Since Hungary and the Community have different priorities for regional development, investment to the amount of the resources transferred from the Community would not have been carried out without EU membership. Not all of this expenditure will generate revenues, and even if it does, it will probably take a long time before those revenues become budget revenues, which in turn will not necessarily increase the central budget. The same mechanism applies to the pre-accession programs.

V. TRANSITION OF THE HUNGARIAN CORPORATE SECTOR

1. The initial situation

Prior to the change of regime in 1988/89, the characteristics of the Hungarian corporate sector were somewhat controversial.

After 1968, Hungarian corporations—unlike those in other socialist countries of the eastern bloc—enjoyed significant autonomy in terms of their management. Many large companies developed a management that was capable of negotiating and competing even on the level of world markets.

At the same time, in the economy as a whole there was an extremely high organizational concentration. As a result of nationalization in the 1940s and 1950s and the vigorous concentration campaigns carried out at intervals, more than 90 per cent of the statistically monitored production was in the hands of fewer than 5,000, mostly very large, state-owned companies and cooperatives. In several sectors large state-owned monopolies emerged. The average size of corporations in many branches—for instance in agriculture and in certain industries—significantly exceeded that of corporations in many industrially developed countries, despite the fact that in these branches, besides the "big ones", middle-sized cooperatives were also to be found. In other areas, chiefly the maintenance industry, the big corporations were complemented by small tradesmen (working without employees).

The economic dominance of the inevitably inflexible large corporations contributed significantly to the shortage economy related problems common to centrally directed economies. The big companies themselves lacked external suppliers, and because of its inflexibility the productive sphere was unable to satisfy consumer demand by adapting its products. In Hungary, however, these problems were greatly reduced in many spheres due to the significant greyand black economies. In the agrarian sector the so-called household economies (in the form of farming on individual crofts, not exceeding one hectare, belonging to farmers who were, in theory at least, members of the producers' cooperatives; and animal husbandry on homesteads) proved to be very efficient. In the 1980s, in the industrial sphere, "business partnerships" (small collectives formed from a company's most efficient employees, who worked as entrepreneurs outside official working hours) played a similar role.

This corporate structure underwent a rapid and dramatic transformation in the years immediately following the political changes of 1989/90.[117]

2. The growth in the number of enterprises

The significant growth in the number of enterprises in Hungary—which was again an exception in the region—began in the early 1980s with the legalization of small enterprises. However, it took on a more rapid pace after 1989, with the coming into force of laws concerning commercial enterprises and individual entrepreneurs. The source of the growth was predominantly the founding of new (private) enterprises, but the dividing up of the former large state-owned companies into smaller units, as well as the dissolution of agricultural cooperatives, also played a part. Between early 1989 and late 1995 the total number of officially registered economic organizations rose more than threefold, increasing from 326 thousand to 1.1 million. (Since 1995 there has been little further change.) The number of companies in relation to the size of the population (that is, more than ten enterprises per one hundred inhabitants) greatly exceeded both the western and the central European averages. However, the majority of new enterprises were created mainly for taxation purposes or underpressure of circumstances, therefore attitudes were characterized by an employee mentality rather than by risk taking.

The number of (registered) economic organizations (year ending)

*Total number of corporate enterprises

	1988	1995	1999
Limited liability company	10.711*	102.697	160.647
Joint-stock company		3.186	4.340
Other incorporated enterprises		11.062	12.449
Unincorporated enterprises	24.657	144.816	211.835
Individual entrepreneurs	290.877	791 .496	660.139
Total	326.245	1.053.257	1.049.410

Source: KSH, Central Statistical Office, Statistical Yearbooks

Approximately one-third of officially registered enterprises are not involved in real activities (because, for example, they were only formed in order to benefit from the investment concessions offered between 1990 and 1993; some never even began—legal—activities, and others went out of business without having their names removed from the registers). Since 1995 the Central Statistical Office has therefore also registered the number of "functioning" companies (i.e. those that pay tax and/or provide statistical data regarding their activities).

The number of functioning companies, 31 December 1998

Branch	Companies with employees of				Total
	-10	11-50	51-300	301-	
Agriculture	36.881	1.280	820	61	39.042
Industry	76.112	5.063	2.069	555	83.799
Building industry	63.551	2.316	362	28	66.257
Trade	255.260	4.894	784	106	261.044
Transportation, Communication	45.322	718	143	56	46.239
Economic services	202.522	2.218	463	69	190.608
Education	11.780	112	7	-	11.899
Health	18.068	113	15	4	18.199
Other	47.187	382	136	14	47.719
Total	756.682	17.096	4.799	893	779.470

Source: *Hungarian Statistical Yearbook 1998*. Central Statistical Office, 1999.

Growth in the number of enterprises was obviously accompanied by a decrease in the average size of companies. Today, the corporate structure is much healthier than the highly concentrated structure that existed in the socialist period, when individual small and medium-sized enterprises were suppressed. Nevertheless, the situation is far from problem free. The majority of the numerous small organizations are smaller than optimal; lacking in capital and occasionally badly managed. They are therefore unlikely to have a long-term future. There was therefore a high level of differentiation among companies in the 1990s, and this will remain the case over the next few years.

3. Changes in ownership structure and company management methods

In the course of the transition, ownership structure in the corporate sphere also changed. While at the beginning of the period under discussion the private sector provided about one-quarter of the GDP, today it produces almost four-fifths and in the coming years its share will slightly increase. The expansion of the private sector, as measured by the number of enterprises, was largely a result of the establishment of new corporations. However, the growth of the sector's weight within the national economy was due partly to privatization and partly to the inflow of direct investment.

Modifications to ownership structure have resulted in fundamental changes in the organization of company management. Earlier, state-owned companies were managed by directors who were appointed (and could be removed at any time) by the relevant government ministries. This resulted in relationships characterized by paternalistic dependency. Following the political changes, the few vestiges of this system that have prevailed are to be found in the ever-narrowing domain of state-owned companies; however, the wholesale removal of company directors following each change of government is clear proof of the survival of certain traditions. The new owners of large companies that have been transferred into foreign ownership have applied the kind of organizational solutions for corporate governance that are used worldwide, establishing boards of directors and supervisory boards and employing independent auditors etc., in the expectation that modern methods of company management will also be used by the—partly foreign—members of these bodies (?). The majority of joint-stock companies and limited liability companies managed by Hungarian owners—struggling with a lack of competent experts—have attempted to adopt the same methods. On the other hand, companies owned by a single owner, typically small scale, are usually managed by the owner him- or herself.[118]

In the course of the transition from a shortage economy to a market economy, corporate conditions have also undergone a rapid transformation. With the liberalization of imports resources are no longer limited, and with the deregulation of wages the labor shortage has been turned into unemployment. Significant changes have also taken place in the financial situation of companies. In the 1980s, lack of capital was one of the primary characteristics of the Hungarian economy, and the significant losses in the corporate sphere caused permanent problems. Following 1990 the inflow of direct investment has effectively helped to remedy the lack capital, and according to surveys carried out by the GKI Economic Research Company, currently "only" one-third of companies regard lack of capital as a serious obstacle to development. The profit-making capacity of enterprises has also improved significantly.

Changes in the operating income of companies
(in billions of forints)

Number of employees	1992	1993	1994	1995	1996	1997	1998
0- 9			-40.1	-26.6	5.0	43.1	85.4
10 – 49			65.6	74.5	81.3	129.4	140.3
50 – 249			-8.1	47.9	85.9	140.5	125.4
Over 250			-68.1	-6.6	96.8	392.6	409.6
Other			-	-	-	-	-
Total	-43.7	81.5	-50.7	89.2	269.0	705.6	760.7

Source: Pitti

4. Changes in entrepreneurial attitudes

In the 1990s, competition and the increased significance of financial criteria etc. forced Hungarian companies to adapt to market conditions. As reflected in surveys[119] carried out by GKI and other similar research organizations, there have been fundamental—although markedly different—changes in company attitudes.

In international practice, companies working in conditions of market economy regard high-quality customer service, and—with some reservations—profit, as their main goals (or "mission"). In similar surveys Hungarian responses typically also mention increased profits (or the closely related increase in income and reduction in costs) as their "ultimate" goals. In the case of majority foreign-owned companies the importance of the profit criteria is even higher than average. Thus, those who responded to the surveys displayed a "rational" attitude regarding their general intentions. (In general the socialist companies declared that increased employee incomes were just as important as profitability. Since the shortage-economy practice of the preceding decades proved that this—at first sight—sympathetic attitude stands in direct opposition to the interests of consumers—and of the company—its modification must be regarded as favorable.)

In most companies significant changes occurred in relation to strategic goals. The bureaucracy common to shortage economies has largely disappeared, as has the luxury of being in a monopolistic position. Instead, effort has been devoted to the development of the company.

On a positive note, the corporate strategy of the majority of companies (following a practice of extensive expansion over several decades) has, for the last few years, been focused on improving the quality of their marketing activities. In recent years an increasing number of companies—that is, over half of those who responded to the surveys—have informed GKI about significant efforts to improve market research, to develop the retail network, and to optimize market conditions. Bearing in mind the general standard of Hungarian marketing activities, these goals are well justified. However, since the standard of marketing activities in the Hungarian economy is, almost everywhere, lower than in developed countries, the modernization of this activity would be justified on a much wider scale than is mentioned above.

Proportion of companies aiming at particular strategic activities*

(%)

Activity	**1993**	**1997**	**2000**
Research		10	37
Purchasing patents, licences or know-how	4	4	8
Free-of-charge technology transfer	-	-	15
Large-scale investment	10	23	48
Small-scale developments	32		-
Expansion of cooperation	12		-
Reduction of cooperation	0		-
Redevelopment of outdated structures	9	-	-
Advertising, PR	-	26	54
Improvement of marketing conditions	-	40	61
Improvement of post-sales services	-	1	

* We have adjusted our questions to the actual economic situation (although this has made it difficult to compare the time-columns). In 1993 we asked questions about the modernization of technology; after 1995 we asked about activities aimed at the improvement of competitiveness; after 1998 we also asked for activities to be rated according to their significance. (The above data also indicate the frequency of fundamental or significant activities).
Source: GKI, Spring Corporate Surveys.

The companies' intentions as regards "technical" developments are also Janus-faced. On the one hand, it can be seen as positive that many companies are carrying out successful innovations on a very significant scale, and that the pressure for redevelopment (?) experienced in the early 1990s has long since vanished. On the other hand, following a well-established tendency, an insufficient number (especially in the light of the "technological" deficit in the economy) of the development measures planned by Hungarian companies are aimed at the modernization of production activities. In an international comparison, it is a particularly negative tendency that even today, only one-third of respondents intend to improve their competitiveness by means of conducting research or buying patents, licences or know-how (nor is the proportion much higher in industry). Even more disconcerting is that only about half of companies undertake significant investments. Smaller enterprises show the least willingness to invest. (In Austria, for example, between 66 and 77 percent of entrepreneurs, as well as about half of small and medium-sized businesses, carry out their own R&D activities, and 44 percent commission external experts to assist them in these tasks.) Another negative factor is that a large proportion of companies has no plans either to improve the quality of their products or to increase their efforts with respect to environmental protection.[120]

Numbers employed in R&D*

Institution	Total number		Scientific developer, researcher	
	1990	1998	1990	1998
R&D Institution	11.931	5.012	5.189	3.061
Higher-education research department	8.843	7.561	5.204	4.398
Company	13.017	4.939	5.681	2.725
Other	2.593	2.803	1.476	1.547
Total	36.384	20.315	17.550	11.731

* Based on full-time employees
Source: *Hungarian Statistical Yearbook 1988.* Hungarian Statistical Office, 1989.

The companies' "average" strategy is the sum of efforts that differ according to property, size, branch and location. In the recently emerging group of companies with foreign majority ownership (occasionally large in international terms but mostly, in fact, medium-sized), the amount of research conducted by the company itself is more or less average. Technological transfer, however, is significantly more frequent, and a willingness to invest is more widespread. Companies in this group are more oriented towards profit and efforts towards domestic expansion are significantly more important than in domestically owned companies. Traditionally, plans for larger investments most frequently occur in big, state-owned companies (in contrast with tradition, however, due to difficulties in financing, the reality of such investments is often questionable). Another characteristic feature is that companies aiming at improving their advertising activities are to be found most commonly in this latter group.[121]

- In certain groups of Hungarian companies it can be shown that globalization and the joining worldwide networks has improved productivity. According to the surveys carried out by GKI, intensive international cooperation has emerged predominantly in the following areas.
- In certain Hungarian branches, predominantly in the textile industry, simple production cooperation, such as occasional contract work, was frequent before the beginning of privatization. It made it possible for many companies—at the cost of part of their corporate independence—to exploit more or less competitive production capacities and to finance production or investment, where it would not otherwise have been possible. After 1990, previously successful contract-work cooperation often became the basis for a foreign partner's acquisition of title. However, in other sectors—for example in the chemical, and especially in the pharmaceutical, industry and in certain engineering branches—foreign acquisition of title served as the basis for a wider ranging cooperation, which included contract work.
- In recent years, with the broadening of international relations, R&D cooperation, and especially the transfer of tech-

nology, has accelerated in several Hungarian companies. At times this has meant fundamental help for the creation of competitiveness in the company in question. This was especially successful if the transfer was accompanied by regular international research cooperation; companies who gave information about such cooperation in our surveys also reported enhanced competitiveness and improved dynamism.

- International marketing experience has been utilized by many Hungarian companies. Cooperation aimed at the adoption of modern market strategies has proved to be outstandingly successful, which, in the recent past (due to the rapid improvement of the former Hungarian deficit in the quality of Hungarian marketing activity), has done most to improve the competitiveness of domestic companies.
- With increasing frequency Hungarian companies are establishing international financial cooperation aimed at the modernization of the productive sphere and at the financing of this modernization. In a company under foreign ownership, international financial relations naturally exist within the company itself. Inter-company financial relations, including mainly those between large Hungarian companies and foreign banks, are increasingly common. Direct borrowing is explained by the lower interest rates and the greater flexibility of foreign banks. Today, foreign investment by Hungarian companies is no longer an exception.

As a result of the efforts of the corporate sector that we have detailed above, the competitiveness of Hungarian companies has significantly improved on the world market in recent years. This fact is illustrated both by the trebling of exports to EU countries over the past few years, and by the figures presented in the corporate surveys below.

The division of company sales in terms of the international competitiveness of products (%)

Product characteristic	1973*	2000**			
	Total	State-owned	Domestic, privately owned	Foreign-owned	Total
Competitive on the world market	18	41(34)	45 (48)	83 (85)	51(44)
Could be competitive with slight development	42	28 (20)	30 (27)	11(11)	26 (21)
Not exportable	40	31(46)	25 (25)	6 (4)	23 (35)
Total	**100**	**100**	**100**	**100**	**100**

* Unweighted averages for industry.
Source: Román.
** Figures for all three main branches of the national economy; figures not in brackets are unweighted, figures inside brackets are averages weighted according to the number of employees in the responding companies.
Source: GKI Co.'s Spring 2000 survey.

The development outlined is not, of course, free of problems. One typical problem is that although today, as is commonly acknowledged, the significance of human resources is equal to that of capital, the handling of these human resources remains a weak element in corporate strategy. Although productivity in industry increased dramatically, it remained low in agriculture and in the large scale (state-owned) service sectors. Wage levels still lag behind the levels common in the EU.[122] In recent years, only companies in certain sectors (for example companies in the processing industry that were acquired by foreign owners) have managed to improve the ways in which they utilized their employees' capabilities. In the state sector, the "resources" have remained practically unchanged, and the importance of a knowledge-based economy has not been recognized. Increasing unemployment has produced high levels of unutilized resources.

5. Problems caused by "unfair" competition

The dynamic enlargement of the private sector, the increasing number of enterprises, the dismantling of a large proportion of the state monopolies—as well as the liberalization of imports, the appearance of transnational companies in Hungary, etc.—have given rise to increased competition in many areas of the economy. This increased competition, as we have outlined above, has had a very positive impact on a formerly rather autarkic market that also showed signs of the shortage economy. This has led to a widening of choice, improvements in quality and in technical standards, some curbing of inflation, and the development of a marketing culture. Other results, however, have not met expectations.

In many places, attitudes that have been held for decades are dying hard. Rather than lowering prices and improving services and quality, a large proportion of entrepreneurs reacted to the fall in domestic sales opportunities by raising prices and neglecting their contractual obligations in order to make up for the losses brought about by decreased turnover by means of reducing costs. In certain sectors the former state monopolies were not replaced by free competition, but by the monopoly of private companies or their oligopolistic situation. This problem is exacerbated by the fact that those institutions that are meant to prevent the abuse of monopolies lack both courage and experience. Respectful of the freedom of enterprise they remain passive observers, even in situations that would have provoked strict intervention in a developed market economy.

In many areas, expectations that foreign companies investing in Hungary would bring with them a culture of customer service have remained unfulfilled. These companies generally create discipline within the company with respect to production and finance, and consistently apply modern methods of management. However, as everywhere in the world, they readily follow the received (and in this case, therefore, lax) norms of the given country in terms of customer service.

Following the political changes, Hungarian governments have invested great resources in the formation of an institutional system for the market economy. Important regulations have been created in the field of competition law, fiscal law, taxation, customs laws, the protection of copyrights, consumer protection and criminal law.[123] Despite this, "unfair" competition has caused increasingly serious problems for Hungarian companies during the past decade. Corruption, according to Transparency International's 1999 survey, has been reduced to "medium" levels, while at the same time, according to surveys by GKI (and EBRD), many other abuses have become common.

The main obstructions to increased production/service
(frequency of mention, in percentage of respondents)

Type of obstruction	1993	1995	1997	1998	1999
Lack of demand ? on the domestic market ? abroad	 65 20	 50 14	 55 10	 66 20	 71 22
Weak competitiveness of the product/services	5	4	3	5	7
Lack of capital	33	30	27	39	42
Unfair competition	15	23	27	32	31
Delayed payments from customers	25	25	22	28	33
Unpredictable state behavior	19	43	28	31	38

Source: GKI Co.'s autumn surveys

One should not, perhaps, be surprised at the consistent response given by those surveyed that the unfair business practices of competitors cause more frequent problems in small and medium-sized—and occasionally domestically owned—companies, than in large state- and foreign-owned companies that are more able to enforce their own interests,[124] etc. According to GKI's survey a wide range of unfair practices have emerged.

Proportion of companies suffering a given level of loss as a result of the illegal business practices of competitors (%)

Form of unfair practice	Losses arising as a result of the given activity			Total
	more than 1% of annual costs	less, but significant	slight	
Taking advantage of mistakes made in the records of the court of registration and in real estate registers	2	6	12	20
Infringement of rights with respect to intellectual property	1	3	6	10
Corruption in relation to public procurement	5	14	10	29
Black-market competition	15	28	16	59
Incomplete performance, or failure to perform, on the part of sub-contractors or external suppliers	6	17	36	59
Demands for protection money	0	1	2	3
Delayed payments or failure to pay	18	30	33	81
Erratic, careless or corrupt attitudes on the part of public institutions	4	15	21	40
Other	7	18	29	54

Source: GKI Co.'s autumn 1998 survey

Our findings indicate that late payment or non-payment is frequent in every sector. Corruption related to public procurement is most frequent in the building industry and in certain financial services (where it can affect between half and three-quarters of companies). In the building industry and especially in commerce, the black market causes even more concentrated losses. The unreliability of court of registration records and of real estate registers most frequently lead to problems in the agricultural sector.

Having said this, it is important to add that in Hungary the "unfair" business practices outlined above occur with only "medium" frequency in comparison with international surveys (e.g. *EBRD*), and that by Central-Eastern European standards the frequency of occurrence is rather low. Criticism of, and efforts to reduce, this phenomenon are justified by the fact that inadequate legal safeguards—as revealed in the first table in this chapter—hinder economic progress on a wide scale.

6. Economic policy for the development of companies

It is clear that due to the kind of significant differences between Hungarian companies suggested above, the development of enterprises can only be supported by a similarly differentiated economic policy. Such policy must take into account the fact that, following the changes over the past few years; companies can be classed according to three main categories on the basis of their attitude.

a) In the Hungarian economy there are increasing numbers of companies, although still not as many as necessary, which, by adopting ambitious strategies, compete successfully—or at least in the hope of success—against imports on the domestic market, and prove their competitiveness by significant exports on world markets. This kind of company is common among those that are now partly, or entirely, in foreign ownership, and/or that cultivate intensive international contacts (partly because the development of an international system of contacts is often an element of their ambitious strategy). However, in contrast to widespread beliefs, successful companies do not only include the sister companies of multinationals. Many middle-sized, or even small, companies—among them Hungarian companies and even, exceptionally, a few (well-managed) state-owned companies—have undeniably become competitive (in terms of exports).

Economic policy can help the development of this class of companies, mainly by means of "classical"—indirect—methods. The creation of legal safeguards is essential. It is very important to create a high quality economic infrastructure (education, transportation and communication, financial sector, etc.). The predictability of the government's work can be a major help. In many cases competent economic diplomacy is important. Hungarian economic policy attempts to meet these expectations (especially the demands of the large multinationals that have obtained significant property). So far, however, certain economic policy institutions (over-politicized and lacking in expertise) have not been able fully to meet these expectations.

b) The second, very large, class of Hungarian companies is (mostly, but not exclusively) made up of small companies that focus on transient opportunities without undertaking serious development. The majority of these companies are predominantly domestically oriented, lack significant international contacts, and have no strategy for improving their typically low level of competitiveness.

More powerful measures in terms of economic policy could (or rather should) be applied to this class than to the previous class. Management training and the more vigorous development of company-related economic advising might often be useful, for example. The organization of the professional safeguarding of interests should be supported. Direct support of R&D, etc. may also be necessary. Our surveys paint a fairly dismal picture of the recent economic role of institutions that are meant to perform such tasks.

The distribution of surveyed companies with respect to their judgement on the significance of assistance received for innovations (%)

Institution providing assistance	Frequent, significant assistance	Occasional assistance	No assistance	Total
Universities, colleges	8	21	71	100
R&D institutions	4	15	81	100
Domestic documentary, information and advising organizations	10	26	64	100
Patent Office	1	5	94	100
Domestic companies	6	19	75	100
Foreign parent-company	16	6	84	100
Other foreign organizations	6	8	86	100

Source: GKI Co.'s autumn 1999 survey

Wide-scale alleviation of the lack of capital typical of this class of companies would be justified, since, in the Hungarian economy, the system of financing innovations, characteristic of developed market economies, has not emerged. So-called business angels, who provide initial support in the practical application of research results, do not exist in Hungary. While elsewhere venture capital investors and banks undertake wide-scale part financing of "industrial" activities related to the introduction of new products and technology but that can no longer be regarded as R&D, in Hungary the role of business credit from these sources is very modest. Companies are obliged to fund most innovations using their own resources. The assistance available (from OMFB or other funds) for the realization of certain developments does little to alleviate the extent of these problems.

c) In the third class of companies, created for the purposes of tax evasion, efforts to improve competitiveness, or expectations of any improvement in this respect, would be misplaced.

NOTES

1. In Hungary, from 1979, a peculiar "stop-go" economic policy was in place, in which every boost to economic growth was accompanied by a disequilibrium in the budget and balance of payments position, and was therefore halted.
2. For different concepts of privatization—in the terminology of the time, property reform—see, for example: Bauer, Tamás (1982), Liska, Tibor (1988), Bársony (1988), Kopátsy, Sándor (1988), Matolcsy, György (1988), Tardos, Márton (1988) and Diczházi, Bertalan (1988).
3. See Act XXXIX of 1995 "On the selling of state-owned property" 2, para. 1. The second paragraph of this article—the article consists of only two paragraphs!—at the same time states that "from among the aspects mentioned in paragraph 1, the State Privatization and Holding Company (ÁPV Rt.) or its representative, when issuing a privatization tender, is bound to state those particular concrete objectives, the realization of which it expects from the given privatization transaction, or the evaluation criteria of such objectives when judging the bids submitted."
4. Act XXXI of 1989.
5. The Law on Business Organizations in practice reinstitutionalized the four traditional forms of trade organization—partnership, limited partnership, limited liability company, and public limited company—and by introducing normative conditions it made way for the creation of a market economy.
6. Tamás Sárközy (1966): p. 135.
7. This law was intended to create the legal foundations for the administration of state property.
8. Act LXIV of 1992 "On the Employees" Share Ownership Program", Act LIII of 1992 "On the Administration and Utilization of Entrepreneurial Assets Remaining in Long-Term State Ownership", Act LIV of 1992 "On the Sale, Utilization and Protection of Assets in Short-Term State Ownership", and Act XX of 1993 "On the Small Businesspersons" Warranty Fund".
9. Sárközy, Tamás: op..cit., pp. 197-198.

10. Mihályi, Péter (1998), p. 163.
11. The privatization tender for HUNGEXPO had been issued by the outgoing government and the applications had already been judged. However, the new ÁŐV Management, appointed by the newly formed Center-Right government, declared the tender invalid and took the privatization of the company off its agenda.
12. Voszka, Éva (1995).
13. Voszka, Éva: op. cit. p. 199. The fact that this topic—and the creation of a new homogeneous organization—was included in the two parties" coalition agreement also reflects the clear-cut privatization views of the Socialist-Liberal coalition.
14. Sárközy, Tamás: op. cit. p. 205.
15. Each of the parliamentary parties delegates one member of the Board. Members are also delegated by employers" and employees" organizations and by certain economic interest representation organizations.
16. Until 1998 this was KPMG Pete Marwick, and since 1998 it has been Ernst & Young.
17. On the use of Existence Credit in relation to privatization, see Giday, András (1998).
18. See on this subject, Boda, Dorottya – Neumann, László (1999).
19. See on this subject, Vanicsek, Mária (1998).
20. In the case of this particular company, unspecified demands for the alleviation of environmental damage and the inextricable links between the infrastructure of the factory and the town made selling impossible.
21. As of early 2000 there are compensation vouchers in circulation with a nominal value, increased by state-guaranteed interest, of approximately HUF 12 billion, and with a stock-exchange value of approximately HUF 5 billion.
22. See: Mihályi, Péter (1998), p. 70.
23. This expression is used by Mihályi, Péter: op. cit. p. 71.
24. If we compare the hard-currency privatization revenues with the total foreign direct investment in flows realized from 1972, the proportion is approximately 40 percent. The remaining 60 percent is divided roughly equally between greenfield investment and follow-up investment. Hard-currency privatization revenues were also realized before 1990, in relation to spontaneous privatization. Major transactions, such as the sale of Tungsram first to Girozentrale then to

General Electric, were carried out in this period. However, this did not reach the state treasury since there were no standardized asset sales or records. At the same time it is obvious that in this period neither privatization nor acquisition-type working capital imports were characteristic.

25. Diczházi, Bertalan (1998), p. 88.
26. The size of further investment in energetics basically depends on mid- and long-term energy politics: the spread of gas power plants and—above all—the method of reconstruction and the changes in capacity of Hungary's only nuclear power station, due to be carried out in 2008-2010.
27. Here we are thinking of the relation between the costs of bank consolidation and privatization revenues: according to the general professional concept, the costs of bank consolidation, or, more exactly, of credit, bank, and debt consolidation, cannot be compared with privatization revenues because these costs reflect the debts formerly accumulated by the Hungarian economy as a whole (in the state-socialist period) rather than the banks' real performance or their realistic market value. Therefore, in professional circles political attempts to compare the two sums have always been rejected.
28. Although it cannot be documented it can be regarded as "common knowledge" that in 1989-1990 there were serious foreign offers to buy state-owned commercial banks, but since these transactions did not take place at the time the subsequent decline in performance simply took these offers off the agenda.
29. Várhegyi, Éva (1998), p. 34-35.
30. See, for instance, the interview with Tibor Pongrácz, the head of the Bank Privatization Committee, in *Népszabadság*, 10 December 1993.
31. Várhegyi, Éva: op. cit., p. 46.
32. In reality, the first bank privatization had the characteristics of spontaneous privatization: in 1989 the Banco San Paolo di Torino acquired a 22 percent stake in InterEuropa Bank by means of a capital increase; and as a result of negotiations initiated by the foreign purchaser, an American financial investor acquired a 50 percent stake in Általános Értékforgalmi Bank (ÁÉB). In Agrobank, the buy-out of small shareholders resulted in significant, and eventually majority, foreign ownership in 1991/2.

33. The relatively large mass of own shares was the result of the cross-ownership that existed after the creation of the two-tier banking system. (See the source mentioned in note 25.) The banks subsequently acquired their own shares, little by little, from the large state-owned corporations that were heading towards bankruptcy. In the case of MKB, the names of these corporations frequently included the suffix "impex": the corporations had embodied the state"s former monopoly in foreign trade and most of them were eventually dissolved.
34. Várhegyi, Éva: op. cit., pp. 54-55. (Emphases in the original.)
35. After the new government nationalized the assets of the Social Security in fall 1998, OTP's 17 percent share package fell into state hands again. Its sell-off took place in fall 1999. Thus, today, the state in fact owns only one single golden share in the Hungarian bank with the largest balance-sheet total.
36. Várhegyi, Éva: op. cit., pp. 55-56.
37. We mention only by way of a note that neither GE Capital nor EBRD can be regarded as a strategic investor, therefore the extent of their purchase should have been just as problematic (in other words, contrary to the Bank Act then in force) as, Soros's Quantum Fund effort a few months earlier, in early 1995, to acquire 25 percent ownership in OTP, which had not been allowed to take place. The bank's weak performance following privatization is probably due to the fact that the investor is not a trade bank, therefore it cannot create a better trade bank than the earlier management from which, in early 1998, the general manager Béla Singlovits was removed.
38. Purchase by Creditanstalt would have been unproblematic since, on the basis of their Hungarian activities, also, their professional qualities and ability to manage MHB was obvious. The decision by the management of ÁPV Rt. was motivated only by the differences between the two applications. Nevertheless, it is fortuitous that it was not the much smaller—practically regional, that is, Central European—Austrian bank, which is already present by means of its daughter-banks in practically all countries of the region, that became the owner of MHB.
39. Deutsche Genossenschaft Bank, GiroCredit, Österreichisches Volksbanken, (the French) Caisse Nationale de Crédit Agricole and (the Canadian) Caisse Centrale Desjardins.
40. Within Takarékbank the savings cooperatives preserved a share of over 25 percent.

41. The second postponement created some—rather tasteless—political debates. The management of ÁPV Rt. had to make a decision about the pricing and the date of the launch three days after the second round of the general elections in 1998. According to the plans, the pricing had to be decided on 23 June and the date of the launch on 24 June. However, the "minicrisis" on the stock exchange, caused by political uncertainty around the time of the elections, made it entirely unreasonable to stick to the original dates that would have resulted in an unfavorable launch price. The management of ÁPV Rt. therefore decided, on 27 May 1998, to postpone the launch. All the more so, since in order to "help" Postabank (details will not be given here) ÁPV Rt, had bought the Finance Ministry"s K&H shares in line with a government decree and did not want to launch the share at a lower price than the price it had paid. Since a postponement required a governmental decree (the government set the date for the launch because it affected the Budget Act, due to the involvement of the social security self-governments), the management of ÁPV Rt. instructed its administration to compile a draft government decree by 3 June. The second/third-in-charge of the election-wining FIDESZ Party, accused the management of ÁPV Rt. several times through the press of intending to make decisions before the change of government that would seriously harm state assets.
42. The privatization organization had no intention of participating in any kind of capital increase as it did not intend to spend on K&H, but to sell its still existing shares—after the nationalization of the assets owned by the social security self-governments it again had significant stakes in the bank.
43. Dr. Kovács, Árpád - Dr. Szabó, Pál: (1998), p. 37.
44. Várhegyi, Éva (1998/a), p. 34.
45. Ibid. p. 35.
46. Tiszai Vegyi Kombinát: Hungary's biggest chemical company.
47. The Hungarian "national" telecommunications company—at that time the majority owner of which was Deutsche Telekom and the minority owner Ameritech. Since then, DT took over Ameritech's stake.
48. *"Az ÁPV Rt. 1997. évi tőkepiaci politikájának érvényesülése."* (ÁPV's Capital Market Policy in 1997) ÁPV Rt. 6/12/IG/1998
49. Mihályi, Péter (1998), p. 430.

50. A typical example of this are the troubles experienced in early 2000 by the second-largest and only Hungarian-owned large dairy producer. This company, created by the merger of four former county dairy producers that purchased the parent company from the state by privatization and subsequently merged with three further smaller dairy producers, went bankrupt at the end of 1999 and faces liquidation. The outcome can scarcely be in doubt: oligopolistic concentration will further increase in the Hungarian milk industry, no Hungarian-owned company will be left, and suppliers who are not paid in full in the course of liquidation and who are unable to establish a fruitful supply relationship with a new purchaser, will lose out.
51. Mihályi, Péter (1998/a), p. 71.
52. Ibid., p. 72. The management of ÁPV Rt. decided in 1988 to create two investment funds for the utilization of compensation vouchers. One of them was to buy vouchers from their original owners; the second was to buy vouchers that had passed into the hands of new owners. The funds were to be based on the non-cash capital contribution making up the minority shareholding in the electricity supplier, which was in the hands of ÁPV Rt. In the first round of the agency tender, OTP Bróker and K&H Bróker qualified. However, it was the wish of the election-winning FIDESZ-MPP parties that the declaration of the winner of the tender take place only after the elections. The new government put a stop to the whole process, however, and it is clear that compensation vouchers will not be taken entirely out of circulation even in 2000.
53. Ibid.
54. On these problems, see Csanádi, Mária (1999) and Laky – Neuman – Boda (1999).
55. In 1997, for example, the employees of SZÜV, in order to prevent the company from going bankrupt, petitioned the management of ÁPV Rt. to mollify the sanctions imposed on it for contravention of the employment clause in the company"s privatization contract drawn up in 1994.
56. In these two Central European countries—and also in Slovakia—whatever was not included in the sphere of voucher-based privatization and whatever is/was being sold to foreign strategic investors, could be sold by the government via individual negotiations, entirely excluding the issuing of tenders. In the majority of cases, not even the selling price is made public. One important example of this was

the Volkswagen/Škoda deal, in which neither the number of shares acquired by the German owner nor the price were made known, although Volkswagen"s investment and the related foreign supplier"s investment—according to official Czech information—represented approximately 40 (!) percent of Czech working-capital imports up to late 1996.

57. *Népszabadság*, 18 May 1998. Between 1 November 1996 and 30 September 1997, Árpád Kovács was chairman of the management of ÁPV Rt. and since then has been head of the State Audit Office.
58. In early 2000 there was much talk of the fact that—at least in the capital markets—the last year of the millennium would be the year of the upcoming markets of Central Europe: this is bound to have a significant impact on foreign direct investment as well.
59. The uncertainty in the relevant statistical data and the difficulties in making comparisons within the region are almost as significant in 2000 as they were ten years ago...
60. An analysis of the statistics for foreign direct investment inflow into Central Europe (that is, CEFTA countries) during the past ten years leads inevitably to the basic conclusion that there is no correlation between the given country's macroeconomic performance—that is, economic growth, balance of payments and budget deficit—and its ability to attract foreign direct investment. Even in absolute terms, Hungary attracted by far the largest amount of foreign direct investment compared to its regional competitors up to 1995–96, when the country's macroeconomic performance was perhaps the worst in the region. During the same period the Czech Republic scarcely attracted any foreign direct investment, in spite of the fact that the Klaus government was at the time the favorite of the entire Western world—although this favoritism was based on a misunderstanding, investors might have been expected to believe what they heard on a daily basis from their governments and their media. Nevertheless, the amount of Czech foreign direct investment inflow rose rapidly in 1998 and remained at the same high level in 1999 once it had become obvious that "the emperor had no clothes" and that the Czech national economy was struggling with serious macro- and microeconomic problems. Also difficult to understand is why, especially following the extremely successful year 1995, Poland's popularity decreased in the very years when the country produced economic growth of 6 to 7 percent and when the growth of the region's

largest market exceeded even these high levels. A really accurate answer will doubtless only emerge with time. However, an approximate idea is probably to be found in the investment strategy of certain major international corporations. In any case, it remains puzzling that macroeconomic performance and the country's image were much less attractive to foreign investors than might have been expected. At the same time, the effect of a given government's economic policy might be found to be more significant than supposed—perhaps because in the main it determines the economy's liberalization and the regulative environment.

61. According to the Hungarian National Bank's balance of payment figures, repatriated profits reached USD 1 billion in 1998: the total amount of repatriated profits was doubled in both 1997 and 1998. The reason for the sudden increase in 1998 was most probably the change in the taxation system: after 1998 the option of transferring earlier profits according to the old taxation regulations was abolished. (At the same time, the panic caused by the Russian financial crisis in the summer of 1998 may also have played a role.)
62. http://mnb.hu/index-n.httm
63. The 18 percent corporate income tax, which is very low by international standards, and the fairly low profit tax of 20 percent would stimulate foreign investors to repatriate profits gained in Hungary if transfer pricing and the price of management services were not more favorable methods of taking income out of the country.
64. See: *Világgazdaság*, 19 January 2000, pp. 1-2.
65. In absolute terms, in 1997 and 1998 the difference was between HUF 713,497 and HUF 1,050,195, and between HUF 853,914 and HUF 1,255,002 average annual gross payments. Source: Central Statistical Office 1999, 2000.
66. It should not be forgotten that foreign companies are included in the branch average, therefore the real differences are much higher than the Central Statistical Office tables quoted here would suggest.
67. The export surplus in Hungarian-German trade—EURO 1 billion—is equal to the deficit in Russian trade relations, due to crude oil and natural gas imports.
68. On the basis of freight documents the entire exports of IBM Hungary, worth USD 2 billion (!), are directed to Germany, since the "importer", IBM Deutschland, has its headquarter in Worms and this is therefore the destination of the "exports" of all European IBM daughter companies.

69. These data are taken from Pitti (1999).
70. Dunning John H. (1993): p. 565.
71. Pitti, Zoltán (1997) and Hamar, Judit (1999).
72. Medicines, computers and office technology, telecommunications equipment, electrical appliances and equipment, medical instruments and precision tools, aircraft and space vehicles and parts.
73. Éltető, Andrea (2000) p. 162.
74. This fund is co-financed by employers and employees in a proportion fixed by the Budgetary Law.
75. Personal income tax is obviously paid by employees, nevertheless we take these payments as an indirect contribution of the employers: they had established the employment possibility by investing into Hungary.
76. Hunya, Gábor and Stankovsky, Jan (1999): p. 4.
77. Several studies reflected years ago on this phenomenon: see, for example, Csáki – Sass- Szalavetz(1996).
78. Coca Cola might soon be followed by Pepsi Cola, UTC Otis by Schindler, Schöller by Eskimo (that is, UNILEVER), or vice versa.
79. "The French banks are ready to accompany their domestic clients to Hungary", was the reply given by Dominique Chatillon, the president of the French Bankers' Association, when asked why French banks are not more active in Hungary. The answer is clear. The French banks' daughter companies limit their activities almost exclusively to serving their domestic clients in Hungary. One of the few exceptions is BNP-Dresdner, which, employing a type of cooperation with which it experimented first in Hungary (involving, for instance, the financing of bus maker IKARUSZ's exports to Russia), has created joint daughter banks in several CEE countries.
80. This was how Opel Hungary Ltd. was transformed into Opel Southeast Europe and became a regional dealer in nine countries. Similarly, Ericsson's software development center became the regional development base for twenty-nine south, east, and southeast European countries.
81. Here we are naturally not taking into consideration the multiplier effects of foreign-owned companies spreading company organizational, business ethical, technical, organizational, and marketing methods at the level of the national economy.
82. GE represents a special example, since besides the USD 800 million invested by GE Lightings Europe in Tungsram, of which about USD 300 million was the cost of the acquisition, GE Aircraft Engines has

invested USD 15 million in Veresegyháza; GE Power Systems has put USD 27 million into another greenfield investment in Ózd; and GE Medical Systems has recently acquired a majority stake in MEDICOR Röntgen Ltd. As is well known, GE Capital has been the main owner of Budapest Bank since 1995, thus five out of the thirteen divisions of GE are already present in Hungary. See *Világgazdaság* (2000/d), p. 5.

83. Matáv Rt., the national telecommunications company, which is the legal successor of a former state monopoly, had been part-owner of two out of the four Hungarian mobile providers. From now on it will be the 100 percent owner, since Deutsche Telekom immediately gave a purchase option for the two mobile phone companies to Matáv Rt., in which they have a major stake and which is, in practice, directed by them. One of the interesting consequences of this transaction will be that in 2001, in the event that Matáv pays Deutsche Telekom, there will be an enormous outflow of capital. Thus, in the balance of payments for 2001, a much lower figure of foreign direct investment inflow will be recorded than in previous years.
84. See: *Népszabadság*, 11 February 2000, p. 11. A. R. and K. Sz. A.: "Megvásárolhatja a Matáv a két Westel-céget?" (Can Matáv buy the two Westel companies?)
85. See: *Világgazdaság* (2000/c).
86. This statement does not contradict the fact that, according to one OECD analysis, "more than three-quarters of Hungarian R&D expenditures in 1997 came from foreign-owned companies in Hungary". See: *Világgazdaság* (2000/a), pp. 1-2. The statement only reflects the sad fact that in the first decade of the economic transition in Hungary the ratio of R&D expenditure to GDP fell to an unprecedented low, even by international standards.
87. See: Farkas, Péter (1995).
88. See: Farkas, Péter (2000): p. 132.
89. See: Papanek, Gábor (1998).
90. See: Sztankó, Éva(1998).
91. This is a joint venture producing medical products for veterinary use.
92. See: *Világgazdaság* (2000/b), p. 7.
93. See: *Világgazdaság*, 25 January 2000, pp. 1. and 15.
94. See: *Világgazdaság*, 1 February 2000. p. 1.
95. Using the categories of Dunning's well-known eclectic theory.
96. It is a professional commonplace—which, on the basis of the experience of developing countries has been included in every handbook

for decades—that tax benefits will not attract foreign direct investment into a country into which capital would otherwise not flow. It is also a fact that in the predominantly working-capital importing countries investment support offered to foreign investors has been inflated to such an extent that offering such benefits has become almost "compulsory". Investors can easily blackmail the government of the target country, claiming that "We are negotiating in three countries and have received ten years' exemption from corporate income tax from the governments of the other two…". The case of BMW is a good example: they openly declared that if they did not get the required tax benefits from the British government—within the EU!—they would relocate their production capacities to Hungary. It is hard to tell to what extent such threats can be taken seriously—that is, to what extent Hungary will have to be prepared to take such enormous investments—and it is even harder to decide what concessions could or should be made to gain such investments…

In terms of individual concessions—on the basis of international experience—it is more sensible to provide support that is related to the real estate required for the investment, such as providing public utilities or infrastructure (e.g. service roads).

97. From this point of view it is extremely important to enlarge the country's motorway network as quickly as possible, regardless of how realistic the government's recent objectives might be and regardless of the less than encouraging achievements in this area so far. It should not be forgotten, however, that the railroads still represent the weakest link in the transportation infrastructure "chain". Not to mention the failure to exploit the full capacities of water transportation on the Danube, in the wake of the over-politicized debate over the Bős-Nagymaros dam…
98. BB: 21-21%; KHB: 8-8.4%; MHB: 8-11.3%; MTB: 9.8-14.4%.
99. Expenditure on Hungarian bank consolidation (approximately USD 3 billion capital costs and approximately the same amount on current expenditure) was not high by international standards. By the end of 1995 the Czech Republic had spent a similar amount for the same purpose, and its banking system is still far from healthy. Finland, which is less populous than Hungary, spent at least 50 percent more on capitalizing and strengthening its banks.
100. See Várhegyi (1997): pp. 71-83.
101. Jones (2001): p. 84.

102. Hypovereinsbank made a general acquisition of BA-CA, thus in Germany and Austria, as well as everywhere else, Hypovereinsbank, that is, the bidder, will incorporate local BA-CA divisions into itself. In Central Europe the locally much stronger BA-CA affiliates are leading the merger. This is also the case in Hungary.
103. The equity capital of Postabank is HUF 44 billion, and as a result of state rehabilitation at the considerable cost of HUF 158 billion, which took place only in 1998/1999, the bank had a minimal net profit in the fiscal year 2000.
104. That is, a "naturally" unprofitable public service provider will "buy" a not very profitable retail bank. Irrespective of the undoubtedly nationwide network (of NPO), neither its capital nor its professional experience will help to revitalize Postabank.
105. Jones: *op. cit.*
106. The approximately HUF 50 billion capital shortfall was extremely significant bearing in mind the size of the insurance sector. The consolidation of the banking system—which, both in terms of size and capital, far surpassed the insurance sector—as mentioned earlier, cost HUF 350 to 400 billion.
107. Taking the hidden economy into account, the amount spent on insurance is even lower by international standards, and the insurance market has an even larger potential.
108. The high level of damage payments in 1999 was primarily caused by the occurrence of serious "acts of God". The sum of damage payments practically equalled the 1998 levels, while charge-related revenues increased by more than 50 percent over the two years.
109. Not taking into account the 100-percent state-owned Hungarian Export Credit Insurance Company.
110. Hungária is the Hungarian daughter company of the Allianz group, while its originally only, then its major, competitor—as its name suggests—is the Hungarian daughter company of the Dutch Aegon group.
111. See: Annual Report 2000. Budapest Stock Exchange Business Development Department, Budapest, January 2000.
112. Balázs, Péter (1993) pp. 1038-1039.
113. See: White Pape (1995). [COM(95) 163 final] p. 508.
114. The real economic conditions of Hungary's ability to assume the obligations of EU membership were first examined by Béla Kádár in the Hungarian economic literature.

115. Companies operating in the customs-free zones provide 42 percent of total Hungarian exports.
116. The analysis by Deutsche Morgan Grenfell is quoted by *Világgazdaság*, 10 March 2000, p. 4.
117. Several general works have been published on the changes that took place in the Hungarian economy in the 1990s. See, for example, Barát (1994), Vértes (1997), the EBRD Transition Reports, etc.
118. We have scarcely any detailed empirical data concerning company management methods in East Central Europe. Research on this subject would be extremely valuable.
119. In its surveys GKI uses eight thousand randomly selected companies from among those companies employing more than twenty employees. For surveys carried out by post, the regular return rate is around 10 percent. See "Ahogy…".
120. Recently, wide-ranging research was carried out on this subject with the methodological support of OECD. See Papanek (1999/a).
121 Ibid.
122. However, the generally low wage levels conceal significant inequalities, which, according to certain authors, in no way reflect production. See: Tsuneo (1999).
123. According to certain authors, the standard of Hungarian economic policy is, in practice, lower than the standard of the (now professional) management in (industrial) companies. See, for example, Lengyel (2000).
124 See: Papanek (1999/b) and Tóth and Semjén (1998).

REFERENCES

"A bankrendszer jövője – egy kérdőíves felmérés alapján"(2000) (The future of the banking system: experiences of a poll.) *National Bank of Hungary*, Budapest, May.

"Ahogy a vállalkozások látják..." ("According to the companies...) *GKI Co.*'s half-yearly publication series.

"Jelentés a a pénzügyi stabilitásról" (2000) (Report on the financial stability) *National Bank of Hungary*, Budapest, August.

"Monetary Policy in Hungary" (2000) *National Bank of Hungary*, Budapest, May.

Balázs, Péter (1993): "Adalékok a közép- és kelet-európai gazdasági átalakulás nemzetközi feltételeihez." (Contributions to the international conditions of the transformation in Central and Eastern Europe), *Közgazdasági Szemle*, Vol. XL., No. 12., pp. 1038-1059.

Barát Miklós (ed.) (1994): "A magyar gazdaság vargabetűje." (The detour of the Hungarian economy) *Aula*.

Bársony, Jenő (1988), "A vagyonérdekeltség érvényesítésének lehetőségei és irányzatainak kritikája." (Possibilies and of interest in assets and their ctitics) *Gazdaság*, no. 3.

Bauer, Tamás (1982), "A második gazdasági reform és a tulajdonviszonyok." (The Second Reform and the Ownership System) *Mozgó Világ*, no. 11.

Boda, Dorottya – Neumann, László (1999), "MRP és MBO a hazai privatizációban." (ESOP and MBO in the Hungarian Privatization) *SZÁMADÁS A TALENTUMRÓL. ÁPV GJW Consultáció*, 1999.

Central Statistical Office (1999 and 2000) "Külföldi működő tőke Magyarországon 1996-1997" and "Külföldi működő tőke

Magyarországon 1997-1998" (Foreign direct investment in Hungary 1996-1997 and 1997 - 1998).

Csáki György – Pitti Zoltán(2000): "Magyarország a világgazdaságban – a nemzetközi működőtőke-áramlás." (Hungary in the World Economy: International FDI-flows) *Külpolitika* (new series) No. 3-4.

Csáki, György – Sass, Magdolna – Szalavetz, Andrea(1996): "A magyarországi külföldi működőtőke-befektetések modernizációs hatása" (The modernizing effect of foreign direct investment in Hungary). *Külpolitika* (new series) No. 2.

Csanádi, Mária (1999), "Szerzõdéses kötelezettségek - Környezetvédelem." (Contractual Obligations – Environmental Protection) *SZÁMADÁS A TALENTUMRÓL. ÁPV – GJW Consultáció*.

Diczházi, Bertalan (1988) "A népi részvényszocializmus vázlata." (Draft for a Popular Shareholders" Socialism) *Figyelő,* 10 November.

Diczházi, Bertalan (1998), "A külföldi tőke szerepe a privatizációban." (The Role of Foreign capital in the Hungarian Privatization) *SZÁMADÁS A TALENTUMRÓL. ÁPV Rt. – KULTURTRADE* Kiadó Kft.

Dr. Kovács, Árpád – Dr. Szabó, Pál (1998), "A magyar privatizációs folyamat összegzése (1990-1997)" (A Summery of the Hungarian Privatization Process: 1990-1997. – draft) Budapest: *ÁPV Rt.*, p. 37.

Dunning John H. (1993): "Multinational Enterprises and the Global Economy" *Addison-Wesley* Publishing Co.

EBRD (1999): "Transition Report." London.

Éltető, Andrea (2000): "A külföldi működőtőke-befektetések hatása az export technológiai szerkezetére nemzetközi összehasonlításban." (The impact of foreign direct investment investments on the technological structure of exports, by international comparison). In (*MTA VKI*) "A működőtőke kivitele és a technikai fejlődés a 21. század küszöbén." (The export of foreign direct investment and technical developments on the verge of the twenty-first century). (Research No. OMFB TAN 99-01.) *Ministry of Education, Budapest.*

European Commission [1995]: "The preparation of the associated countries of Central and Eastern Europe for the integration to the single market of the European Union." (A Communication of the Commission), White Paper, Brussels, V. 03. Com(95) 163, final.

European Commission [1999]: "Regular Report from the Commission on Progress towards Accession." October 13, 1999, http://europa.eu.int/eu/Info/

European Commission [2000]: "Regular Report from the Commission on Progress towards Accession." November 8, 2000, http://www.mfa.gov.hu/euanyag/hu/en.html

Farkas, Péter (1995): "A külföldi működőtőke-beáramlás hatása a K+F-re és az innovációra Magyarországon." (The impact of foreign foreign direct investment inflow on R&D and on innovation in Hungary). *Institute for World Economics,* 1995 (manuscript).

Farkas, Péter (2000): "A külföldi működőtőke hatása a K+F-re és az innovációra Magyarországon." (The impact of foreign foreign direct investment on R&D and on innovation in Hungary). In: (*MTA VKI*) "A működőtőke kivitele és a technikai fejlődés a 21. század küszöbén." (The export of foreign direct investment and technical developments on the verge of the twenty-first century). (Research No. OMFB TAN 99-01.) *Ministry of Education, Budapest.*

Giday, András (1998), "Kedvezményes privatizációs technikák." (Preferential Privatization techniques) *SZÁMADÁS A TALENTUMRÓL.* ÁPV Rt. - Kulturtrade Kiadó Kft.

GKI Economic Research Co. (2000): "Az EU-csatlakozás és Magyarország versenyképessége, felzárkózása." GKI Economic Research Co. [2000]: Accession to the EU and Hungary's competitiveness and catching up, Budapest, November, pp. 119.

GKI Economic Research Co. (2000): "The Role of Foreign Firms in the Hungarian Economy." (Compiled and written by Gy. Csáki) 16+15 pages.

Hamar, Judit (1999): "Regional Aspects of FDI-Inflows in Hungary." *KOPINT-DATORG* Discussion Papers No. 59, September.

Hunya, Gábor and Stankovsky, Jan (1999): "Foreign Direct Investment in Central and East European Countries and the Former Soviet Union." *WIIW-WIFO Database,* 1999/258/ L/2196, September.

Jones, Colin (2001): "First glimpses of consolidation." *The Banker,* January.

Kádár, Béla (2000): "Magyarország európai integrálódásának makrogazdasági összefüggései." (The macro-economic implications of Hungary's integration into Europe), In: Forgács, Imre – Inotai, András – Wéber, Attila (eds.) (2000): *Az Európai Unió évkönyve 1999-2000.* (The Yearbook of the European Union 1999-2000), DHV Magyarország – Osiris, Budapest.

Kopátsy, Sándor (1988), "Gondolatok a tulajdonreformról." (Thoughts about Ownership reform) In: *A tulajdon reformja* (The Ownership Reform), Pénzügykutató Rt.

Laky, Teréz –Neumann, László – Boda, Dorottya (1999), "A privatizáció foglalkoztatási hatásai." (Employment impacts of Privatization) *SZÁMADÁS A TALENTUMRÓL. ÁPV – GJW Consultáció.*

Lengyel, László (2000): "Agyelszívás Magyarországra?" (Brain drain to Hungary?) *Boss.* No. 1.

Liska, Tibor (1988), *Ökonosztát*, Budapest: Közgazdasági és Jogi Könyvkiadó.

Losoncz, Miklós (1999): "A közösségi támogatáspolitika és Magyarország." (The regional policy of the Community and Hungary), *Közgazdasági Szemle,* Vol. XLVI., No. 11., November, pp. 1030-1038.

MAGYAR PÉNZÜGYI ÉS TŐZSDEI ALMANACH (Hungarian Financial and Stock Exchange Yearbook) – different issues.

Matolay, Réka (2001): "Életigenlők." (Yes for life.) *Figyelő,* March 1-7. pp. 60-61.

Matolcsy, György (1988), "Változatok a tulajdonreformra." (Versions of Ownership Reform) *Gazdaság,* no. 4.

Mihályi, Péter (1998), *A magyar privatizáció krónikája 1989-1997.* (The Chronics of the Hungarian Privatization: 1987-1997) Budapest: Közgazdasági és Jogi könyvkiadó.

Mihályi, Péter (1998/a) "A kárpótlás." (The compenzation) *SZÁMADÁS A TÁLENTUMRÓL.* ÁPV Rt. – KULTUR-TRADE Kiadó Kft.

Monthly Report. National Bank of Hungary – different issues.

Népszabadság (2000), A. R. and K. Sz. A.: "Megvásárolhatja a Matáv a két Westel-céget?" (Can Matáv buy the two Westel companies?) 11 February.

Papanek, Gábor – Petz, Raymund –Vértes, András (1997): "EU-harmonized Enterprise Surveys in Hungary." *Hungarian Statistical Review, Special English Issue.*

Papanek, Gábor (1998): "Az innovációs folyamatok sikerei és gondjai a magyar gazdaságban." (Successes and problems of innovation processes in the Hungarian economy). *Európai Tükör,* December.

Papanek, Gábor (ed.) (1999/a): "A magyar innovációs rendszer főbb összefüggései." *OMFB.* In English: National Innovation System in Hungary. OMFB. [1999]

Papanek, Gábor (ed.) (1999/b): "Jogbiztonság a magyar gazdasági életben." *Filum.* In English: "Business Ethics and Legal Environment in Hungary." *GKI's Economic Trends and Research Summaries.* (1999) No.2.

Pitti, Zoltán (1997): "Egészen eredeti tőkefelhalmozás Magyarországon." (Very primitive original capital accumulation in Hungary). *Társadalmi Szemle* Nos. 8–9.

Pitti, Zoltán (1999): *Külföldi érdekeltségű vállakozások térnyerése és a hazai gazdaság 1998. évi fejlődése* (The rise in the number of companies with foreign interest and the development of the domestic economy in 1998), mimeo, GKI Economic Research Co.

Pitti, Zoltán (2000): *A hazai társas vállalkozások működési jellemzőinek értékelése és a gazdálkodás beszállítói programot érintő összefüggéseinek bemutatása.* (The evaluation of the operation of the Hungarian-owned companies – with special regard to the "suppliers' program") *GKI Co.*

Román, Zoltán (1973): *Termelékenységünk az iparban.* (Productivity in the industry) KJK.

Sárközy, Tamás (1966), *A hatékonyabb kormányzásért (avagy egy technokrata reménytelen bozótharca az államapparátussal és a politikával szemben)* (For an effective governance: a partisan's hopeless fights against burecracy) Budapest: Magvető, p. 135.

Sztankó, Éva (1998): "Kutatás és technológia-fejlesztés az iparban." (Research and technological development in the industry). *Építőipar,* No. 9–10.

Tardos, Márton (1988), "A gazdasági szervezetek és a tulajdon." (EconomicOrganizations and the Ownership) *Gazdaság*, no. 3.

Tóth, István János – Semjén, András (1998): "Tax Behaviour and Financial Discipline of Hungarian Enterprises." In: Csaba, László (ed): *The Hungarian SME Sector Development in Comparative Perspective.* CIPE-KOPINT

Transparency International: (1999) "Bribe. Payers Index and Corruption Perceptions Index." www: transparency.de/documents.

Tsuneo, M. (1999): "Felemás piacgazdaság és a régi rendszer öröksége." (A contradictory market economy and the 'heritage' of the 'ancien régime') *Külgazdaság* No. 10.

Vanicsek, Mária (1998), "Elosztásos privatizáció." (Distribution-type privatization) *SZÁMADÁS A TALENTUMRÓL*. ÁPV – KULTURTRADE Kiadó Kft.

Várhegyi Éva (1998): "Bankprivatizáció." (Banking privatization) *SZÁMADÁS A TÁLENTUMRÓL* ÁPV Rt. - KULTURTRADE Kiadó Kft. Budapest.

Várhegyi, Éva (1998/a), "Magyar bankprivatizáció: Kényszerből erény." (Hungarian Bank Privatization: from Must to Virtue) *FIGYELŐ*, 28 May.

Vértes, András (ed.) (1997): *A kapitalizmus alapjainak lerakása Magyarországon (1990-2002).* (The laying down of the basis of capitalism in Hungary: 1990-2002) GKI Co.

Világgazdaság (2000/a): "Kiugró a külföldi tőke szerepe Magyarországon. A multik magasabb fizetést adnak és termelékenyebbek, mint a magyar tulajdonú cégek." (The outstanding role of foreign capital in Hungary. Multis pay higher wages and are more productive than Hungarian-owned companies). 19 January.

Világgazdaság (2000/b): "A szellemi tőke értéke. Bázisok Magyarországon" (The value of intellectual capital. Bases in Hungary). 1 February.

Világgazdaság, (2000/c): "Több támogatás a beszállítóknak. Egyetlen multi sem kap egyedi kedvezményt – Székesfehérvár megtelt." (More support for subcontractors. Not a single multinational gets individual benefits – Székesfehérvár is "full"). 7 February.

Világgazdaság (2000/d): "Nyolcszázmillió dollárt ölt a Tungsramba a GE" (GE invests eight hundred million dollars in Tungsram). 17 February.

Világgazdaság (2001): "Adatok, tények, tendenciák. – 2001." A VILÁGGAZDASÁG évkönyve. (World Economy 2001: data, facts, tendencies – a Yearbook of the daily VILÁGGAZDASÁG)

Voszka, Éva (1995), *Az agyaglábakon álló óriás* (The Giant with Feet of Clay) Budapest: Pénzügykutató Rt.

World Bank (1999): "Hungary. On the Road to the EU." Washington.

Yearbook. National Bank of Hungary – different issues.

CHAPTER III
SHORT-TERM MACROECONOMIC FORECAST (2001-2002)

I. MACROECONOMIC PERFORMANCE AND INDICATORS

In the coming years the relatively rapid development of the Hungarian economy is expected to continue, and its external and internal balance will probably be maintained within tolerable margins.*

External conditions are basically favorable. The economic growth of the EU, which represents Hungary's main export market, has accelerated, although in the year 2000 increasing fuel prices have worsened the terms of trade.

Between 2000 and 2002, average growth in the Hungarian economy will reach an annual 5 percent. Significant amounts of foreign direct investment will flow into the country. Growth will be largely export and investment oriented, although consumption will also increase. Telecommunications, manufacturing as well as the construction industry will see the most dynamic development (by an annual average of between 8 and 11 percent). The development of the service sector will accelerate, while developments in agriculture will stagnate further.

The main question to be examined is how Hungarian economic policy will adapt to the changes in the domestic and world economy. The main issues in the coming years will be the preparation for EU accession, the handling of sectors in crisis (agriculture and health), and the avoidance of overheating in the economy.

In 2001/2002 (prior to the general election in Hungary), fiscal attitudes will probably be somewhat more relaxed. However, income policy will not go as far as to fulfil unrealistic promises.

* This chapter is based upon GKI Economic Research Company's most recent forecasts which were prepared in early March, 2001.

Financial indicators, 1999-2002

	1999 (1998 = 100)	2000. (1999=100)	2002	2000-2002 annual average
Inflation (previous year = 100)	110.0	109.8	106-107	108.8
Budget deficit / GDP (percent)*	5.1	3.4	4.9	5.1
Foreign trade deficit (EURO billion)	2.9	4.3	4.9	4.7
Current account deficit (EURO billion)	2.0	1.9	2.7	2.5

Note: Data for 2000 are preliminary figures as of March 2001. Data for 2002 are based on forecasts by GKI Co.

* Taking extra-government financing into account, the budget deficit is typically higher by 0.5-1 percentage points.

Under such conditions the balance of payments deficit in relation to GDP will increase only slightly (or perhaps stagnate). In 2001/2002, due to electoral considerations, economic policy (according to GKI Co.'s forecasts) will allow for a growth in internal consumption slightly exceeding the growth of GDP, and thus a slight disequilibrium will emerge. Significant reform measures will probably not take place until 2002.

The net influx of foreign direct investment will amount to between EURO 3 and 4 billion over the coming two years (while the current account deficit will be between EURO 5 and 6 billion). The difference will be covered by the further influx of non debt-generating external sources. This way, the country's net external debt will decrease significantly compared to the increasing export performance, and will decrease both in relative and absolute terms.

Macroeconomic indicators, 1999-2002
(volume indexes)

	2000 (1999=100)	2002 (2000=100)	2000-2002 annual average
GDP	105.3	116.0	105.0
Of which:			
Agriculture	100.0	101.0	100.5
Industry	118.3	145.3	113.4
Construction industry	105.8	125.0	109.3
Trade	131.0	129.0	110.0
Transportation, telecoms	104.0	110.3	103.5
Services	102.0	104.5	102.0
Domestic utilization of GDP	105.1	116.7	105.0
Of which:			
Individual consumption	104.0	109.2	104.5
Investment	106.5	117.5	108.0
Exports (goods and services)	122.5	124.3	115.0
Imports (goods and services)	121.5	125.5	114.5

Note: Data for 2000 preliminary figures as of March 2000. Data for 2002 are GKI Co.'s forecasts.

The domestic utilization of GDP will increase significantly. Investments will increase much more rapidly than average. The accumulation of fixed assets will increase by an annual average of approximately 10 percent, thus by 2002 the investment rate will have increased by 3 percent as compared to 1999, that is, to about 27.5 percent.

The employment situation will further improve. The employment level will increase by an average of 0.5 to 1 percent annually. The unemployment rate will fall (to about 5 percent). However, social tensions will prevail among the elderly, the less highly qualified people, as well as among those living in disadvantaged areas, and those living in the eastern part of the country. Efficiency on the level of the national economy (GDP per employee) will increase by more than 12 percent over the three years period of 2000–2002.

Public consumption will increase by an annual 4.5 percent. This will allow for some improvement in the situation of the least well off. However, the incomes of the most affluent will continue to increase at the fastest rate, thus differentiation in terms of incomes and assets will continue. Public savings will increase, especially in the form of pension funds. However, the savings rate will remain low in the long term.

From the second half of 2001 onward, inflation will steadily decrease and by the end of 2002 it will fall to between 6 and 7 percent. A very slow increase in the real rate of interest can be expected, while nominal interest will slowly but steadily be reduced. Significant fluctuations are likely on the money and capital markets. In 2001, crawling devaluation will probably be abolished and the HUF exchange rate—perhaps with wider fluctuation margins—will be pegged to the EURO. During the period of crawling devaluation, and even after it has been abolished, there will be a continuous currency appreciation (at the level of consumer prices) but without putting competitiveness at risk.

During this period, the Hungarian economy will reach or surpass its 1989 level in every important aspect, (that is, the levels that existed before the change of system). (GDP has just surpassed its 1989 level in the fiscal year 2000.)

Significant integration will take place with Western Europe. By the end of 2002 Hungary will, in most respects, be ready for membership of the European Union (although, naturally, its development and income levels will remain much lower than the EU average). The actual decision regarding membership will be predominantly of a political nature. At the same time, important institutional and budget reforms remain to be introduced.

Compared to the most likely course of events as detailed above—partly due to unfavorable world-economic trends and partly to Hungary's inadequate adaptation to them—it is possible that a worse course of development might take place. This would involve a slower increase in exports and weaker economic growth (of an annual 3 to 3.5 percent). In the context of more advantageous foreign economic conditions (for example, rapid accession to the EU and successful internal reforms) a more favorable course of development would be possible. In this case, GDP would increase at an annual average of 5.5 to 6 percent and inflation would fall to 4 or 5 percent by 2002.

II. INSTITUTIONAL, ORGANIZATIONAL AND LEGAL CHANGES

1. Changes in ownership and organization, and competition

In the coming years, the rise in the number of enterprises in Hungary will gradually slowdown. Fewer new companies will be formed, while centralization/concentration processes will continue.

In more and more areas, large corporations will replace small ones. In terms of the corporate structure of the national economy, the proportion of large corporations is already significant: it corresponds to levels in the developed industrial countries. These corporations are almost entirely foreign (sometimes state-)owned and play a decisive role in exports and technical development. Their numbers, weight and importance will increase in the coming years. Although the position of small and medium-sized companies is improving, they continue to face difficulties: not many of them will survive into the year 2002.

The number of micro-enterprises is very high compared to international levels. Many of them are formed as a result of coercion, or are "virtual" enterprises, only created in order to avoid paying high personal income tax and/or welfare charges. In the next two or three years their numbers will fall the most dramatically. On the other hand, the number of micro-enterprises will increase.

In the coming years the position, sales opportunities, and profitability of domestic private companies will improve. Their capital and performance will increase in absolute terms. However, the proportion of such companies will slightly decrease, mostly due to the dynamic expansion of foreign-owned companies. Foreign-owned

The number of enterprises at the end of the period 1995-2002
(1000)

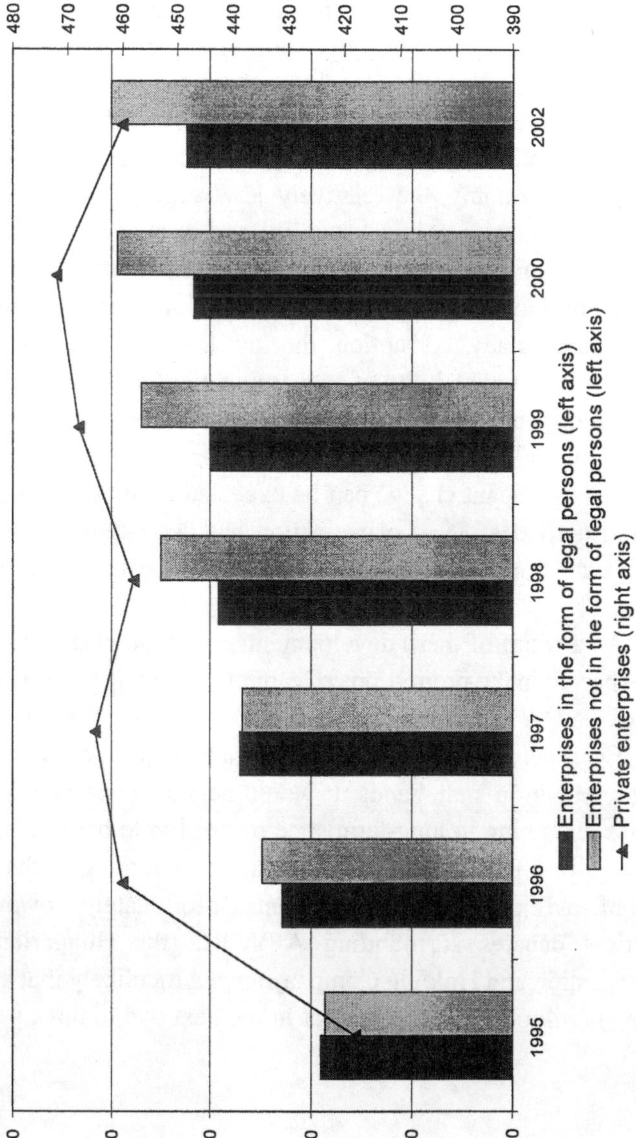

Source: Central Statistical Office; and GKI Co.'s forecasts.

companies are the most dynamic players in the economy. They dominate the key branches and their further expansion can be expected. The size of the state sector will slightly decrease but its role will remain essentially unchanged.

The interest of foreign investors in investment opportunities in Hungary is still high. They are attracted by the recovery of the Hungarian economy, the relatively low wages, the high level of skills, the country's political stability, and its expected accession to the EU (in spite of the uncertainty that remains about the date of accession). However, foreign investors still have many complaints about bureaucracy, corruption, the low level of legal guarantees, crime, the unpredictability of economic policy, and the condition of the country's infrastructure. Despite this, the overwhelming majority are basically satisfied and plan to expand their presence.

No significant change can be expected in the state's entrepreneurial activities. Mass privatization has been completed and no significant transactions can be foreseen in the next two or three years.

As a result of these developments, the following changes can be expected in the proportions of capital ownership in the corporate sector.

Even so, significant entrepreneurial or quasi-entrepreneurial assets remain in state hands. It would be very important for companies remaining in long-term state ownership to be supervised by a specialized profit-oriented organization, according to the principles of traditional asset management. Unfortunately, however, the political debates surrounding ÁPV Rt. (the Hungarian State Privatization and Holding Company) make it unlikely that a breakthrough will occur in this respect in the next two to three years.

Composition of the subscribed capital of business organisations according to ownerssship
(at the end of the period, in percent)

Type of ownership	1992	1995	1997	1998	1999	2002
Domestic private person	9.8	12.4	10.9	11.2		
Domestic company	12.4	19.9	24.2	26.2		
Cooperative	2.8	2.1	1.6	1.7		
Employees' share ownership organization (ESOPs)	0.1	1.0	0.8	0.6		
Domestic private total	25.1	35.4	37.5	39.7	39.5	39
Foreign natural and legal persons	10.1	27.9	35.4	37.6	38.5	42
Private total	35.2	63.3	72.9	77.3	78.0	81
Central government	58.9	29.5	15.9	13.3		
Local governments	5.1	6.3	8.9	7.6		
Other	0.8	0.9	2.3	1.8		
State and other	64.8	36.7	27.1	22.7	22.0	19
Total subscribed capital	100	100	100	100	100	100

Source: 1992-98: data from State Tax Authority.

In the recent past, important initiatives have been made to expand competition into areas in which the provider's natural monopoly had previously rendered competition impossible (electricity and gas supply, fixed-track transportation, telephony, etc.). In this context, "natural monopoly" implies that the service requires some kind of network (cables, rail-tracks, pipelines, etc.) and that the provider owns the network and refuses to allow other's "goods" to pass through it. Since the creation of new networks is not lucrative enough, it is practically impossible for new market players to compete. Natural monopolies are often accompanied by concession contracts for a given area (and/or period), which exclude competition by legal means.

The market liberalization can be expected in the period up to 2002, which means, on the one hand, that the owners of networks (pipelines, cables, power-lines, railroad tracks, etc.) will be forced, in return for appropriate payment, to allow others' "goods" through. On the other hand, by decreasing or ending concessions, the various service providers (e.g. telephone, cable TV, Internet) will be allowed onto each other's territory.

The greatest progress is taking place in the field of telecommunications and information technologies. The rapid spread of mobile phones has decreased the monopolistic situation previously enjoyed by MATÁV. Technical developments are expected to generate competition among the local telephone and cable TV companies. The conditions for liberalization will probably be regulated by the Communication Act, expected to be passed in 2002.

In terms of electricity supply, in the long term every user will be able to decide from whom they choose to purchase electricity, forcing producers to provide reliable services and favorable tariffs for consumers. The present levels of technological development mean that this opportunity will only be available to large-scale consumers. Household users will profit from this indirectly via the lower costs to the electricity providers.

From the technological and legal point of view, liberalization could take place immediately. One problem, however, is that the electricity distributor MVM has a long-term contract with the domestic power plants to buy at a higher price than the expected price of imports. The liberalization of the electricity industry, which would still affect only large-scale consumers, could optimally take place at the end of the period under discussion.

In the gas sector, MOL, interestingly enough, is one of the most vocal advocates of liberalization, since its expectation is that competition, and the related freedom with respect to pricing, will release it from the pressure of officially imposed prices. Liberalization will bring about opportunities for other distributors (using the pipelines at present owned by MOL) to appear on the Hungarian market, but also for MOL to maneuver better among the sources of purchase, to express its costs more realistically in its prices, and even to export Hungarian gas. However, because of government attitudes, no rapid breakthrough can be expected.

2. Innovative tendencies

In the year 2000, the character of the innovative tendencies that have become prominent over the last decade does change once again. Firstly, unprofitable production has been halted. An increasing number of industries have subsequently become internationally competitive as a result of the technology transfer that has accompanied the increasing imports of capital. Innovations have now transformed all sectors of the economy, increasing its efficiency. The tripling of Hungarian exports in recent years testifies to the significant progress made over the last decade.

Despite this progress, the innovative efforts of the microsphere still cannot be regarded as satisfactory. The circle of those who have been left entirely untouched by progress is too wide. A significant percentage of companies do not regard it as possible to improve the quality of their products. The problem is particularly serious in the otherwise crisis-stricken agricultural and transportation industries as well as in small enterprises. At the same time, developments in information technologies have generated increased efforts towards R&D-development in every sector.

3. Reforms and the performance of public services

The Hungarian economy's period of growth between 2000 and 2002 will probably not contribute to the reforms that are needed. The last two years of a political cycle are not a suitable time for such undertakings. At the same time, a step backwards occurred in the principally positive old-age pension reforms during 1999 and 2000.

Health-service reforms are the most pressing. However, an overall professionally and socially acceptable concept has not yet been developed.

The reform of the country's administrative system and its financing, and above all the introduction of regional administrations, is also an urgent requirement, so that by the time of EU accession, EU resources can be handled at regional level.

The harmonization of the taxation system will continue but will not have been completed by 2002. The most difficult problem will to be raise the minimum VAT to 5 percent. Although conceptual changes cannot be expected, actual amounts might change. Social security contributions will decrease and tax benefits for families with children will increase. All this will particularly favour multinational companies and families with higher incomes.

The freezing of membership fees paid to private pension funds at 6 percent (rather than the 8 percent prescribed by law) has slowed down the progress of old-age-pension reforms. This will lower confidence in the pension system and also reduce the pensions later received by members of these pension funds. When indexing pensions, problems arise as a result of the underestimation of inflation, as well as the subsequent end-of-year corrections.

The significant rise in the minimum wage—which includes the wages of state employees—will temporarily accelerate the countrywide rise in wages, distort the wage structure, lower employment rates, and strengthen the gray economy. There are serious tensions within the social insurance system. Changes to family benefits and allowances have put families on lower incomes at a disadvantage. Changes to the unemployment benefit system have reduced the number of those entitled to benefit as well as the level of support provided, while the organization of public work has fallen below demand.

In the housing benefit system, the focus has been shifted to state-subsidised credits. The result will be an upsurge in the number of flats being built, although this will only slightly ease the problems that have accumulated over the years.

III. REAL PROCESSES

1. Changes in the industrial structure

In the coming years rapid growth of about 5 percent, which has characterized the Hungarian economy since 1997, will continue. This growth will lead to pronounced structural changes, which, in turn, will contribute to further growth. The most rapid development will be seen in manufacturing industry, the construction industry and telecommunications.

a) Industry and the construction industry

By the end of the 1990s substantial structural changes had taken place in Hungarian industry in terms of branch structure, the size of corporations, and ownership structure. In the coming years this process will continue, although at a slower pace. No significant progress has been made in terms ofregional structures, which means that several regions have remained at a disadvantage. In this respect, only a modest improvement can be expected by 2002.

The improvement of the production structure, indicated by various performance indicators—such as export intensity, productivity, energy consumption, and transportation requirements—will continue.

The majority of industrial exports are sold on the markets of the European Union. Transnational companies engaged in global activities have proved to be a stabilizing force during the crisis in Hungarian industry. They will continue to play this role in the future, provided that no political or economic development—unlikely from the current perspective—worsens the security or competitiveness of production in Hungary.

In the coming years the output of currently successful branches will continue to grow dynamically, although their difference from the average will gradually decrease since an annual growth rate of 50 to 130 percent cannot be sustained even for a few years.

In other branches, further slight intra-sectoral transformations can be expected. In the chemical industry, based on the petrochemical industry, high oil prices on the long-term would be a significant obstacle. The solution will be to increase the proportions of labor-intensive products.

Industrial structure according to production values, 1985-2002

(proportions in percent)

	1985	1990	1995	1999	2002*
Mining	2	1.8	1.1	0.6	0.4
Food and tobacco industry	20.7	22.2	23.6	15.2	12.6
Textile and clothing industry	8.1	6.3	4.6	3.9	3.5
Wood, paper, and printing industry	3.5	4.3	5.4	4.8	4.6
Chemical industry	21.5	21.9	20.0	13.9	11.5
Manufacturing of non-metallic mineral products	3.2	3.4	3.2	2.6	2.5
Metallurgy and metal production	11.3	11.0	9.7	7.2	6.5
Machinery industry	17.0	15.3	17.9	40.4	49.6
Other processing industries	1.7	1.6	1.3	1.1	1.0
Electrical energy, gas, heat and water supply	11.0	13.2	13.2	10.3	7.8
Industry total	100.0	100.0	100.0	100.0	100.0

Source: Central Statistical Office; figures for 2002 based on GKI Co.'s forecast.

In the coming years development will continue to be rapid and largely export oriented.

Major industrial indicators, 2000-2002
(volume indexes, percent)

	Average annual growth	2002 1999=100
Production	10	135
Domestic sales	5	115
Exports	14	150

The expected growth will be given a solid foundation by the continuing high level of industrial investments and the expected increase in such investments. In the second half of the 1990s, industrial production capacities increased by more than 150 percent. Within investments, the proportion of machine acquisitions was about 60 percent. Investment in information technologies is growing rapidly.

According to entrepreneurs, the main obstacle to the realization of investment plans is still the shortage of owners' capital. Companies regard the scarcity of capital as a very serious risk and are very cautious about taking out long-term credit. (72 percent of companies do not borrow long-term investment credit at all.)

Since 1996, energy consumption has stagnated despite an annual growth in GDP of over 4 percent, This can be explained partly by the rapid changes in sectoral and product structure and the far higher than average development of more energy-efficient activities; partly by the modernization of certain areas, such as the car industry, computer technology, and telecommunications; and, finally, by the rise in energy prices, which has necessitated a more rational handling of energy both in terms of production and consumption. The combined effect is that energy provision is stable, with surpluses predominantly on the supply side, especially in terms of energy provision via cable.

According to GKI Co.'s forecasts for the period up until 2002, energy consumption in the production sector will stagnate, while the consumption of electricity will increase by an annual 1.3 to 1.4 percent. Total public energy consumption up to 2002 will increase by 0.6 to 0.8 percent, and by 1.5 percent with respect to electricity.

Restructuring that gives imported natural gas an advantage over domestically produced coal will continue. The use of crude oil and its derivatives for energy, and the weight of atomic energy and renewable energy sources, will barely change in terms of domestic supply. The uneconomical nature of domestic energy resources and the limited amounts of hydrocarbons make a further increase in imports fairly likely.

At present, power-plant capacity exceeds demand. The construction of new plants could only take place as a result of closures necessitated by economic or environmental protection concerns.

During the last three years, the volume of output in the construction industry increased by 32 percent. It is likely that this growth rate will be sustained: in the period between 2000 and 2002, GKI Co. expects an annual average growth of 8 percent in the volume of building and construction activities, that is, a total of 26 percent growth over the next three years.

On the supply side, conditions for the development of the construction industry are mostly available. This branch is one of the most competitive in the economy, although it is, at the same time, affected by a number of problems: among the most pressing ones are unfair competition, illegal employment, and frequent construction errors.

Two-thirds of construction commissions come from the economic sphere, about 30 percent from budget organizations, and about 5 percent from the public. Demand from the economic sphere in the period between 2000 and 2002 is expected to rise fairly steadily. With the exception of the agriculture, demand will increase in every sector. The volume of investments in construction on the part of budget organizations will increase significantly by

2002. The development, renewal, and maintenance of the transport infrastructure and flood-protection systems represents a significant task for constructors.

After several years of stagnation, the construction of apartments will increase, primarily as a result of the government's package of measures encouraging the construction of private or rented apartments. However, the positive effects of this will only be felt in the second half of the period examined here.

b) Agriculture

It can be expected that between 2000 and 2002 the agriculture will be characterized by stagnation (as it has been don in 1999-2000), as well as by further differentiation and selectivity. An annual average growth in production of 1 percent can be expected in the medium term. Internal demand will increase by an annual 2 or 3 percent. Agrarian exports will amount to approximately USD 5.2 billion. The proportion of agrarian exports within the total exports of the national economy will further decrease. The exploitation of opportunities offered by foreign markets is hampered not so much on the demand side as on the supply side (quality, marketing, etc.).

On the basis of the recent situation (a virtually defunct domestic land market and non-marketable forms of land ownership) the increased prevalence of landholdings of a manageable size and with a rational structure cannot be expected. Within this branch a "secondary" change of ownership—that is, the concentration into fewer hands of easy to manage landholdings and assets—is yet to take place. Due to the limitations on land acquisitions and low profitability, no capital inflow can be expected—thus agriculture will continue to suffer from a lack of resources.

On the medium term—in this case including the period beyond 2002—agriculture will be characterized by three typical types of operation. Large landholdings (business organizations, co-operatives, corporations) will inevitably be the decisive organizational form within the agriculture. These farms, which will continue to own between 45 and 50 percent of arable land, have emerged, and will emerge, partly as the successors of former state farms and co-operatives, and partly as the farms of new private producers.

Medium-sized farms of between 15 and 50 hectares, based on family ownership and predominantly on a family labor force, might come to represent 30 percent of arable land. A more significant growth in medium-sized farms would take place in Hungary only in case of stronger government support. However, this is unlikely.

Nevertheless, small producers and part-time farmers must still be taken into consideration. It is possible that the approximately one million small producers might join the Hungarian market successfully, mainly in the production of fruits and vegetables and the raising of small livestock. In other respects they will be less and less capable of competing successfully on the markets. However, even in the long term, the majority will only produce enough to be self-sufficient. Alternatively, they will be forced to become entrepreneurs, although the profitability of such enterprises will be low and it will be difficult for them to make a living.

Medium-term opportunities in agriculture will be determined to a significant extent by loss of income and the using up of assets. In the medium-term period examined here, producers' prices—compared to the extremely depressed levels of previous years—will rise. Agricultural producers, however, with their weak bargaining position, will remain unable to realize their justified claims for higher prices. Nevertheless, a reduction in the gap in earnings can be expected in the medium term.

With levels of investment remaining dramatically low, the competitiveness and efficiency of Hungarian agriculture will have further worsened by the end of the period under examination. The main branches of domestic agronomy and livestock rearing will fall further behind EU levels.

The most desirable situation would be for the state to take a role in promoting the acceleration of landholding concentration, the co-ordination and control of markets, the integration of producers (into co-operatives, etc.), and the improvement of efficiency, rather than preserving recent production and market structures. This policy hampers further agrarian transition and makes agriculture to be unable to serve the initial social and political goals of transition.

Based on the recent and foreseeable future situation, there is no chance that agricultural production will approach 1990 levels by the end of the mid-term period: production levels will remain around 25 percent lower. The conditions required for a more rapid expansion are not in place: such conditions would most importantly include fixed ownership and organizational relationships, the stable use of land, a functioning land market, a rational farm structure, market-based cooperation among agricultural producers (wholesale co-operatives), machinery pools, and the strong representation of agrarian interests. Also—in order to put in place these missing conditions—the clear and dependable involvement of the state is essential.

c) Services

In the broad sense, services include transportation, telecommunications, trade, tourism, and business and public services.

Freight transportation productivity, measured in terms of GDP, is not currently as high as the levels reached in the late 1980s—due mainly to the almost 50 percent decline in railroad freight carrying. However, road and pipeline transportation does approach 1990 GDP levels, while air transportation significantly exceeds them.

One of the most important questions with respect to the development of the freight transportation is whether any progress can be made in renewing the infrastructure of railroad and road transportation, in modernizing vehicles, and in improving companies'

The volume of production in agriculture and food processing industries 1990-2002

(1990=100)

Percentage

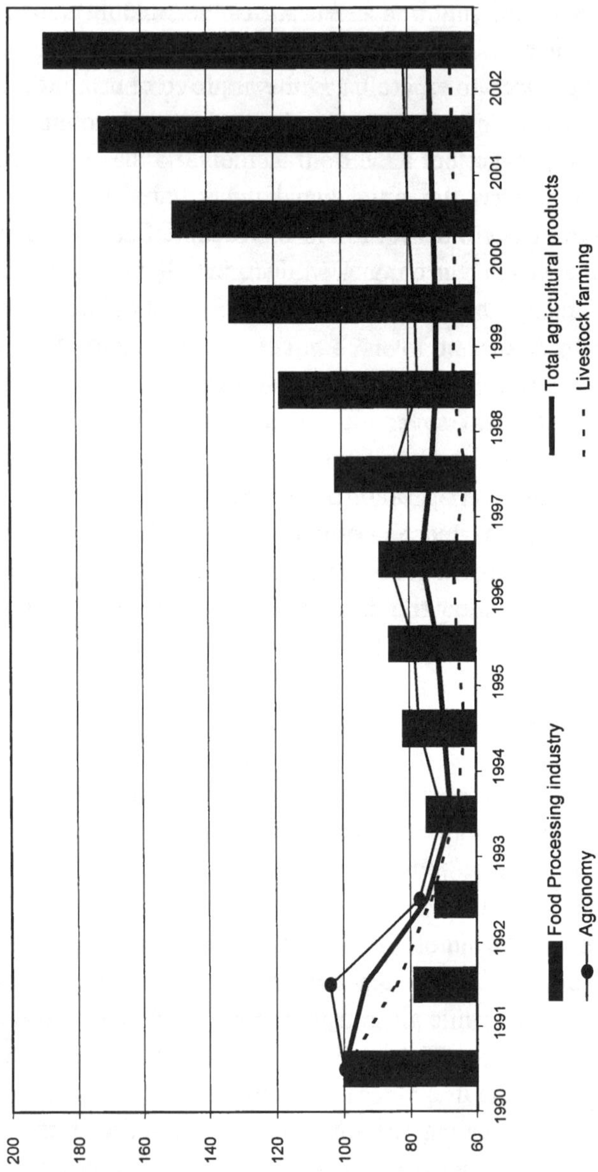

Source: Central Statistical Office; GKI Co.'s forecasts.

competitiveness. The growth of demand for domestic transportation up until 2002 will remain behind the expected growth rate of the GDP. At the same time, participation in the expanding area of transit transportation will be a decisive issue with respect to competitiveness.

Sadly, however, potential investment sources are not in proportion to the demand, therefore no improvement can be expected either in road or in railroad transportation. The financial resources for a full-scale modernization of the railroads are more uncertain than ever. The recently declared accelerated highway-construction program will improve the chances of making the necessary progress, but it will not produce meaningful results during the period examined here.

Transportation productivity measured in terms of GDP up to 2002 might altogether increase by 6 to 7 percent.

The railroads will continue to lose ground, although to a lesser extent than earlier. Waterways transportation will remain modest, while the role of pipeline transportation will remain unchanged. The role of road and air transportation will gradually increase.

In the period since the change of system telephony is the only significant sub-branch of telecommunications to produce an annual average growth in double digits, without any regression. The number of telephone-line subscribers between 1990 and 1999 increased from 1 million to 4 million, and the number of mobile phone subscribers rose from zero to over 1.5 million. Despite this, the number of telephone lines per thousand inhabitants is about half the average in developed countries, nor is the situation any better with respect to mobile telephones.

The so far significant quantitative development will, in the next two or three years, undergo a qualitative modification. On the one hand, technical developments will open up new areas of use; on the other hand, they will weaken monopolistic positions, which will probably lead to a reduction in prices. By 2003 the use of the

Internet will have become general even among small enterprises. The Telecommunications Act, which is currently in preparation, will have a serious impact on the expansion of competition.

Up to 2002 the volume of retail turnover will increase by an annual average of 5 percent. The proportion of the labor force employed in trade will decrease due to the modernization of this branch, since labor, both in terms of services and administration, will be replaced by capital.

The structural transformation of the retail industry will comprise partly the further increase of the market share of shopping malls and hypermarkets, and partly closer cooperation and mergers within the already existing networks. It follows that the number of market players will further decrease.

The shopping malls' share of retail turnover in fiscal 2000 reached 12 percent, and by 2002 might reach 14 to 15 percent. There is currently 49 square meters of shopping mall space per one thousand inhabitants in Hungary, which is less than a third of the average in West European countries. At the same time, retailers in Hungary compete for much lower levels of consumer power than in the West, while the costs of construction are scarcely any lower than in Western countries.

The service industry in its narrow sense (without the so-called production infrastructure) is a multifaceted complex of various activities.

Between 2000 and 2002 the total growth rate of GDP in these service branches will not even achieve half of the average of the growth rate of the national economy. Up to 2002 the Hungarian economy will not be transformed from an industry-driven economy to a service-driven one. According to GKI Co.'s forecast, the service sector's GDP will increase by an annual 2+ percent in the given period.

No substantial progress is to be expected in terms of budget reform (apart from the transformation of the Treasury) prior to 2002, thus there will be no significant impact on the service sphere.

Real estate development and turnover have become increasingly dynamic since the end of 1997. This has predominantly been caused by the higher real incomes of entrepreneurs and by the presence of increasingly wealthy citizens. Supply, in terms of business space, has also dramatically improved. At the same time, the demand side has begun to narrow. Clients are less and less able to afford the high rents, thus the demand for space in the shopping malls will decrease. Some of this space is being transformed into offices. However, this will further increase the already existing surplus in the supply of office space.

The construction of hotels, apartments, and guest-houses has accelerated since 1998, when capital-rich real estate developers and hotel chains appeared on the market. In Budapest alone the number of hotel rooms will increase by 100 percent over the next two years. Income from tourism is rapidly increasing, and the market players expect its further expansion.

The program for the building of rented apartments also promises to be successful. In the course of this program the state intends to provide non-refundable support for local governments in return for the building of social flats that will be available for rent. However, the local governments themselves will have to contribute between 25 to 30 percent of the costs, something which the smaller local governments will not be able to afford.

The land market will remain legally closed to foreigners. This, along with the low profitability of agriculture, will keep land prices low. Because of the absence of demand, no significant rise in land prices can be expected in the period examined in the present study. Should it became legally possible for business organizations with a domestic majority to obtain ownership of land exceeding 300 hectares, land prices would immediately rise.

On the real estate market foreign investors expect to achieve an annual profit of 12 to 15 percent in US dollars. This will have to be achieved from rental fees and increased value, while, in the meantime, they have debts to repay: real estate developers normally have minimal owner's capital and mostly finance constructions from bank loans, which, during booms at the real estate markets, promote more rapid development activities. However, in times of recession the repayment of these loans might be problematic.

In the branches of public administration and compulsory social security, a fall in personnel of a few percentage points is to be expected, generated by "rationalization" aimed at reducing costs. Reductions in personnel will not necessarily take place in areas where it would be justified by the size of the tasks to be performed. Without a qualitative transformation the public administration will barely be able to meet the challenges created by the requirements of accession to the EU.

Education and health care are struggling amid ever-changing reform concepts. The overall reform of health care, even according to official statements, will be postponed until after 2002.

The development of the financial institutional system is not reflected in the structure of the GDP. The proportion of financial activities within the GDP in 1991 was 2.2 percent; it had increased to 4.5 percent by 1995, but subsequently decreased. According to the latest figures it was 4.1 in 1998, while both the quality and quantity of the services had risen.

In the forthcoming period the regulation of the important players on the money market will be made uniform. Thus they will be given ever wider opportunities for the complex performance of various activities.

The number of financial institutions will fall radically by 2002, since, on the small Hungarian market, only a smaller number of institutions than there are at present can work efficiently as universal trade banks. Strong specialization might represent a way out for the smaller institutions.

In the period 2001-2002 the dynamic growth in the insurance market will be unbroken. In this branch, by 2002, net income is expected to increase by almost 50 percent compared to 1999. (This means an annual average growth of almost 15 percent in 2000-2002.)

From 2000, membership of voluntary pension funds will increase only modestly since the majority of those interested in the fund system have already become members. However, the increase in assets will remain dynamic. By the end of 2002 the voluntary funds will have a membership of almost 1.3 million persons, and their assets will be around HUF 350 billion.

The membership of the compulsory pension funds stood at around 2.07 million persons on 31 December 1999, which means an almost 40 percent growth compared to the end of 1998. From 2000 the growth in membership will be limited to the recruitment of those in first-time employment. Thus in the forthcoming years the membership will increase by an annual 100,000 to 130,000 persons. On the other hand, the assets of the funds will dynamically increase since in the next ten to fifteen years practically no services will be provided. The assets of the funds are expected to exceed HUF 550 billion on 31 December 2002.

d) Foreign trade

Between 1995 and 1999 the volume of both exports and imports increased by an extremely dynamic annual average of 15 percent. This high rate was partly due to competitiveness based on low wages compared to international levels, which also contributed to favorable changes in productivity. It was also helped by the exchange rate policy based on previously declared crawling peg devaluation.

Exports directed to the European Union grew the most rapidly, representing more than 70 percent of total Hungarian exports. The German economy plays an important role: 40 percent of exports and 30 percent of imports are carried out in relation to

Germany. More than two-thirds of exports are by multinational companies, which form an organic part of the global economy.

In 2001–2002 the Hungarian economy will further integrate into the European Union and the global economy. However, it should be borne in mind that the already very low rate of crawling devaluation, which will further decreased by October 2000 and which might be entirely abolished by 2001 or 2002, will not counterbalance the rapid increase in processing industry prices, and that the real price index in 2001–2002 will be less favorable than last year by 90 to 92 percent. This level of appreciation cannot be sustained in the long term.

Cost-related competitive advantages might also be reduced. The growth rate of productivity in the processing industry might be reduced to an annual 5 to 6 percent. Real incomes will increase more rapidly, while the number of employees cannot be expected to decrease.

As a result of the high rate of economic growth in EU countries, exports were more dynamic in 2000, following the previous year's deceleration, and reached an annual figure of around 17 percent. However, in 2001 and 2002, in keeping with the expected slowdown in European prosperity, export dynamism will be reduced to 10 percent. Changes in import rates between 2000 and 2002 will be similar to those in export rates.

By 2002 the proportion of exports (of goods and services) will be 67 percent of GDP, compared to 33 percent in 1991 or 55 percent in 1999, while the proportion of imports (of goods and services) will be 70 percent of GDP in 2002, compared to 34 percent in 1991 and 57 percent in 1999.

Growth rate of the volume of exports and imports, 1985-2002

(percent, 1985 = 100)

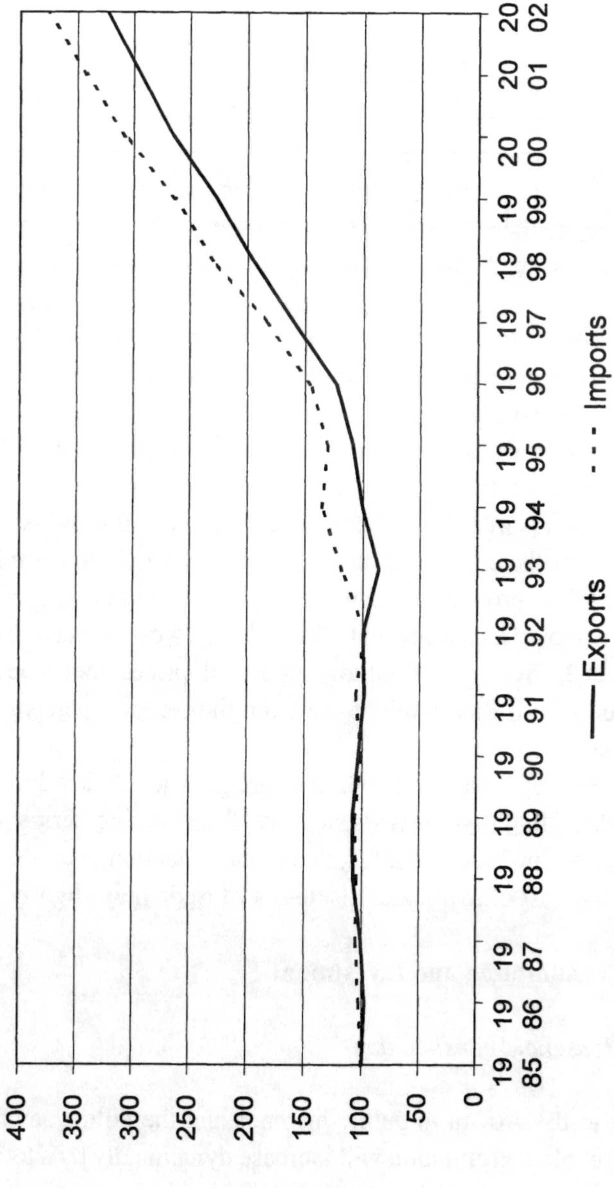

Source: Central Statistical Office; GKI Co.'s forecasts.

Foreign-trade ratios, 1991-2002
(percent)

	Imports/exports	Exports/GDP	Imports/GDP
1991	102.9	32.7	33.7
1999	103.3	54.8	56.7
2000	103.4	63.3	65.0
2002	103.7	72.4	73.6

Source: Central Statistical Office; GKI Co.'s forecasts.

The system of foreign-trade relations, in which 85 percent of exports and 75 percent of imports are carried out with developed countries, will not change significantly. The proportion of exports and imports carried out with EU countries will be around 75 and 65 percent respectively.

The resurgence of the Russian market will provide an opportunity for the expansion of Hungarian exports in the coming three years. The proportion of these exports in terms of total exports might grow from the recent –2 percent to 4 or 5 percent by the end of 2002. Because of falling crude oil prices the proportion of imports from Russia might fall from the recent 7 percent to 4 or 5 percent.

Between 2000 and 2002 the foreign-trade deficit does increase steadily. In 2000 it worsened by deteriorating terms of trade. However, in 2001 and 2002, due to the reduction in crude oil prices and the cost of raw materials, terms of trade may slightly improve.

2. Consumption and investment

a) Household consumption

Due to the growth in public incomes and the falling savings rates, household consumption will increase dynamically by a total of 14.4 percent in the period examined here, that is, by an annual average of 4.6 percent. This means that in 2002 the volume of consumption might exceed the 1989 level by almost 7 percent. The dramatic rise in the minimum wage, planned to take place by 2001, might temporarily make growth more dynamic by 1 to 2 percent.

The various strata of society will be affected differently by a rise in income, and the consumption of entrepreneurial households and wage-earning families with children will increase at the highest rate. Consumption among other wage earners will increase more slowly, and consumption among old-age pensioners even more slowly still. Consumption in households excluded from employment will decrease. These changes will have an impact on the structure of consumption. The proportion of food consumption will decrease, while the proportion of consumer durables (cars, furniture, electronic and electrical appliances), clothing, and services (tourism, education, health, telecommunications) will increase.

The volume of household energy consumption will increase very slightly, while fuel consumption will show a definite rise. In terms of foodstuffs, demand for products that had a falling turnover in the period when real public incomes were lower (fruits, dairy products, vegetables, meat) will increase, while demand for basic foodstuffs and non-essentials will either remain unchanged or will slightly decrease.

b) Investment, savings

Following last year's temporary slowdown, in the three years from 2000 to 2002 an annual average growth in investments of 10 percent can be expected. Over the three years this will mean an increase of over 30 percent. Such rapid growth in the volume of investments is partly due to the willingness and ability of the private sphere to save, and partly to the increase in developments financed from the state budget. The rate of investments will increase to almost 28 percent by 2002, from the 24 percent level of 1999.

The volume of household consumption, 1989-2002
(1989 = 100)

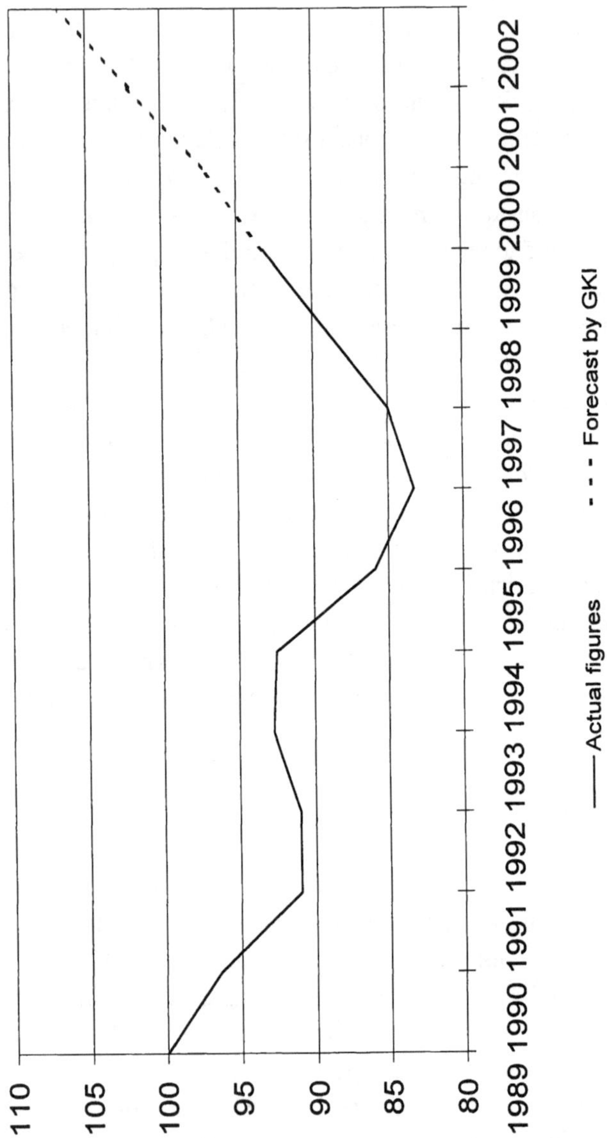

Source: Central Statistical Office; GKI Co.'s forecasts.

Corporate investment activity will be extremely vivid. Due to favorable foreign-market conditions, export-oriented enterprises will realize further large-scale developments, especially in the machinery industry but increasingly also in electronics.

With the forthcoming accession to the EU, further greenfield investments can be expected in industry (especially in the machinery industry, the engineering industry, and the textile industry). In the more developed western parts of the country, labor force resources are nearing exhaustion. The available labor force demanded by certain larger-scale investments can only be found east of the Danube.

In the electric energy industry significant developments will be made, especially in terms of reducing losses within the grid and increasing the efficiency of power plants. The telecommunications and data transfer industries will show higher than average development in the coming three years. The 1,800 megahertz mobile-phone network will be completed in its entirety, and the Internet will become more widely accessible. Investments begun earlier in trade, hospitality and tourism will continue. In the financial sector, lack of technical development is still a significant factor. Banking, insurance, and insurance-related electronic systems still do not meet modern standards.

In the state's investment policy, priority is given to the construction of highways and apartment buildings, and to the development of tourism. The construction of highways, which was halted in 1999, has been relaunched in 2000. However, real acceleration can only be expected from 2001. At the same time, there is only a little money available for renewing the existing road network.

There are also hold-ups in the development of the railroads due to a shortage of money, although smaller-scale investments are in progress (mostly in the area of electrification). Following the unsuccessful privatization attempt of Malév, the Hungarian national airlines, Hungarian air transportation system might face great difficulties—except for a successful privatization in the near future, which would help bring about fresh capital and a major technical renewal of the company.

Although the EU regards investments in environmental protection as of primary importance, Hungarian resources in this respect did not increase significantly between 1998 and 2000. The state/local governments are targeting their investments at the expansion of the sewage system and at increasing the capacity of solid waste disposal.

Among investments by the state the renovation of the downtown areas of various former royal seats in connection with the thousandth anniversary of the foundation of the Hungarian state, the construction of the National Theatre, and the reconstruction of the Budapest Sports Palace can be regarded as significant individual investments.

The local governments are the losers in terms of the changes in state redistribution. The state budget regularly under-finances their tasks, thus part of their income from the utilization of assets must be spent on actual running costs. The ever-decreasing resources for development come from their own income, credits, the issuing of bonds, and grants (mostly from the EU).

The combined resources of entrepreneurial investments are abundant. Enterprises produce significant profits, and amortization is increasing. With the reduction in forint interest rates, financial institutions will offer large amounts of credit to entrepreneurs. However, the main source of investments will remain their own resources.

3. Employment and unemployment

In 2001–2002, growth in employment possibilities will continue—although at a slower rate than it has grown since 1997. According to GKI Economic Research Co.'s forecast, employment will increase in this two years long period by 2.5 percent, that is, by 90,000 to 100,000 persons.

The volume of accumulated fix assets, 1990-2002
(1989 = 100)

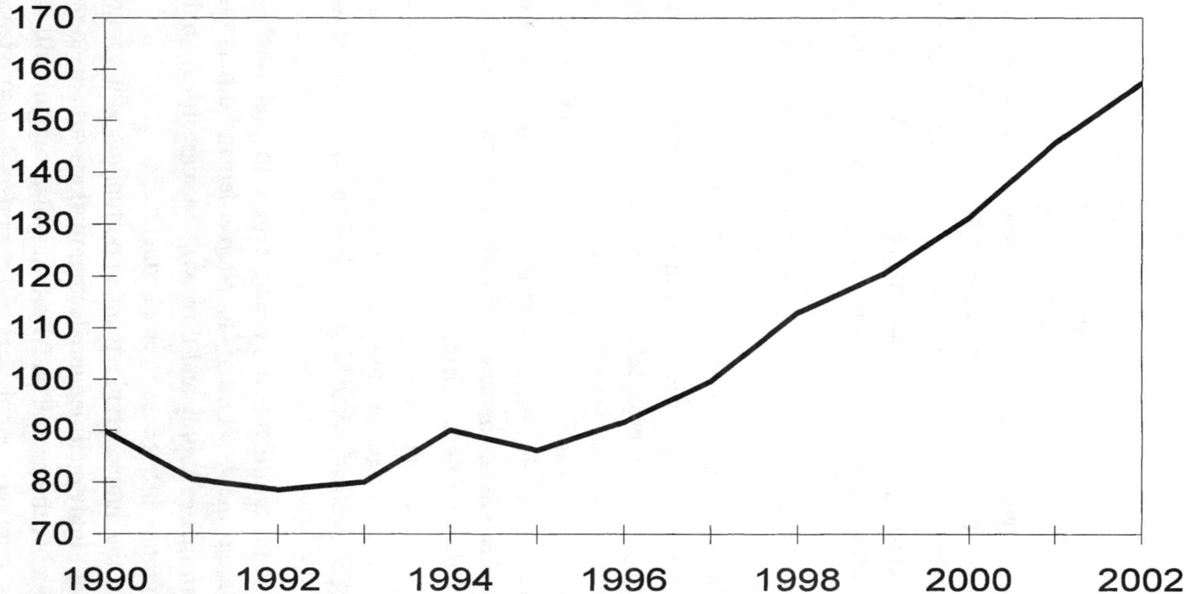

Source: Central Statistical Office; GKI Co.'s forecasts.

The increase in labor force demand only compensates for a fragment of the workplaces previously shut down. The average economic growth of 5 percent will mainly be due to improvements in efficiency. In the competitive sphere it is predominantly the launching of new investments that requires additional labor force.

There will be hardly any change in the available labor force. The baby boomers born between 1970 and 1975 have already appeared on the labor-force market. The gradual raising of the retirement age will, in the coming years, lead to a steady increase in the presence of older employees. In theory, restrictions to the unemployment benefit system generate higher numbers of workers. However, the long-term unemployed seldom find jobs in the primary labor-force markets.

The demand for employees will become increasingly differentiated but, taken as a whole, will increase. Despite relatively favorable employment prospects large-scale illegal employment will have to be tolerated. The dramatic rise in the minimum wage might also lead to the expansion of the black/gray economy. The modification of the employment structure will continue to be slow, and the job market will be characterized both by shortages and surpluses of labor force in different fields.

In the coming years a great deal of tension will remain in the labor-force market. Bringing the retirement age closer to the West European average, something that is otherwise justified and necessary, will, even in the event of favorable economic conditions, make it more difficult for young people to find employment. In some areas the structure of labor-force demand differs dramatically from that of supply and there will be scarcely any reduction in the regional differences in employment.

In the future, employment opportunities will continue to be best for highly qualified intellectual workers with up-to-date skills. Regionally, the central and Transdanubian regions will absorb the highest number of employees. All regions will absorb labor force in the period under discussion, but the dynamics of the less-developed regions will not allow for the compensation of earlier disadvantages.

The growth of efficiency at the level of the national economy (GDP per employee) will be around 13 percent over the whole of the period examined here.

In the most developed regions of the country the unemployment rate is around 4 to 5 percent—that is, it has fallen to the level of "natural" unemployment—while in the less developed regions, the rate is two to two and a half times higher.

In the first half of 2000 the unemployment benefit system, which is otherwise stricter than the average among EU countries, underwent further restriction (i.e., a reduction of the period for which benefit can be paid and the elimination of income compensation). By this method, unemployment statistics can be radically improved and one of the most unpleasant types of unemployment, that is, long-term unemployment, can be "eliminated". However, the "elimination" of unemployment by changes in the regulations is rather harmful than useful. Individuals lose all contact with institutions and with channels that might lead them back onto the labor-force market, while the country's entitlement to EU grants that also take unemployment levels into account is reduced.

By the end of the period under discussion unemployment will be in the range of 200,000 to 220,000 people, that is, a rate of approximately 5 percent. By international standards this would in practice mean the end of unemployment. In reality, however, the rise in employment rates will be too slow to absorb those who fall outside the benefit system.

Of the structural tensions caused by unemployment, regional tensions will continue to exist. The situation of young people might slightly improve due to their higher levels of education, greater adaptability, and lower wage demands.

IV. MONETARY PROCESSES

1. Monetary and capital market processes

a) Inflation

One of the phenomena that accompanied the change of regime was the significant acceleration of inflation. Domestic inflation over the past decade has mostly been connected with the transformation of production and cost structures and the restructuring of price ratios. Besides this, the rapid increase in trade margins has also generated inflation.

The reduction of inflation might be helped by budget and income policies as well as by reduced inflation expectations.In fiscal 1999–2000, the dampening of expectations has been be made difficult due to the dramatic rise in the price of crude oil and other fuels. Exchange rate policy means have also been exhausted: the monthly 0.3 percent devaluation in fiscal 2000 made hardly any impression.

Inflation in the coming two years will total more than 15 percent, but the rate will fall year by year. The basis for this fall will be provided by the stabilization of energy prices on the world markets, as well as the expected changes in real incomes, price controls, and imported inflation.

Favorable economic growth and the rapid improvement of productivity leads to a sensible increase in real wages without generating a serious risk of inflation. Productivity will increase more rapidly than the combined total of real wages and real appreciation.

Industry's domestic sale price index reflects the effects of high international crude oil prices. From the second half of 2001 this will not affect the price index since further increases in the price of crude oil on the world market are not expected. Due to the rapid improvement in productivity and efficiency, changes in the input prices of industrial production will only be slightly reflected in the producer price index. Imported inflation will only reflect the—probably modest—impact of the world markets, since devaluation will increase import prices by 4 percent this year and next year by only 2 percent.

On the basis of recent government policy no liberalization of energy prices can be expected before 2002. Only centrally controlled price rises that do not accelerate inflation can be expected in this area. With the approaching elections it is unlikely that taxation will cause a rise in producers' or consumer prices.

With respect to food products, no increase in real prices can be expected. The low profitability of agriculture would justify a more rapid increase in prices than the general consumer price index, but the government will probably alleviate this problem by increasing subsidies rather than by liberalizing prices.

Changes in the price of beverages and tobacco products, which already make up 10 percent of the consumer price index, will be more dynamic than the average, which can be explained by the large increase in excise tax. This tendency is likely to continue, since the tax on tobacco products will have to be significantly increased before accession to the EU.

With respect to consumer durables a very modest price increase can be expected. This is mainly due to competition from imports.

In terms of domestic fuel supplies and services, independent of world market levels and other cost factors, price changes can be expected to remain close to general inflation rates as a result of the government's administrative intervention.

Domestic sales prices in the processing industry, 1999–2002
(percent)

Period	Mid-term average price index	End of period price index (previous year, same month = 100)
1999	107.0	113.1
Mid-2000	115.8	115.9
2000	109.8	110.2
2001	108.5	108.2
2002	106.5	106.0

Source: Central Statistical Office; GKI Co.'s forecasts.

According to GKI Economic Research Co., by the end of the period up to December 2002, a month/month inflation rate of around 6 percent, or slightly higher, can be expected. Even in the event of slightly more rapid economic growth and a more favorable world market climate it is unlikely that a more rapid reduction in prices can be achieved. The expected fall in the prices of raw materials will be cancelled out by the increase in wages.

b) Exchange rates

Permanent devaluation in the crawling peg exchange rate system (that is, the method of declaring in advance changes in exchange rates), which was introduced in 1995, has proved effective. During the past five years the forint has mainly been at the strong end of the intervention band, and the Central Bank has intervened to prevent the forint from becoming too strong.

Because of the gradual fall in inflation the abolition of crawling peg devaluation system is now in sight. Inflation, and the dynamics of previous years, would justify the completion of this process by early 2002, but it might easily be the case that crawling devaluation will be abolished by the middle of 2001. After this, the forint will probably be pegged to the EURO. The question remains as to how wide an intervention band the forint can move in. A relatively wide band might provide opportunities for "silent" appreciation or devaluation. On the other hand, because of the relatively small market and the free flow of capital, maintaining a narrower band can also be justified.

In the period following the pegging of rates there will be a marked appreciation in the forint's real exchange rate due to domestic inflation. The unfavorable impact of this real appreciation will be compensated by the improvement in productivity (that is, its significantly more rapid increase than the EU average).

In the coming period relatively balanced money and capital markets can be expected. The EURO is expected to strengthen against the dollar. In this respect a slow change can be foreseen, in which, over the two years, the EURO will improve from the recent 0.95 level to 1.02.

c) Interest rates

In recent years the interbank and money market interest rates have virtually followed inflation. The interest on deposits has followed falling inflation more rapidly, while debit interest has followed it more slowly.

In 1995/1996, a very high real rate of interest appeared, since in order to finance the state budget deficit it was necessary to increase savings. By 2000 the initial return or real interest rate of 10 percent had fallen significantly to either 2 or 3 percent, depending on inflation (and the method of calculation).

In the next two or three years the recent real interest level is expected to be sustained. This does not particularly encourage foreign investment. The relatively low level of real interest is made possible by the gradual improvement in Hungary's risk grading.

In the coming three years the public debit interest will decrease, since a significant broadening of credit supply can be expected from domestic and foreign financial providers.

The active influencing of interest will play an increasing role in reducing inflation. As long as a strict budget policy is maintained the Central Bank can pursue a relatively more relaxed monetary policy. However, as the elections approach, the Hungarian National Bank (if it remains faithful to its own principles) will have to follow a slightly restrictive policy. The reduction in interest levels is unfavorable in terms of savings, therefore the encouragement of saving is worth supporting by appropriate tax and pension policies.

Interest rates, 1999–2002

Period	Overnight deposit rate	1 year reference return	Retail deposit within a year	Entrepreneurial deposit within a year	Entrepreneurial credit within a year
Dec. 2000	9.5	9.0	7.8	8.2	11.3
Dec. 2001	8.0	7.5	6.0	6.5	10.0
Dec. 2002	7.5	7.0	5.5	6.0	9.5

Source: Hungarian National Bank Monthly Report; GKI Co.'s forecasts.

d) The capital markets

Although the recent past of the Budapest Stock Exchange has been really pretty sad, and the stock exchange index is in March 2001 at around 7,000, equal to level which was once reached five years ago, in the coming years the economic environment will improve for domestic enterprises. The output of companies listed on the stock exchange is expected to show greater than average improvement. For this reason, the nominal return of the stock exchange index might be around 100 percent over the three years. However, if this is to happen new listings must take place. A stock-exchange-friendly rethinking of the government's economic policy would also be necessary, since one of the reasons for the fall in stock exchange prices is the impact of unpredictable and hectic government reactions. (Controversy currently surrounds the degree of price rises for gas and medicines, and the regulation of the telecommunications market.) In a favorable case, however, by the end of 2002 the stock exchange index might rise back to around the level of 10,000 points.

The corporational and local government bond market is likely to expand. Over the next two years the value of issued corporate bonds might reach altogether HUF 100 to 120 billion. Local governments issue bonds mainly to finance their investment plans. For financing highways, the appearance of an annual HUF 60 to 70 billion is likely.

The credit portfolio of forint investments will increase more rapidly than in previous years. This will partly be due to preferential loans in connection with the building of apartments, partly to changing the foreign currency credits of corporations into forint credits, and partly to the financing of new developments.

The proportion of domestic institutional investors on the securities market will further increase. Voluntary and private pension funds and life insurance companies will place new capital of HUF 950 to 1,000 billion in the securities market over the next three years. In addition, there will be new savings in investment funds, which, over the next two years, will amount to HUF 500 billion.

2. Household incomes and savings

The real income of households up to 2002 is expected to increase by an annual rate of 4 to 5 percent. This is mostly as a result of the rise in wages. Following the planned dramatic rise in the minimum wage an additional increase of 1 or 2 percent might take place.

An annual 2 to 2.5 percent rise in real old-age pensions can be expected, which, over the two-year period, will result in a total increase of about 5 percent in the standard of living. Thus the value of old-age pensions compared to other incomes will naturally further decrease. The real value of social benefits is also expected to increase steadily, especially the value of tax benefits. One of the disadvantages of this is that it does not affect the less well off, which will lead to an increase in social tensions.

In terms of capital incomes, the role of interest will rapidly decrease due to the drop in interest rates. Entrepreneurial income will increase at a rate slightly exceeding the GDP.

The incomes of the various strata of society will naturally increase at different rates. Up to 2002 the incomes of entrepreneurial households or households living on employee wages will increase more rapidly than the average. Incomes of households living on old-age pensions will increase somewhat more slowly, while the incomes of disadvantaged families living on unemployment benefits or family allowance and other welfare benefits will fall further behind. The differences in income, which already exceed the EU average, will therefore further increase.

The savings rate will fall. In 1999, out of total financial incomes excluding interest and capital gains, 5 percent were invested as savings. The equivalent figure in 2000 will remain below 4 percent, and in 2001 and 2002 it will be around 3 percent. This is extremely low.

An increasing amount of savings will flow into fixed forms (pension funds, life insurance). While 35 percent of annual financial transactions flowed into fixed forms in 1999, the proportion by 2002 might approach 60 percent. An insignificant number of households took out credit up to 1998. From 1999, however, mostly due to the increasingly widespread practice of purchasing cars by installment, these households became active credit beneficiaries. State-subsidized credit for the construction of apartments will lead to a significant increase in household debt portfolios. Thus, by 2002, household debt portfolios might be over double the size of the 1999 debt portfolios.

These tendencies will be accompanied by unfavorable macroeconomic effects. Since household savings will decrease while households become active players in the credit market, a shortage of credit will arise. While over the next three years expected net savings of HUF 1,500 billion will be produced, the state budget, over the same period, will require credit of around HUF 1,300 billion. On top of this, highway construction, which was intended to be financed by the Hungarian Development Bank, as well as the entrepreneurial sphere, will also present a significant demand for credit. This will necessitate the increased involvement of foreign resources.

3. State household processes

Between 1997 and 1999 the state budget deficit—measured in terms of meaningful economic indicators—was stuck at a level representing 4 to 5 percent of the GDP. Compared to this, there will be an improvement in 2001: a formal deficit of 3 percent can be expected, and even including highway-related credits in the calculations the deficit will not exceed 3.3 percent. In the next two years—using similar calculations—a 3.5 to 4 percent deficit is to be expected.

Calculating according to EU methods will result in a deficit 1 to 1.5 percent higher in relation to GDP (especially due to State Property Agency's expenditures and expenditures related to highway construction, which are non-budget items, and the entire exclusion of privatization income from the calculations).

Dynamic economic growth, high public incomes, and a rapid rise in consumption will significantly increase the state budget's tax and contributions income. This means that—in the event that other conditions remain unchanged—the real value of the potential income that can be used for tax deductions and the increasing of expenditure might rise by an annual 5 percent. In addition, the drop in interest rates in early 2000—and their expected continued fall—

will result in the shrinking of the state's interest-related expenditures.

The question is how the government will make use of its increasing room for maneuver. The most likely course of events is that the public burdens (especially social security contributions) will be lowered, but that the majority of the surpluses will finance selective increases in expenditure.

In the course of the distribution the following preferences are expected to play the most important role:

- a marked increase in expenditure with respect to central state operations (due to the requirements of NATO membership and the reinforcement of the police force and of the justice system);
- a significant increase in family tax benefits;
- a significant increase in wages in certain professional groups belonging to the public sphere (mostly doctors, teachers and nurses).

The realization of programs included in the Széchenyi Plan (a medium-term development plan which covers the development of tourism, motorway-building, SME-promotion, rental apartment building and a central development project is informatics) and related programs for further development will probably also receive preferential treatment, but their financing will formally take place mostly from off-budget sources.

The financial resources of local government will increase much more slowly than the resources of the national administration can be expected to increase.

Since the reduction in public burdens is expected predominantly to affect social security contributions, the deficit of the social security funds is likely to increase.

The indications are that the budgets in 2000 to 2002 will be characterized by the underestimation of inflation. This will have serious negative consequences. On the one hand, the official forecasts, which discredited themselves because of their over-optimism, were unable to influence inflation expectations. On the other hand, the underestimation of incomes might necessitate mid-year corrective measures in the case of old-age pensions and public-sector wages. According to various drafts of the budget for 2001, inflation will yet again be underestimated, and, furthermore, these calculations are based on the already underestimated incomes for the year 2000.

Besides the budget processes outlined above, centralization of incomes and redistribution will slightly decrease. By 2001 the state debt in relation to GDP will fall slightly, and will certainly be lower than 60 percent.

4. External balance positions

Hungary began the period 2000 to 2002 amid favorable foreign market conditions. However, due to the relatively high rate of economic growth and the significant import requirements for the further increasing of exports and growth, the country's external balance in the coming years will slightly worsen. By the end of 2001 the current account deficit will increase from the 1999 level of EURO 2 billion to EURO 2.7 billion, and GDP will increase to around 4.5-5.0 percent, which is still tolerable and does not require economic policy intervention.

The current account balance of payments deficit will continue to increase, predominantly due to the continuing worsening of the balance of trade. Throughout the period exports will increase at the same rate as imports, therefore the gap between them will remain the same.

The overall balance of services will improve: the largest item, tourism, will produce increasing profits. The balance of technical-cultural services will remain in deficit. Due to the sectors' increasing foreign market activities the balance of public and freight transportation will be increasingly positive. As a result of profit transfers in relation to the further increasing direct investments of foreign capital, the outflow of income will increase, while interest-type payments will slightly decrease.

In the period between 2000 and 2002, foreign direct investment of a net EURO 5 to 6 billion can be expected to flow in (including owners' credits but decreased by capital exports), which will not compensate for the deficit of EURO 7 to 8 billion within the current account balance of payments deficit. However, taking EU transfers and portfolio investments into account the country's indebtedness in absolute terms will decrease slightly and, as a percentage of the GDP, will decrease significantly.

The country will continue to remain an attractive target for direct foreign capital investments. After the decision has been made regarding the date of EU accession, these advantages will further increase. An annual average of almost EURO 2 billion foreign direct investment (including owners' credits) can be expected. At the same time, an increase in the outflow of foreign direct investment must be expected, up to an annual amount of EURO 400 to 500 million.

5. Fulfillment of the Maastricht criteria

Approximation to the Maastricht criteria is one of the important long-term goals of Hungarian economic policy. Although fulfillment of the criteria is not a condition for EU accession it is important for Hungary to demonstrate that its crucial financial indicators approximate to the required levels. The better the situation Hungary can achieve in relation to these criteria by around 2002, the more rapid and straightforward will be its accession to the EU.

According to the Maastricht criteria the inflation rate may only exceed by 1.5 percent the average of the three best performing EMU member states in the year prior to accession to the EMU. In 1999 this average did not reach 1 percent, thus the condition for joining the EMU is to achieve an inflation rate below 2.5 percent. The Hungarian situation in 2002 (5 percent) will be a long way off this level.

Nevertheless, a continued fall in inflation is likely, since the strict monetary policy—and the fiscal policy (more or less) supporting it—have created an opportunity for a lasting fall in inflation. However, a too-high rise in wages, mistakes in economic policy, and "imported inflation" might affect the falling inflation trend.

The reduction in long-term interest rates and their approximation to required levels (according to the criteria long-term interest rates may exceed by a maximum of 2 percent the average of the three countries with the lowest inflation) will be made possible partly by the reduction in inflation, in terms of the domestic economy, and partly by the open capital market, in terms of the international economy.

According to the criteria the state budget deficit cannot exceed 3 percent of GDP, which, between 2000 and 2002, unfavorable conditions, might be formally fulfilled. In reality, however (including, according to the EMU definition, items financed by the state alongside those currently financed from off-budget resources). Deficit in fiscal 2001 will most probably exceed 4 percent of GDP. Hungary is in a relatively good position in terms of fulfilling the requirements in relation to total state debts. According to the requirements total state debts must not exceed 60 percent of GDP. However, the average among eleven EMU countries has exceeded this proportion, while the Hungarian figure was only slightly above it.

The stability of the exchange rate is a further requirement, although only devaluation is forbidden. According to the regulations, countries joining the Monetary Union must participate in the Exchange Rate Mechanism of the European Monetary System for two years. Their exchange rate must remain within a prescribed band and no official devaluation can take place.

By 2003 the Hungarian economy will closely approximate to the criteria for EMU accession but will not be able to fulfill them. However, for the present this is not necessary, since too much haste would create disadvantages for the Hungarian economy as well. Hungary's joining of the economic and monetary union might take place between 2005 and 2010.

STATISTICAL APPENDIX

Table 1

GDP per capita

	HUF	US dollar	PPS	Value indices, US dollar	Volume indices, HUF	Exchange rates, HUF/ US dollar
1990	202640	3150	6240	113.1	101.0	63.20
1991	241476	3228	6252	102.5	96.7	74.81
1992	285040	3608	6267	111.8	88.2	79.00
1993	344707	3745	6281	103.8	97.2	92.03
1994	425365	4046	6296	108.0	99.7	105.13
1995	548836	4367	6310	107.9	103.2	125.69
1996	676315	4433	6392	101.5	101.7	152.57
1997	841039	4504	6616	101.6	105.0	186.75
1998	997238	4651	n.a.	103.2	105.4	214.45
1999	1151521	4769	n.a.	102.5	104.7	237.31
2000	1285000	4941	n.a.	103.6	105.2	260.06

Table 2/a

Gross output by industries,
Volume index, previous year = 100.0

	1990	1991	1992	1993	1994	1995	1996	1997	1998	1999
Gross output (at purchasers' prices)	94.5	85.9	94.6	99.6	104.0	102.1	102.3	107,0	107.2	106.5
Gross output of industries (at basic prices)	94.3	86.2	94.0	100.0	104.1	102.2	103.2	107,5	107.5	106.7
Agric., hunting, forestry, fishing	91.9	86.1	89.0	89.4	99.8	101.9	103.4	98,7	100.4	100.5
Mining, manuf., el., gas and water supply	91.4	81.1	87.1	100.5	106.0	108.0	104.2	115,0	112.6	110.3
Construction	79.0	82.9	103.1	95.8	113.4	98.7	102.0	106,3	100.1	105.3
Trade,repair, hotels and restaurants	114.7	95.8	98.2	92.5	100.4	99.1	99.0	104,5	108.0	102.6
Transport, storage and communications	91.5	86.2	104.0	95.9	103.3	109.4	101.7	108,7	101.5	108.3
Other services	104.2	96.2	102.5	109.7	102.6	93.3	104.4	101,0	104.6	104.4
Net taxes on products	-	-	106.1	93.2	102.7	101.1	92.1	101,4	103.1	104.3

Table 2/b

The final use of gross domestic product
Volume indices, previous year = 100.0

	1990	1991	1992	1993	1994	1995	1996	1997	1998	1999	2000
Total domestic use	96.9	90.9	96.4	109.9	102.2	96.9	100.8	104.4	107.8	104.0	105.0
-Annual final consumption, total	97.3	94.9	100.6	105.4	97.7	93.4	97.1	102.3	104.1	104.2	103.1
-Annual final consumption of households	96.4	94.4	100.0	101.9	99.8	92.9	97.3	101.7	104.9	104.6	103.3
-Annual final consumption of government	102.6	97.3	104.9	127.5	87.3	95.9	95.8	105.7	99.7	101.8	101.6
-Gross capital formation	95.8	78.9	79.6	132.3	119.8	108.2	113.9	108.7	117.1	103.3	109.9
-Gross fixed capital formation	92.9	89.6	97.4	102.0	112.5	95.7	106.7	109.2	113.3	105.9	106.6
-Changes in inventories											
-Statistical discrepancy											
Exports	94.7	86.1	102.1	89.9	113.7	113.4	108.4	126.4	116.7	113.1	121.8
Imports	95.7	93.9	100.2	120.2	108.8	99.3	106.2	124.6	122.8	112.3	121.1

Table 3

Volume indices of industrial production and sales

previous year = 100

	1990	1991	1992	1993	1994	1995	1996	1997	1998	1999	2000
Production	90.7	81.7	90.3	104.0	109.6	104.6	103.4	111.1	112.5	110.4	118.3
Sales											
-Domestic sales	87.9	82.6	93.4	103.8	106.4	98.4	98.5	98.7	103.2	101.4	109.0
-Exports	88.7	76.3	96.6	100.1	121.0	118.8	117.6	134.1	128.4	123.0	127.4
-Total	88.0	81.7	76.1	102.9	109.8	103.8	104.1	110.3	113.2	110.9	117.7

Table 4

Index of productivity in the industry
at constant prices, previous year=100

	1990*	1991*	1992**	1993	1994	1995	1996	1997	1998	1999	2000
Mining and quarrying	99.5	116.0		139.6	129.4	98.8	112.9	110.1	108.0	116.2	120.5
Food, beverage, tobacco	98.9	102.0		110.5	113.2	111.1	105.9	99.2	98.9	105.1	100.8
Text., dress, leather pr.				101.9	109.7	103.3	97.7	100.6	105.2	115.6	84.5
Wood, paper, printing pr.				95.8	113.0	109.5	102.1	116.6	122.5	103.2	98.9
Chemical products	94.4	89.5		101.4	110.8	102.2	98.3	109.0	121.7	95.7	102.7
Non-metallic mineral pr.	99.4	84.6		115.3	115.7	107.2	104.2	104.3	110.5	103.2	101.0
Man. of basic metals	97.7	80.7		123.6	127.2	108.6	106.6	109.1	114.2	95.7	111.4
Manufacture of machinery	87.2	96.0		113.2	130.8	127.8	123.2	141.5	128.8	113.3	108.7
Other manufacturing				139.0	117.5	111.7	93.0	110.9	111.4	94.0	98.9
Manufacturing, total				114.4	111.6	111.5	106.8	114.6	113.4	110.7	117.9
Electr., gas, water, heat	98.0	100.4		97.8	96.9	106.6	110.9	108.2	100.5	104.3	105.5
Industry, total	95.7	96.5		113.4	115.7	110.9	107.5	113.8	111.9	109.9	116.7

* Different structure
** Data missing

Table 5

Export indices by branches
previous year = 100

	1990	1991	1992	1993	1994	1995	1996	1997	1998	1999	2000
Mining and quarrying	78.6	47.3	122.2	112.2	97.0	101.4	144.6	57.9	142.0	190.3	59.4
Food. beverageand tobacco	90.0	98.1	78.5	96.6	115.2	120.0	113.8	103.9	94.0	96.8	105.8
Text.. dress.. leather pr	86.5	71.6	93.9	111.9	114.9	100.5	103.8	103.8	116.5	116.3	113.2
Wood. paper and printing pr.	94.7	123.9	123.8	99.2	127.6	111.4	115.1	134.6	115.4	95.7	130.0
Chemical products	80.4	73.1	89.2	106.2	111.4	99.7	96.6	103.8	95.3	95.1	111.0
Non-metallic mineral pr.	-	-	-	101.3	102.7	107.6	111.2	123.7	134.8	97.7	110.7
Man. of basic metals	94.3	78.6	113.7	104.4	127.6	110.3	98.8	119.4	110.0	99.2	110.9
Machinery	75.8	68.3	86.7	96.6	128.8	144.6	148.4	177.2	152.8	143.0	139.9
Other manufacturing	-	-	-	114.8	99.5	155.4	90.4	104.8	124.5	119.7	133.2
Manufacturing. total	-	-	-	99.2	119.3	118.5	118.5	136.9	129.0	123.4	127.5
Electr., gas, heat, water	320.7	30.2	-	71.8	712.0	139.0	540.7	142.0	86.1	69.0	121.6
Industry, total	83.5	78.1	92.0	100.1	121.0	118.8	117.6	134.1	128.4	123.0	127.4

Table 6

Procurement price indices of agricultural products
previous year = 100

	1990	1991	1992	1993	1994	1995	1996	1997	1998	1999	2000*
Crop cultiv.,horticult. prod.	135.0	96.3	101.7	122.7	118.8	124.8	152.2	101.0	93.7	110.1	130.8
- crops.	143.0	94.9	104.1	125.1	118.9	121.7	163.8	97.0	91.2	110.8	132.8
-vegetables	125.9	92.3	111.6	132.4	106.4	108.0	126.9	124.0	94.9	101.1	129.9
-fruits	119.6	144.6	76.1	98.7	131.4	187.3	74.7	126.1	109.5	111.6	117.0
-wine-grape, must wine	95.8	80.1	99.3	106.1	122.4	148.0	127.0	107.1	108.4	118.7	120.5
Live animals and products	124.4	101.5	113.8	115.5	129.2	128.8	111.6	124.7	113.8	95.4	112.3
-cattle live, animal prod.						124.5	113.5	121.9	126.3	105.2	103.6
-pig live, animal prod.						143.7	100.7	129.5	103.5	84.8	122.3
- poultry live, animal prod.						115.1	127.3	120.0	103.0	95.3	106.8
Total	128.5	99.1	108.6	118.5	124.9	127.1	128.4	113.4	103.9	100.9	122.5

* Producer price indices

Table 7/a

Inland transport of goods

Quantity of goods transported, 1000 metric tons

	1990	1991	1992	1993	1994	1995	1996	1997	1998	1999	2000
Rail transport	47397	33492	23977	19971	21531	20838	21842	20390	20512	18811	16844
Road transport	115361	79068	50329	38155	39425	-	-	82794	123757	136610	137196
Waterway transport	1272	1306	1198	975	901	1107	692	698	747	806	1075
Transport by pipeline	-	6030	10368	11044	10279	10233	9645	9324	9167	8471	8594
Transport,total	-	119896	85872	70145	72136	-	-	113206	154183	164698	163709

Table 7/b

International transport of goods

Quantity of goods transported, 1000 metric tons

	1990	1991	1992	1993	1994	1995	1996	1997	1998	1999	2000
Rail transport	40325	33596	29141	22658	26707	30093	27193	29874	31898	30930	33271
Road transport	3403	2849	1993	1600	1491	-	-	7263	4908	4706	5194
Waterway transport	3025	1757	1515	853	838	2206	1416	1376	1643	1292	1345
Transport by pipeline	-	13474	11961	11267	11117	11360	12692	12996	14423	13782	12405
Transport, total	-	51683	44618	36390	40140	-	-	53268	54132	50726	52237

Table 7/c

Total transport of goods

Quantity of goods transported, 1000 metric tons

	1990	1991	1992	1993	1994	1995	1996	1997	1998	1999	2000
Rail transport	87722	67088	53118	43573	48238	51032	49035	52005	53655	49741	50115
Road transport	118764	81917	52188	39752	40916	104618	90527	90057	128666	141316	142390
Waterway transport	4297	3063	2713	1828	1739	2279	2108	2074	2390	2098	2420
Transport by pipeline	25642	25469	22329	22294	21396	21684	22337	22320	23590	22253	20999
Transport, total	230112	171579	130356	107454	112300	179626	164022	166474	208316	215424	215946

Table 8

Principal data of construction-installation activity

volume indices, previous year = 100

	1990	1991	1992	1993	1994	1995	1996	1997	1998	1999	2000
Overground construction	82.1	82.6	87.3	98.6	99.4	84.3	108.4	129.4	103.4		
Civil engineering	86.3	100.9	124.7	117.4	138.6	75.1	89.9	105.0	127.6	105.4	102.6
Building inst. and compl.	91.7	88.4	118.3	102.2	105.8	88.5	109.6	96.7	122.7	117.9	108.2
Maintenance,modernization	84.5	81.3	72.7	80.8	95.5	82.0	107.2	101.8	67.9	120.6	108.6
Total	86.2	87.4	101.5	103.2	112.4	82.4	102.7	108.1	115.3	109.0	105.8

Table 9/a

Price index of industrial production and sales

previous year = 100

	1990	1991	1992	1993	1994	1995	1996	1997	1998	1999	2000
Producer's prices	122.0	132.6	111.5	110.8	111.3	128.9	121.8	120.4	111.3	105.1	111.7
Domestic sales prices	124.2	131.9	109.3	110.5	110.2	127.3	122.6	120.8	110.6	107.1	114.5
Sales price of ext. trade	112.4	130.2	115.2	112.5	115.0	134.0	119.7	119.5	112.5	102.8	108.6

Table 9/b

Price index of construction and assembling

previous year = 100

	1990	1991	1992	1993	1994	1995	1996	1997	1998	1999	2000
Overground construction	116.7	122.0	114.2	112.1	113.7	125.7	123.4	119.5	110.9		
Civil engineering	115.6	114.4	121.7	113.5	116.0	128.7	127.9	121.5	110.8	110.9	112.0
Installation, completion	116	116.2	116.3	110.9	113.8	125.6	123.1	118.9	111.1	108.8	109.6
Maintenace, modernization	-	-	117.2	111.8	114.2	127.3	122.5	119.0	105.1	108.7	108.8
Construction, total	116.3	119.2	117.2	112.0	114.5	126.6	124.8	119.9	110.7	110.3	111.2

Table 10

Consumer price index by main groups of expenditure

previous year = 100

	1990	1991	1992	1993	1994	1995	1996	1997	1998	1999	2000
Food	135.2	121.9	119.4	129.2	123.4	131.1	117.3	117.5	114.4	102.9	109.2
Beverages, tobacco	130.7	125.1	119.6	118.6	116.4	120.1	126.6	118.9	115.3	111.5	111.0
Clothing	123.3	132.1	123.0	116.7	116.1	120.2	125.6	118.7	114.1	110.6	105.8
Consumer durable products	120.8	131.7	114.3	111.0	111.8	124.0	119.2	108.5	108.1	106.6	101.7
Fuel and power	127.6	181.0	143.2	120.3	111.7	150.0	132.5	129.9	117.9	109.4	109.1
Other industrial goods	128.9	143.4	127.2	121.6	119.0	127.3	125.7	116.1	110.7	114.7	115.0
Services	125.6	141.9	126.0	124.1	120.3	126.0	126.4	119.2	116.2	114.8	109.7
Total	128.9	135.0	123.0	122.5	118.8	128.2	123.6	118.3	114.3	110.0	109.8

Table 11

Number of persons employed by staff groups

Corresponding period of the previous year = 100

				1993	1994	1995	1996	1997	1998	1999	2000
Agriculture, fishing				75.9	93.8	90.1	102.5	95.2	96.8	97.0	91.6
Mining and quarrying				80.1	92.9	86.7	96.5	82.9	94.5	94.9	76.1
Manufacturing				89.0	94.8	95.7	100.1	101.6	105.6	101.8	101.3
Electr., gas, heat, water				97.3	103.0	89.2	91.9	109.7	99.1	102.5	93.0
Construction				95.5	97.1	108.1	100.2	100.7	104.9	110.0	104.6
Wholesale, retail trade				97.7	99.6	98.4	105.9	102.0	95.0	109.6	105.1
Hotels and restaurants				95.5	100.2	105.4	97.9	106.0	100.6	109.5	103.5
Transp., storage, commun.				97.1	93.5	101.6	100.5	96.5	97.4	102.1	100.6
Financial intermediation				105.7	100.4	112.8	101.3	100.0	98.2	98.9	94.7
Real estate				98.1	91.3	104.0	98.2	114.1	111.4	112.8	107.1
Publ. adm., social secur.				102.0	106.9	99.3	96.4	95.8	100.2	102.6	99.0
Education				109.9	98.8	99.1	95.3	92.9	102.9	100.5	100.9
Health and social work				102.2	98.9	96.8	97.5	102.9	102.5	100.6	100.4
Other community,soc. acts				89.6	113.4	97.0	88.7	100.4	103.6	98.1	97.9
Total				93.7	98.0	98.1	99.2	100.0	101.4	103.1	101.0

Data of 1990, 1991, 1992 are not comparatable because of the changes of statistical classification.

Table 12

The number of unemployed persons by regions

	1990	1991	1992	1993	1994	1995	1996	1997	1998	1999	2000
Budapest	3 803	31 037	64 637	63 600	54 512	54 358	45 835	40 620	31 071	27154	21 269
Baranya	5 388	18 890	29 470	25 837	22 673	22 178	22 456	22 528	19 157	19181	17 926
Bács-Kiskun	4 786	31 680	47 235	40 369	29 147	24 919	24 370	24 711	21 970	22829	21 248
Békés	5 486	28 109	36 157	32 310	27 141	23 296	23 597	23 889	20 651	21462	18 963
Borsod-Abaúj-Zemplén	14 011	50 757	75 873	74 287	55 036	56 351	57 385	58 168	54 533	55998	56 359
Csongrád	4 089	18 260	27 843	26 118	20 732	18 347	17 543	18 118	15 391	15783	15 141
Fejér	4 005	15 974	27 370	26 217	21 632	20 003	17 387	17 956	14 612	14542	12 158
Győr-Moson-Sopron	2 732	12 690	19 192	18 314	14 235	13 319	13 214	11 514	8 588	8860	7 643
Hajdú-Bihar	4 645	25 554	42 338	43 041	35 342	33 489	35 726	34 656	31 594	32956	31 630
Heves	4 879	17 099	26 148	23 696	18 415	18 171	17 265	16 181	15 682	15337	14 557
Jász-Nagykun-Szolnok	5 904	26 862	38 740	35 296	29 271	28 421	26 958	25 025	21 548	21702	20 748
Komárom-Esztergom	2 032	13 467	23 337	21 585	17 627	16 085	16 244	14 829	12 925	11978	9 735
Nógrád	4 924	16 997	23 818	21 218	17 230	16 122	15 525	14 283	13 442	13324	12 955
Pest	5 119	29 811	52 681	44 704	34 540	33 146	29 912	29 805	25 308	22895	19 913
Somogy	3 985	14 104	20 437	19 943	16 395	17 532	18 112	17 490	15 719	16481	15 409
Szabolcs-Szatmár-Bereg	13 530	41 295	63 926	52 861	47 288	44 725	42 091	43 060	37 538	40215	38 373
Tolna	3 693	13 813	19 795	18 058	14 646	13 720	14 881	14 730	12 536	12815	11 361
Vas	955	8 776	13 469	13 512	10 433	9 712	9 433	8 380	7 099	7562	6 154
Veszprém	4 265	17 520	25 224	23 631	19 588	18 483	16 657	15 817	13 670	13056	11 646
Zala	2 329	9 837	16 293	16 258	13 709	13 516	12 768	12 199	11 060	10379	9 221
Total	100 526	442 532	693 983	640 855	519 592	495 893	477 459	463 962	404 094	404509	372 409

Table 13

Rate of unemployment at the end of the year

percentage

	1990	1991	1992	1993	1994	1995	1996	1997	1998	1999	2000
Budapest	0.3	2.9	6.4	6.3	5.4	5.7	5.0	4.5	3.6	3.3	3.4
Baranya	2.7	8.9	14.1	12.6	11.1	11.6	12.0	13.3	11.0	11.6	12.3
Bács-Kiskun	1.9	11.1	17.4	15.7	11.4	10.1	10.3	10.5	9.4	10.1	10.9
Békés	3.0	13.6	17.7	16.9	14.2	12.9	13.6	14.0	12.3	13.2	15.5
Borsod-Abaúj-Zemplén	3.9	13.1	20.3	21.1	15.6	16.6	18.4	19.2	17.7	19.8	21.2
Csongrád	2.0	8.0	11.9	12.2	9.7	9.0	9.0	9.2	7.8	8.5	9.5
Fejér	2.1	7.1	12.6	12.5	10.4	10.2	9.0	9.4	7.6	7.9	8.1
Győr-Moson-Sopron	1.3	5.6	8.3	8.8	6.9	6.5	6.7	5.8	4.4	4.6	5.4
Hajdú-Bihar	1.9	9.4	16.7	17.3	14.2	13.7	15.7	15.2	13.7	15.7	16.3
Heves	3.3	10.2	15.7	15.8	12.3	12.4	12.8	11.8	11.6	12.1	12.8
Jász-Nagykun-Szolnok	3.1	12.3	18.1	17.5	14.5	14.5	14.4	14.6	12.4	13.2	14.9
Komárom-Esztergom	1.4	8.1	14.6	14.0	11.4	10.7	11.5	11.0	9.5	9.4	9.3
Nógrád	5.0	14.0	21.7	19.1	15.5	15.4	16.3	15.6	14.7	15.6	16.1
Pest	1.6	5.9	11.3	9.3	7.2	7.4	6.9	6.9	5.9	5.4	5.6
Somogy	2.7	8.1	11.8	12.8	10.5	11.9	12.6	12.8	11.2	12.5	13.6
Szabolcs-Szatmár-Bereg	5.9	15.0	23.0	20.6	18.5	18.8	19.0	19.3	16.9	19.4	21.1
Tolna	3.1	10.2	15.3	14.9	12.1	11.7	13.6	13.5	11.5	12.8	13.3
Vas	0.7	5.9	9.1	9.5	7.3	7.1	6.8	6.3	5.2	5.8	6.6
Veszprém	2.4	8.5	12.7	12.5	10.3	10.0	9.4	9.1	7.9	8.1	8.8
Zala	1.6	6.1	10.4	10.8	9.1	9.4	9.2	8.9	8.0	7.8	8.5
Total	2.1	8.2	13.3	12.8	10.4	10.4	10.5	10.4	9.1	9.6	6.4

Table 14

Average monthly gross earnings of employees

previous year = 100

	1990*	1991*	1992	1993	1994	1995	1996	1997	1998	1999	2000
Mining and quarrying	121.7	134.3	118.1	130.0	118.1	113.0	118.4	128.0	110.4	113.5	117.9
Manufacturing, total			125.9	124.7	123.5	116.0	121.6	122.1	116.6	115.8	115.0
Food, beverage, tobacco	123.8	124.9	125.6	127.7	123.2	114.5	118.9	118.6	117.5	115.3	115.7
Text., clothing, leather			121.9	117.7	119.8	118.4	120.7	121.9	115.1	115.3	112.4
Wood, paper, printing			132.3	122.9	121.2	113.6	117.6	125.8	111.6	112.1	112.3
Chemical products	123.1	130.3	126.7	126.0	124.4	116.3	123.5	123.0	116.3	116.9	115.3
Non-metallic mineral pr.			127.8	124.7	123.5	116.1	123.3	121.3	117.6	118.5	112.8
Manufact. of basic metals	122.5	122.8	124.5	123.1	127.6	116.3	119.8	122.1	116.4	110.9	117.4
Machinery	121.4	127.7	127.8	125.9	123.6	115.6	124.2	122.3	118.6	117.4	116.0
Electr., gas, heat, water	133.9	140.6	127.5	124.7	122.7	114.7	123.1	121.1	119.2	116.1	114.3
Industry, total	122.9	127.6	125.7	124.9	123.3	115.8	121.7	121.8	116.6	115.5	115.5
Construction	118.5	120.9	122.8	120.6	126.0	113.3	118.0	122.1	115.4	112.7	113.2
Wholesale, retail trade			126.7	121.3	120.6	113.1	125.2	118.2	116.7	112.4	116.2
Hotels and restaurants			130.6	121.6	120.4	111.1	120.1	116.3	113.2	115.4	113.0
Transp., storage, commun.	133.1	140.4	130.3	120.0	125.9	112.6	124.3	122.9	120.3	117.4	112.0
Financial intermediation			130.6	124.8	118.5	109.5	124.7	128.5	124.8	116.5	114.6
Total	127.9	130.0	125.1	121.9	124.9	112.6	120.4	122.3	118.3	116.1	113.5

* In these years changes were introduced in the classification of staff groups

Table 15

Number of registered business units

	1990	1991	1992	1993	1994	1995	1996	1997	1998	1999	2000
Corporation with legal entity	29470	52756	69386	85638	91229	106245	125940	147388	162588	165093	171495
Partnership without legal entity	26807	43439	60000	85116	92393	111057	132119	144552	166863	175979	196009
General partnership	418	463	1187	2492	3348	3951	4394	4509	5006	5217	7873
Limited partnership	5789	22977	41218	67301	89045	107106	127725	140043	161857	170762	188136
Other partnership without legal entity	7288	8697	10597	12920	16335	19913	22712	24269	26182	26998	27255
Sole proprietor	393450	510459	606207	688843	778036	791496	745247	659690	648701	660139	682925
Government institutions	-	15915	15091	14853	14888	14879	14696	14520	14844	15300	15436
of which central	-	1422	1488	1356	1328	-	-	-	-	-	-
of which local	-	14493	13603	13346	13560	-	-	-	-	-	-
Non-profit institutions	22296	27407	33891	38493	42604	46804	50601	54418	58866	62121	65335

Table 16

Number of business units with legal status declared bankruptcy at the end of the year

	1992	1993	1994	1995	1996*	1997*	1998*	1999	2000*
Enterprises**	262	308	310	309	542	526	495		302
Business organization	1433	2054	2119	2144	19007	24197	25985		18353
Cooperative	599	698	704	701	2462	2610	2641		1715
Total	2294	3074	3147	3175	24054	29498	31255		29569

* Under bankruptcy or liquidation

** Companies forced to change the form of the organisation

Table 17

Energy balance (in petajoule)

	1990	1991	1992	1993	1994	1995	1996	1997	1998	1999
Production	603.4	593.5	561.2	552.8	549.7	553.9	536.7	523.5	489.2	472.1
Of which:										
Coal	188.2	178.8	151.6	132.9	128.5	130.5	134.4	138.1	127.5	125.8
Hydrocarbons	264.4	262.1	255.4	256.6	254.8	254.4	238.9	222.9	201.0	184.0
Within it: Crude oil	78.5	75.5	74.8	67.8	66.7	68.4	60.6	55.8	51.7	50.9
PB gas from mining	10.2	9.9	10.7	10.0	11.4	11.3	9.6	10.5	10.3	9.9
Natural gas	159.6	161.2	154.6	162.9	156.9	158.6	150.8	140.7	124.2	109.9
Natural gasoline	16.1	15.5	15.3	15.9	19.8	16.3	18.0	15.9	14.8	13.3
Electricity generated by nuclear power station	137.3	137.3	139.6	138.0	140.5	140.3	141.8	139.7	139.5	141.0
Electricity generated by hidroelectric power station	1.8	1.9	1.6	1.7	1.6	1.6	2.1	2.2	1.6	1.8
Firewood	11.7	13.4	13.0	23.7	24.3	27.5	19.5	20.6	19.7	19.6
Imports	724.7	620.1	531.3	597.9	565.3	609.4	651.6	630.9	659.5	649.6
Sources, total	1328.1	1213.6	1092.5	1150.7	1115.0	1163.3	1188.3	1154.4	1148.7	1121.7
Exports	70.8	47.1	51.0	74.1	87.0	87.6	80.2	78.3	74.3	79.7
Change in stocks	13.1	-13.1	-8.5	18.3	-10.0	8.6	27.9	23.2	28.4	-0.9
Energy consumption	1244.2	1179.6	1050.0	1058.4	1038.0	1067.1	1080.2	1053.0	1046.0	1042.9

* Data have not published yet

Table 18

Investments by form of management

at current prices, HUF million

	1990	1991	1992	1993	1994	1995	1996	1997	1998	1999	2000
Corporation with legal entity		313382	338799	373163	510895	627336	836736	1061815	1345320	1335800	1483500
Company with legal entity		127273	247692	330197	476192	608626	812767	103854	132725	1318000	1468000
Co-operative		24020	13291	12515	11083	15796	20624	25930	31220	16500	14400
Corp. without legal entity	118193	108399	110080	133277	10175	626340	39433	48262	62692	6100	7100
Partnership without legal entity					6880	2536	2081	5706			
Organisation bound to transform					21672	21111	8375	9138	13323	21700	4700
Corp. and unincorp. enterprises		162200	77961	30305	524075	674787	884544	1119215	1412449	1363600	1495400
Govern. and Soc. security	n.d.	70069	106690	131919	179536	166350	172391	257565	351576	299200	373900
Government		697783			177280	162659	169760	254337			
-Central government		29391	41018	49257	72312	63948	65427	88401	102899	112200	147200
-Local government		40392	65351	78895	104968	98711	104333	165936	246083	184700	221800
Social security		-	-	3437	2256	3691	2631	3228	3916	2300	4900
Total	459694	491850	555569	638309	842737	1038764	1337561	1709876	1764026	2427143	1869300

Table 19

Investment by industries and branches

at current prices, HUF million

	1990*	1991	1992*	1993	1994	1995	1996	1997	1998*	1999	2000
Total	262487	383451	445489	505082	690431	1038764	1337561	1709876	2137879	2427143	2830400
Agriculture, hunting and forestry	18895	15085	9252	9565	17702	29608	46133	61462	76677	79388	83000
Fishing	-	73	59	85	114	291	67	371	842	720	
Mining and quarrying	-	4298	3605	3413	4345	4232	4349	5360	10650	12137	8700
Manufacturing	95467	100547	132174	124512	155903	223523	312821	396018	548458	696584	726900
Electr., gas, heat and water supply	19594	41016	39897	53486	74811	90874	94305	115046	162414	175631	189800
Construction	4050	7428	8935	10331	16995	16549	27615	29177	41107	47579	49400
Wholesale and retail trade; repair ser.	24085	23070	27193	29793	35818	48566	105157	109137	144366	191334	208500
Hotels and restaurants		6864	10804	6324	5827	8424	10515	16439	19524	26106	31500
Transp., storage and comm.	59575	87519	84555	112084	171662	196886	216354	323930	354274	361170	504800
Financial intermediation		19209	25056	29750	33888	53081	44033	42880	60743	53963	70500
Real esttate renting and business activities		22509	25340	31442	43284	232743	324230	386857	393983	469745	584900
Public administration and social security		16589	23983	26727	38074	37761	40394	66194	127307	111474	136400
Education		9935	15315	17914	20206	25168	28837	36735	42554	52378	57600
Health and soc. work		13646	20997	24047	32310	34443	31563	43657	50489	47942	56900
Other comm., social and personal services		15663	18324	25609	39492	36615	51188	76613	104491	100992	121500

* In these years changes were introduced in the classification of staff groups

Table 20

Volume indices of investments by different categories

pevious year = 100, investments put into operation

	1990	1991	1992	1993	1994	1995	1996	1997	1998	1999*	2000
Total	77.0	95.0	89.1	97.0	111.6	94.7	105.2	108.5	112.7	106.6	106.5
Construction	69.9	98.7	83.6	94.4	110.9	92.9	104.5	106.3	103.3	103.2	105.8
Machines	93.7	94.8	98.0	100.7	113.5	98.2	105.7	111.3	127.6	110.6	107.6
-Domestic machines	96.7	110.0	78.9	101.1	118.2	106.3	110.9	116.0	146.2	n.a.	n.a.
-Import machines	89.5	79.9	111.0	100.5	110.2	92.4	102.0	107.9	113.2	n.a.	n.a.
Other	43.9	83.4	95.5	93.7	106.5	90.2	106.6	110.4	103.7	n.a.	n.a.

* In that year there was a change in data collection

Table 21

Volume indices of imports by groups of countries and value indices of imports by main commodity groups

previous year = 100

Countries/year	1990	1991	1992	1993	1994	1995	1996	1997	1998	1999	2000
Total	94.8	105.5	92.4	120.9	114.5	96.1	105.5	126.4	124.9	114.3	136.4
Developed countries	96.5	132.5	93.6	110.1	124.0	96.0	104.2	130.8	125.0	114.3	127.9
Developing countries	141.8	108.7	60.1	127.1	114.2	115.6	105.9	146.8	150.9	122.3	154.3
Central and Eastern Europe		56.3	98.4	149.8	90.2	92.8	108.0	105.3	112.1	106.0	162.2
European Union		115.2	93.8	111.6	129.4	97.3	103.9	129.7	123.8	114.6	123.7
Commodity groups											
Food, beverages, tobacco	110.2	97.8	98.1	117.4	122.6	80.9	96.8	114.1	113.9	98.7	112.3
Crude materials		79.8	80.7	103.8	125.3	100.1	104.9	118.3	108.5	89.3	113.0
Fuels, electric energy	117.2	86.1	95.9	115.8	106.2	96.7	112.8	94.1	105.8	98.5	105.1
Manufactured goods		123.1	96.4	108.4	121.4	102.6	106.5	118.6	120.1	108.5	111.9
Machinery and transport equipment		100.7	85.3	146.3	104.9	89.8	102.6	149.9	135.7	124.4	131.1
Total	94.8	105.5	92.4	120.9	114.5	96.1	105.5	126.4	124.9	114.3	120.8

Table 22

Volume indices of export by groups of countries and value indices of export by main commodity groups

previous year = 100

Countries/year	1990*	1991	1992	1993	1994	1995	1996	1997	1998	1999	2000
Total	95.9	95.1	101.0	86.9	116.6	108.4	104.6	129.9	122.1	115.9	133.8
Developed countries	112.0	121.7	105.5	84.3	123.3	103.2	105.7	132.3	125.5	120.9	133.2
Developing countries	94.8	105.6	68.8	87.1	85.5	101.5	96.2	106.4	151.6	116.9	137.4
Central and Eastern European countries		52.4	101.2	96.9	105.1	119.2	104.3	125.2	104.7	90.7	139.4
European Union		128.1	108.0	82.8	127.8	105.1	105.7	133.6	124.1	120.6	131.8
Commodity groups											
Food, beverages, tobacco	95.3	107.4	92.0	72.4	109.8	125.4	93.5	112.2	108.0	90.1	103.6
Crude materials		128.0	94.8	83.8	97.7	94.6	107.8	117.7	91.7	101.9	116.2
Fuels, electric energy	81.4	91.2	130.6	104.0	122.7	93.3	114.8	93.7	94.7	98.5	100.1
Manufactured goods		94.0	110.0	86.5	115.4	105.0	110.0	114.1	112.1	106.8	111.7
Machinery and transport equipment		79.9	91.4	101.1	121.9	111.4	101.5	159.7	137.9	128.5	130.8
Total	95.9	95.1	101.0	86.9	116.6	108.4	104.6	129.9	122.1	115.9	121.7

* This year changes were introduced in the classification of commodity groups.

Table 23

Balance of trade

	1990	1991	1992	1993	1994	1995	1996	1997	1998	1999	2000
Total (billions of HUF)	58.7	-91.4	-34.9	-342.5	-408.3	-314.4	-371.6	-394.3	-577.0	-707.0	-1121.2
Of which:											
billion HUF	-	-85	-34	-	-	-	-	-	-	-	-
million USD	945.0	-1110.6	-361.4	-3623.4	-3853.0	-2599.3	-3064.2	-2037.1	-2025.2	-2995.7	-3988.0

Table 24/a **Lending and deposit rates of the National Bank of Hungary**

interest rate (p.a.), %, at the end of the year

	1990	1991	1992	1993	1994	1995	1996	1997	1998	1999	2000
I.NBH refinancing rates											
Base rate	22.00	22.00	21.00	22.00	25.00	28.00	23.00	20.50	17.00	14.50	11.00
1.Long-term refinancing credits at base rate											
a)Credits financing the budget since 1991	-	25.00	21.00	22.00	25.00	28.00	23.00	20.50	17.00	14.50	11.00
c)Credits refinancing banks maturing over a year	22.00	22.00	21.00	22.00	25.00	28.00	23.00	20.50	17.00	14.50	11.00
2.For rediscounting bills of exchange if the period between rediscounting and maturity is 0-90 days	21.00	27.00	20.00	22.20	28.20	30.11	21.75	19.50	20.00	20.00	20.00
3.Preferential refinancing											
a)Export credits											
-maturing within 180 days	12.00	10.00	10.00	10.00	10.00	10.00	10.00	10.00	10.00	10.00	10.00
-maturing over 180 days but within one year	13.00	11.00	11.00	11.00	11.00	11.00	11.00	11.00	11.00	11.00	11.00
-maturing over one year	14.00	12.00	12.00	12.00	12.00	12.00	12.00	12.00	12.00	12.00	12.00
b)Discounting negotiable export documents	-	10.00	10.00	10.00	10.00	10.00	8.50	7.50	7.50	7.50	7.50
c)Forint loan for export prefin.	-	11.00	11.00	-	-	-	-	-	-	-	-
d)Loans disbursed und. tourism facility (70% of br)	-	15.40	14.70	15.40	17.50	19.60	16.10	14.35	11.90	10.15	-

(Table 24/a - continued)

e)Loans to refinance existence loans	-	16.50	-	3.00	3.00	3.00	3.00	3.00	3.00	3.00	3.00
f)Loans to refinance start and Japanese loans (75% of base rate)	-	16.50	12.60	16.50	18.75	21.00	17.25	15.38	12.75	11.88	8.25
g)Loans for re-starting & starting(75% of base r.)	-	16.50	15.75	16.50	18.75	21.00	17.25	15.38	12.75	11.88	8.25
4.Interest on debt of the Budget inc. before 1991	-	9.00	8.4	8.72	8.72	8.20	7.89	8.18	8.05	8.22	8.22
II.Interest rates on voluntary deposit held with the NBH interst on not official deposits	-	-	5.0	5.00	5.00	5.00	5.00	5.00	5.00	5.00	5.00
Interest on deposits fixed at least for 1 month	-	-	-	1.00	1.00	-	-	-	-	-	-
III.Interest rates on the state liquidity fund	-	9.00	8.4	-	-	-	-	-	-	-	-
IV.Deposit of budgetary institutions fixed at least for one month	-	-	13.0	10.00	10.00	20.00	23.00	20.50	17.00	14.50	-
V.Interest rates on mandatory reserves											
On reserves generated ag. HUF liabilitie	-	1.00	3.0	2.00	8.00	14.00	14.00	-	-	8.25	6.00
On forint reserves generated against forex liab.	-	-	12.0	11.00	18.00	29.00	18.00	-	-	8.25	6.00
VI.The highest central bank penalty rate of the NBH	-	-	-	10.00	10.00	10.00	10.00	10.00	10.00	10.00	10.00

Table 24/b

Central Bank interest on repurchase agreements (repo) interest rates

Interest rate (p.a.), %, At the end of the year

	1993	1994	1995	1996	1997	1998	1999	2000
Active interest rates								
-overnight	23.00	31.25	31.00	27.75	25.25	19.50	16.25	13.75
-1 week	23.00	31.25	31.00	27.75	25.25	22.50	-	-
-1 month	23.00	-	-	-	-	-	-	-
-3 month	23.50	-	-	-	-	-	-	-
Passive interest rates								
-overnight	-	-	19.00	17.50	14.50	14.00	12.25	9.75
-1 week	-	28.00	26.25	21.75	19.25	16.50	-	-
-1 month	18.00	28.00	-	22.25	19.75	16.75	16.00	-
-3 month	18.50	-	-	-	-	-	-	-

Table 25 **The Central Government Gross Debt and Interest Payment Obligations**

in the percentage of the GDP

	1990	1991	1992	1993	1994	1995	1996	1997	1998	1999	2000*
Debt											
1.Deficit financing debt	22.3	23.2	27.1	28.6	27.9	25.2	25.9	25.8	28.1	34.8	35.7
1.1.Loans	21.2	19.8	16.7	13.4	10	7.5	5.5	3.2	2.3	1.6	1.1
1.2.T-Bills	0.5	2.4	5.4	6.2	7.2	7.4	9.9	10.6	10.3	11.3	10.3
1.3.Bonds	0.6	1.1	5.1	9	10.7	10.2	10.5	12.1	15.5	21.9	16.5
2.Others	17.4	15	16.6	21.2	19.8	59.1	45.6	37	33.1	25.0	20.5
2.1.Loans	16	13.8	11.1	8.7	7.1	47.9	30.1	28	25.5	18.4	15.0
2.2.Bonds	1.4	1.2	5.4	12.5	12.7	11.2	15.5	9.1	7.6	6.6	5.5
Gross debt of the central government(1+2)	39.7	38.3	43.7	49.8	47.7	84.3	71.5	62.9	61.2	59.9	56.1
Interest payments											
1.Interests paid on deficit financing debt	1.7	2.2	3	3	3.9	5	4.9	4.7	4	4.2	1.1
1.1.Loans	1.5	1.9	1.8	1.3	1.1	0.9	0.6	0.4	0.2	0.2	0.0
1.2.T-Bills	0.1	0.2	0.9	0.9	1.3	1.8	1.7	1.9	1.6	1.6	0.3
1.3.Bonds	0.1	0.1	0.4	0.8	1.4	2.2	2.6	2.4	2.2	2.5	0.7
2.Others	1	1.4	2.1	1.4	2.7	3.6	2.8	4.8	3.4	3.1	0.3
2.1.Loans	0.9	1.3	1	0.7	0.6	0.5	0.4	2.3	2.0	2.0	0.2
2.2.Bonds	0	0	1.1	0.6	2	3	2.4	2.5	1.4	1.1	0.1
Interest payments on gross debt of the central government(1+2)	2.7	3.5	5.2	4.4	6.5	8.5	7.7	9.5	7.4	7.3	1.4

* Estimated value

Table 26/a

The Budapest Stock Indices

Yearly data, arithmetical average

		1991	1992	1993	1994	1995	1996	1997	1998	1999	2000
Budapest Stock Exchange Index		1007	899	879.78	1611.81	1425.0	2968.56	6509.09	7081.84	6708.46	7849.75

Table 26/b

The breakdown of the turnover

(HUF billion)

	1990	1991	1992	1993	1994	1995	1996	1997	1998	1999	2000
Equities	6.1	9.8	6	18.3	57.1	82.3	490.5	2873	6921	6863	6834
Government bonds	-	0.3	12.4	73.4	53.9	77.2	418.2	1959	4800	6509	1268
T- bills	-	-	15.1	85	81.2	81.1	206.3	1818	2071	2559	307
Other	-	-	0.2	9	19	12.6	30.4	86	20	75	104
Total turnover	6.1	10.1	33.7	185.7	211.2	253.2	1145.4	6736	13848	16006	8513

Table 26/c

Market Capitalization

(HUF billion)

	1990	1991	1992	1993	1994	1995	1996	1997	1998	1999	2000
Equities	16.4	38.2	47.2	81.7	181.5	327.8	852.5	3058	3020	4144.9	3393.9
Government bonds	0	15.3	82.3	241.7	392.9	454	703.4	952	1408	2040.3	2607.8
T- bills	0	0	54.4	74	239.6	376.3	697.2	908	917	968.4	797.3
Other	0	0.1	18	59.6	69.4	63.2	139.8	196	213.6	152.2	146.4
Total	16.4	53.6	201.9	457	883.4	1221.3	2392.9	5114	5558.6	7305.8	6945.4

Table 27

Gross and net foreign debt in convertible currencies
(excluding intercompany loans)

										Million Euro	
USD million	**1990**	**1991**	**1992**	**1993**	**1994**	**1995**	**1996**	**1997**	**1998**	**1999**	**1999**	**2000**
Gross foreign debt	21270	22658	21438	24560	28521	31660	27956	24395	27280	29279	29060	33055
Gross foreign assets		8104	8386	9633	9585.5	15324	13367	12409	14286			
Net debt	15938	14555	13052	14927	18935	16817	14184	11157	12344	11312	11250	12236
In billions of HUF												
Gross foreign debt		1713.4	1800.1	2473.2	3157	4415.6	4315.2	4490.3				
Gross foreign assets		612.8	704.2	970.1	1061	2137.2	2204.7	2525.2				
Net debt		1100.6	1095.9	1503.1	2096	2278.4	2110.5	1965.1				

Table 28

Balance of payments

USD million, Euro million in 1999-2000

	1990	1991	1992	1993	1994	1995	1996	1997	1998	1999	1999	2000
Export	6346	9258	10028	8093	7613	12810	14183	19637	20749	21842	20521	27560
Import	5998	9069	10076	11340	11248	15252	16828	21371	22870	24020	22574	29855
Trade balance	348	189	-49	-3247	-3635	-2442	-2645	-1734	-2121	-2178	-2054	-2296
Freight and shipment, net	-164	-80	-116	-106	-176	-186						
Travel: -receipts	818	1006	1231	1181	1428	1714	2246	2582	2504	3394	3197	3722
-expenditures	473	446	641	739	925	1056	957	1153	1205	1191	1119	1190
-net	345	560	590	442	503	659	1288	1428	1298	2203	2078	2533
Government -expenditures, net	17	63	78	-17	-12	-13	0	-13	-19	-35	-32	-20
Investment income:												
-receipts	230	297	420	456	661	758					388	554
-expenditures	1644	1628	1635	1586	1947	2357					919	1077
-net	-1414	-1331	-1216	-1130	-1286	-1599					-530	-523
Direct investment income -net	-24	-32	-45	-56	-117	-194	-238	-431	-936	-834	-809	-870
Unrequired transfers -net	727	860	859	732	909	1127	922	996	1018	346	320	442
Services -net	302	67	103	-104	-55	195				1779	1315	1939
Labor & property income: -net	18	-20	9	-6	-43	-52						
Other current payments -net	-28	-9	110	37	1	25	73	-	-			

(Table 28 - continued)

Current account balance	127	267	324	-3455	-3911	-2480	-1678	-981	-2298	-2076	-1975	-1620
Capital account	-127	-267	-324	3455	3911	2480	156	117	188	33	31	298
Medium- and long-term capital:	204	3070	432	5632	2295	5601						
Assets: - net	-76	-57	-146	237	36	118						
Liabilities:- net	-31	1668	-894	3066	1161	1072						
Inflow	2516	4077	2204	6388	5429	7131						
Outflow	2547	2409	3098	-3322	4267	6058						
Direct investment income -net	311	1459	1471	2339	1146	4453	2279	1741	1555	1696	1851	-426
Basic balance	331	3337	756	2177	-1616	3121						
Short-term capital:	-893	-617	5	459	960	1411						
Assets	-324	141	-152	-165	189	-9						
Liabilities	-569	-758	157	624	771	1420						
Overall balance	-562	2720	761	2635	-656	4532	-1458	-170	797	-2326	-2241	1158
Changes of reserves	562	-2720	-761	-2635	656	-4532						

Table 29

Annual averages of exchange rates

average of previous year

	1990	1991	1992	1993	1994	1995	1996	1997	1998	1999	2000
Ann. average of the movement of exchange rates the currency basket	16.4	16.4.	7.9	10.8	15.6	26.9	19	15.1	13.8	7.4	4.5
Real effective exchange rate of HUF based on prices of industrial output:											
-according to international publication policy	99.8	105.5	99.6	103.8	95.3	94.1	103.8	105.4	96.3	100.3	95.4
-according to Hungarian policy, reciprocal indicators	100.2	94.8	100.4	96.3	105.0	106.3	96.3	94.9	103.8	99.7	93.2

Table 30

Economic sentiment index
of GKI Co.

	1996	1997	1998	1999	2000
The economic sentiment	-15.24	-7.88	-3.96	-13.95	-7.10

Source: GKI Co., Sonda Ipsos

Table 31

Consumer confidence indices in Hungary

1993	1994	1995	1996	1997	1998	1999	2000
-62.63	-49.98	-71.25	-49.00	-33.30	-24.80	-32.50	-22.00

Table 32

Population by age-groups (as of January 1)
total (thousands)

	1990	1991*	1992*	1993*	1994	1995	1996	1997	1998	1999	2000
-14	2130.5	2063.7	2009.8	1958.0	1910.8	1869.9	1836.5	1802.0	1771.7	1744.6	n.a.
15-29	2065.8	2120.4	2170.2	2221.6	2261.9	2294.3	2314.4	2323.9	2314.0	2291.8	2234.8
30-39	1621.8	1587.9	1551.5	1508.7	1450.6	1377.6	1317.6	1276.8	1267.1	1269.7	1278.3
40-59	2596.9	2609.3	2625.8	2637.4	2668.0	2717.5	2758.7	2792.0	2804.6	2808.0	2785.9
60-69	1115.6	1973.6	1980.0	1984.5	1067.9	1058.3	1040.2	1022.7	1010.8	998.4	n.a.
70-	844.3				917.7	928.0	945.0	957.1	967.2	979.1	n.a.
Total	10374.9	10354.9	10337.3	10310.2	10276.9	10245.6	10212.4	10174.5	10135.4	10091.6	10036.0

* There are no data about the age-group of 70 or more because there was not such a group then (just age 60 or more)

Table 33

Economicly activity of population aged 15-74

thousand

	1990	1991	1992	1993	1994	1995	1996	1997	1998	1999	2000
Economically active population (15-74)	5496.1	5400.2	4776.7	4596.0	4443.2	4375.0	4048.2	3995.1	4010.7	4096.2	4111.6
Of which:											
-employed	4795.2	4668.7	4332.5	4077.1	3992.0	3958.5	3648.1	3646.3	3697.7	3811.5	3849.1
-unemployed	24.2	100.5	444.2	518.9	451.2	416.5	400.1	348.8	313.0	284.7	262.5
Economically inactive population (15-74)	945.5	1016.8	2952.2	3167.3	3336.4	3444.7	3759.8	3804.9	3745.1	3620.8	3574.3
Of which: -passive unemployed			153.0	115.6	107.0	105.4	101.8	94.7	110.4	109.1	106.9
Participation rate	85.3	84.0	61.8	59.2	57.1	55.9	51.8	51.2	51.7	53.1	53.5
Unemployment rate	0.4	1.9	9.3	11.3	10.2	9.5	9.9	8.7	7.8	7.0	6.4

Table 34

Number of employed persons by highest qualification
thousands

	1993	1994	1995	1996	1997	1998	1999
Less than 8 grades of primary (general) school	79.9	59.3	47.7	42.6	34.3	29.9	32.5
Primary (general) school	949.6	871.2	809.5	772	770.9	770.6	668.5
Apprentice school and specialized secondary school	1008.2	1091.6	1094.6	1099.1	1119.6	1128.9	1211.9
General secondary school	362	407.3	407.5	412.2	454.3	419.3	308.5
Vocational secondary school	418.5	720.8	704.6	693.5	685.7	731.5	943.9
College	333.1	325.4	334.9	347.8	332.6	350.4	381
University	227.4	216.9	224.1	237.9	212.9	244.1	245.2
Total	3770.3	3692.5	3622.8	3605.1	3610.3	3674.7	3791.5
Of which: with manual qualification	1923.6	1980.2	1932.1	1898.4			

* Data have not available yet.

Table 35 **Development level on basis of gross domestic product (GDP) by counties**

GDP per capita as a percentage of the national average	1994	1995	1996	1997	1998	1999
Budapest	180	181	185	187	186	191
Baranya	84	80	78	80	79	78
Bács-Kiskun	77	79	76	73	71	70
Békés	81	78	76	72	69	68
Borsod-Abaúj-Zemplén	69	76	71	69	69	67
Csongrád	94	93	93	90	89	86
Fejér	96	99	103	117	124	114
Győr-Moson-Sopron	106	109	111	109	121	131
Hajdú-Bihar	83	78	78	76	76	72
Heves	71	75	74	72	73	72
Jász-Nagykun-Szolnok	79	77	76	75	72	67
Komárom-Esztergom	80	106	89	86	84	83
Nógrád	62	59	57	53	57	55
Pest	76	73	73	78	78	80
Somogy	77	76	75	70	69	69
Szabolcs-Szatmár-Bereg	59	61	59	58	57	55
Tolna	95	92	91	84	86	89
Vas	105	107	109	114	117	118
Veszprém	79	84	81	80	81	80
Zala	95	92	93	91	90	90

ABOUT THE EDITORS

György Csáki, born in 1953, completed his BA and MA degrees at the Budapest University of Economics and attained his Ph.D. in International economics at the Hungarian Academy of Sciences in 1985. Between 1976 and 1989 he taught macro-economics and international economics at the Budapest College of Politics, in 1989 moved to the Institute for World Economics of the Hungarian Academy of Sciences as senior Research fellow, an later he became Deputy General Director. Since 1997 he is working for GKI Economic Research Co. as Research Director. At the same time he is the Head of the Department of International Relations at the Budapest Business College.

Dr Csáki has published extensively about FDI in central Europe and Hungary, financial sector reforms in the central European transition economies as well as about privatization. Among his most important publications some books are to be mentioned as follows: "What to know about the IMF and the World Bank?" Kossuth Publishing House, Budapest, 1988; "The Reunification of Europe in the age of global networks." Promethée/Paris - IWE/Budapest. 1992. (Editor); "Experiences with privatization in Hungary: the early transition period." In: 'Privatization and Economic Reform in Central Europe.' Edited by Dennis A. Rondinelli. Quorum Books, Westport, Connecticut - London. 1994.; "Foreign Direct Investments in Hungary - a Basic Issue of the Transformation. In: Zloch, Iliona (ed.): "Privatisation and Foreign Investment in Eastern Europe" Praeger Greenwood Publishing Group, New York, 1995.; 11.; "Transformation of the financial systems in East-Central Europe." In: Pál Gáspár (ed.): 'Changes and Challenges. Economic Transformation in East-Central Europe.' Akadémiai Kiadó, Budapest, 1995; "Reinforcing the Modernization Role of Foreign Direct Investment in Hungary." Working Papers No 62. Institute for World Economics, Budapest, 1996; "Foreign Direct Investment and Transition: The Case of the Visegrád countries." (Editor) Trends in World Economy No 78. Institute for World Economics of the Hungarian Academy of Sciences, Budapest, 1996; "Privatisation in Hungary I." (editor) GJW Consultáció, Budapest, 2000.

Gábor Karsai, born in 1953, completed his BA and MA degrees at the Budapest University of Economics and attained his Ph.D. in Macroeconomics at the Hungarian Academy of Sciences in 1988. From 1976 to 1995 he worked for the leading Hungarian economic weekly *'Figyelő'* as columnist and staff editor of economic policy issues. In the 1980s he coordinated a critical scientific review on the subject of economic planning and policy in Hungary. Since 1996 he has been working for GKI Economic Research Company, initially as Research Director later promoted to Managing Director.

Dr Karsai has had published four books to date. In the first, 'Supply Responsibility or Market Orientation' (1988) he used the example of the domestic trade sector to illustrate the changes in the centralized planning system in Hungary. The sequel to this book (2000) is a study of the privatization process of the same sector. Dr Karsai is the co-author of the 'Dictionary of a Change of Regime' (1992), which illustrates the correlation among the elements of transition to market economy presented in a dictionary-type format. His fourth book, 'Diminishing Illusions' (1994) presents an analytic portrait of the lives of leading Hungarian economists.

No. 27 *Germans in America: Aspects of German-American Relations in the Nineteenth Century.* Edited by Allen McCormick. 1983.

No. 28 *A Question of Empire: Leopold I and the War of Spanish Succession, 1701-1705.* Linda and Marsha Frey. 1983.

No. 29 *The Beginning of Cyrillic Printing — Cracow, 1491. From the Orthodox Past in Poland.* Szczepan K. Zimmer. Edited by Ludwik Krzyżanowski and Irene Nagurski. 1983.

No. 29a *A Grand Ecole for the Grand Corps: The Recruitment and Training of the French Administration.* Thomas R. Osborne. 1983.

No. 30
Vol. XI *The First War between Socialist States: The Hungarian Revolution of 1956 and Its Impact.* Edited by Béla K. Király, Barbara Lotze, Nandor Dreisziger. 1984.

No. 31
Vol. XII *The Effects of World War I, The Uprooted: Hungarian Refugees and Their Impact on Hungary's Domestic Politics.* István Mócsy. 1983.

No. 32
Vol. XIII *The Effects of World War I: The Class War after the Great War: The Rise Of Communist Parties in East Central Europe, 1918-1921.* Edited by Ivo Banac. 1983.

No. 33
Vol. XIV *The Crucial Decade: East Central European Society and National Defense, 1859-1870.* Edited by Béla K. Király. 1984.

No. 35
Vol. XVI *Effects of World War I: War Communism in Hungary, 1919.* György Péteri. 1984.

No. 36
Vol. XVII *Insurrections, Wars, and the Eastern Crisis in the 1870s.* Edited by B. K. Király and Gale Stokes. 1985.

No. 37
Vol. XVIII *East Central European Society and the Balkan Wars, 1912-1913.* Edited by B. K. Király and Dimitrije Djordjevic. 1986.

No. 38
Vol. XIX *East Central European Society in World War I.* Edited by B. K. Király and N. F. Dreisziger, Assistant Editor Albert A. Nofi. 1985.

No. 39
Vol. XX *Revolutions and Interventions in Hungary and Its Neighbor States, 1918-1919.* Edited by Peter Pastor. 1988.

No. 41 Vol. XXII *Essays on East Central European Society and War, 1740-1920.* Edited by Stephen Fischer-Galati and Béla K. Király. 1988.

No. 42 Vol. XXIII *East Central European Maritime Commerce and Naval Policies, 1789-1913.* Edited by Apostolos E. Vacalopoulos, Constantinos D. Svolopoulos, and Béla K. Király. 1988.

No. 43 Vol. XXIV *Selections, Social Origins, Education and Training of East Central European Officers Corps.* Edited by Béla K. Király and Walter Scott Dillard. 1988.

No. 44 Vol. XXV *East Central European War Leaders: Civilian and Military.* Edited by Béla K. Király and Albert Nofi. 1988.

No. 46 *Germany's International Monetary Policy and the European Monetary System.* Hugo Kaufmann. 1985.

No. 47 *Iran Since the Revolution—Internal Dynamics, Regional Conflicts and the Superpowers.* Edited by Barry M. Rosen. 1985.

No. 48 Vol. XXVII *The Press During the Hungarian Revolution of 1848-1849.* Domokos Kosáry. 1986.

No. 49 *The Spanish Inquisition and the Inquisitional Mind.* Edited by Angel Alcala. 1987.

No. 50 *Catholics, the State and the European Radical Right, 1919-1945.* Edited by Richard Wolff and Jorg K. Hoensch. 1987.

No. 51 Vol.XXVIII *The Boer War and Military Reforms.* Jay Stone and Erwin A. Schmidl. 1987.

No. 52 *Baron Joseph Eötvös, A Literary Biography.* Steven B. Várdy. 1987.

No. 53 *Towards the Renaissance of Puerto Rican Studies: Ethnic and Area Studies in University Education.* Maria Sanchez and Antonio M. Stevens. 1987.

No. 54 *The Brazilian Diamonds in Contracts, Contraband and Capital.* Harry Bernstein. 1987.

No. 55 *Christians, Jews and Other Worlds: Patterns of Conflict and Accommodation.* Edited by Philip F. Gallagher. 1988.

No. 56 Vol. XXVI *The Fall of the Medieval Kingdom of Hungary: Mohács 1526, Buda 1541.* Géza Perjés. 1989.

No. 57 *The Lord Mayor of Lisbon: The Portuguese Tribune of the People and His 24 Guilds.* Harry Bernstein. 1989.

No. 58 *Hungarian Statesmen of Destiny: 1860-1960.* Edited by Paul Bödy. 1989.

No. 59 *For China: The Memoirs of T. G. Li, Former Major General in the Chinese Nationalist Army.* T. G. Li. Written in collaboration with Roman Rome. 1989.

No. 60 *Politics in Hungary: For A Democratic Alternative.* János Kis, with an Introduction by Timothy Garton Ash. 1989.

No. 61 *Hungarian Worker's Councils in 1956.* Edited by Bill Lomax. 1990.

No. 62 *Essays on the Structure and Reform of Centrally Planned Economic Systems.* Paul Jonas. A joint publication with Corvina Kiadó, Budapest. 1990.

No. 63 *Kossuth as a Journalist in England.* Éva H. Haraszti. A joint publication with Akadémiai Kiadó, Budapest. 1990.

No. 64 *From Padua to the Trianon, 1918-1920.* Mária Ormos. A joint publication with Akadémiai Kiadó, Budapest. 1990.

No. 65 *Towns in Medieval Hungary.* Edited by László Gerevich. A joint publication with Akadémiai Kiadó, Budapest. 1990.

No. 66 *The Nationalities Problem in Transylvania, 1867-1940.* Sándor Bíró. 1992.

No. 67 *Hungarian Exiles and the Romanian National Movement, 1849-1867.* Béla Borsi-Kálmán. 1991.

No. 68 *The Hungarian Minority's Situation in Ceausescu's Romania.* Edited by Rudolf Joó and Andrew Ludanyi. 1994.

No. 69 *Democracy, Revolution, Self-Determination. Selected Writings.* István Bibó. Edited by Károly Nagy. 1991.

No. 70 *Trianon and the Protection of Minorities.* József Galántai. A joint publication with Corvina Kiadó, Budapest. 1991.

No. 71 *King Saint Stephen of Hungary.* György Györffy. 1994.

No. 72 *Dynasty, Politics and Culture. Selected Essays.* Robert A. Kann. Edited by Stanley B. Winters. 1991.

No. 73 *Jadwiga of Anjou and the Rise of East Central Europe.* Oscar Halecki. Edited by Thaddeus V. Gromada. A joint publication with the Polish Institute of Arts and Sciences of America, New York. 1991.

No. 74 Vol. XXIX *Hungarian Economy and Society during World War Two.* Edited by György Lengyel. 1993.

No. 75 *The Life of a Communist Revolutionary, Béla Kun.* György Borsányi. 1993.

No. 76 *Yugoslavia: The Process of Disintegration.* Laslo Sekelj. 1993.

No. 77 Vol. XXX *Wartime American Plans for a New Hungary. Documents from the U.S. Department of State, 1942-1944.* Edited by Ignác Romsics. 1992.

No. 78 Vol. XXXI *Planning for War against Russia and Serbia. Austro-Hungarian and German Military Strategies, 1871-1914.* Graydon A. Tunstall, Jr. 1993.

No. 79 *American Effects on Hungarian Imagination and Political Thought, 1559-1848.* Géza Závodszky. 1995.

No. 80 Vol. XXXII *Trianon and East Central Europe: Antecedents and Repercussions.* Edited by Béla K. Király and László Veszprémy. 1995.

No. 81 *Hungarians and Their Neighbors in Modern Times, 1867-1950.* Edited by Ferenc Glatz. 1995.

No. 82 *István Bethlen: A Great Conservative Statesman of Hungary, 1874-1946.* Ignác Romsics. 1995.

No. 83 Vol. XXXIII *20th Century Hungary and the Great Powers.* Edited by Ignác Romsics. 1995.

No. 84 *Lawful Revolution in Hungary, 1989-1994.* Edited by Béla K. Király. András Bozóki Associate Editor. 1995.

No. 85 *The Demography of Contemporary Hungarian Society.* Edited by Pál Péter Tóth and Emil Valkovics. 1996.

No. 86 *Budapest, A History from Its Beginnings to 1996.* Edited By András Gerő and János Poór. 1996.

No. 87 *The Dominant Ideas of the Nineteenth Century and Their Impact on the State.* Volume 1. *Diagnosis.* József Eötvös.

Translated, edited, annotated and indexed with an introductory essay by D. Mervyn Jones. 1997.

No. 88 *The Dominant Ideas of the Nineteenth Century and Their Impact on the State.* Volume 2. *Remedy.* József Eötvös. Translated, edited, annotated and indexed with an introductory essay by D. Mervyn Jones. 1997.

No. 89 *The Social History of the Hungarian Intelligentsia in the "Long Nineteenth Century," 1825-1914.* János Mazsu. 1997.

No. 90 Vol.XXXIV *Pax Britannica: Wartime Foreign Office Documents Regarding Plans for a Post Bellum East Central Europe.* Edited by András D. Bán. 1997.

No. 91 *National Identity in Contemporary Hungary.* György Csepeli. 1997.

No. 92 *The Hungarian Parliament, 1867-1918: A Mirage of Power.* András Gerő. 1997.

No. 93 Vol. XXXV *The Hungarian Revolution and War of Independence, 1848-1849. A Military History.* Edited by Gábor Bona. 1999.

No. 94 *Academia and State Socialism: Essays on the Political History of Academic Life in Post-1945 Hungary and East Central Europe.* György Péteri. 1998.

No. 95 Vol.XXXVI *Through the Prism of the Habsburg Monarchy: Hungary in American Diplomacy and Public Opinion during World War I.* Tibor Glant. 1998.

No. 96 *Appeal of Sovereignty in Hungary, Austria and Russia.* Edited by Csaba Gombár, Elemér Hankiss, László Lengyel and Györgyi Várnai. 1997.

No. 97 *Geopolitics in the Danube Region. Hungarian Reconciliation Efforts, 1848-1998.* Edited by Ignác Romsics and Béla K. Király. 1998.

No. 98 *Hungarian Agrarian Society from the Emancipation of Serfs (1848) to Re-privatization of Land (1998).* Edited by Péter Gunst. 1999.

No. 99 *"The Jewish Question" in Europe. The Case of Hungary.* Tamás Ungvári. 2000.

No. 100 *Soviet Military Intervention in Hungary, 1956.* Edited by Jenő Györkei and Miklós Horváth. 1999.

No. 101 *Jewish Budapest.* Edited by Géza Komoróczy. 1999.

No. 102 *Evolution of the Hungarian Economy, 1848-1998.* Vol. I. *One-and-a-Half Centuries of Semi-Successful Modernization, 1848-1989.* Edited by Iván T. Berend and Tamás Csató. 2001.

No. 103 *Evolution of the Hungarian Economy, 1848-1998.* Vol. II. *Paying the Bill for Goulash-Communism.* János Kornai. 2000.

No. 104 *Evolution of the Hungarian Economy, 1848-2000.* Vol. III. *Hungary: from Transition to Integration.* Edited by György Csáki and Gábor Karsai. 2001.

No. 105 *From Habsburg Agent to Victorian Scholar: G. G. Zerffi (1820-1892).* Tibor Frank. 2000.

No. 106 *A History of Transylvania from the Beginning to 1919.* Vol. I. Edited by Zoltán Szász and Béla Köpeczi. 2001.

No. 107 *A History of Transylvania from the Beginning to 1919.* Vol. II. Edited by Zoltán Szász and Béla Köpeczi. 2001.

No. 108 *A History of Transylvania from the Beginning to 1919.* Vol. III. Edited by Zoltán Szász and Béla Köpeczi. 2002.

No. 109 *Hungary: Governments and Politics, 1848–2000.* Edited by Mária Ormos and Béla K. Király. 2001.

No. 110 *Hungarian Minority in the Voivodina.* Edited by Enikő A. Sajti. 2001.

No. 111 *Hungarian Successes.* Edited by László Somlyódy. 2002.

No. 112 *Hungary and International Politics in 1848–1849.* Edited by Domokos Kosáry. 2001.

No. 113 *Social History of Hungary from the Reform Era to the End of the Twentieth Century.* Edited by Gábor Gyáni, György Kövér and Tibor Valuch. 2002.

No. 114 *A Millennium of Hungarian Military History.* Edited by László Veszprémy and Béla K. Király. 2001.

No. 115 *Hungarian Relics. A History of the Battle Banners of the 1848-49 Hungarian Revolution and War of Independence.* Jenő Györkei and Györgyi Cs. Kottra. 2000.

No. 116 *From Totalitarian to Democratic Hungary. Evolution and Transformation, 1990-2000.* Edited by Mária Schmidt and László Gy. Tóth. 2000.

No. 117 *Credit*. István Széchenyi. 2002.
No. 118 *The Ideas of the Hungarian Revolution, Suppressed (1956), Victorious (1999-2000)*. Edited by Lee W. Congdon and Béla K. Király. 2002.
No. 119 *Ten Years in Freedom. The Birth and Consolidation of Democracy in East Central Europe, 1990-2000*. Edited by Mária Schmidt and János Simon. 2002.
No. 120 *Ten Years in Freedom. The Birth and Consolidation of Democracy in East Central Europe, 1990-2000*. Edited by Mária Schmidt and János Simon. 2002.
No. 121 *The Highest Price. Povl Bang-Jensen and the UN, 1955-1959*. Bo Lidegaard. 2002.